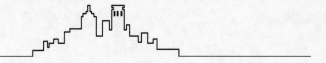

Understanding the Developing Metropolis

Lessons from the City Study of Bogotá and Cali, Colombia

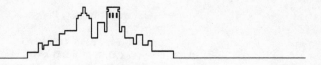

Understanding the Developing Metropolis

Lessons from the City Study of Bogotá and Cali, Colombia

Rakesh Mohan

Published for The World Bank
Oxford University Press

Oxford University Press

OXFORD NEW YORK TORONTO
DELHI BOMBAY CALCUTTA MADRAS KARACHI
KUALA LUMPUR SINGAPORE HONG KONG TOKYO
NAIROBI DAR ES SALAAM CAPE TOWN
MELBOURNE AUCKLAND

and associated companies in
BERLIN IBADAN

Published by Oxford University Press, Inc.
200 Madison Avenue, New York, N.Y. 10016

Oxford is a registered trademark of Oxford University Press

Manufactured in the United States of America
First printing April 1994

Library of Congress Cataloging-in-Publication Data

Mohan, Rakesh, 1948–
    Understanding the developing metropolis : lessons from the city
study of Bogotá and Cali, Colombia / Rakesh Mohan.
        p.   cm.
    Includes bibliographical references and index.
    ISBN 0-19-520882-X
    1. Bogotá (Colombia)—Economic conditions.   2. Cali (Colombia)—
Economic conditions.   3. Urban policy—Developing countries.
I. Title.
HC198.B5M633   1994
333.9861'48—dc20
                                                              93-41140
                                                                  CIP

Contents

v

Tables

Foreword

This book summarizes extensive empirical work on Bogotá and Cali, Colombia, carried out under one of the first comprehensive studies of its kind in a developing country. A few similar studies have been done on cities in industrial countries, the first being *Anatomy of a Metropolis,* by Edgar M. Hoover and Raymond Vernon (Harvard University Press, 1959). Although not a model for this work, it was a source of inspiration.

Our expectation when beginning this research was that the development patterns and behavior in Bogotá and Cali would resemble those observed in industrial countries in the early decades of the twentieth century. In fact, the research revealed strong behavioral similarities of households, workers, and firms to those contemporaneously observed in industrial countries. This is true of patterns of decentralization and movement of firms, of determinants of household demand for housing, of travel demand and choice of mode, and of general urban residential growth patterns. Of course, there are differences—household incomes are lower, residential densities are higher, transit use is greater, and service levels are lower in the two cities studied than in industrial countries. But it is the similarities, not the differences, that have been most striking.

These similarities in behavior support the view that the basic tenets of urban economic theory are applicable in large cities where household and firm decisions are determined in market settings and where passenger travel and freight transport are motorized. A basic conclusion is that cities are not chaotic collections of unpredictable activities. Their strong common patterns of behavior enable us to formulate policies for transport, housing, urban labor markets, and local public finance and to improve the management of cities.

Those of us who worked on the project are particularly indebted to Colombia for collaborating in this effort and for sharing with us its extensive data, intellectual resources, and institutional support.

Gregory K. Ingram
Administrator
Research Advisory Staff

Preface and Acknowledgments

This monograph attempts to summarize the main findings of the World Bank research program known as the City Study. The study, which was under the overall direction of Gregory K. Ingram, examined five major urban sectors—housing, transportation, employment location, labor markets, and public finance—in Bogotá (officially, Santa Fe de Bogotá) and Cali, Colombia. The goal of the study was to increase understanding of these sectors in order to assess the effect of policies and projects on cities in developing countries.[1]

The idea of the City Study was initiated in 1975–76 by Hollis Chenery, then Vice President of the Development Policy Staff of the World Bank. It was his broad vision of development policy research that enabled us to contemplate and then implement such an intensive program of research in urban economics. The research reported in this volume was conducted over a period of about five years, 1977 through 1981, by a large team at the Urban and Regional Economics Division (headed by Douglas H. Keare) of what was then the Development Economics Department of the World Bank in Washington, in cooperation with the Area de Distribución Espacial de la Población (headed by Ramiro Cardona) of the Corporación Centro Regional de Población (CCRP), Bogotá, and the Departmental and Municipal Planning Offices (Planeación Departamental and Planeación Municipal) of Cali. Participants in the study directed by Gregory Ingram were Alan Carroll, Andrew Hamer, Valerie Kozel, Kyu Sik Lee, Johannes F. Linn, Rakesh Mohan, Alvaro Pachon, Anna Sant'Anna, and Richard Westin of the World Bank; in Bogotá, Alberto Hernandez, Rodrigo Villamizar, and Amparo de Ardila were led by José Fernando Pineda. About twenty-five consultants and research assistants based in both Bogotá and Washington assisted. In addition to World Bank research funds, funding was provided by Colombia's National Statistical Agency (Departamento Administrativo Nacional de Estadística, DANE) for the 1978 Household Survey and by the Bogotá Chamber of Commerce for dissemination of study results. The project also benefited from the direction of the Colombian Advisory Committee, consisting of Eduardo Aldana, Rodrigo Botero, Bernardo Gaitan, Pedro Gómez, Jorge Méndez, Miguel Urrutia, Eduardo Wiesner, and the Resident Representative of the World Bank at the time, Ian Scott. At the World Bank, the consistent interest and encouragement given by Ardy Stoutjesdijk and Anthony Churchill were very helpful.

In this volume, I attempt to integrate the main findings of the different segments of the project. Although I have presented the findings as I have interpreted them from the work of the whole team, the primary credit for each portion of the research should go to its originators (italicized in the entries).

LAND MARKETS: *Rakesh Mohan,* Rodrigo Villamizar, Gregory K. Ingram, Ricardo Paredes, Guillermo Wiesner, M. Wilhelm Wagner.

HOUSING AND RESIDENTIAL LOCATION: *Gregory K. Ingram,* Andrew Hamer, Amparo de Ardila, Alan Carroll, José Fernando Pineda, Rafael Stevenson, Oscar Borrero, Anna Sant'Anna.

TRANSPORTATION: *Alvaro Pachon,* Valerie Kozel, Richard Westin, Gregory K. Ingram, Alberto Hernandez, José Cifuentes, Emilio Latorre.

EMPLOYMENT LOCATION: *Kyu Sik Lee,* Yoon Joo Lee.

LABOR MARKETS, POVERTY, INCOME DISTRIBUTION: *Rakesh Mohan,* Gary Fields, Jorge García, M. Wilhelm Wagner.

PUBLIC FINANCE: *Johannes F. Linn,* Alberto Hernandez, Jeffrey Lewis, Caroline Fawcett, Juergen Wolff, David Greytak.

OVERALL PATTERNS: *Gregory K. Ingram,* Rakesh Mohan, José Fernando Pineda, Alvaro Pachon.

DATA DOCUMENTATION: Yoon Joo Lee, Nelson Valverde.

As may be expected from the quantitative research in this volume, a legion of research assistants has contributed to the work. Thanks are due to Yoon Joo Lee, Sung Yong Kang, Robert Marshall, Kathie Terrell, Wili Wagner, Jon Roseman, Nancy Hartline, Mark Snyderman, Leslie Kramer, and Nelson Valverde, all of whom gave much beyond the call of duty in managing the vast volumes of data processed in this study. In Colombia we also received assistance from Sonia Rodriguez, Marco Tulio Ruiz, María Clara de Posada, and Alejandro Vivas.

We received extensive cooperation from many organizations in Colombia. Work in Cali was carried out with staff from the Departmental Planning Office (Planeación Departamental), headed by Lacides Reyes, and from the Municipal Planning Office (Planeación Municipal), headed by Jaime Cifuentes. We collaborated with the Integrated Plan for the Development of Cali (Plan Integral para el Desarrollo de Cali, PIDECA), directed by Julian Velasco. Among the staff associated with our work in Cali were M. Sanchez, Hugo García, M. V. Fuentes, J. Osorio, F. Fajardo, M. Santacruz, S. Prado, A. Rivera, and G. López. We were also generously assisted by the staff of the Bogotá District Planning Office (Departamento Administrativo de Planeación Distrital), the National Centre for Building Industry Studies (Centro Nacional de Estudios de la Construcción, CENAC), the Social Security Institute (Instituto Colombiano de Seguaros Social, ICSS), and the Superintendencia Bancaria. Enrique Low and Clara Eugenia Lopez, Controllers (Contralores) of Bogotá District, took special interest in the public finance work and gave generously of their staff time.

We were particularly fortunate to have been able to collaborate with members of DANE, who provided us with unfailing and careful assistance.They agreed to incorporate our requirements into their schedule of quarterly household surveys, which resulted in the World Bank–DANE City Study Household Survey of 1978, on which many of our results are based. The high quality of this survey owed much to the diligence of its DANE supervisors, Roberto Pinilla and María Christina Jimenez. The contributions of Gary Losee, Alfredo Aliaga, Jairo Arias, Alvaro Pachon, and José Fernando Pineda to its design and implementation were notable. We would like to thank the authorities of DANE for so readily providing all the data sets used in the study. My own participation in the organization and collection of the data in the 1978 Household Survey taught me much about the practical difficulties and pitfalls involved in the collection of primary data, on which we economists are so dependent but which we seldom understand.

For me, this work has spanned a period of what I presume will be about a third of my professional life. Douglas Keare inducted me into the World Bank in December 1976 to work in the study. Although most of the research had been completed by late 1981, the changing interests and reassignment of all participants made it very difficult to bring to final form all the work that had been done. Since 1980, I have returned to the Government of India twice to work on housing, urban development, and industrial development in a policymaking capacity. Greg Ingram, in his various incarnations in the 1980s, was able to find the resources to enable me to extricate myself from the government of India at various times, first to return to the World Bank in 1984, then again in 1989 and 1990 to write this volume as well as the earlier monograph (Mohan 1986). I appreciate his efforts in providing me these opportunities to conclude an enterprise we started jointly in January 1977. These "sabbaticals" have been invaluable in helping me keep up my research interests and in giving me respite from the pressures of normal governmental work. It was also generous of Otima Bordia and A. N.

Varma, Secretary, Industrial Development, Government of India, in 1989 and 1990, respectively, to give me time off from the ministry during difficult times of onerous work. The constant encouragement received over the years from Doug Keare and Johannes Linn has also been instrumental in enabling me to finish this work.

In Colombia, we benefited greatly from having as our main collaborators Ramiro Cardona and José Fernando Pineda. Their warm hospitality, generously extended to the whole team, made every visit to Colombia a pleasure. They contributed greatly to our knowledge and understanding of Colombia, making possible a truly collaborative project.

Geri Mitchell organized the final processing of this manuscript, doing much of it herself. She was assisted by Jean Ponchamni, Maria Dimatulac, María E. Sánchez, and Helen Lee. I am grateful to them for being able to do this in addition to their normal duties.

The final production of this book has taken as long as its creation. Well-considered comments from three anonymous referees led to very useful revisions. Its readability owes a lot to the careful editing of Willa Speiser, Jeanne Rosen, Kathryn Kline Dahl, and Deirdre Murphy.

Our quest in this study was to find general approaches to studying the workings of large cities in developing countries and to achieve modes of understanding the behavior of and interactions among the participants in the myriad activities in a developing metropolis. We feel that we achieved some success in this quest and that our findings have general relevance to understanding the growth of large cities. Our approach was to describe and analyze the various patterns of behavior that are found to be stable over time. For example, some of our work has been corroborated by the subsequent works of Steve Mayo and Steve Malpezzi on housing and by Kyu Sik Lee's continuing efforts on employment location. On other issues, our results are still among the few available for cities in developing countries. In writing this book, delayed though it is, I hope that large cities will begin to be better understood by professionals and policymakers alike. I also hope that more detailed work of this kind will be forthcoming so that we can continue to improve our understanding of the developing metropolis.

My greatest debt, intellectual and otherwise, in being able to conduct this study and to bring it to a close in this book is to Gregory Ingram. To him, my deepest gratitude.

I dedicate this book to my wife, Rasika Khanna, for allowing me to desert her at various times in the raw summer heat of Delhi in order to finish this work, which has followed me for more than a decade. My children, Tarini and Rasesh, who have appeared during the course of the writing of this book, will have to wait for my next effort to be eligible for dedication.

Note

1. Two monographs have been published: Rakesh Mohan, *Work, Wages, and Welfare in a Developing Metropolis: Consequences of Growth in Bogotá, Colombia* (New York: Oxford University Press, 1986); and Kyu Sik Lee, *The Location of Jobs in a Developing Metropolis: Patterns of Growth in Bogotá and Cali, Colombia* (New York: Oxford University Press, 1989).

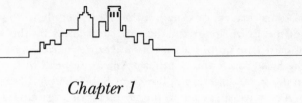

Chapter 1

Introduction

The total urban population in developing countries has roughly quadrupled in the past four decades, from less than 300 million in 1950 to more than 1.2 billion in 1990. The rapid growth of cities is among the more striking features of the developing world. In 1950 there were only three cities in the developing world with more than 5 million people; now there are at least twenty-four such cities in developing countries, compared with only ten in developed countries. The word "metropolis" used to describe Western cities such as New York, Chicago, London, Paris, and Rome. Today it is as likely to bring to mind Buenos Aires, São Paulo, Mexico City, Tokyo, Manila, Seoul, Bombay, New Delhi, or Cairo. More often than not, current discussions of urban or metropolitan problems concern cities in developing countries.

Since large metropolitan centers did not appear in what are today's developed countries until their economies had reached a comparatively advanced stage, the emergence of such cities in poor countries has frequently been regarded as an unusual phenomenon. A metropolis, once a source of national pride, now inspires awe if not fear. To many, large cities in developing countries conjure up images of gigantic slums, floods of destitute migrants congregating in ramshackle shanty towns, cacophonous traffic choking the main arteries, and ineffective local government struggling to provide basic public services. Because of this widespread negative view and the alarm it evokes, urban policies often attempt to slow the growth of large cities rather than to manage their growth in a healthy fashion.

Despite misdirected and even counterproductive policies, large cities have continued to expand and have usually prospered in the process. By the end of the century the developing world is expected to have more than fifteen "megacities" with at least 10 million people each and more than a hundred cities with at least 1 million people each. United

Nations' projections suggest that more people in the developing world will be living in urban than in rural areas by the year 2020. This is already true in most countries in Latin America, East Asia, and the Middle East. South and Southeast Asia as well as China are rapidly moving in the same direction, followed by Sub-Saharan Africa.

A positive approach to the problems of large cities is a must if governments are to meet the challenges posed by city growth. In the preindustrial age the concentration of people in cities was a religious, political, or military phenomenon. Today it is an economic phenomenon, and it must be analyzed as such. Evolving constructive metropolitan policies requires an understanding of how cities work.

The need for such understanding led the World Bank to launch a research program in the 1970s known as the City Study. This effort, for reasons outlined below, has focused primarily on Bogotá and secondarily on Cali in Colombia. The main objective of this study has been to learn more about the intrinsically complex and interrelated phenomena that underlie the rapid growth of a city. Those of us involved in the study have sought to understand how the components of a city's economy—its housing, employment, labor force, land market, transportation systems, and public services—interact and behave in the context of rapid city growth. Our ultimate goal has been to bring about a more positive orientation to urban policy.

Considerable research exists on the old cities in Europe and North America, and their structures are reasonably well understood. The workings of their housing and labor markets, the locational decisions of their residents and employers, and the patterns of their traffic and transport are all regarded as tractable. There are stylized facts about these cities that appear to have wide applicability. But how relevant is this knowledge for cities in developing countries? Do we need to apply different modes of understanding to these cities? How have their populations responded to rapid growth? What do project and city planners need to know about the processes and patterns in these cities so they can contribute more effectively to urban development? How much intervention in different markets is necessary for a city to accommodate rapid growth? The City Study was designed to illuminate these and many related questions.

The broad theme of the City Study is behavioral adaptation to rapid change in the context of rapidly growing cities in developing countries. The impetus for this work arose from the World Bank's increasing involvement in urban projects, beginning in the early 1970s. Along with this involvement came a greater awareness of the existence of urban poverty and its concomitant problems. Whereas the manifold problems of rural poverty had been studied for a long time, little information was available on the dimensions and nature of urban poverty. This led to the formation of an Urban Poverty Task Force at the World Bank in 1974. The Task Force assembled a group of academics working on these issues and commissioned a series of studies. These efforts did not produce a coherent program for addressing the issues of urban poverty, but they did result in greater attention to urban problems and greater appreciation of the complexity and interrelatedness of urban phenomena. It also became clear that one feature of the City Study should be a focus on urban poverty.

At the time this study was being launched, the notion that everything in a city is interrelated had taken hold, and it was widely accepted that these interrelationships were best captured in large-scale urban models. Researchers in the 1960s and early 1970s, especially in North America and the United Kingdom, had been very optimistic about the utility and feasibility of constructing such models and using them to understand how cities work and hence to plan better. Two broad modeling approaches were prevalent: behavioral or analytical models and operational or planning models. A critical review of these modeling efforts was conducted as a prelude to the City Study (see Mohan 1979), and it led to considerable skepticism about the utility and practicality of large-scale models. In designing the City Study, we opted instead for detailed investigations of each area of urban decisionmaking. It was more important, we decided, to understand and model the behavior of the various actors and markets that constitute a city than to replicate its functions in a large-scale model.

The approach we adopted was therefore to model different markets, as well as the behavior of individuals, households, firms, and the public sector within those markets. We wanted especially to examine the responses of these actors in the face of extremely rapid change. How, for example, do people react to shifting prices in the housing market? How much do people do for themselves, and how should the public sector intervene? What kinds of supply responses can be expected when demand for housing burgeons? How does the public sector cope with widespread illegality in land transactions? How do people choose their mode of transport? What kind of transport services appear in response to a variegated demand? How are incomes determined in an urban setting, and how are they affected by changes in labor market conditions? How do people decide whether or not to participate in the labor market? These are the kinds of questions we sought to address through the behavioral modeling of actors and markets. We felt that urban policies could be much more effectively designed if there were better appreciation of the underlying behavior that results in the phenomena observed.

The objective of the City Study was not to propose a specific program to guide city growth, but rather to develop tools (models as well as other analytical methods) that could be used to estimate the spatial and economic effects of different kinds of policy intervention. The research strategy was threefold: (a) to systematically describe the current spatial patterns of the various economic activities that constitute a city, along with recent changes in the observed patterns; (b) to model behavior and to estimate parameters useful for understanding how the main urban constituents respond to rapidly changing conditions; and (c) to assess the policy impact of these findings. The systematic description would enable us to determine how the spatial patterns of activities evolve in response to changes such as the decentralization of jobs and residences in a growing city. These descriptions would in turn help us formulate hypotheses to be tested, and the empirical estimations of models would yield the parameter estimates. We would also be able to observe the apparent effects of policies that attempt to alter the spatial distribution of activities.

The magnitude of this task, we knew, would depend critically on how similar the fundamental processes of urban development are at different stages of economic development. If existing tools designed to study cities in rich countries could be applied or adapted for use in poorer countries, the task would be that much easier. We looked for clues about the transferability of these tools by comparing the spatial patterns of cities in rich and poor countries. Our assessment was that the similarities outweighed the dissimilarities (see Ingram and Carroll 1981). The research was therefore also designed to test whether familiar tools devised to study cities in industrial countries could be transferred to the study of growing cities in developing countries.

Most urban studies concentrate exclusively on issues related to the supply of infrastructure, housing, and transport services. The City Study addresses these issues in detail. But it gives equal attention to the working of the labor market and the resulting income distribution, because the emphasis is on the behavior of people and firms in a situation of rapid growth. A prior knowledge of household behavior and the labor market activity of individuals and their employers is necessary before the housing, transport, and infrastructure issues can be addressed. Mapping the spatial distribution of income and explaining its overall trend are crucial to comprehending and predicting the nature of demands for infrastructure, housing, and transport that are likely to arise in a growing city.

City Selection

Having decided to launch a program of research designed to improve understanding of how cities in developing countries work, we next decided to study one city in detail rather than to attempt to draw conclusions from cross-country patterns. This seemed the appropriate strategy, given our intention to focus on understanding the intracity patterns and behavior that characterize a rapidly growing city. Resources, both financial and human, did not permit a simultaneous, in-depth study of several cities in different countries.

Once the decision had been made to focus on a single city, it became apparent that Latin America was the place to look. The urbanization experience of Latin America in the 1950s, 1960s, and early 1970s was a precursor of the fast urban growth phenomenon common to most developing countries. Many Latin American countries had already reached levels of urbanization that exceeded 50 percent, and there were a number of large cities from which to choose. Furthermore, the proximity of the region to Washington, D.C., where the World Bank's headquarters are located, was a big advantage, since the study was expected to involve intensive work in the selected city and hence frequent travel.

Certain additional criteria led us to choose Bogotá as the primary site for this study. First, the policy and planning climate in the city and in the country had to be receptive to such a study. We wanted the policymakers, planners, and administrators to be interested in the results and capable of absorbing them. This depended on the availability of professionals working on urban issues both within and outside the government, and on the interest of the national and local governments in the management of city growth. The potential for the World Bank to make future urban-related investments was another consideration.

The second criterion was a favorable research climate in the selected city and country. To carry out the study in a reasonable time, it was desirable for the city to have both a rich data base and competent individuals or institutions that could participate in the work. Moreover, the potential usefulness of the study would be enhanced if the local research capability existed to utilize the results so that the knowledge could be transferred to other researchers when the study was concluded. The availability of existing data bases in time series, cross-sectional, and disaggregated form was an important asset to be considered, as was the availability of relevant studies.

A third criterion was the absence of an atypical development pattern that would limit the transferability of the findings. The city had to be large enough to exhibit adequate variation in land prices, travel patterns, density levels, and the like so that the analyses could be applied to a wide range of situations. Accordingly, idiosyncratic administrative cities such as Brasília were excluded. The relative stability of the national economy was also important. A cultural context common to many countries was an added asset.

Given these criteria, the choice was narrowed down to four countries: Brazil, Colombia, Mexico, and Peru. Rio de Janeiro was eliminated because of its highly unusual geography, and São Paulo and Mexico City because they are far too large, complex, and unmanageable for practical study. Government interest was found to be keenest in Colombia. From discussions with government officials, consultants, and academics, it also became apparent that a concern for intracity problems was widespread in that country.

Bogotá exhibited characteristics representative of a cross-section of Latin American cities (see Ingram and Carroll 1981), which greatly enhanced the chances that the findings would be transferable to other cities. It also had a rich data base on which to build (see the appendix to this volume for details). Moreover, Colombia had a history of policy-related analytical work on urban issues, influenced in part by the life-long interest of Lauchlin Currie. The importance of urbanization in economic development and of housing as an economic activity had long been emphasized by Currie. In 1950 he led the first World Bank mission to a developing country, which happened to be to Colombia. He later moved there and exerted a lasting influence on national planning. It is also worth noting that Albert Hirschman derived the crucial insights for his book, *The Strategy of Economic Development* (1958), during a three-year stint in Colombia's National Planning Department; that the International Labour Organisation (ILO) sent an influential employment mission headed by Dudley Seers to Colombia in 1967 (see ILO 1970); and that a detailed country report on Colombia was among the early World Bank country economic reports published (Avramovic and associates 1972). Of direct relevance to our study was the important urban development study of Bogotá undertaken with support from the United Nations Development Programme (UNDP) in 1970–74 (known as the Phase II Study). This work had generated a substantial amount of benchmark data, in particular a comprehensive household survey in 1972.

At the time we began the City Study in 1977, other scholars had recently completed or were engaged in research on Bogotá. Albert Berry and Miguel Urrutia had been working for years on issues concerning the labor market and income distribution (see Berry 1975a, 1975b; Berry and Soligo 1980; Berry and Urrutia 1976; Urrutia 1969, 1985). Gary Fields and Helena Ribe were interested in similar issues (see Fields 1975; Fields and Marulanda 1976; Fields and Schultz 1980; Ribe 1979). Richard Nelson, T. Paul Schultz, and Robert Slighton (1971) had also worked earlier on the interrelated issues of population growth, internal migration, and labor market adjustment. Peter Amato (1968, 1970a, 1970b) had documented patterns of urban residential location a decade earlier. Georges Vernez (1973) and Rodrigo Losada and Hernando Gomez (1976), among others, had worked on *pirata* developments and incremental housing development. Harold Lubell and Douglas McCallum (1978) had addressed the relation of employment issues and urban development. At the World Bank, several studies on Colombia had been conducted or were in progress in the mid-1970s: Johannes Linn was carrying out a large program of research on urban public finance (see Linn 1976a, 1976b, 1979, 1980a, 1980b); Marcelo Selowsky was working on a study on the distribution of public services (see Selowsky 1979); William Doebele and Orville Grimes had conducted studies on the working of the urban land market (see Doebele 1975; Doebele, Grimes, and Linn 1979); and Mariluz Cortes was involved in a project investigating the role of small-scale enterprises (Cortes, Berry, and Ishaq 1987). Thus a vibrant research ambience existed both in Bogotá and at the World Bank that was very conducive to initiating the City Study in Colombia.

The active involvement of local researchers was essential to the success of this endeavor. Bogotá was well endowed with research institutions and university departments that had some experience working on urban issues. It was therefore easy to find researchers who could participate in the study. The work was eventually based in the Corporation Central Regional de Poblacíon (CCRP)—an institution engaged in population studies, urban studies, and economics research.

The interest that different levels of government have taken in this study is borne out by the many contributions of public institutions. The National Planning Department (Departamento Nacional de Planeación) was active in initiating and facilitating the study; the National Statistical Agency (Departamento Administrativo Nacional de Estadística, DANE) shared raw data from past surveys and conducted the 1978 City Study survey; and the Banking Regulatory Agency (Superintendencia Bancaria) provided data on pirate land developments and contributed staff resources. The city government of Bogotá made staff available to help conduct the public finance portion of the study.

When we were getting under way, the city government of Cali, along with the State Planning Office (Planeación Departamental) of Valle, the state in which Cali is situated, expressed great interest in our work. They invited us to broaden the study to include Cali, which we did. The City Planning Office (Planeación Municipal) provided extensive staff resources to implement the study in Cali.

Finally, the World Bank had a large program in Colombia. It was therefore expected that the results of the study would find a ready audience within the institution.

In short, Bogotá satisfied all the criteria that had been laid out for selecting a site for the City Study. Cali was added because of the local interest expressed. It proved very useful as a comparator for assessing the generality of the findings. Whereas the primary studies were undertaken in Bogotá, an attempt was made to duplicate the research wherever possible in Cali. Wherever significant differences exist, they have been noted. Otherwise, most general conclusions apply to both cities.

The Macroeconomic Setting: Were the 1970s Exceptional?

This study is being published many years after completion of the field research, which was carried out from 1977 to 1980. The question arises whether the results were unduly influenced by any special conditions prevailing in Colombia from 1972 to 1980, the period covered by the study. A related question is whether any developments during the 1980s give cause for reassessing the results. It is also useful to place the city-related issues addressed in this study within the national economic context of the time.

Since the study was designed to enhance our understanding of the behavioral underpinnings of how cities work, especially in the context of rapid growth and change, the delay in publication should not make our findings obsolete. Indeed, the economic changes that have occurred during the 1980s underscore the usefulness of taking a behavioral look at how a city functions rather than adopting a prescriptive approach to planning.

Viewed in retrospect, the economic environment in Colombia was more buoyant in the 1970s than in most other recent decades, although not exceptionally so. In the early 1980s Colombia was on the verge of economic crisis for reasons that were in part exogenous: a drop in coffee prices, high world interest rates, an international recession, and the backwash of the debt crisis affecting the rest of Latin America. These externally induced economic difficulties were exacerbated by burgeoning domestic problems, including high fiscal deficits and a significant appreciation of the real exchange rate. Growth in employment slowed, unemployment rose, and the external trade deficit widened. Although the situation in Colombia was not nearly as strained as it was in most other Latin American countries, many of which were highly indebted, international banks, facing difficulties elsewhere on that continent, hardened credit terms for Colombia. The optimistic tone of this study, a reflection of the economic environment of the 1970s, would probably have been tempered if the period of observation had been the 1980s. Nonetheless, most of our findings are unaffected by the events of those years.

The three decades prior to the 1980s marked an important demographic and economic transition for Colombia. In the 1960s the rural labor force ceased to grow (Urrutia 1985) and the urban labor force expanded rapidly. People living in urban areas began to outnumber rural dwellers: they increased from 39 percent of the population in 1951 to 52 percent in 1964 and 60 percent in 1973. By the late 1970s two-thirds of Colombians resided in towns and cities. Colombia, like most countries experiencing urban growth, had undergone a striking demographic transition in a short time.

In the 1980s this process slowed down; urban residents accounted for 68 percent of the population in 1986. The urbanization process during the 1950s, 1960s, and 1970s was therefore somewhat different from that in the 1980s. That some of our findings differ from those of earlier studies (for example, ILO 1970; Lubell and McCallum 1978) is partly because we were observing the consolidation phase of Colombia's urban history, whereas others had observed the effervescent phase, when urban growth seemed excessively rapid and endless. One of the lessons drawn in this study is that understanding the growth processes in a specific city requires an appreciation of the national urban growth context.

Colombia's demographic transition is also evident from dramatic changes in other social indicators during the 1960s and 1970s. The crude birth rate (CBR) fell from 45 per thousand population in 1963 to 31 per thousand in 1974. The CBR then declined more gradually, reaching 27 per thousand by 1985. Similarly, infant mortality fell from 6.5 per thousand births in 1963 to 4.0 per thousand births in 1974 and to 3.2 per thousand births in 1985. Primary schooling became universal in the 1970s, and secondary school enrollment increased from 17 percent of the school-age population in 1963 to 39 percent in 1974 and 50 percent in 1985. These indicators confirm the extremely rapid changes that took place in the 1960s and 1970s and the slowdown that followed in the late 1970s and early 1980s.

The economic impact of these social and demographic shifts was far-reaching. The rapid growth in population, particularly in urban population, placed severe strains on the suppliers of urban services. The slowing of change toward the late 1970s made it easier for the housing supply and other urban amenities to catch up with the backlog of urgent demand. Similarly, the impressive expansion in the supply of education starting in the 1960s, especially for females, transformed the quality of the labor force within two decades. Some of the employment pressures during the 1980s may be related to this expansion, which had the effect of reducing the returns to secondary and higher education and so contributed to improving the distribution of income (see chapter 4 in this volume; Mohan and Sabot 1988).

Colombia sustained a respectable but not exceptionally high rate of economic growth in the decades following World War II (see table 1-1). From 1950 to 1966, the gross domestic product (GDP) grew an average of almost 5 percent a year. This accelerated to about 6.4 percent a year between 1967 and 1974 but fell back to about 5.5 percent for the rest of the decade. Then came the exceptional deceleration of the 1980s. Income per capita dropped during 1980–83 for the first time in three decades. Whereas economic growth was just respectable, the increase in employment growth in the late 1970s was exceptional (see table 1-1 and chapter 5).

The existence of relatively tight labor markets, the absence of notable segmentation, and the measurable increase in real wages, all of which were observed in our study, were clearly influenced by unusually high growth in employment during the period. In our judgment, however, this phenomenon was not entirely fortuitous but was in part the consequence of appropriate policies and sound macroeconomic management.

Indeed, Colombia has benefited from a long record of sound macroeconomic management, which has usually responded successfully to changes in the economic environment. Like most other developing countries, especially those in Latin America, Colombia emphasized import-substitution industrialization policies during the 1950s and 1960s. Its periods of economic growth and stagnation have been linked to its terms of trade, especially to the movement of world coffee prices. In the late 1970s coffee prices were booming and the economy was doing well; in the early 1980s the opposite was true. The post–World War II import-substituting strategy led to the consolidation of industrial growth, particularly in Bogotá, which rapidly surpassed Medellín as Colombia's prime manufacturing center.

The Lleras government (1966–70) introduced policy changes that helped lay the foundation for some of the income and employment gains of the 1970s. Export promotion was pursued actively by introducing various incentives; a crawling peg exchange rate policy was adopted to maintain a realistic real exchange rate; fiscal discipline was exercised; and a mild program for the deregulation of some import controls was put in place. This policy package was largely continued by the Pastrana government (1970–74), which, in addition, consciously introduced an

Table 1-1. Economic Growth in Colombia, 1950–86
(percent)

| Period | Average annual growth | | | Share of capital in GDP |
	GDP	Employment	Capital	
1950–57	4.9	2.5	5.3	44.1
1958–66	4.9	2.4	3.9	43.3
1967–74	6.4	2.8	4.1	42.7
1974–80	5.5	4.1	4.9	40.7
1981–86	2.7	2.8	4.2	37.8

Source: García (1988).

urban development thrust by promoting construction activities. The result was improved utilization of capacity in the industrial sector and a significant increase in noncoffee exports. The construction boom was concentrated primarily in Bogotá and secondarily in Medellín and Cali.

In the field of housing, the most significant development was the introduction of a new savings instrument that assured savers a real rate of return on their accounts through indexation. The funds mobilized through this instrument could then be used to finance housing. Although there is some debate about the overall impact on housing of this financial innovation, it undoubtedly helped foster middle- and upper-middle-income housing activity (see chapter 7). Housing and financial markets did become better linked as a result.

The López administration (1974–78) deemphasized support for construction and adopted an explicit urban deconcentration program to direct economic activities away from the largest cities of Bogotá, Medellín, Cali, and Barranquilla. Emphasis was also put on using public resources to help the poor: spending on public health and education was promoted, whereas investments in infrastructure for energy and transport were downgraded.

The net result of the policy environment that originated in the mid-1960s was that sectors with low ratios of capital to labor grew faster than other sectors, noncoffee exports increased, and education expanded rapidly along with other social services (see Urrutia 1985). This led to the remarkable employment boom in the late 1970s.

At about the same time, however, the policy package began to unravel. World coffee prices shot up to unprecedented levels, as did unrecorded foreign exchange earnings from the drug trade. The balance of payments went into surplus. Since it was difficult to sterilize these foreign exchange inflows, the real exchange rate appreciated significantly, and noncoffee exports began to falter. When coffee prices crashed in the early 1980s, as shown in table 1-2, a severe balance of payments crisis ensued; the current account deficit was 6 percent of GDP in 1984. The policy response was to impose stringent controls on almost all imports. The economic difficulties were compounded by rising budget deficits, which reached 6.8 percent of GDP in 1984. These were caused in part by the bunching of some large infrastructure investments, especially in the power sector, and by the drop in coffee revenues. The economic downturn during 1980–84 caused significant unemployment.

Other related developments may have contributed to the slowdown in employment growth, most notably in organized manufacturing. As was documented in a 1987 internal World Bank report, wages in the organized sector began to rise in the late 1970s, and the differential between wages in the organized and the unorganized sectors may have widened. Wage agreements, which had usually been concluded every other year,

Table 1-2. Prices and Wages in Colombia

Indicators	1971	1972	1973	1974	1975	1976	1977	1978	1979	1980	1981	1982	1983	1984	1985	1986	1987	1988
Indexes																		
Exchange rate																		
Nominal (pesos per dollar)	20.1	22.0	23.8	27.1	31.2	35.0	36.8	39.1	42.6	47.3	54.5	64.1	78.9	100.8	142.3	196.1	243.0	299.0
Real (average)	n.a.	n.a.	n.a.	n.a.	100.0	95.4	85.7	85.5	81.7	83.5	81.6	75.6	73.6	79.9	91.4	108.5	108.2	105.6
Wages[a]	105.2	108.6	110.5	111.8	111.3	109.2	109.7	121.7	127.6	129.5	134.2	132.6	132.9	132.4	n.a.	n.a.	n.a.	n.a.
Coffee price index	80.9	89.3	104.8	98.6	100.0	172.6	215.7	151.0	131.2	111.4	74.9	77.0	74.2	77.2	81.7	115.2	64.7	74.8
Annual growth rate (percent)																		
GDP deflator (1975=100)	10.8	13.0	20.2	25.4	22.8	25.5	29.1	17.1	24.0	27.6	22.8	24.8	20.4	22.2	23.2	24.0	22.8	27.0
Exchange rate																		
Nominal	9.4	9.7	8.2	13.8	15.1	12.1	5.1	6.3	8.8	11.2	15.2	17.6	23.1	27.8	41.2	37.8	24.0	23.0
Real	n.a.	n.a.	n.a.	n.a.	n.a.	-4.6	-10.1	-0.3	-4.4	2.2	-2.3	-7.3	-2.7	8.5	14.4	18.7	-0.3	-2.4
Wholesale prices	n.a.	n.a.	n.a.	n.a.	n.a.	22.9	26.7	17.6	27.8	37.5	23.5	24.6	18.0	21.2	23.0	24.4	25.2	283

n.a. Not available.

a. 1970 = 100.

Source: Internal World Bank documents (unpublished 1987 and 1989 country economic memoranda); Thomas (1985).

became an annual occurrence in the late 1970s. This put added pressure on real wages. One feature of the rising wage costs in the organized sector was the increasing share represented by employment benefits. The appreciation in the real exchange rate was exacerbated by these developments, and the growth of the manufacturing sector, especially in export-oriented industries, was adversely affected. Although this study did not find significant evidence of segmentation in the labor market (see chapter 5), some observers in the 1980s did. It is possible that certain developments noted in the 1970s could have led to increasing segmentation later.

A specific feature of the rising unemployment in the 1980s was high unemployment among educated women. As this study documents at length in chapter 5 (see also Mohan 1985), the supply of women in the labor force grew as access to education expanded in the 1960s and 1970s. Some of the rise in urban unemployment rates in the early 1980s stemmed from the increasing numbers of women desiring to work outside the home.

The travails of the early 1980s have led more recent administrations to adopt policies encouraging the use of labor. The government has also kept the real exchange rate on a par with rates of the mid-1970s, reduced the fiscal deficit to manageable levels (1.4 percent of GDP by 1987), and brought the current account back into balance by 1987. These initiatives have been helped by higher coffee prices. An attempt has also been made to shift public spending away from capital-intensive projects. A war on poverty, launched by the Barco government (1987–90), emphasized extending services to the backward regions of the country and providing health and nutrition services, education, and basic utilities to the poor.

Shelter is an important component of this war on poverty. A welcome change in approach is the recognition that slum upgrading is a key component of housing strategy and that community participation is a must in this process. Less welcome is the return to an earlier strategy of directly investing in housing through the National Housing Agency (Instituto de Crédito Territorial) (see World Bank 1990). Moreover, inadequate attention is being given to rental housing as a vehicle for satisfying the needs of the poorest (see chapter 7). In light of Colombia's experience in the 1980s, our analysis of shelter needs and patterns from a behavioral viewpoint, and our findings about effective policy initiatives, remains valid (see chapter 10).

A final feature of Colombia's economic environment in the 1970s is relevant to our study. Government policies after the mid-1960s did not discriminate against agriculture. Helped by the favorable terms of trade that emerged, the agricultural sector prospered (García 1983; Thomas 1985). The coffee boom from about 1974 to 1980 also contributed, as did the prospering drug trade. Furthermore, the introduction of new coffee varieties and of new agronomic practices increased the demand for labor, and that in turn helped tighten Colombia's rural labor market in the late 1970s. Since these policy and economic changes coincided with the demographic transition described earlier, the supply of rural labor tightened further and real wages rose, bringing improvements in income distribution (Urrutia 1985). These developments were reflected in the urban labor market as well, putting pressure on real wages in the late 1970s. But the deterioration in the general economic situation in the early 1980s, coupled with the fall in coffee prices, erased some of the gains of the 1970s.

Overall, the late 1970s may be seen as a transitional period during which the urbanization process in Colombia was traversing the upper bend of the sigmoid path followed by most urbanizing countries.[1] In conducting this study, we observed the rapid changes in Bogotá (and Cali) resulting from the rapid demographic transition that Colombia had gone through in the 1960s and 1970s. We also observed the fruits of macroeconomic policies in place since the mid-1960s that had stimulated labor using economic and urban growth. Conditions in the urban labor market benefited as well from positive developments in the agricultural sector. Moreover, specific government policies adopted in the early 1970s fostered the generally high levels of urban infrastructure services noted in our study. The early 1980s witnessed a reversal of some of the economic gains posted in the 1970s, but the record of the late 1980s encourages renewed optimism for the future.[2]

Given the changing nature and requirements of maturing urbanization (the stage when the urban population in a country exceeds 70 percent), the future growth of Bogotá (and Cali) will undoubtedly exhibit different characteristics than those documented in our study. But many other countries are now undergoing the phase of rapid urbanization. This volume will provide useful approaches to analyzing city growth in those countries. The improved understanding of how cities work that this study attempts to furnish should influence the adoption of more positive policies for managing large cities as they grow further. Developing countries will continue to see the emergence of large cities for a long time to come.

Overview

The striking result of this study is that many of the behavioral relations documented for Bogotá and Cali are similar to those observed for other cities in both developed and developing countries. This suggests that cities exhibit strong regularities in their patterns of development, which in turn suggests that the transferability of basic behavioral findings is great. This conclusion is bolstered by the fact that Bogotá and Cali have many characteristics typical of other large cities in the developing world. Although many of the results pertain specifically to the two cities studied, the research also shows that economic forces strongly condition the course of urban development and that markets play an important role in the allocation of resources to urban areas. Public use of private incentives can help achieve harmonious development. Efficient city growth requires management and administration that is oriented as much to economic issues as it is to physical "bricks and mortar" issues of infrastructure.

The City Study was divided into seven segments covering various aspects of urban growth and the urban economy. These include the spatial patterns of urban development, the operation of urban land markets, employment and income distribution, the location of employment within the city, housing, transportation, and public finance and administration. This book is more or less organized around these seven segments or topics.[3]

Chapter 2 looks at the patterns of city growth across many countries in both the developing and the developed worlds. It offers a rationale for the emergence of large cities and traces patterns of spatial development common to growing cities. The continuing decentralization of both residence and employment is a feature of most cities as they grow.

Chapter 3 introduces the cities of Bogotá and Cali by summarizing their structure in relation to the spatial distribution of population and land values. It then describes their changing spatial patterns by tracing the density and land value gradients as they evolved over time. The main characteristic of growth associated with these cities, as with other expanding cities, is the decentralization of residence and employment that has occurred.

Together, chapters 4 and 5 cover the third segment of the study, on employment and income distribution. Chapter 4 includes an anatomy of the distribution of income in Bogotá and Cali, with specific attention to the distribution and characteristics of poverty. The central issue considered is the existence and measurement of spatial inequality—that is, the concentration of the poor in certain parts of the city. The various correlates of urban poverty are also described, and the measurable reduction in poverty in the late 1970s is documented. Chapter 5 turns to the work force, which is profiled not only by the usual demographic criteria of age, education, and income level, but also by place of residence within the city. Estimates of the returns to education and experience are also presented in this chapter. An interesting feature of these estimates is how the expansion of access to education has affected the returns to higher education. The segmentation of the labor market is then examined. In addition to the usual segmenting variables such as union membership and the size of firms, the influence of workers' backgrounds, as proxied by their places of origin and residence, proves relevant. The interaction of labor markets with city structure in terms of the location of jobs and workers' residences and the extent of workers' spatial mobility emerges as the theme of this chapter.

Chapter 6 reports on the changing locational patterns of employment in Bogotá and Cali, with a focus on the manufacturing sector. The factors influencing decisions about where to locate are identified and the process of movement described. The discussion emphasizes the role of the central city as an incubator for entrepreneurship. The findings are then generalized to provide some guidelines for public policy.

Chapter 7 assesses the housing situation in Bogotá and the response of housing markets to the city's rapid growth. The institutional setting is described, along with the role of government intervention. The concept of unorganized urban housing markets is afflicted with a host of myths and prejudices; the validity of these is examined in the context of the widespread unregulated housing developments in Bogotá. To achieve a better understanding of the working of housing markets, the function of tenure choice and mobility as adjusting mechanisms is investigated in some detail. Similarly, the main parameters of housing demand, such as income and price elasticities, are carefully estimated. Overall, the study finds that Bogotá's housing market functioned relatively well and that the supply of housing improved despite the city's rapid population growth. The study points clearly to the importance of rental options in satisfying the housing demand of the poor.

Chapter 8 takes a detailed look at the transportation sector in Bogotá. The interdependence of the city's structure and its transportation patterns is described. The regulatory apparatus and the supply mechanisms of urban transport are documented, and the distributive impact of the main taxes and subsidies affecting this sector is evaluated. Bogotá has a wide variety of transport modes, which work relatively well. The overall effect of regulation, taxes, and subsidies is progressive. The modeling of mode choice and other aspects of travel demand are also introduced. The widespread availability of transportation in Bogotá at affordable flat rates, made possible in part by government subsidies, has done much to alleviate the spatial disadvantage of poor workers in Bogotá. The importance of providing a range of choices in urban transportation systems is one of the important conclusions of this study.

Chapter 9 offers a window onto the structure and performance of Bogotá's urban government. The seemingly unplanned and decentralized approach to providing urban services has resulted in relative abundance. The financing pattern differs from that found in most cities.

Borrowing to finance investments is common, and user charges service the loans.

Finally, chapter 10 attempts to give an integrated view of the findings from the City Study. The main lesson seems to be that the most practical way of coping with city growth is to endogenize institutional responses to the rapidly changing and unpredictable demands made by the city's residents. The needs of citizens of a growing city are multifaceted. Whereas overall patterns of city growth are predictable, many individual and group needs are not. Institutions and methods of responding to these changing situations must be developed in such a way that little central direction is necessary. The institutions themselves should be flexible enough to respond to the changing requirements of a city.

Notes

1. As the level of per capita income starts growing in a developing country, the level of urbanization first rises slowly, then accelerates, and finally slows down.

2. Because this study has focused on the economic sphere, the repercussions of the deteriorating social and political situation in Colombia have been ignored.

3. Almost all the findings in this study are empirically based. An appendix documents the vast data sets that have been used in the studies that underlie this book.

Chapter 2

The Spatial Structure of Cities in Developing Countries

Urbanization has been the most pervasive development phenomenon in countries whose per capita income has grown from low to high levels. In most countries the emergence of large cities has been part of the urbanization process. In some of these countries, one city dominates the urban system. In others, there are a number of large cities along with a continuum of smaller settlements, with urban activities well distributed among them. However, a notable feature of this century, and particularly the latter half of this century, has been the emergence of the metropolis as a familiar place for habitation. The greatest growth of large cities, both in the size of individual cities and in the number of large cities, has occurred in the developing countries. As late as 1960, the number of large cities (those with a population of over half a million) in developing countries was about the same as in developed countries: about 100. By 1990 there were probably more than 300 such cities in developing countries—about double the number in developed countries. In 1960 such large cities accounted for a third of total urban population in developing countries; now they account for about half, a proportion similar to that in developed countries. As the numbers rise, it becomes increasingly important to understand the reasons behind the emergence of these cities, the dynamics of their growth, and their changing spatial structures. Are there similarities and patterns that can be observed and understood?

The Emergence of Cities

Urbanization takes place when the predominant economic activity in a region shifts from primary production (agriculture, mining, logging, and such) to secondary and tertiary production (processing and servicing activities). Primary activities are characteristically land-intensive and are therefore spatially dispersed. Secondary and tertiary activities are capital- and labor-intensive and are therefore spatially concentrated. Because the elasticity of substitution between land and nonland production factors in secondary and tertiary activities is greater than that in primary activities, a greater use of capital and labor per unit of land is possible in secondary and tertiary activities.

As incomes increase with economic growth, the demand for services and nonfood goods rises, whereas the relative demand for food falls. At the same time, increases in agricultural productivity make it possible to produce more food with a smaller work force. Labor then shifts from rural areas to those where production of nonfood goods and services is concentrated. Those areas thus become urban.

What actually constitutes an urban area? The traditional characteristics of an urban settlement are a population above a given size, a high density of population, and a predominance of nonagricultural activities. Why do secondary and tertiary activities concentrate in such locations? Because such activities typically exhibit economies of scale, their existence requires a spatially concentrated work force. This work force, along with its dependents, requires an increasing number of activities and people to service its needs, as do the industrial activities themselves. Population begins to snowball as more people and businesses move into the area to meet the needs of the existing enterprises. The growing demand for complementary services and products produces agglomeration effects—economies achieved because of the presence of a multitude of activities—and lead to expansion of the economy as a whole. The combination of scale economies, agglomeration effects, transportation needs, and comparatively higher nonland/land substitution elasticities in industry and services produces a concentration of people and economic activity. Thus cities emerge.

Different industries exhibit different levels of economies of scale. The existence of some industries with greater degrees of scale economies leads to the emergence of large cities. The further specialization of such cities into high-level service, governmental, education, and financial sectors adds to their size. These growing cities offer increasingly varied employment possibilities for workers and their households. The concentration of more skilled jobs also attracts more highly skilled workers from the smaller cities and towns. This in turn generates more jobs and better communication, transportation, water, and sewerage systems, all of which make it possible for cities to grow. As an economy switches into production of more "modern" goods and services, its cities continue to expand (Henderson 1988).

Eighteenth- and nineteenth-century urbanization in European countries was dominated by the imperatives of the Industrial Revolution.

Most people who came to the cities did so to work in the new mills and factories. Current urbanization in developing countries is different in that the tertiary sector requires more labor than does the manufacturing sector. The existence and expansion of cities is therefore equally determined by the economies of scale inherent in certain industries and by the localization economies achieved by the agglomeration of different kinds of service activities in one place.

Understanding the reasons for the emergence of large cities is essential to understanding their internal urban structure. The term "urban structure" refers to the kind, location, and density of activities as they are distributed across space in urban areas. The goal of this study is to understand both how this structure changes as a city grows and what determines these changes.

The main constituents of a city are the people who live there, the firms that do business there, and the government. It is the residents who generate the economic activity that supports the city. Their key demands are for housing—which typically accounts for half of land use in cities—and for transportation to get to work, school, shopping, and leisure. The firms in a city employ people in manufacturing, trade, retailing, and other services. They decide where to locate based on the pattern of demand for their products, the technology they use in production, the location of their suppliers, and their distribution capabilities. The government's role is to supply infrastructure and public services and to regulate economic activity. A key area for government intervention, whether through direct supply of services or through regulation, is that of transportation.

Because people, firms, and governments in different countries concentrate in cities for similar reasons, and because there are common and comprehensible patterns of human behavior, cities throughout the world have quite similar structures. Given such broad similarity, the structure of any city can be studied along similar lines. Differences can be understood by examining the functions of the city, the nature of economic activity found there, the characteristics of the people who live there, and the activities of the government.

This chapter lays out the broad characteristics of cities, giving comparative information for rich and poor countries wherever possible. The next chapter describes the changes that have taken place in Bogotá and Cali as their structures have changed with growth and development over the past quarter-century. These two cities' structural similarity to other cities in both developed and developing countries gives credence to the wider applicability of our detailed behavioral studies. The goal, then, is to look for useful ways of describing cities in a summary fashion and to identify the phenomena that are common to all or most of them. Decentralization, which is fundamental and pervasive with city growth, is one such phenomenon.

Growth and Decentralization

The concurrent growth and decentralization of cities is nothing new. Bowden (1975, p. 78) reports that J. Stow described these processes at work in London in "A Survey of London, Written in the Year 1598":

> In 1598 London had a central business district (in the modern sense) but it had not had one for long. The London Stow describes is still predominantly medieval in that merchants, artisans, the rich and poor, storage and manufacturing were found scattered in all wards and parishes. Great parts of the city were residential. Most people (although a declining majority) lived where they worked. . . .
> Yet specialized warehouses were remarked in the parishes . . . and the old district of the Italian galleymen; tenements and squatter settlements of aliens, primarily Flemish refugees, were concentrating in the suburbs, as well as within the city wall, many formerly clustered activities that we think of as dispersed were seen by Stow as dispersing for the first time, e.g., grocers, vintners and cooks, and manufacturing—particularly that associated with the metal and leather trades—was gravitating to the north. . . . From a population of 50,000 in the 1540s, the city's population had probably trebled by the turn of the century . . . the crucial change is the centripetal movement of the progenitors of the retailers of luxury shopping goods. "Men of trades and sellers of wares in this city have often times changed their places as they have found their best advantages." . . . Most of the luxury traders and their great merchant counterparts had moved toward the center of the city (often without moving their residences with them).

This is a good description of the processes of concentration and deconcentration of cities, and one that is quite applicable in developing countries today. Typically, activities first converge in the city center and then deconcentrate later, a process that had clearly begun in London by the sixteenth century. Moreover, the separation of residence and workplace, while not common then, had begun. The central business district (CBD) had begun to gain specialized functions. Adna Weber, in his classic work on the structure of nineteenth-century cities, said that "the most encouraging feature of the whole situation is the tendency . . . toward the development of suburban towns. The significance of this tendency is that it denotes, not a cessation in the movement toward concentration, but a diminution in the intensity of concentration" (Weber 1963, p. 458).

There has been a tendency to think of decentralization mainly in terms of the widespread growth of American suburbs in the 1950s and 1960s, which was remarkable because of the related decline in the city-center activities. That was a special case of decentralization, perhaps typical of the richest countries, but decentralization in general should be regarded as a wider city growth phenomenon. Mills and Song (1979, pp. 82–83) describe this process succinctly:

> The most important causes of urban decentralization are the growth of metropolitan areas, rising real income, and improved urban transportation. In small urban areas, the purchases of an entire urban area's population are needed to support its commercial and industrial activities, and they are therefore located centrally. As the population and real income of an urban area grow, it becomes possible to support shopping and employment centers with the customers and labor force of only part of the urban area.[1] Thus sub-centers of stores and workplaces appear away from the central business district. Thus fewer people are tied to the city center for jobs and shopping, and they are attracted to suburban residences because of lower land values and correspondingly lower population densities. Real income growth has an additional important effect. As income rises, a family's housing demand rises and it is induced to move further from the center to take advantage of low land values. Improved transportation, whether by public transit or automobile, has the same effect. It increases accessibility to the central business district from distant parts of the urban area, thus permitting people to take advantage of cheap suburban land for housing.

Measurement Issues

How is decentralization to be measured? One obvious measure is the proportion of people living or working in the CBD or in the central city. As long as the boundaries of these entities are kept constant, this measure should give a good sense of concentration, if observed at different times during the growth of a city. Such a measure can be supplemented by the proportion of people living or working in successive rings around the city center. The problem with such measures, however, is that boundaries of the CBD, central city, and rings are arbitrary (although often taken to be legal boundaries), and observation of concentration or deconcentration will depend on their inclusiveness. These boundaries are often enlarged as a city grows. Moreover, the concept of the CBD, although clear in principle, is not clear for measurement purposes. Where are its boundaries? As a city grows, the CBD typically expands. For these reasons, it is better to find methods of describing the density pattern of the whole city that are not so sensitive to boundary-definition issues.

Given the observation of and theoretical justification for density patterns that decline from the city center, it is natural to describe them as being given by a function that shows density declining exponentially from the city center: $D_x = D_o\, e^{-gx}$, where D_x is density at distance x from the CBD, D_o is the estimated density at the center, and g is the estimated rate of decline of density. Thus g may be interpreted as the percentage decline in density per unit distance. The larger g is, the greater the rate of decline from the center and the more concentrated the city. The decline in g over time then measures the rate of decentralization of the city. And because g can be measured if there is information on the population density of different parts of a city and because it is expressed in units of density decline per kilometer or mile, its value can be compared across cities. Values are given for a whole range of cities in the next section.

A few issues concerning measurement need to be mentioned. First is the selection of the exponential functional form. Several articles (for example, Griffith 1981; Anderson 1982; Wheaton 1982a, 1982b) have questioned the validity of the simple exponential form and suggested more complex forms for estimation. One criticism is on theoretical as well as econometric grounds. The simple exponential form can be derived from economic theory assuming static equilibrium in the urban area (Mills 1967). It is argued that, in fact, urban areas grow from a historical process of successive accretion, and, because of the durability of structures, the urban area is not in equilibrium at any given time. The density function should therefore be derived from a more realistic model of city growth. Another criticism concerns CBDs with little residential population. There is a doughnut-like hole in the city center (Anderson 1982). Moving outward from the city center, the population density first rises and then begins to decline toward the suburbs. This is observed in some cities in developing countries as well as in most developed countries (see, for example, Asabere and Owusu-Banahere 1983 for African cities).

There is considerable merit in these arguments, and the functional form can clearly be refined. The elegant simplicity of the negative exponential is appealing, however, and although inexact, it is not inconsistent with some of the other formulations suggested. It also has the advantage of being the most common functional form estimated and is therefore available for comparison purposes.[2] The general problem of the empty city center is often solved by excluding city-center observations from the estimation sample. The recent refinements are also useful in interpreting the results of the simple estimation.

Chief Determinants of Decentralization

It is useful to obtain some idea of what the more powerful determinants of decentralization are and which of these are expected to be especially relevant in developing countries. The most important determinant is increase in population. Historically, the decrease in transportation costs has also been very important; this was especially true during the major transition from animal-drawn vehicles to motorized vehicles and later from rail transportation to private automobiles (the latter particularly in developed countries, where the advent of the limited-access highway followed the rise of the automobile). In developing countries many modes of transport coexist, and different classes of people have access to different modes at different prices (see chapter 8). The third key determinant has been rising per capita income. Again, this has been more important for developed countries in the last half-century. The rapid rate of city growth in developing countries has included high rates of immigration; this has meant that, paradoxically, the rate of per capita income growth has been low in the largest cites even when it has been high for the country as a whole. In-migration has essentially been an equilibrating mechanism, reducing the disparities between large city/ other and between overall urban/rural income levels. Rates of income growth have therefore been high for some groups of people and corresponding parts of cities, and low for other groups and parts of cities. Thus, growth in population is a good explanation for residential decentralization in some parts of a city, whereas income growth may explain decentralization in another part.

Rich people often live largely in one area of a city, and as the city expands and income grows, they continue to fill spaces in the same direction as city growth; the poor, meanwhile, live in another area of the city and expand in another direction. The density patterns are quite different for these two segments of the city. The standard residential pattern in cities in developed countries is one of the rich living in outer rings and the poor in inner rings. Theoretically this is because the demand for housing space is highly income elastic for the rich, and lower land prices at the periphery more than offset the increased transportation costs that result from living greater distances from the city center. In cities in developing countries, however, it is now quite common to observe many low-income suburban settlements, as well as a few high-income residential suburbs, on the city periphery. This pattern is documented in detail for Bogotá and Cali in chapters 3 and 4. These low-income settlements are often of high densities. An examination of density gradients, g, in such cases yields the expected flattening out— but the flattening out is at a high density level everywhere. In cities in developed countries, the flattening out is at the low density levels that result from decreases close to the center and increases at the periphery.

It is fascinating to speculate on the reasons for these different patterns. One is explicit government policy. As Asabere and Owusu-Banahere (1983) have documented for African cities, in the pursuit of an ideal Garden City concept, it has been quite common for governments to clear congested central cities, usually populated by the poor, and move the inhabitants to distant locations, often designed as sites-and-services projects.[3] The original idea that concentration was bad emanated from the dismal health conditions in European industrial cities in the eighteenth and nineteenth centuries. This idea has been transferred somewhat uncritically to developing countries. Even when people have not been relocated, it is common to design high-density residential complexes for poor people at the periphery, because that is where land is available and inexpensive.

The second factor in high-density peripheral development has to do with the nature of housing demand and the construction technology available to the poor. As chapter 7 and other studies document, the poor spend considerable portions of their income on shelter; in fact, even for middle-income residents, housing has low income elasticity of demand. Among the poor, price elasticity of demand is also low. Given low income levels, the building technology used is pretty rudimentary, and construction is a mixture of self-help and contracting. There is evidence from Bogotá and Cali that homes in the poorer areas have fewer floors than homes in the richer areas (see chapter 3). Low-income housing is seldom more than three stories, because going higher would require steel, more cement, and formal construction methods. The extent of substitution of capital for land in low-income housing is therefore limited. The high proportions of income spent on shelter and the low income elasticity of demand also suggest some maximum threshold for crowding. The result of these two effects is only a small density gradient in poor parts of the city: the areas near the center are only slightly more densely inhabited than those on the periphery. It is typically larger households with greater space needs that are pushed toward the outskirts to take advantage of lower land prices. In the poorer areas there is little difference in per capita space between the center and the periphery. Transportation costs affect this pattern, too. If there is a flat fare system, the poor can afford to live on the periphery, because they spend only more time traveling—not more money.

Which Came First—Decentralization of Population or Businesses?

In cities in developing countries and industrial countries alike, employment decentralization appears to lag behind residential decentralization. There has been relatively early decentralization of large and polluting manufacturing activities in cities in developing countries. As in residential development, the Garden City philosophy has played a role in locating large—and often even small—industry in peripheral industrial parks. Again, the desire for a clean, arboreal central city has been buttressed by the availability of cheaper land at the periphery. The deindustrialized CBD in these cities then tends to specialize in retail and wholesale trade, banking and finance, and other service functions. Given the paucity of overall demand for services because of low incomes, these functions often become more concentrated during the initial stages of urban growth. If decentralization occurs, it usually happens after the richer residents have left the central city and established communities that can sustain subcenters of employment. There is little decentralization of service functions to the poorer areas, except to meet essential daily retail needs. Overall patterns of employment decentralization can therefore be quite different between manufacturing and tertiary sectors and between rich and poor parts of the city. Given these considerations, we can expect a continuing trend toward employment decentralization in cities in developing countries when those cities exhibit continuing population and income growth and residential decentralization.

The preceding discussion illustrates how changes in the environment and the behavior of firms, households, and individuals are connected to changes in urban structure as measured by density gradients. The next section considers the changes in density gradients that have been observed in cities in both developed and developing countries.

City Characteristics: Evidence from Different Countries

What are some of the broad structural characteristics of cities, and how have they changed over time? This section draws on research reported in Ingram and Carroll (1981); most evidence is taken from Latin American countries so that Bogotá and Cali can be seen in their appropriate context.

In 1970 twenty-four Latin American cities had central-city populations of more than 600,000 or metropolitan populations of more than 1 million. North America had thirty-six metropolitan areas with 1 million or more inhabitants. Of the large Latin American cities, comparable data were available for only thirteen. Twelve large U.S. metropolitan areas from various parts of the country were selected on the basis of comparative size and rate of population growth during 1950–70.

Overall, urban population growth was much higher in the 1950s than in the 1960s in both Latin America and the United States (see table 2-1). In the Latin American cities, the average annual growth rate declined from 5.5 percent in the 1950s to 4.6 percent in the 1960s; in the U.S. cities it declined much more, from about 4.1 to 2.5 percent. Although it is difficult to assemble comparable information for the period since 1970, it is apparent that these trends have continued, and urban population growth has declined further in both regions. In the United States most older large cities lost population during the 1970s while the newer cities, mostly in the Southwest, continued to grow. Table 2-1 shows that except for Mexico City, the larger cities grew somewhat more slowly than the smaller cities, with this tendency being much more pronounced in the United States than in Latin America.

Preston (1979) confirms this general pattern worldwide. This suggests that, for the most populous cities, the advantages of urban agglomeration economies and economies of scale tend to get exhausted, and some urban diseconomies might set in. This should not be overstated, however, since the largest cities in developing countries continue to grow at significant rates. The main reasons for the overall decline in urban population growth in North America and in Western Europe are that these regions are approaching 100 percent urbanization levels and their total population growth has become very small—near zero percent in some countries. Within the developing world, Latin America has the highest urbanization levels, with many countries more than 60 percent urbanized.

A major difference between North American and Latin American cities is that large cities in Latin America (and in developing countries in general) have much lower real income levels. Gross national product (GNP) per capita in 1975 was $7,100[4] (in 1975 dollars) for North America and $1,000 for Latin America (World Bank 1977). Based on growth rates reported by Kuznets (1966), North America would have had a per capita GNP of $1,000 (1975 dollars) in the 1850s. There were no cities of more than 1 million people then. Hence, although some similar changes are observed over time in developed and developing countries, their levels of magnitude are often quite different.

It is interesting to observe changes in the intrametropolitan population distribution as large cities grow. Table 2-2 summarizes data for a twenty-year period for the central and peripheral areas of the ten Latin American cities with available data and the twelve U.S. cities from table 2-1. It is striking that across the cities on both continents, both the central and peripheral densities vary by an order of magnitude: this is an indication of the definitional problems that are encountered when making such comparisons. What is the central city? Where does it end and the periphery begin? In most metropolitan areas worldwide, the area considered to be the central city has a residential density of about 5,000 to 20,000 people per square kilometer (see Mohan 1980). Central densities are continuing to increase in most Latin American cities, whereas they are clearly stabilizing or decreasing in North America. Peripheral densities are rising in nearly all cities in this sample, and rising faster than central-city densities. Thus pervasive decentralization is taking place in both North American and Latin American cities, with the trend more pronounced in the former. The Latin American central densities

Table 2-1. Population and Population Growth in Selected Latin American and U.S. Metropolitan Areas

Latin American city	Population (thousands)			Annual growth rate (percent)	
	1950	1960	1970	1950-60	1960-70
Mexico City	3,180	5,246	8,657	5.1	5.1
São Paulo	2,708	4,818	8,195	5.9	5.5
Buenos Aires	4,723	6,739	8,189	2.8	2.0
Rio de Janeiro[a]	3,298	5,012	7,082	4.3	3.5
Lima[b]	—	1,846	3,302	—	5.4
Bogotá[c]	715	1,697	2,855	6.9	5.9
Santiago[d]	1,509	2,170	2,820	4.6	2.7
Caracas[e]	724	1,388	2,199	6.1	4.7
Recife	819	1,240	1,793	4.2	3.8
Belo Horizonte	475	888	1,606	6.5	6.1
Guadalajara	440	851	1,455	6.8	5.5
Monterrey	376	708	1,213	6.5	5.5
Cali[c]	284	638	898	6.4	3.9

U.S. city	Population (thousands)			Annual growth rate (percent)	
	1950	1960	1970	1950-60	1960-70
New York	9,556	10,695	11,572	1.1	0.8
Los Angeles	4,152	6,039	7,032	3.8	1.5
Chicago	5,178	6,221	6,979	1.9	1.2
Philadelphia	3,671	4,343	4,818	1.7	1.0
Washington, D.C.	1,508	2,077	2,861	3.3	3.3
Boston	2,414	2,595	2,754	0.7	0.6
Houston	936	1,418	1,985	4.2	3.4
San Diego	557	1,033	1,358	6.4	2.8
Miami	495	935	1,268	6.6	3.1
Denver	612	929	1,228	4.3	2.8
San Jose	291	642	1,065	8.2	5.2
Phoenix	332	664	968	7.2	3.8

— Not available.
a. Data are for 1947, 1960, and 1970.
b. Data are for 1950, 1961, and 1972.
c. Data are for 1951, 1964, and 1973.
d. Data are for 1952, 1960, and 1970.
e. Data are for 1950, 1961, and 1971.
Source: Ingram and Carroll (1981).

Table 2-2. Population Density in Central and Peripheral Areas of Selected Latin American and U.S. Cities

Latin American city	Location[a]	Area (square kilometers)	Population per square kilometer		
			1950	1960	1970
Mexico City	C	138	16,225	20,558	21,074
	P	2,192	432	1,101	2,675
São Paulo	C	1,493[b]	1,380	2,287	4,005
	P	6,458	79	172	343
Buenos Aires	C	200	14,952	14,872	14,897
	P	3,860	473	1,025	1,418
Rio de Janeiro	C	1,171	2,030	2,824	3,631
	P	5,293	174	322	535
Bogotá[c]	C	304	2,352	5,582	9,391
	P		—	—	—
Recife	C	290[d]	3,594	3,815	5,075
	P	1,992	148	223	367
Belo Horizonte	C	335	1,053	2,070	3,686
	P	3,335	37	58	111
Guadalajara	C	188	2,204	3,940	6,383
	P	1,164	52	95	220
Cali[c]	C	85	3,341	7,506	10,565
	P	—	—	—	—

U.S. city	Location[a]	Area (square kilometers)	Population per square kilometer		
			1950	1960	1970
New York	C	777	10,157	10,015	10,161
	P	4,758	350	612	773
Los Angeles	C	1,326	1,675	2,130	2,390
	P	9,213	210	350	420
Chicago	C	578	6,275	6,140	5,825
	P	9,054	170	295	400
Philadelphia	C	334	6,202	5,995	5,835
	P	8,868	180	264	325
Washington, D.C.	C	158	5,077	4,835	4,790
	P	5,936	119	221	355
Boston	C	119	6,735	5,860	5,387
	P	2,435	662	780	867
Houston	C	1,028	580	913	1,198
	P	15,250	22	31	49
San Diego	C	552	606	1,038	1,258
	P	10,484	21	44	63
Denver	C	246	1,690	2,008	2,092
	P	9,233	21	47	77
San Jose	C	300	318	681	1,480
	P	3,067	64	143	202
Phoenix	C	642	166	684	906
	P	23,069	10	10	17

— Not available.
a. C = center; P = periphery.
b. 1,622 in 1959 and 1960.
c. Data are for 1951, 1964, and 1973.
d. 146 in 1950.
Source: Ingram and Carroll (1981).

29

Table 2-3. Population Density Gradients in Selected Latin American and U.S. Cities

Latin American city	pb	Parameter[a]	1950	1960	1970
Mexico City	1.0	D_o	69,000	62,000	44,000
		g	0.37	0.27	0.17
São Paulo	1.0	D_o	8,400	12,000	18,000
		g	0.14	0.13	0.12
Buenos Aires	0.6	D_o	54,000	37,000	33,000
		g	0.21	0.14	0.02
Rio de Janeiro	0.5	D_o	8,700	10,000	11,000
		g	0.09	0.08	0.07
Bogotá	0.5	D_o	—	37,000	26,000
		g	—	0.25	0.12
Recife	0.6	D_o	13,000	14,000	17,000
		g	0.25	0.21	0.19
Belo Horizonte	1.0	D_o	5,000	11,000	19,000
		g	0.26	0.28	0.27
Guadalajara	1.0	D_o	14,000	28,000	39,000
		g	0.45	0.46	0.41
Monterrey	1.0	D_o	6,200	8,500	7,400
		g	0.32	0.27	0.19
Cali	0.5	D_o	—	43,000	29,000
		g	—	0.41	0.21

U.S. city	pb	Parameter[a]	1950	1960	1970
New York	0.6	D_o	62,000	45,000	40,000
		g	0.16	0.13	0.11
Los Angeles	0.6	D_o	4,800	5,300	5,800
		g	0.06	0.06	0.05
Chicago	0.5	D_o	27,000	20,000	16,000
		g	0.13	0.10	0.08
Philadelphia	1.0	D_o	20,000	16,000	14,000
		g	0.18	0.15	0.13
Washington, D.C.	1.0	D_o	15,000	11,000	9,000
		g	0.25	0.18	0.14
Boston	0.7	D_o	14,000	11,000	9,300
		g	0.16	0.13	0.12
Houston	1.0	D_o	2,100	3,500	4,200
		g	0.12	0.13	0.12
San Diego	0.5	D_o	2,100	3,200	3,600
		g	0.11	0.10	0.09
Miami	0.5	D_o	8,000	6,800	7,200
		g	0.23	0.15	0.13
Denver	1.0	D_o	6,800	6,000	5,100
		g	0.27	0.20	0.16
San Jose	0.5	D_o	620	1,300	3,500
		g	0.08	0.07	0.10
Phoenix	1.0	D_o	350	2,700	3,100
		g	0.08	0.16	0.14

— Not available.

Note: Density gradients were calculated using the technique described in White (1977).

a. Parameters from density $= D_o e^{-gx}$, where x is the distance in kilometers from the city center, g is the density gradient per kilometer, and D_o is the estimated central city density.

Source: Ingram and Carroll (1981).

are akin to older North American cities, and the newer North American cities are structurally dispersed, with low densities all over.

Data in table 2-2 are based on arbitrary definitions of central and peripheral areas. Density functions are more robust than actual central-city densities as proxies for detecting city structures and for summarizing changes over time. As Mills and Tan (1980) report, urban population density functions have been estimated for almost every developed country in the world, and an increasing number of estimates are available for developing countries as well. As mentioned earlier, the exponential density function provides a good summary indicator of city structure, with g measuring the percentage of decline in density per unit distance and D_0 measuring the theoretical density at the center.

The concept behind this functional form is that of a circular mono-centric city. There has been considerable discussion of the use of other functional forms to account for two problems: cities typically have more than one large employment center, and the city center typically has very little residential population since most land is used for economic activity.[5] These are useful elaborations of the simple theory and provide for more realistic estimation, but they lose the elegant simplicity of the exponential function. Moreover, they cannot be used for comparison purposes because most estimates that exist are for the simple exponential form.

Thus, g is a good summary measure of decentralization. For a fixed radius x of a circular city, the smaller the g, the smaller the proportion of people living within x distance of the city center and the more decentralized the city. Hence, when g declines from one decade to the next, the city can be said to have decentralized.

Table 2-3 displays estimates of density function parameters for the same sample of Latin American and U.S. cities. The density gradient g declined over time in most cites, increasing only in Guadalajara, Belo Horizonte, Houston, San Jose, and Phoenix—and in each case in only one of the two decades. The decline in the population density gradients in Bogotá and Cali was particularly significant: both fell by almost half between 1960 and 1970, implying a notable decentralization of population. Latin American cities generally have steeper gradients than U.S. cities, as do smaller cities compared with larger ones. Intercept (central city) densities (D_0) are significantly higher in Latin American than U.S. cities; the averages are 24,000 and 10,000, respectively. Latin American city centers are also more highly congested in terms of residential population.

When we combine the comparison of intercept densities with that made for density gradients, two major points emerge. First, there is a surprising degree of similarity between the density function parameters of large Latin American and U.S. cities. This similarity is enhanced when we compare the large Latin American cities to only the five older Northeastern cities (New York, Chicago, Philadelphia, Washington, and Boston). The 1970 average intercept and gradient, 17,700 and 0.116, for these five cities are similar to the 1970 averages, 24,600 and 0.12, respectively, for the large Latin American cities. It appears, too, that density function parameters follow different patterns in Latin America and the United States: As size varies, U.S. cities have fairly constant density gradients and varying intercept densities, while Latin American cities have fairly constant intercept densities and varying density gradients. Coupling this pattern with the similarity of parameters for large cities suggests that the relatively smaller Latin American cities have larger intercept densities and steeper gradients than similar U.S. cities and therefore are much more centralized.

These patterns are quite common the world over and in recent history. The regular decline in gradient over the past century (see table 2-4) is remarkable, and the pattern clearly transcends countries and cultures. The picture for a larger sample (see table 2-5) is a little more varied, but the broad patterns continue to hold true. The largest cities—those with population between 5 million and 10 million—appear to have a uniformly low gradient of around 0.1 or less, whereas smaller cities generally have much higher gradients. More densely populated countries, such as India, Japan, and the Republic of Korea, tend to have higher overall densities and higher gradients in their smaller cities than Latin American countries do.

Although density function comparisons have been based on city size to some extent, the data suggest that city age, transportation technology, and per capita income are also important determinants of the decentralization observed in a city (Harrison and Kain 1979; White 1977). For example, density gradients vary for North American cities of different vintage, and they are similar for Latin American cities and older North American cities. Older cities developed during a period when public transit was the dominant mode, as it still is in most developing countries. By the time the newer U.S. cities, like San Jose, Phoenix, Houston, and Los Angeles, emerged and developed, automobiles had become the dominant form of transportation. The older cities in industrial countries and most cities in developing countries are therefore more centralized and have higher densities than the newer North American cities. This also suggests that portions of developing-country cities that are newly developed or inhabited by the rich could be similar to the newer North American patterns of city development.

The level of structural similarity is quite surprising. Living conditions, per capita incomes, patterns of housing, and levels of public service infrastructure vary considerably among North America, Latin America, Europe, Africa, India, and East Asia, as do the histories and cultural

Table 2-4. Population Density Gradients Per Kilometer in Selected Cities Worldwide by Decade, 1880–1960

Year	Average for four U.S. cities[a]	Chicago	London	Paris	Bombay	Kingston (Jamaica)
1880	1.22	0.49	0.38	0.60	0.37	—
1890	1.06	0.32	—	—	0.33	1.02
1900	0.96	0.22	0.23	0.50	0.26	—
1910	0.80	0.23	—	—	0.24	0.90
1920	0.69	0.16	0.17	—	0.20	—
1930	0.63	0.13	0.17	0.50	0.17	—
1940	0.59	0.13	0.14	—	0.17	0.54
1950	0.50	0.11	0.12	0.21	0.13	—
1960	0.31	—	0.09	—	0.10	0.33

— Not available.
a. Baltimore, Milwaukee, Philadelphia, and Rochester.
Source: Mills and Tan (1980).

influences of each of these regions. Yet decentralization of cities has been a pervasive phenomenon accompanying growth. Moreover, judging from North American and Western European cities, decentralization continues even after population growth stops. This is what attracted the most attention in the 1960s and 1970s, because its effects—the emptying out of central cities and the increasing residential separation of the rich in suburbs and the poor in the center—are stark. The phenomenon of decentralization observed in developing countries is then closer to the earlier pattern for cities in developed countries, when growth was accompanied by decentralization. The distinction essentially is that in these periods D_0 continues to increase or remains constant as g declines, whereas in later stages D_0 declines as well.

The documentation for employment density gradients is less abundant because of the difficulty of obtaining spatial data on employment, which is not typically reported in population censuses. However, the pattern of continuing decentralization is well documented for some countries, such as Brazil, Japan, the Republic of Korea, and the United States (for example, see, respectively, Y. J. Lee 1985; Mills and Ohta 1976; Mills and Song 1979; and Mills 1972). Employment density gradients are typically much steeper than those of population density, which suggests the familiar overall pattern of inward commuting for work. Employment decentralization has usually lagged behind residential decentralization. Manufacturing is usually the first sector to begin decentralizing for the technological reasons discussed earlier, essentially connected with the ease of substituting capital for land. The portion of retail trade that serves the daily needs of consumers typically decentralizes with population, but the other portions remain centralized, along with much of wholesale trade. Office activities often remain the most centralized; the possibilities of capital/land substitution are extremely high for these activities. Because commercial activities are the most directly related to consumer buying power, their rate of decentralization is closely related to prevailing income levels (see table 2-6). It is therefore reasonable to expect less centralization of these activities in rich cities and in richer sections of poor cities. Chapter 6 documents these patterns as they apply to Bogotá and Cali.

The Consequences of Growth and Decentralization

Because we can expect continued growth of large cities along with decentralization, it is necessary to examine some of the consequences of these patterns. First, we need to understand that although the process of urban growth and decentralization in developing countries is similar

Table 2-5. Population Density Gradients Per Kilometer in Selected Cities Worldwide, 1950, 1960, 1965, and 1970

City	1950	1960	1965	1970
Large cities				
New York	0.16	0.13	—	0.11
Tokyo	0.06	0.07	0.08	0.08
London	—	0.08	—	0.07
Madras	0.24	0.24	—	—
Great Britain[a]	—	0.10	—	0.06
West Germany[a]	—	0.25	—	0.21
Japan[a]	—	—	—	0.48
Seoul	—	0.35	0.33	0.22
Medium-size cities				
Birmingham	—	0.12	—	0.04
Manchester	—	0.08	—	0.06
Accra	—	0.52	—	0.46
Poona (India)	—	1.05	—	1.07
Pusan (Republic of Korea)	—	—	0.26	0.13
Kumasi (Ghana)	—	—	0.61	0.55
Taegu (Republic of Korea)	—	—	0.78	0.74
Bangalore (India)	0.61	0.53	—	—
Great Britain[b]	—	0.34	—	0.25
West Germany[b]	—	0.31	—	0.31
Japan[b]	—	—	—	0.49

— Not available.

a. Data are averages for cities with populations of more than 1 million.

b. Data are averages for cities with populations of 0.5 million to 1 million.

Source: Ingram and Carroll (1981) for New York; Mills and Ohta (1976) for Tokyo; Mills and Tan (1980) for Madras, Poona, and Bangalore; Mills and Song (1979) for Seoul, Pusan, and Taegu; Asabere and Owusu-Banahere (1983) for Kumasi; Glickman (1979) for all others.

Table 2-6. Central City Shares of Residential Population and Employment, Selected Latin American Cities
(percent)

		Residential population						Employment		
	Year	Economically active population	Professionals/technical workers	Office workers/salespeople	Service workers	Blue-collar workers	Car owners	Manufacturing	Commerce	Service
Mexico City	1950	73	86	81	70[a]	—	—	—	—	—
	1960	59	72	66	49[a]	—	—	—	—	—
	1970	39	52	47	43	28	—	—	—	—
São Paulo	1950	85	—	—	—	—	—	84	95	—
	1960	—	—	—	—	—	82	80	92	90
	1970	75	—	—	—	—	—	71	—	—
Buenos Aires	1950	65	—	—	—	—	—	67	—	—
	1960	46	62	55	57	—	—	49[c]	—	83[b]
	1970	37	56	48	44	—	54	—	—	66[b,c]
Rio de Janeiro	1950	76	—	—	—	—	—	77	—	—
	1960	56	—	—	—	—	—	75	88	—
	1970	68	—	—	—	—	79	76	86	82
Recife	1950	—	—	—	—	—	—	59	—	—
	1960	63	—	—	—	—	—	63	86	—
	1970	77	—	—	—	—	82	63	85	86
Belo Horizonte	1950	—	—	—	—	—	—	56	—	—
	1960	—	—	—	—	—	—	47	91	—
	1970	81	—	—	—	—	90	53	92	88
Guadalajara	1950	87	95	94	91[a]	—	—	94[d]	—	—
	1960	88	96	94	90[a]	—	—	92[e]	—	—
	1970	84	91	89	86	84	—	87	—	—
Monterrey	1950	91	94	95	92[a]	—	—	—	—	—
	1960	86	89	89	85[a]	—	—	—	—	—
	1970	66	78	76	71	70	—	—	—	—

— Not available.
a. Service workers and blue-collar workers combined. b. Commerce and service combined. c. For 1964. d. For 1956. e. For 1965.
Source: Ingram and Carroll (1981).

to that in developed countries, the existence of different initial conditions and behavioral parameters often makes the results quite varied. The emergence of large, low-income, high-density settlements on the peripheries of cities raises the questions of where jobs and transportation networks should be located and how the costs of public services should be structured. For example, the establishment of a flat-fare transportation system would help residents overcome the disadvantage of living far from the center, but such a system would give the wrong signals about the associated resource costs of transportation. The provision and pricing of other essential services, such as water, sewerage, and drainage, present a similar problem. Residential decentralization stretches out the supply networks of these services, which are then expensive to provide. If the poor have little choice about where to live in the first place, however, they can hardly be charged high prices for essential services. Some of these issues are therefore difficult to analyze because of their politico-economic nature.

Another common consequence of residential decentralization is the increased spatial separation of the rich in suburbs and the poor in the central city (see chapter 4). This separation has economic as well as social effects. Employment opportunities are likely to be more plentiful in the better-off areas, where the residents have a greater demand for goods and services. The poor then either commute long distances to work in these areas, or they seek residential land nearby. This often gives rise to squatter settlements and slums in the middle of otherwise rich neighborhoods. Because of the high land values and pressures to use the land more "productively," the government often relocates poor residents, frequently by force.

The decentralization of employment and residences naturally causes a rapid conversion of agricultural land to urban uses. This is often perceived to be a major problem, and fears are expressed about the dwindling supply of agricultural land. This is, on the whole, a false concern. Even in the most densely populated countries, such as Japan and Korea, only a small fraction of total arable land is urbanized. The loss of agricultural land is, however, a legitimate concern for the farmers whose property is urbanized, even if they are fairly compensated. When they lose their livelihood, they often do not receive appropriate training and employment in alternative occupations. The faster the growth and decentralization of a city, the more serious this problem is, as the competition for land at the urban fringe becomes intense. The challenge for policymakers is to ensure that land is allocated to its most economically efficient use and that the legitimate interests of owners and users, both old and new, are protected.

Notes

1. Compare this development with the "dispersing for the first time [of] grocers, vintners and cooks" in sixteenth-century London.

2. For theoretical derivation and review of this functional form, see Mills (1967, 1972) and Mohan (1979).

3. See Berry (1973) chapter 3 and Jacobs (1961) chapter 1 for discussion of the Garden City concept.

4. All dollar amounts are U.S. dollars unless labeled otherwise.

5. For example, Griffith (1981) discusses a generalization of the simple exponential form to account for multicentered cities; Anderson (1982) proposes a cubic spline function to account for an empty center.

Chapter 3

Growth and the Changing Structure
of Bogotá and Cali

Unlike many other Latin American countries—for example, Argentina, Ecuador, Peru, and Venezuela—Colombia has a well-articulated system of cities in which Bogotá accounts for only about 20 percent of the total urban population. Colombia's primacy index (that is, the ratio of the population of the largest city to the total urban population of the country) is the lowest in Latin America except for that of Brazil (see Renaud 1981). However, Bogotá's share of both population and output has increased over the past few decades (see tables 3-1 and 3-2).

Within forty years Colombia was transformed from a predominantly rural country to one that is predominantly urban; its urbanization level rose from about 30 to 65 percent. During the same period Bogotá grew from an intermediate-size city (by today's standards) into a large metropolis. It had a remarkably high and sustained rate of population growth, of about 5 percent a year over almost a half a century (see table 3-1). Tables 3-2 and 3-3 give the comparable growth in economic output since 1950. The growth rate of Bogotá's regional product was 7 percent per year during 1950–75, while that for Colombia was 5.2 percent. But because population grew faster in Bogotá than in the country as a whole, the per capita growth rate for the city's gross product was only 0.6 percent a year, versus 2.1 percent a year nationwide (see table 3-3). Economic opportunities in Bogotá led to substantial labor mobility, and the per capita differential between Bogotá and Colombia as a whole narrowed over the years until it was only about 1.5 by the mid-1970s. It would be even lower if price differentials were accounted for. Bogotá grew faster than other Colombian cities taken as a whole over this period (and earlier—as long ago as the mid-1800s), and it emerged with a high concentration of people and economic activity by the 1970s. Cali,

Table 3-1. Population and Intercensal Population Growth in Colombia

	Population			Annual compound growth rate (percent)		
Year	Total (thousands)	Urban[a] (percent)	Bogotá (percent)	Total	Urban[a]	Bogotá
1938	8,702	31	3.8	n.a.	n.a.	n.a.
1951	11,548	39	5.7	2.2	3.9	5.2
1964	17,485	52	9.5	3.2	5.4	7.3
1973	22,500	60	12.7	2.7	3.7	5.6
1983	26,965[b]	65[b]	15.1[c]	2.0	3.0	4.0[c]

n.a. Not applicable.

a. The urban population is the percentage living in a county seat (*cabecera municipal*). Most county seats have 1,500 people or more, but some have fewer; moreover, not all settlements that large are county seats.

b. Data are estimates from Sokol and others (1984).

c. Bogotá's 1978 population was estimated from the World Bank–DANE Household Survey. The 4.0 percent population growth rate observed from 1973 to 1978 was assumed to continue until 1983.

Source: 1938, 1951, 1964, and 1975 population censuses; Sokol and others (1984).

too, has grown consistently (see table 3-4). This record is consistent with the idea that cities grow because they are more efficient economic producers, benefiting from agglomeration and scale economies.

The average population density of Bogotá shows remarkable stability in the face of rapid population growth. Peak density occurred at the end of the 1950s, the period of most rapid growth. (The area data must be regarded as somewhat dubious because the juridical definition of the area of a city is always somewhat arbitrary, as is more evident in the data for Cali. The extension of a city's boundaries eventually does, however, reflect the area that is regarded as belonging to the city at any given time.) The pattern for Bogotá suggests that the juridical area of the city

Table 3-2. Gross and Per Capita Domestic Product, Colombia and Bogotá

	Colombia		Bogotá		Bogotá's GRP as a percentage of Colombia's GDP	Bogotá's GRP per capita as a percentage of Colombia's GDP per capita
Year	GDP (millions of pesos)	GDP per capita (pesos)	GRP (millions of pesos)	GRP per capita (pesos)		
1960	77,714	5,088	11,996	9,220	15.4	1.81
1965	97,968	5,455	17,208	9,591	17.6	1.76
1970	130,361	6,484	25,920	10,822	19.9	1.67
1975	176,478	7,352	37,671	11,779	21.3	1.60

Note: GDP = gross domestic product. GRP = gross regional product. Pesos are 1970 pesos; the exchange rate was US$1 = Col$18.40.

Source: Colombia (1977).

Table 3-3. Average Annual Growth in Domestic Product, Colombia and Bogotá
(percent)

Period	Colombia		Bogotá	
	GDP	GDP per capita	GRP	GRP per capita
1950–75	5.2	2.1	7.0	0.6
1960–75	5.6	2.5	7.9	1.7
1970–75	6.2	3.2	7.8	1.7

Note: GDP = gross domestic product. GRP = gross regional product.
Source: Table 3-2.

tends to follow growth in population, albeit with a lag. The constant average density implies that Bogotá has always been decentralizing as it has grown, in the sense that the central parts of the city have housed a successively smaller proportion of the total population. It would be interesting to see whether such a pattern holds for other cities. If so, it would go against the general notion that cities become increasingly congested as their populations grow. Cali's density pattern is more erratic because the juridical area has been changed in fits and starts, but there, too, density stabilized in the 1970s and is now comparable to Bogotá's. Overall land development has clearly kept pace with population growth in these cities, and the city area appears to have become an endogenous variable.

How does Bogotá compare with other cities in the world in terms of density? Bogotá falls midway between the world's densest cities, such as Bombay (140 people per hectare) and Calcutta (120 per hectare), and such North American cities as Chicago, Philadelphia, Detroit, and San Francisco, which have about 40 to 60 people per hectare. New York City (including the boroughs of the Bronx, Manhattan, Queens, and Brooklyn) is about as dense as Bogotá, with more than 100 people per hectare. There is a large degree of similarity in overall population densities in large cities in the world, and Bogotá falls somewhere in the middle.

How has the physical character of Bogotá changed as it has grown? Its original design was the traditional rectangular grid of streets and avenues, with the Plaza Principal as the focus of the city. Until the early twentieth century the entire built-up area of the city occupied what is now only the central business district (CBD). The city was primarily a commercial, political, and religious center; Medellín was the industrial capital of the country. (Medellín had more manufacturing employment than Bogotá until about the late 1960s. It has since become better known for more dubious activities.) High- and middle-income residents of Bogotá began to move north in the second quarter of this century as the southern and western parts of the city began to fill up with lower-

Table 3-4. Area, Population, Population Growth, and Density in Bogotá and Cali

City and year	Area (hectares)	Population (thousands)	Average annual growth rate (percent)	Density (population per hectare)
Bogotá				
1560	20	—	—	—
1600	56	—	—	—
1670	129	3	—	23
1720	—	20[a]	3.9	—
1800	—	22[a]	0.1	—
1850	294	30	0.6	100
1886	610	64	2.2	105
1900	909	100	3.2	110
1928[b]	1,958	235	3.1	120
1938[b]	2,514	330	3.5	131
1951	—	660	5.5	—
1958	8,084	1,130	8.0	140
1964[b]	14,615	1,730	7.4	118
1973[b]	30,423	2,877	5.8	95
1978[c]	30,886	3,500	4.0	113
Cali				
1800	50[d]	6[e]	—	120
1880	114[d]	15[e]	1.1	127
1900	—	24[e]	2.5	—
1918	—	45[e]	3.6	—
1938	400[d]	88[b]	3.4	255
1951	1,290[d]	284[b]	9.0	187
1958	1,850[d]	428[e]	6.0	231
1964	9,100[f]	638[b]	6.3	70
1973	9,100[f]	930[b]	4.2	103
1978[c]	9,100[f]	1,100	3.4	121

— Not available.

a. Data are from Lubell and McCallum (1978), table 2.1.

b. Data are from population census estimates.

c. Data are from the 1978 World Bank–DANE Household Survey. All data for Bogotá—except for the years marked a, b, and c—are from Wiesner (1980), table 1.

d. Data are from the "Plan General de Desarrolo de Cali y su Area Metropolitana, 1970–1985–2000," an internal document of the Planeación Municipal de Cali.

e. Tabares (1979).

f. Area for Cali is from the Planeación Municipal de Cali.

and lower-middle-income residents. In the mid-1950s Chapinero, originally an outlying suburb north of the city, began to replace the city center as the primary commercial area. The city became elongated north to south, being bounded on the east by high mountains and on the west by valuable agricultural land and by low-lying land that discouraged development. Only in the 1960s and 1970s did the western parts of the city begin to fill, giving the city its present almost semicircular shape.

Cali, which nestles into the base of the mountains to its west, has had a somewhat similar history. Until the early part of the century the built-up area was a compact, traditional rectangular grid of streets around the central plaza (Plaza Mayor), and the city was mainly a commercial, religious, and political center for the state of Valle del Cauca. Being small, it was mixed in character until it began to expand in the mid-twentieth century, when the rich occupied the western part of the city and the poor the eastern parts. Like Bogotá, Cali developed linearly north to south, with greater development taking place toward the south. The eastern part of the city consists of low-lying lands populated by the poor, who settled there in great numbers during the major land invasions of the 1950s and early 1960s. Since then, the city has filled out and has acquired a semicircular shape—almost a mirror image of Bogotá, although smaller.

As in other cities, it is difficult to separate the effects of institutional decisions on the spatial development of a city from those arising from individual preferences as revealed by the market. Because much is made in this study of the particular spatial income pattern found in both cities, it is interesting to note some of the main planning exercises that have been carried out in Bogotá. The two main influences on the shape of the city were Karl Brunner in 1935 and Le Corbusier in 1951. Much of Bogotá's existing zoning and planning structure can be attributed to Brunner, who organized a city planning department. The northern part of the city was zoned for low-density residential development, while the south was zoned for high-density development. Le Corbusier's main contribution was the creation of an industrial zone to the west of the city; intentionally or fortuitously, this separated the poor south—zoned for high-density development under Brunner's plan—from the rich north. These basic zoning and planning regulations have had a powerful impact on the structure of city growth. The low-density residential development zoned for the northern part of the city has effectively segregated it for the rich. Similarly, the high-density residential zoning in the southern part of the city made it possible for the poor to locate there. The industrial zone in the west houses the main industries located in Bogotá.

This pattern of growth is typical of cities as they expand, except that in Bogotá land is probably more effectively segregated by use—between low- and high-density residential development, and among residential, commercial, and industrial uses—than is typical for many cities in developing countries. In Bogotá and Cali the central cities were densely packed to begin with and could become only a little denser as the city grew. New growth, in both residential and employment activities, took place largely outside the city center. Although land use planning had significant effects on land use segregation, it is difficult to clearly identify the sequence of causation. Land use regulations may essentially have followed existing land use patterns and perpetuated their continuance. The rich suburbanized from the center in successive waves toward the north; the poor replaced them, to some extent, in the center, as is typical in North American cities, but they also decentralized toward the south.

As Bogotá grew, its employment structure diversified, and now about 25 percent of its labor force is engaged in manufacturing, another 25 percent in commerce, and about 37 percent in services. This distribution is typical of well-diversified cities—almost all large cities in the developing world have more than 20 percent employment in manufacturing activities (see Mohan 1986, chap. 3)—but some manufacturing noncapital cities, such as Bombay, Calcutta, and São Paulo, have as much as 40 percent of their labor force in manufacturing. The presence of the national government in a capital city clearly increases the proportion of people employed in tertiary activities. Cali has a higher proportion of manufacturing employment and a lower share in the service sector than does Bogotá. It is important to look at the overall employment structure in a growing city because different employment structures have different implications for the spatial pattern of city growth, and, as shown later, the location patterns of various activities have changed as Bogotá has grown. Specifically, manufacturing has led the trend toward decentralization of employment location.

To summarize, both Bogotá and Cali have grown at very high sustained rates for more than a century. Income has grown faster than population over at least the past three or four decades, and real per capita income has therefore grown substantially. The result of growth in both population and income has been a considerable physical expansion of the city, and both population and economic activity have decentralized. The following sections document the magnitude of this decentralization and note the departures from the general pattern that might be expected from a growing, primarily monocentric city.

Growth and the Spatial Distribution of Population and Income

Maps 3-1 and 3-2 show the boundary lines for rings and sectors within Bogotá and Cali. They also show the *comunas*—smaller divisions marked by two-digit numbers—that make up each ring or sector.[1] Map 3-3 illustrates the spread and densities of population in Bogotá. As might be expected, the outskirts are relatively sparsely populated, whereas the center is denser; the southern part of the city is clearly more densely populated than the north. The center (CBD, *comuna* 31) is less dense than some surrounding areas. The densest areas are more than ten

Map 3-1. Bogotá: Ring and Sector Systems Based on 1973 *Comunas*

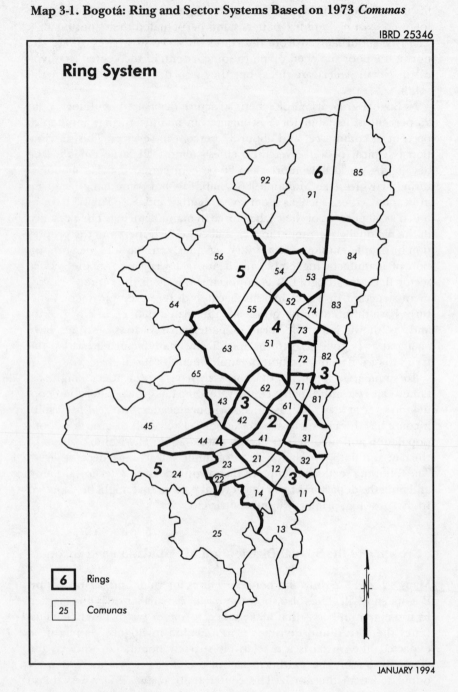

IBRD 25346

Ring System

| 6 | Rings |
| 25 | Comunas |

JANUARY 1994

Source: Mohan 1986, map 3-1.

IBRD 25347

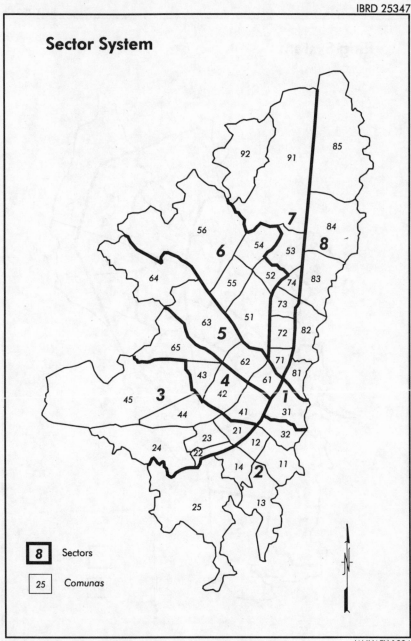

Sector System

8 Sectors

25 Comunas

N

JANUARY 1994

Map 3-2. Cali: Ring and Sector Systems

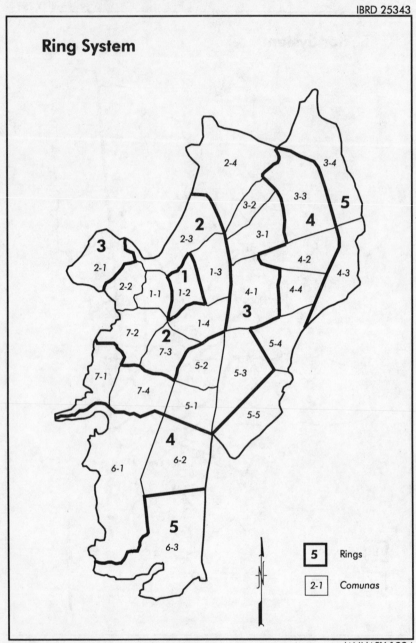

Source: Mohan 1986, map 3-2.

IBRD 25344

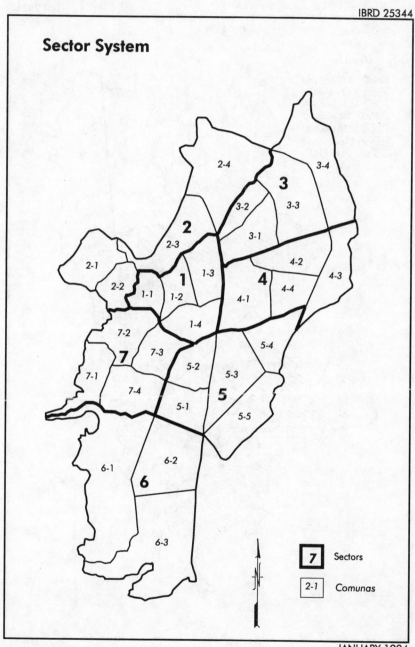

Sector System

2-4

3

3-4

3-2   3-3

2

2-3   3-1

2-1

2-2   1-1   1   1-3   4   4-2   4-3

1-2   4-4

4-1

1-4

7-2   5-4

7   7-3   5-2

7-1   5-3   5

7-4   5-1

5-5

6-2

6-1   6

6-3

7 Sectors

2-1 Comunas

JANUARY 1994

Map 3-3. Bogotá: Population Density by *Comuna*

IBRD 25348

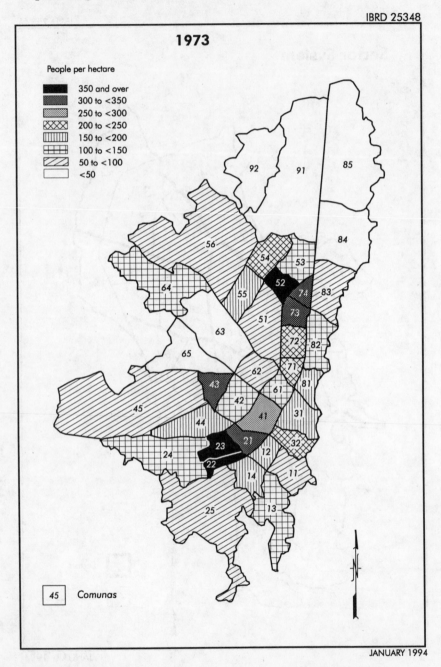

JANUARY 1994

Source: Mohan 1986, map 3-3.

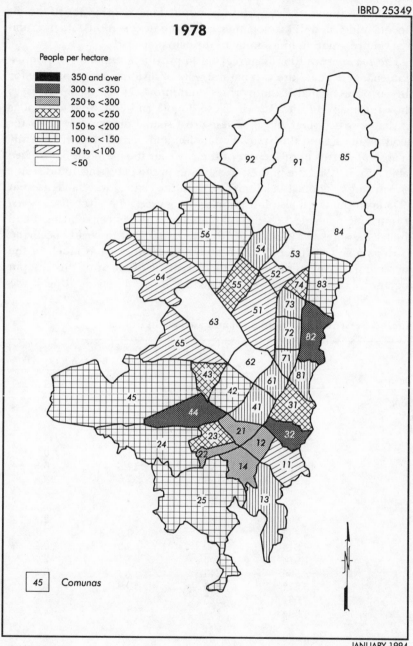

IBRD 25349

1978

People per hectare

- 350 and over
- 300 to <350
- 250 to <300
- 200 to <250
- 150 to <200
- 100 to <150
- 50 to <100
- <50

45   Comunas

JANUARY 1994

times denser than the least dense, but some of the outlying areas in the south are about as densely populated as some of the inner ones. Thus, although exponentially declining population density functions fit Bogotá and Cali well (as documented in the next section), such a summary representation hides some of the actual diversity.

The *comunas* are too disaggregated to provide a summary of population changes. There are two natural ways of dividing a city spatially for the purposes of analysis: into "rings" and into "sectors," or pie slices, as shown in maps 3-1 and 3-2. (Because Bogotá and Cali are semicircular in shape, so are their rings.) These gross spatial divisions are used for analysis throughout this study. Population and density declined slightly in absolute terms in the center of the city over the period 1964–78 (see table 3-5). In 1964 the highest density was in the CBD (ring 1 and sector 1), but ring 2 (about 1–3 kilometers from the center) was the densest in 1973 even though it also lost population between the two census years. It is striking that ring 3 (3–6 kilometers from the center) and ring 4 had similar densities in 1973 and 1978. The fastest growth clearly occurred in rings 5 and 6. Indeed, ring 5 accommodated twice as much of the incremental population during those years as the rest of the city put together. Land prices also increased the most in ring 5. Ring 6 was

Table 3-5. Growth in Population and Density in Bogotá

Division	Area, 1973 (hectares)	Population, 1978 (thousands)	Average annual rate of growth in population and density (percent)	
			1964–73	*1973–78*
Ring				
1	398	82	−1.8	2.4
2	1,357	280	−0.2	−0.3
3	2,575	426	3.2	3.4
4	5,960	923	5.7	0.7
5	14,329	1,592	14.6	6.3
6	5,804	189	37.6	13.8
Sector				
1	398	82	−1.8	2.4
2	4,357	696	5.8	7.1
3	5,313	859	8.3	2.8
4	1,914	250	7.1	−2.7
5	3,066	213	7.4	0.2
6	5,673	680	10.9	6.0
7	5,064	325	5.7	−1.9
8	4,638	388	7.1	14.5
City	30,424	3,492	7.2	3.9

Note: Density for all years has been calculated based on the 1973 area.
Source: 1964 and 1973 population censuses; 1978 World Bank–DANE Household Survey.

almost uninhabited in 1964. The main part of population growth in Bogotá in the period covered by table 3-5 has clearly been in the outlying rings. There has been some decentralization of population, partly because population in the two inner rings has declined somewhat, but mainly because of the much larger additions in the outskirts. The lower panel of table 3-5 gives the same information for the radial sectors. Sector 1, the CBD, is identical to ring 1. The southern sectors (2, 3, and 4) are almost twice as densely populated as the northern sectors (6, 7, and 8). The sectors have grown somewhat uniformly, although sector 6 grew faster than the others. Not until the early 1960s did the western part of the city began to fill up; before then the city had largely been a north-south strip stretching along the mountains. Sectors 4 and 5 form the industrial corridor that Le Corbusier established in 1951. On average, the densities of rings 3 and 4 are very similar to those of sectors 3 and 4. The northern part of sector 8 is even sparser than the average.

We now turn to the spatial distribution of income (see chapter 4 for a systematic discussion of this subject). Again, *comunas* are too disaggregated to provide a useful picture. It should be noted, however, that the income of the poorest *comuna* was only one-twelfth that of the richest. Each *comuna* was relatively homogeneous within itself. A glance at map 3-4, which illustrates the distribution of household income per capita (HINCAP) by *comuna* for 1973 and 1978, shows that mean income varied across the city in a remarkably regular fashion, increasing in income as one follows the map clockwise from south to north. There is no discernible pattern from the center to the periphery, however (see table 3-6). Only a mild pattern is discernible by rings. There is a tendency for income to rise somewhat from the center toward the periphery and then to decline; ring 5 is poorer than the rest. The differences, however, are small, and the coefficients of variation are large. For most of the rings, the proportion of households in the ring is not very different from the share of income, except for ring 5. Thus it is clear that the income distribution pattern is quite different from that in U.S. cities, where income, in general, increases as one moves from the center to the periphery.

The data partially support the idea that the poor in cities in developing countries get pushed to the periphery. The pattern is more distinct when viewed by sectors. The richest sector (sector 8) has a mean HINCAP more than five times that of the poorest (sector 2). Except for sector 6, which is relatively poor, income increases as one moves from sector 2 to sector 8. The most heterogeneous zone is the CBD, with a very high coefficient of variation. The share of income received by the poor sectors is much less than their share of households. The ranking of the sectors did not change between 1973 and 1978. It is therefore clear that a spatial analysis of Bogotá is of more interest when done by radial sectors

Map 3-4. Bogotá: Distribution of Mean Household Income Per Capita by *Comuna*

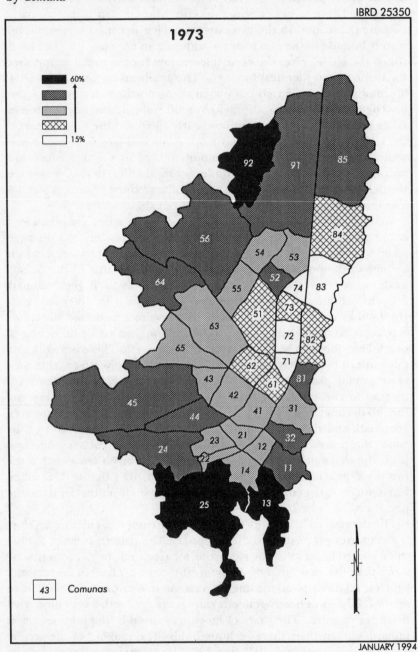

IBRD 25350

1973

60%

15%

92   91   85

56

54   53   84

64   55   52   74   83

51   73

63   72   82

65   62   71   81

43   61

45   42   31

44   41   32

23   21   12

24   22   11

14

25   13

│ 43 │ Comunas

N

JANUARY 1994

Source: Mohan 1986, map 3-4.

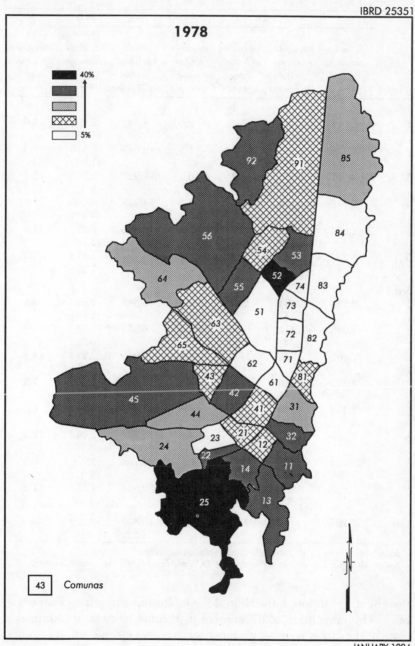

Table 3-6. Spatial Distribution of Monthly Income and Population in Bogotá

| | 1973 | | | | 1978 | | |
Division	Mean household income (1973 pesos)	Mean household income per capita (1973 pesos)	Distribution of households (percent)	Share of income in ring or sector (percent)	Mean household income (1978 pesos)	Mean household income per capita (1978 pesos)	Distribution of households (percent)
Ring							
1	2,114	884 (2.10)	3.5	2.6	8,343	2,490 (1.03)	3.0
2	2,976	1,016 (1.92)	10.8	11.5	16,047	5,570 (1.04)	9.8
3	3,722	1,073 (1.59)	12.7	16.9	19,928	5,913 (0.93)	13.1
4	3,046	788 (1.94)	30.7	33.5	14,772	4,105 (1.40)	27.2
5	2,264	533 (1.86)	39.1	31.7	10,818	2,277 (1.10)	41.6
6	3,202	753 (1.93)	3.3	3.8	15,999	3,178 (1.26)	5.3
Sector							
1	2,114	884 (2.11)	3.5	2.6	8,343	2,490 (1.03)	3.0
2	1,583	414 (1.44)	18.1	10.2	6,833	1,585 (0.52)	19.9
3	2,002	484 (1.41)	24.4	17.5	9,930	2,234 (0.86)	24.6
4	2,347	646 (1.68)	9.8	8.2	12,843	2,800 (0.88)	7.2
5	2,453	700 (1.68)	7.7	6.8	13,893	3,067 (1.04)	6.1
6	2,349	5,561 (1.66)	17.0	14.3	12,801	2,744 (0.98)	19.5
7	45,791	1,265 (1.61)	12.6	20.6	16,163	3,750 (1.07)	9.3
8	7,895	2,258 (1.50)	7.0	19.7	32,804	11,354 (0.90)	11.1
City	2,791 (1.89)	751	100.0	100.0	13,805 (1.22)	3,629	100.0

Note: Numbers in parentheses are coefficients of variation.
Source: 1973 population census sample; 1978 World Bank–DANE Household Survey.

than by rings, although the rings do exhibit some interesting characteristics. The magnitude of differences in income between the different parts of the city is surprisingly large for averages taken over large numbers (see table 3-6).

Such differences are seldom encountered between different regions of a country. In Bogotá (as in Cali) the rich clearly concentrate in certain locations. Although the poor are to be found in most parts of the city, the declining coefficient of variation between 1973 and 1978 indicates increasing spatial segregation of income classes. The growth of the northern part of the city, the resulting gradients for land values and population density, the use of transportation, and the type of housing all conform much more to patterns found in developed countries than in the city's southern section.

One other ring characteristic should be mentioned: household size, which increases from 3.83 in the city center to 5.3 in ring 5 and 4.9 at the periphery (ring 6). Larger households require more space and hence are more likely to locate away from the center. In addition, although larger households earn higher total incomes, the added compensation is not enough to offset larger household size. Thus household income per capita declines with increasing household size. The periphery of Bogotá therefore contains larger as well as somewhat poorer households, the household income per capita measure being a more meaningful measure of welfare than total household income.

A broad picture of the changing structure of Bogotá is now beginning to emerge. Growth has entailed the densification of successive rings moving outward from the center, but this densification is not uniform between different sectors of the city. The rich have continued to move north (sectors 7 and 8) and to settle in relatively low-density neighborhoods, whereas the poor have largely moved toward the south and southwest (sectors 2 and 3) and to some extent toward the west (sector 5). The striking element of this pattern is the relatively high constant density that is observed as one moves from the center toward the southern periphery. The poor appear to live in settlements of similar densities whether in the center or on the outskirts. There is a clear increase in household size toward the periphery, and the density of dwelling units would therefore be expected to decline outward in the poor sectors as well. A similar pattern can be observed in Cali.

The Evolution of Land Values and Population and Employment Densities

Table 3-7 expands on the information presented in table 3-5. The maximum distance from the city center is about 15 kilometers (to ring 6) in Bogotá and about 10 kilometers (to ring 5) in Cali. Growth has clearly occurred by accretion in the outer rings; density in the CBD has remained at about 200 persons per hectare. Growth on the fringes of

Table 3-7. Change in Population Density by Ring, Bogotá and Cali

	Bogotá				Cali			
	Area (hectares)	Density (population per hectare)			Area (hectares)	Density (population per hectare)		
Ring		1964	1973	1978		1964	1973	1978
1	398	220	180	205	140	210	150	160
2	1,357	210	210	220	1,500	140	125	135
3	2,575	100	140	140	3,000	95	135	160
4	5,960	90	150	155	3,000	25	70	100
5	14,329	25	80	110	1,500	25	50	70
6	5,804	1	17	32	n.a.	n.a.	n.a.	n.a.
City[a]	30,424	50	95	115	9,100	70	103	121
Density gradient (g)		0.18	0.15	0.12		0.51	0.44	0.25

n.a. Not applicable.

Note: All figures are rounded.

a. City area has been kept constant for all calculations of city density, unlike in table 3-4. In fact, both cities have grown during the period in question, and many peripheral areas included here were outside the 1964 city boundaries.

Source: Data for Bogotá are from 1964 and 1973 population censuses and 1978 World Bank–DANE Household Survey. Data for Cali were calculated from data in Tabares (1979).

the existing cities has accompanied densification of the inner rings. This process is somewhat different from the growth pattern observed in most U.S. cities in the early twentieth century. Thus, while Bogotá and Cali have decentralized with growth in the sense that a smaller proportion of the total population lives within any area of constant radius, they have not yet decentralized in the manner of many cities in the United States, where central cities have actually lost populations in substantial magnitudes.

The last line in table 3-7 gives the measured density gradients from 1964 to 1978 for the two cities. The unit of observation is the barrio, or neighborhood.[2] These density gradients were estimated for Bogotá from about 300 observations in 1964 and about 450 in 1973 and 1978 and for Cali from about 130 observations in 1964 and about 200 in 1973 and 1978. These data are more disaggregated than those usually available for such calculations. The gradients reported for different cities in chapter 2, for example, are based on far fewer data points in each case. As noted in chapter 2, g declines as expected for both cities and is higher for Cali, the smaller city, than for Bogotá. For purposes of comparison, we may recall that, around 1970, g was 0.11 for New York, 0.08 for Chicago, 0.08 for Tokyo, 0.07 for London, 0.22 for Seoul, 0.17 for Mexico City, 0.12 for São Paulo, and 0.12 for Bogotá. Among smaller cities like Cali, it was 0.19 for Monterrey, 0.41 for Guadalajara (Mexico), 0.27 for Belo Horizonte, 0.19 for Recife (Brazil), 0.25 for medium-size cities in Great Britain, and 0.31 for similar cities in Germany. Thus Bogotá and Cali have population density gradients that are typical for cities of their income levels, size, and available transport systems. The gradients have declined over time with increases in population and income, much as would be expected. Both cities exhibit substantial decentralization with growth but with successive densification of inner rings, unlike many North American cities.

Simple urban economic theory (Mills 1972) leads us to expect that the land value and density patterns should be broadly consistent. The competition for land for its highest economic use gives land its value. Higher density implies higher relative use, and, conversely, higher land value gives people an incentive to use land more intensively. In a fully developed urban model, land values and population densities would both be endogenous variables that would be expected to move in a consistent fashion.

For most cities it is typically difficult to obtain good information on land values, especially comparable information over a long period of time. It is also difficult to separate the value of land from that of the structures built on it. We were fortunate in obtaining a unique data set of about 6,000 transactions in Bogotá covering the period 1955–78 from Guillermo Wiesner of Wiesner and Cía. Ltda., a long-established Bogotá

Table 3-8. Evolution of Land Values by Ring, Bogotá and Cali

	Bogotá					Cali			
	Average distance from the center (kilometers)	Land values (1978 pesos per square meter)			Average annual growth rate, 1964–78 (percent)	Average distance from the center (kilometers)	Land values (1978 pesos per square meter)			Average annual growth rate, 1963–79 (percent)
		1963–65	1972–74	1975–77			1963	1974	1979	
Ring										
1	0	4,250	3,900	3,100	−2.3	0	5,900	4,600	6,400	0.6
2	2.2	1,850	1,660	1,550	−1.3	1.8	1,100	1,100	2,400	5.6
3	3.8	1,350	1,350	1,320	−0.2	3.4	520	480	1,030	4.9
4	6.5	870	1,080	1,130	1.9	5.4	380	410	960	6.6
5	9.8	570	800	850	2.9	6.9	150	370	810	12.0
6	15.4	370	700	730	4.9	n.a.	n.a.	n.a.	n.a.	n.a.
Gradient[a] (h)	n.a.	0.16	0.08	0.07	n.a.	n.a.	0.55	0.51	0.25	n.a.

n.a. Not applicable.

Note: 1978 exchange rate: US$1 = Col$38.

a. Land value gradients were calculated as $V_x = V_0 e^{-hx}$, where V_x is the price of land x from the center, V_0 is the theoretical value at the center, and h is the gradient.

Source: For Bogotá, Villamizar (1981). For Cali, Velasco and Mier (1980).

real estate firm. Because all transactions observed were for land that was not built on, we did not have to artificially separate the values of the land and the structures. (For detailed analysis of land values in Bogotá, see Villamizar 1981; Mohan and Villamizar 1982; and Wagner 1984.) The data set for Cali was obtained from the Cali Planning Office.

Table 3-8, which shows the pattern of the evolving land price surface for Bogotá and Cali by rings, is remarkable for the highly regular pattern that emerges and is consistent with expectations. The prices are given in constant 1978 Colombian pesos because the earlier prices were inflated by the consumer price index. For both Bogotá and Cali, land prices decrease from the center toward the periphery in a regular fashion; central land values remain broadly constant in real terms, whereas considerable and consistent increases are recorded toward the periphery. This is in keeping with the evolution of density patterns shown in table 3-7.

The constancy of real land prices in the central areas of Bogotá during the 1960s and 1970s is remarkable. A word of caution is necessary regarding the significant decline in the CBD (ring 1). Wagner (1984) has demonstrated the existence of some biases in the measurement of central land values. As may be expected, less and less vacant land is available in central areas over time; the number of vacant-land transactions therefore falls, and larger lots became even scarcer. In the CBD larger lots fetched higher unit prices than smaller lots, but since the number of smaller-lot transactions was higher, the unweighted averaging process biased the average CBD land values downward. Hence, the fall in real urban land values in the Bogotá CBD during the 1960s and 1970s is partially illusory. Land values may be regarded as having been constant over the period.

It is also important to note some findings that go against the conventional wisdom. It is widely thought that land values have been skyrocketing in cities in developing countries and that they will do so indefinitely. In fact, in Bogotá between 1955 and 1977 they grew at only about 3 percent a year in real terms, a rate not far from either the per capita GNP growth rate for the country or the return on any alternative asset. The absolute land prices were not very different for Cali, a finding consistent with those of Mills and Song (1979). They found that, in the Republic of Korea, land values in larger and smaller cities were not very different, and the rate of increase was marginally higher among cities categorized as second-largest than among the largest cities.

The main point is that cities grow in a regular fashion and that the evidence from Bogotá and Cali is quite consistent with the theoretical expectations outlined in chapter 2. These regularities are, moreover, results of the regularities in human behavior that are investigated in the rest of this study. This evolving pattern of land value gradients confirms that land values have essentially been determined by the economic competition for access to space according to its best use. Distance from the city center emerges as the best explanation for variance in land value around the city. It is therefore the access characteristics of each plot of land that are the principal determinants of its value. Other variables, such as amenities, availability of infrastructure, neighborhood characteristics, and zoning, are less significant explanators of land value variance in Bogotá. The next section shows that although distance from the CBD is the prime determinant of land values, other factors, such as access to subsidiary shopping centers and main transport arteries, are also significant in explaining the ridges and values encountered in the land value surface of Bogotá. There is little evidence that the land market has not been working competitively in Bogotá.

Why have real urban land prices in Bogotá and Cali risen at moderate rates? First, during the period under consideration the supply of housing generally matched the rapid growth in demand (see chapter 7). The rapid land development that took place in the *barrios piratas* (extralegal developments) essentially kept up the supply of developed or semideveloped land in response to constantly rising demand. Second, explicit government policy aimed at rapid investment in urban infrastructure helped provide at least a minimal level of services to the emerging new developments—both legal and extralegal. Third, the availability of different sets of instruments for investment in Colombia discouraged overcrowding in real estate investment. Fourth, the competition between developers, who had relatively free entry into the housing and land markets, helped keep the returns to land development within moderate limits, which more or less matched national income growth per capita over this period.

Comparing the density and land value gradients in tables 3-7 and 3-8 provides further evidence:

	Bogotá		Cali	
	Land value	Density	Land value	Density
1964	−0.15	−0.18	−0.51	−0.51
1973	−0.08	−0.15	−0.25	−0.44
1978	−0.07	−0.12	−0.23	−0.25

According to standard urban economic theory, we would expect the pattern of land value gradients to be similar to density gradients. Furthermore, their levels are consistently lower than the density gradients, as is often theorized (Mills and Song 1979). A comparison of estimated V_0 (land value at the center of the city) with actual V_0 reveals that our estimates are consistently lower than the actual values. This implies that the gradient of the curve should, in fact, be much steeper at the center of the city than we have estimated. Because of the high concentration of economic activity at the center, one can expect land values to be determined much more by employment density than by residential density. The latter falls rapidly from the center, and it is quite plausible that land values will exhibit a similar decline. Estimated V_0 is therefore likely to be lower than this central peak. The estimated densities were consistently higher than the actual densities for the CBD, whereas estimated land values were consistently lower than real land values. What is to be expected is that residential densities will increase somewhat from the CBD and then decline, whereas land values should show a rapid decline from the city center at first and then a slower decrease.

Land values are expected to be extremely high at the city center because of the concentration of economic activity there. It was suggested in the last chapter that employment densities are expected to be higher in the center and that they typically have a steeper gradient. Table 3-9 vividly illustrates this for Bogotá and Cali. Estimates of employment density gradients are more difficult to come by than estimates of population density because employment data are not usually available by location. The gradients for Bogotá in 1978 appear to be similar to those calculated by Mills (1972) for a sample of U.S. cities in 1963. The table shows that manufacturing has decentralized most, as expected, followed by commerce and services. Financial activities are heavily concentrated in the center and might have become more so during the 1970s.

Table 3-9. Employment Density in Bogotá
(jobs per hectare)

Item	All	Manu-facturing	Commerce	Finance	Services
Jobs per hectare, 1978					
Ring 1	425	43	97	102	128
Ring 2	158	28	36	21	54
Ring 3	77	24	14	4.4	26
Ring 4	42	12	8.0	1.8	15
Ring 5	21	5.6	4.8	0.4	6.0
Ring 6	7.0	1.1	0.6	0.1	3.0
Employment density gradients					
Bogotá, 1978	0.30	0.21	0.30	0.56	0.29
Bogotá, 1972	0.33	0.33	0.32	0.44	0.35
Cali, 1978	0.72	0.71	1.00	—	0.64
Average for selected U.S. cities, 1963	0.26	0.27	0.35	—	0.33

— Not available.

Source: Colombian data were calculated from K. S. Lee (1989), 1972 Phase II Household Survey, and 1978 World Bank–DANE Household Survey. U.S. data are from Mills (1972).

Table 3-10. Distribution and Density of Workers' Residences and Workplaces, Bogotá

		Distribution of workers				Density of workers			
		1972[a]		1978[b]		1972	1978	1972	1978
Division	Area (hectares)	By residence (percent)	By workplace (percent)	By residence (percent)	By workplace (percent)	By residence per hectare	By residence per hectare	By workplace per hectare	By workplace per hectare
Ring									
1	398	1.7	25.7	2.4	14.5	37	73	507	420
2	1,357	10.9	15.0	9.7	18.3	70	85	87	155
3	2,575	13.1	16.3	13.3	17.0	44	61	50	76
4	5,960	34.5	20.7	26.0	21.2	50	52	27	41
5	14,330	37.6	20.4	43.0	25.5	23	36	11	20
6	5,804	2.2	1.8	5.5	3.6	3	11	2	7
Sector									
1	398	1.7	25.7	2.4	14.5	37	73	507	420
2	4,357	18.3	7.6	19.1	8.5	36	52	14	22
3	5,313	25.1	13.4	23.4	13.4	41	52	20	29
4	1,914	9.5	9.3	6.5	9.2	43	40	38	55
5	3,065	7.1	10.9	6.3	12.6	20	24	28	47
6	5,673	16.3	9.8	17.8	12.4	25	37	14	25
7	5,065	13.3	9.9	10.1	10.2	23	24	15	23
8	4,638	8.8	13.4	14.3	19.0	10	37	23	47
City	30,423	100.0	100.0	100.0	100.0	28	39	26	38

Note. The survey included 877,000 workers in 1972 (including 786,000 whose workplaces were identified) and 1,185,000 workers in 1978 (including 1,150,000 whose workplaces were identified). Information on the workplaces of some workers was unavailable.

a. Data are from Pachon (1979), table 5. Primary data for workers by residence was from the 1972 Phase II Household Survey household file, and by workplace from the 1972 Phase II Household Survey person file.

b. Data are from 1978 World Bank–DANE Household Survey.

Employment density gradients are much steeper than population density gradients.

Cali is still very centralized. It really has only one major employment concentration—the center. Because we do not have reliable data for earlier years, it is difficult to say whether employment has decentralized in Cali yet, except in manufacturing.

The employment pattern is examined in more detail in chapter 6. Here we merely need to establish that the employment structure of Bogotá and Cali is consistent with the expected pattern of growth and decentralization. Bogotá's CBD had a net loss of jobs in the 1970s, primarily in manufacturing. Some of the CBD functions shifted to ring 2, in the northern sector, which is more easily accessible to the rich living in sector 8.

The Changing Structure of Bogotá: Some Wrinkles

So far we have treated the city in a relatively simple manner. The measurement of each gradient assumes that the city is symmetric around the city center and is essentially monocentric. This is justified in the main because both Bogotá and Cali are roughly semicircular, though constrained by mountains on one side, with the city center roughly at the geographic center of the semicircle in each case. The income and population distributions are not, however, symmetric. In Bogotá the northern sectors (7 and 8) were characterized as particularly rich and the southern sectors (2 and 3) as poor. In Cali the picture is more mixed, but broadly, the western sectors (2, 6, and 7) are richer than the eastern sectors (3, 4, and 5). In general, jobs exceed the number of resident workers in the rich sectors, and the converse is true in the poorer sectors (see table 3-10). As might be expected, population density is higher in the poor than in the rich sectors. This suggests that the smooth patterns depicted in the preceding discussion hide considerable diversity and that it would be useful to look at the density and land value patterns in different sectors to observe the extent to which earlier generalities remain true. These patterns are particularly important for housing and transport decisions. For example, the density information presented in tables 3-9 and 3-10 shows that employment densities are greater than residential densities in the inner rings but less in the outer rings. Although the commuting pattern would be predominantly inward, the decentralization of both employment and residence suggests that a decreasing proportion of trips for work would be made toward the center as time goes on.

A more interesting residential and work pattern is shown in the bottom part of table 3-10. Most striking is the job deficit in poor sector 2 (in the south) and the job surplus in rich sector 8 (in the north), which leads one to expect considerable crosstown commuting in addition to radial commuting. This changing pattern points to the need to increase the number of circumferential routes so that north-south crosstown traffic can avoid inner-city congestion. This is possible only if appropriate investments and changes are made in the prevailing road structure. It is therefore important to observe and understand trends in transportation patterns in order to design workable transportation routes and make appropriate policy decisions about public investment in infrastructure.

One anomaly may be observed in table 3-10: In contrast to the general pattern of decentralization, there seems to have been an increase in the density of population of workers in Bogotá's CBD between 1972 and 1978. Table 3-7 also shows some increase in population density in the CBD (from 180 persons per hectare to 220 persons per hectare). This is partly explained by the rapid change in the character of the CBD's resident population during the 1970s. Many families moved to outer locations and were replaced by single-member households (single workers). The housing structure also changed from apartments to rooming houses (popularly known as *inquilinatos* in Bogotá). Single-member households, which are characteristically difficult to cover in household surveys, were probably undercounted in the 1972 survey. Repeat visits in the 1978 World Bank–DANE survey ensured better coverage. The substantial shift over time toward single-worker residences in central cities is quite common; it is well known in North America and European cities and has also begun to appear in the central cities in some developing countries.

Until now the distance from the city center has been emphasized as the key variable affecting the access characteristics—that is, the proximity of land parcels to economic opportunities—of a particular location and, therefore, the value of land. The hypothesis is that large or dense agglomerations of people are instrumental in increasing these economic opportunities, and this is the reason for the clustering of population near the city center. Thus a concentration of economic activity in the center produces relatively high population densities and correspondingly high land values, both of which decline with distance.

The observation that the rich live in some parts of the city and the poor live in other areas leads to the revision of some of these ideas. That more jobs are located in rich sectors means that those sectors are economically more attractive and firms have a greater tendency to locate there. The lower population densities of those areas are more than enhanced by the purchasing power of the resident population. Access characteristics conferred by proximity to the city center or by short distance from workers' residences are heightened by the greater purchasing power of richer households. Thus the access characteristics of locations within close proximity to richer areas of the city are improved, and land prices are bid up. There is more competition for retail space, for example, in these areas. The establishment of shopping centers and other activities then attracts greater employment, contributing further to the positive access characteristics of these locations.

The product of population and mean income is probably not a good measure of purchasing power because the requirements of a large number of poor people do not aggregate: each household has meager demands, so poor sectors can support only a limited number of economic activities—small retail activity for subsistence daily needs but little else. Thus, in Bogotá, much other retail and wholesale activity continues to be concentrated in the center, and more people live in the poor southern part of the city than there are jobs there. Conversely, the rich neighborhoods in the north have a much higher demand for goods and services than their population densities would suggest. Moreover, office and other professional activity has tended to move north in the same direction as the rich. Thus the access characteristics of these neighborhoods have improved further and are not adequately measured by population densities. In addition, because the infrastructure (for example, roads, lighting, water supply, and sewerage) is better in the richer areas, the quality of life and the intrinsic characteristics of the sites are better as well. All these factors combine to produce land values that are higher in the rich areas than in other neighborhoods no farther from the city center.

The estimates of population density and land value gradients for each sector in Bogotá and Cali (table 3-11) are striking. The declining exponential function is still a good approximation of land values for each sector. The population densities do not do as well; the estimated density gradients are not significantly different from zero in a number of sectors. Indeed, in Cali sectors 4 and 5 exhibit mildly positive gradients, whereas in Bogotá the density gradients are low or insignificant for sectors 2, 3, 5, and 6. What these sectors have in common is relatively low mean income. The land value gradients, however, are not significantly different from those in other sectors.

To understand these phenomena, we need to delve further into the role of land values and their effect on urban structure. When land values are high, capital is substituted for land, and the result is the construction of taller buildings. We can therefore expect to observe, on average, taller buildings in city centers and in zones in which land prices are high. As land prices increase, single-family homes are replaced by multifamily dwellings (apartments), and residential densities rise. Although residential densities rise per unit of land area, living space per person does not necessarily decrease in wealthy areas. These options, however, are not open to the poor.

Table 3-11. **Land Value and Population Density Gradients in Bogotá and Cali, by Sector**

	Bogotá						Cali					
	Household mean income index[a,c]	Land value[b]		Population density[c]			Household mean income index[a,c]	Land value[d]		Population density[c]		
Sector		g	R²	h	R²			g	R²	h	R²	
1	61	n.a.	n.a.	n.a.	n.a.		163	n.a.	n.a.	n.a.	n.a.	
2	52	−0.15	0.54	−0.11	0.06		212	−0.42	0.69	−0.13*	0.00	
3	74	−0.01	0.09	−0.02*	0.01		84	−0.45	0.73	−0.10*	0.00	
4	96	−0.08	{ 0.46	−0.12	0.09		58	−0.42	0.69	+0.13	0.11	
5	103			−0.05*	0.03		82	−0.55	0.77	+0.07*	0.02	
6	97	−0.10	0.71	−0.05*	0.02		125	−0.21	0.41	−0.26	0.16	
7	122	−0.08	0.72	−0.16	0.50		219	−0.86	0.59	−0.13*	0.05	
8	236	−0.07	0.55	−0.14	0.32		n.a.	n.a.	n.a.	n.a.	n.a.	

n.a. Not applicable.

Note: All coefficients are significant at the 0.01 level except those marked with an asterisk.

a. Percentage of mean household income for the city.
b. Data are for 1975–78.
c. Data are for 1978.
d. Data are for 1979.

Source: Velasco and Mier (1980); Tabares (1979); Pachon (1979); Villamizar (1981); City Study barrio file.

The rates of price increase were no higher in the rich areas than in the poor ones (Villamizar 1981). In Bogotá the rate of increase (adjusted for inflation) in the rich sector (sector 8) was about 2.5 percent a year between 1955 and 1977; it was about 4 to 7 percent a year in the poorer sectors (2, 3, and 6). The price levels, however, were consistently lower in the poor areas. These data indicate that although each land parcel is nonsubstitutive to some extent, a citywide land market is functioning. Whereas land prices in poor areas continued to be lower than in richer areas, a catch-up phenomenon was observed: prices of land parcels equidistant from the city center were not too dissimilar. The natural result of this phenomenon is that while the rich substitute for land with capital, the poor substitute for land by crowding.

Much of the housing in Bogotá still has fewer than two floors. The number of floors declines rapidly from the CBD, and the northern part of the city, the richer sector 8, has taller buildings than other areas (table 3-12). The average number of floors declines systematically by ring, as does the average age of dwellings, and the proportion of single-family homes increases with distance from the center. These patterns are very much according to expectations: capital is being substituted for land in the shape of taller buildings in the inner rings; the city has grown by accretion at its edges, and therefore the outer rings have newer houses; and apartment buildings or semidetached houses are replacing single-family houses as prices increase near the CBD. Land

Table 3-12. Spatial Pattern of Housing in Bogotá, 1978

Division	Mean household income index	Single-family units (percent)	Average age of dwelling unit (years)	Average number of floors	Average dwelling space per person (square meters)
Ring					
1	62	39	16	7.1	14
2	116	57	21	3.5	23
3	124	74	16	2.8	30
4	112	86	12	1.7	23
5	82	95	9	1.8	18
6	122	100	8	1.5	26
Sector					
1	61	39	16	7.1	14
2	53	96	13	1.4	12
3	74	91	10	1.8	19
4	96	91	11	1.9	25
5	103	72	18	3.4	20
6	97	92	10	2.1	21
7	122	84	17	1.9	30
8	236	59	10	2.9	45
City	100	85	12	2.1	21

Source: Mohan and Villamizar (1982).

prices are performing their function well, and the housing market seems to be responding as expected.

There is no clear pattern of average dwelling-unit space per person except that it is low in the CBD. We would expect that living space per person would be greater in the outer rings because people would be trading space for higher transport costs. If we now look at the sectoral pattern, it is clear that the poorest sectors (2 and 3) in the south have much less living space per person than the rich northern sectors. Thus the poor are substituting crowding for land, and the rich are substituting capital. (Chapter 7 analyzes the housing market in detail. One of the important findings reported there is that housing demand is inelastic among low-income residents, and they spend a high proportion of their incomes on housing.) Crowding in sector 2 is about the same as in the CBD; lower land prices at the periphery have not led to more space per person. It would seem that the poor have limited choices and that there is a limit to substitution by crowding. The percentage of single-family units increases consistently toward the periphery, while the average number of floors per structure declines. The population density in the poorer peripheral residential areas is not lower than in the center, but the density of dwelling units and households is. Larger households can take advantage of lower land prices at the periphery and live in larger dwelling units to have about as much per-person living space as smaller households nearer the city center.

We now begin to understand why the land value gradients hold up even when the cities are disaggregated into sectors, whereas the density gradients do not. The way the land market functions results in land values that are not too different at similar distances from the center. The rich sectors have higher land values because of better employment opportunities, as well as better neighborhoods and infrastructure. Because land values are relatively regular, the poor have no choice but to substitute for land by crowding. Since it is the larger households that locate on the periphery, they still have to live at high densities to compensate for the land prices, which are similar to land prices in the rich suburbs. They cannot buy more space by substituting capital for land because housing would be too expensive. For example, the average number of floors is 2.9 in sector 8 and only 1.4 to 1.8 in sectors 2 and 3; average dwelling unit space per person is lowest in sector 2 and is also low in peripheral ring 5 (see table 3-12). It would have been instructive to see how these indicators had changed since the early 1970s, but comparable data were not readily available. In any event, we observe high population densities on the periphery of some parts of the city, and consequently there is no measurable density gradient in those sectors. The rich sectors still have a density gradient, and we can therefore observe gradients for the city as a whole. Nonexistent density gradients in some sectors of the city are consistent with relatively strong land value gradients. This suggests a need for caution in interpreting similarities between citywide population density and land value gradients.

One other important aspect of land value patterns merits further discussion. As a large city grows, it acquires many new competing commercial centers that begin to rival the old CBD. These alternative (or additional) economic centers, in turn, are strong motivating forces for the decentralization of residential population.

We examined this process by looking at the land value peaks along key urban corridors in Bogotá (see Villamizar 1981 for details of the pattern). The detailed analysis along ridges of the land value surface reveals small hills, in accordance with the access characteristics that go with the higher levels of economic activity in the developing subcenters of a rapidly growing city. Because of such developments, the gradient of land prices decreased as the city grew. The relative importance of the CBD declined, and secondary gradients developed around the subcenters. In general, as a city grows, the smooth land price surface centered around the CBD develops wrinkles in the form of ridges, valleys, and small hills, as observed around Bogotá's new subcenters.

Mills and Song (1979) found that in Korean cities commercial land values were always higher than residential land values in the CBD and in the rest of the city at points equidistant from the center. The evidence we have found is consistent with their findings. Indeed, at equal distances from the CBD, the proportion of area covered by commercial activity in any neighborhood is a good predictor of land values in that area. These results are consistent with our expectations about access characteristics of neighborhood and with the observed higher land values in the richer areas of the city. Commercial activity locates in the rich areas of the city.

The purpose of this section has been to illustrate the complexity that is usually hidden behind regularities in city structure. We have shown, however, that these complexities are also the results of economic behavior on the part of households and firms—specifically the pattern of housing demand by households and the location decisions of firms—in combination with governmental decisions regarding zoning and infrastructure. Physical characteristics such as building heights and residential and employment densities are appreciated better when behavior is understood; conversely, behavior is affected by the prevailing structure. Thus, it is important to study both the overall structure of a city and the behavior of its elements.

Summary

The growth of Bogotá and Cali has been characterized by continuing decentralization of population and, to some extent, of employment.

Although cities in developed countries have experienced a similar phenomenon, in that the concentration of population and employment in city centers has declined, there are some significant differences. Lower suburban population densities in North American cities are mainly attributable to the much larger size of residential lots in the suburbs relative to those in the central city. In Bogotá and Cali residential lot size increases only moderately with distance from the city center. Although both the rich and poor have dispersed their residences, neither group has developed the large-lot, low-density suburbs typical of developed countries. The poor have moved wherever there is available space, and they continue to live in high densities at the periphery as well. In Bogotá and Cali some peripheral densities are as high as central densities.

It is important to understand how these high peripheral densities are consistent with a land value structure that conforms to the expectations of a regular decline from the city center. The functioning of the land market is such that land values at similar distances from the city center are quite similar, although they are slightly higher in the richer areas because of the higher level of economic activity there. Nevertheless, the poor have to pay roughly equivalent prices, and hence they substitute for land by crowding. Larger poor households, in particular, have to locate in crowded conditions at the periphery. The poor cannot substitute more capital for land because that would make the housing too expensive.

The high level and growth of land prices, often attributed to undesirable speculation and monopoly ownership, are usually regarded as unwarranted and hence as villains in city growth. Impressions are often based on faulty observation or inadequate analysis, however, as the analysis of a unique data set spanning the past quarter century of Bogotá's development suggests. A careful analysis of this data set indicates that the pattern of land values is consistent with the evolving density pattern of residence and employment, with land values remaining nearly constant in the CBD and rising at the periphery. Land prices follow a regular pattern: they are highest within the CBD and decline as distance from the center increases. They are determined much more by standard accessibility considerations than by availability and quality of infrastructure. Lot size also increases price. Large lots in central locations are rare and are priced higher per unit of area than smaller lots similarly located. By contrast, large lots on the city periphery are lower in price per unit of area than smaller lots similarly located. Land use on the periphery is not as intensive, and large parcels are common, so large parcels of land are offered for sale at a discount.

There was no explosive increase in real land prices; overall land values in Bogotá grew in step with the city's economic activity as measured by this real product. This implies that the aggregate rents from land remained a roughly constant proportion of Bogotá's product and suggests that land has a unitary elasticity of substitution with other factors of urban production. The indications in Bogotá and Cali were that land, on average, had returns quite comparable to and not higher than returns to other assets. The land market in these cities should therefore be judged as operating quite efficiently and as giving appropriate signals for the allocation of resources. Increases in land prices are much more the result of increasing opportunity costs resulting from growth and agglomeration than of the market imperfection or "rampant speculation" that is usually thought to characterize the operation of urban land markets.

These observations have a number of significant implications for policy approaches to expanding cities. First, the economic forces resulting from household and firm behavior are powerful in pushing city structure toward relatively well-understood and predictable changes as a city's population grows. This suggests that planning for land-use zoning, infrastructure, transport, and other areas of urban development would do well to conform to these general trends rather than fight them, as planning authorities often do, sometimes unwittingly and sometimes intentionally. Second, fast-rising land prices at the periphery should not be a matter of concern; they come part and parcel with city growth, and artificial measures that attempt to stem such growth in prices will seldom succeed. Third, given the requirements of an expanding urban population, the utmost must be done to let the supply of developed urban land expand in response to demand; this is the surest way of keeping land prices roughly consistent with the growth of the rest of the economy.

The decentralization of employment in Bogotá and Cali has been led by the decentralization of manufacturing employment, as has happened in cities in developed countries. Yet the CBDs continue to attract service employment and to retain large retail and wholesale trade activity. In Bogotá the result has been that overall CBD employment has remained almost constant in absolute terms, although its share has been falling—to about one-sixth of all city employment by the late 1970s. The center has become more specialized in its service and retail functions. The analysis indicates that decentralization can be expected to continue because the underlying causes—increases in real income, urban population growth, and transport improvements—are also expected to continue. This important feature of rapid city growth is often neglected in the planning of urban services; for example, transport investments are often based on forecasts of rising rather than constant employment in a city's CBD. The existing radially oriented system, with transport primarily focused toward the city center, should be supplemented with circumferential services.

Although decentralization has many benefits, it also has accompanying costs. It requires more extensive utility networks and therefore additional investment in public infrastructure. The per-household costs of many of these services are inversely related to density. Because the net residential densities of most new developments in Bogotá and Cali continue to be high, infrastructure costs per household are not as high as they might otherwise be. But the location of many poor households near and on the periphery raises the costs of infrastructure extension, and these costs could be difficult to recover from the poor through user charges.

Notes

1. The size of the *comunas* varies significantly, the smallest being about 174 hectares and the largest twenty times that size at 3,680 hectares. The population ranges from about 25,000 to 400,000. See the appendix for a description of the main data sets used in the study and more details about the spatial classification adopted.

2. The barrio, or neighborhood, is the smallest observation unit in the census. Because it is much smaller than a *comuna*, many more observations can be used to estimate the density gradient functions.

Chapter 4

Poverty, Distribution of Income, and Growth

In studying the growth of a country, it is common to look at the changing distribution of income to assess the distribution of the gains resulting from growth.[1] We study the distribution of income in Bogotá in a similar context but with one added dimension—that of spatial distribution within the city. This is crucial for understanding the spatial pattern of housing, transportation, and public services and for projecting the future demand for these services. One problem in studying the spatial distribution of income is that there are few established patterns for making comparisons and no robust theory for making predictions. The only theory that exists (for example, Muth 1969) has grown out of patterns observed in cities in developed countries and depends on two crucial assumptions. The first is that the income elasticity for the demand for housing (n_H) be greater than 1; the second is that the elasticity of the marginal cost of transport (as distance increases) with respect to income be small relative to n_H.

Under these assumptions, in a monocentric city in equilibrium, one would expect higher-income households to live farther from the city center than lower-income households do. There is increasing evidence that the income elasticity for housing demand is less than 1 (see chapter 7). Hence, although the theory explains the existing patterns of income distribution in cities in developed countries, its methodological basis can be called into question. Moreover, in situations where many transport modes exist and traffic is slow, the second assumption may also be not true for cities in poor countries. Chapter 3 established that there is little evidence of systematic variation of income by distance from the city center but that the pattern is much more distinct by radial sector. There is evidence of some segregation in residence by income, which also affects the distribution of employment. This chapter is therefore necessarily exploratory and primarily descriptive, concentrating on establishing the existing patterns in Bogotá and Cali and exploring useful methods of measurement and description. It is difficult to generalize from these findings, but it is hoped that similar measurement for other cities will, over time, establish recognizable patterns that are also explicable from a theoretical point of view. Recognition of the patterns is necessary for understanding how Bogotá functions.

There is considerable concern about the existence of "excessive" poverty in rapidly growing cities. Sometimes this is expressed as concern about the growth and characteristics of the informal sector (see, for example, Mazumdar 1976; Sethuraman 1974; Gilbert and Gugler 1982; and Webb 1977) and sometimes as concern about the location of the poor in undesirable parts of cities and the inferior conditions under which they live. Much of the literature supports the belief that the quality of life for the poor has worsened in large cities in developing countries. There is also a widespread impression that "unemployment, underemployment and misemployment add up to a massive problem in third world cities related to dimensions of inequality" (Gilbert and Gugler 1982, p. 70). Much normative evaluation has characterized the work that many of the poor do (particularly in the service sector, as domestic servants, street vendors, and shoeshine boys, for example) as socially wasteful or unproductive. The other most common concern is with the housing conditions of the poor. Earlier, slums and squatter resettlements were regarded as evidence of a culture of poverty; the new view, now widely accepted, usually sees the incremental housing typical of many poor settlements as evidence of hope, innovation, and opportunity. It is therefore illuminating to assess the actual existence of poverty in cities like Bogotá and Cali and to confront impressions and beliefs with empirical evidence.

This chapter illustrates some of the difficulties of even identifying the poor, despite a plethora of data for these two cities. It then examines the correlates of poverty (given plausible ranges of measurement errors). The interest is as much in measurement techniques and methods of analysis as in the description of the situation in Bogotá and Cali per se.

The changes in income distribution and poverty in Bogotá during the 1970s are better appreciated with some understanding of the overall economic conditions in Colombia during this period and in the economic preconditions of recent decades. The late 1940s and early 1950s in Colombia saw rapid industrialization and creation of new industries under conditions of substantial protection. It has been argued that nonagricultural income distribution probably worsened from the mid-1930s until the early 1950s while this industrialization was taking place (Berry and Urrutia 1976). Many of the protected industries that emerged were relatively capital-intensive and not labor-intensive. Given the skewed and highly concentrated ownership of capital, such industrialization could be expected to lead to a lower share of labor earnings. Because rural-urban migration was also very high during this period, providing almost "unlimited supplies of labor" at the low end, it was possible to keep blue-collar wages down. Conversely, this burst of industrialization created a sudden demand for highly skilled and educated workers, whose real earnings rose rapidly.

The whole period from the 1930s to the mid-1950s could be described as involving major structural changes in the Colombian economy—in particular, a shift from a predominantly agricultural rural economy to one based on urban industries and services. These structural changes continued apace until the mid-1960s, but the latter part of the period, from the mid-1950s to the mid-1960s, witnessed dramatic increases in blue-collar wages. Berry and Urrutia hypothesized that during this period the degree of protected import substitution may have decreased, and small-scale competitive enterprises may have become more successful. The expansion of primary education in the 1950s also contributed to higher average levels of workers' skills. The period between the mid-1950s and mid-1960s was one of slower economic growth and was in many ways a period of consolidation. Surprisingly, lower-skilled workers' incomes rose rapidly, even though rural-urban migration continued at high rates.

The overall income distribution in Colombia has remained highly unequal and is probably among the most unequal in the world. The share of the bottom 40 percent has remained around 10 percent of total income, whereas the share of the top 5 percent has been about one-third.[2] This is a little worse than in some comparable middle-income countries. In Malaysia, for example, the share of the bottom 40 percent was estimated to be 12 to 18 percent and that of the top 5 percent was a little less than 30 percent (Anand 1983). The Gini coefficient for Colombia is consistently estimated to be above 0.5. For comparison, in developed countries the share of the bottom 40 percent of households is typically estimated to be about 15 to 20 percent and that of the top 20 percent, between 35 and 45 percent of total income, with Gini coefficients of between 0.3 and 0.4.[3] Our estimates, which are only for Bogotá and Cali between 1973 and 1978, suggest some improvement in the late 1970s. The poverty estimates corroborate this tendency, so there probably was some improvement in income distribution in Colombia as a whole.

If such improvement did occur, it would be consistent with a number of other developments in the Colombian economy during this period. With declines in fertility rates and the progressively smaller proportion of people left in the rural areas, the rates of rural-urban migration and of urbanization have slowed. Moreover, there is evidence that the wages of rural unskilled workers rose significantly in the late 1970s (Urrutia

1985). The Colombian agricultural economy benefitted greatly from relatively high coffee prices throughout the 1970s and particularly from 1975, when a boom began that lasted until almost the end of the decade. Overall growth in agriculture was also consistently high over this decade, with an average annual growth rate of 5 percent (see Sokol and others 1984). Thomas (1985) has forcefully argued that these changes were not entirely fortuitous but rather resulted from good macroeconomic management along with progressive policies that supported agricultural development. The net result was that the demographic transition taking place in Colombia in the 1970s, coupled with robust growth in the agriculture sector, produced a relatively tight rural labor market. This in turn applied pressure on the urban labor market, and real wages rose at the same time as urban employment expanded substantially.

Correspondingly, it appears that the nonagricultural sectors were also following a labor-using strategy that led to a rate of growth of employment that exceeded output growth in the 1970s (Sokol and others 1984). Again, apart from fortuitous circumstances, this success can be attributed to successful fiscal and trade policies that promoted labor-using manufactured exports. The extensive expansion of urban public services involving the public sector also contributed significantly to the expansion of demand for labor. A major result of the expanded demand for labor was the increased participation of unskilled women in the labor force, which increased the household income of poorer households (see Mohan 1986, Urrutia 1985, and chapter 5 of this book for details).

Distribution of Income in Bogotá and Cali, 1973–78

An assessment of income distribution is typically plagued by measurement problems. Most censuses in developing countries do not include an income question, and those that do merit considerable skepticism about the veracity of responses. Household surveys are usually regarded as more accurate because they are more carefully done, with smaller samples. Rural income surveys present greater problems than urban surveys because it is difficult to evaluate both outputs and inputs. In urban surveys, wage earnings are easier to evaluate than income from property. The main sources of data that were used in this study were the 1973 population census for Bogotá and Cali and household surveys in 1975, 1977, and 1978 conducted by DANE, the Colombian national statistical agency. The 1978 survey was conducted especially for the City Study, and the income question was more detailed than in other surveys. The 1973 census seemed to have covered only about 50 percent of total personal income, whereas the 1978 survey may have covered as much as 90 percent and the other surveys perhaps 60 to 65 percent.

Although it is difficult to assess accurately the extent of undercoverage for each income group and for different years, our overall judgment is that coverage is probably better at the low end than at the top end of the income distribution. The evidence was conflicting, but the earnings of the least-skilled occupational categories recorded in the 1973 census were broadly comparable with other data on the labor earnings of these categories of workers. Female participation in the labor force, however, may have been undercounted in the 1973 census, contributing to some underestimation of household incomes. Overall, although there was substantial undercoverage of income in the 1973 population census, the *distribution* of income may be regarded as reliable and comparable with other data sets (see Mohan 1984 and Mohan, Wagner, and Garcia 1981). Hence, despite problems with the comparability of different data sets over time, it is possible to conclude from the evidence that the distribution of income improved marginally over the late 1970s in Bogotá and Cali. These details illustrate typical issues that are encountered in estimating income distribution trends in just two cities that are data-rich in comparison with most others in developing countries.

Table 4-1, which gives the decile shares of income for 1973 and 1978 for Bogotá and Cali and the values of two indexes of inequality—the Gini coefficient and the Theil index[4]—reflects the striking inequality that exists in Colombia. The income share of the bottom 40 percent of households is less than half the share received by the top 5 percent. Even in 1978, when the income coverage was greater than 90 percent, it appeared that there was substantial undercoverage of income from capital. Since such income is likely to accrue to the richer households, the actual distribution would be even worse than that apparent from this table. The results are similar for Bogotá and Cali and for the different income measures and rankings.[5]

The overall improvement in distribution between 1973 and 1978 is evident. These results were also consistent for different income concepts, different ranking procedures, and intermediate years (1975 and 1977) for both cities,[6] implying a high degree of confidence in these results. One general result obtained but not reported here was that all the indexes used yield higher inequality of households when ranked by HINCAP. This implies that even though households of larger size tend to have higher total household income, their per capita household income tends to be lower.

In summary, the levels of overall inequality found in Bogotá and Cali are not substantially different from earlier estimates for urban Colombia, although a slight tendency toward improvement is observed in the late 1970s. The distribution of income is slightly worse in Bogotá than in Cali.

Table 4-1. Distribution of Income in Bogotá and Cali
(percentage shares of total income)

Category	Bogotá		Cali	
	1973	1978	1973	1978
Households ranked by household income				
Bottom 20 percent	3.3	4.0	3.4	4.1
Bottom 40 percent	9.8	11.9	10.4	12.4
Top 20 percent	62.5	55.5	60.0	54.1
Top 5 percent	30.2	25.1	31.7	25.0
Gini coefficient	0.565	0.507	0.553	0.487
Theil index	0.610	0.458	0.601	0.429
Individuals ranked by household income per capita				
Bottom 20 percent	3.3	4.0	3.4	4.2
Bottom 40 percent	9.9	11.5	10.5	12.4
Top 20 percent	62.6	58.0	60.5	55.5
Top 5 percent	30.8	29.0	31.4	27.3
Gini coefficient	0.568	0.522	0.554	0.500
Theil index	0.649	0.508	0.632	0.470

Source: 1973 population census; 1978 World Bank–DANE Household Survey.

We now address the issue of the distribution of income across space in Bogotá and Cali. What are the spatial patterns? How do we measure them systematically? Can we trace trends over time? Both Bogotá and Cali exhibit striking patterns of income segregation by space. The ratio between mean incomes in different zones of the city is as much as 1 to 6, with the means taken over relatively large zones. This kind of spatial disparity in incomes is unusual even among the regions of a country, but because there is little information of this type for other cities, it is difficult to say what the norm would be for spatial distribution within a city. Discussion of the extent of spatial inequality within a city and comparison with others are difficult because there are no natural units of analysis. Unlike the world, which can be divided into countries, or a country, which can be divided into states or regions, there are no natural divisions within a city. In the United States much discussion focuses on the contrasting characteristics of central cities and suburbs, but even in this case there is no natural definition of what constitutes a central city. Any division of a city is arbitrary.

In this study we continue to use the two systems of zonification introduced in chapter 3—that is, rings and sectors. Much urban economic theory for a monocentric city would suggest systematic differences by distance from the city center—that is, by rings—but there is also a respectable tradition, originating with Homer Hoyt (1939, 1966), that divides the city into pie slices (sectors) for studying the distribution of income. Hoyt traced the historical development of a large number of North American cities. He concluded that income groups tended to locate in one section of the city and that as the city developed, the rich continued to locate in the same direction as that in which the city was expanding. Peter Amato (1968) established a similar pattern for Bogotá: he focused on the elite and showed that they have tended to locate predominantly in the northern part of the city and have continued to move in that direction. In later articles Amato (1970a, 1970b) noted patterns in Quito, Lima, and Santiago that were broadly similar to those in Bogotá, although not always as distinct.

In this exploratory section we suggest the use of a more systematic method of inequality measurement to assess the extent of spatial inequality and its trend over time. As indicated in table 4-2, in 1978 mean household income per capita in the poorest sector (2) in Bogotá was about one-fifth of that in the richest sector (8). In Cali the poorest sector (4) had about one-quarter the mean household income of the richest (2). Some anomalies may be noted in the data for Cali. The data for the CBD sector in 1978 seems to have suffered from some sample errors: population is shown to have fallen from about 4.3 percent of total population in 1973 to only 1.1 percent in 1978, whereas mean household income as a proportion of the overall mean increased from about 1.03 to 1.78. This is not plausible. The data for Cali do suggest, however, that the decentralization process for rich households had just begun in the 1970s. Many rich households continued to live within or near the central city. The movement of households from the rich sector 2, located near the central city, to sector 6, a developing suburban residential area, was just starting. Our observations in the late 1970s were made over this period of rapid transformation. Cali, being a much smaller city than Bogotá, still had a long way to go in terms of growth and decentralization, although the process of suburbanization of the rich had begun. Overall, however, the patterns for Bogotá and Cali were similar in terms of segregation of the rich and poor.

How much is hidden behind the means in table 4-2? Are there large variances around these means, so that the means do not necessarily imply differing characteristics in the sectors? The measurement of inequality is essentially the measurement of variance in a distribution. What we now seek to do is to decompose this variance into two parts: the variance between the means of income in rings, or sectors, or any other grouping of people and the variance in incomes between people within a group. The Theil index can be decomposed in this way. Total inequality can be decomposed into within-group (or within-sector, within-ring)

Table 4-2. Spatial Distribution of Income in Bogotá and Cali

	Bogotá				Cali			
	1973		1978		1973		1978	
Sector	Share of sector in city population (percent)	Mean HINCAP[a]	Share of sector in city population (percent)	Mean HINCAP[a]	Share of sector in city population (percent)	Mean HINCAP[a]	Share of sector in city population (percent)	Mean HINCAP[a]
1	2.3	1.07	2.4	0.80	4.3	1.03	1.1	1.78
2	18.2	0.57	20.6	0.50	4.2	3.68	4.8	2.36
3	26.0	0.68	25.2	0.73	19.5	0.89	15.2	0.88
4	9.3	0.90	7.2	0.98	21.2	0.69	17.8	0.64
5	7.3	0.98	6.2	1.03	35.1	0.68	42.2	0.73
6	18.2	0.80	20.0	0.91	11.1	1.61	12.8	1.42
7	12.0	1.71	9.1	1.44	4.5	1.37	6.0	2.13
8	6.6	2.87	9.1	2.60	n.a.	n.a.	6.0	2.13
City[b]	100.0	697[b]	100.0	1,012[b]	100.0	594[b]	100.0	2,425[b]

n.a. Not applicable.
a. Mean household monthly income per capita taken across individuals in the sector as a multiple of overall mean HINCAP.
b. Mean household monthly income per capita taken across individuals in Bogotá or Cali, expressed in current pesos. Consumer price index (1970 = 100): 1973 = 150; 1978 = 400.

Source: 1973 population census; 1978 World Bank–DANE Household Survey.

contribution and between-group (or between-sector, between-ring) contributions. The latter can be regarded as an index of spatial inequality in
incomes.[7]

The Theil inequality indexes in table 4-3 show the level of inequality
within each sector of the two cities. In general, the Theil index for each
sector is lower than for the city as a whole; that is, inequality within each
sector is less than overall inequality (see table 4-3). The lowest inequality
is found within the poor sectors (sectors 2 and 3 in Bogotá and sector 4
in Cali). Similarly, in 1978 the richest sectors (sector 8 in Bogotá and
sector 2 in Cali) also have low levels of inequality. This is a clear indication that the rich and poor parts of both cities became more homogeneous over the 1970s. The degree of spatial income segregation
increased during that period, and the rich and poor areas of the city
became more recognizable as such.

The lower part of table 4-3 presents measures of the between-group
contribution of the sectors and rings. The decomposition of inequality
permitted a calculation of this between-group measure, which has been
interpreted as a measure of the spatial inequality in income within a city.
The spatial contribution of groupings by sector is substantial—about 20
to 25 percent of total inequality. Because each sector is distinct and
internally homogeneous, spatial inequality between sectors is high in
both cities. A low spatial contribution (4–5 percent) by rings confirms
that the level of inequality within rings is not very different from overall
income inequality within the whole city (see Mohan 1986). Each ring is
about as heterogeneous as the whole city. For *comunas*, shown in the last
row of the table, spatial inequality is between 32 and 40 percent, showing that these smaller spatial units are even more distinct in character.

These systematic measures confirm once again that there is no discernible pattern in household income according to distance from the
central city in either Bogotá or Cali—as is often observed in cities in
developed countries. Income groups are significantly segregated by sector. Like households have been gravitating toward each other in different parts of the city. The methodology used here suggests a systematic
measure of spatial inequality that can be used to make similar measure-
ments in other cities.

It is difficult to judge the magnitude of such spatial inequality. Is 20–
25 percent spatial inequality low or high? I have seen no similar indexes
for other cities. Anand's (1984) work on Malaysia, however, provides
some estimates for comparison. He found interstate and rural-urban
contributions to inequality in Malaysia to be 9.1 and 13.7, respectively,
according to the Theil index. By these standards, Bogotá and Cali must
be judged to be highly segregated spatially by income. Moreover, this
inequality is increasing, despite evidence of some overall decrease in
income inequality. If spatial segregation of income groups has long-

Table 4-3. Spatial Inequality in Bogotá and Cali: Individuals Ranked by HINCAP

		Bogotá					Cali			
	Income ranking[a] (1978)	1973		1978		Income ranking[a] (1978)	1973		1978	
Item		Theil index	Ranking[b]	Theil index	Ranking[b]		Theil index	Ranking[b]	Theil index	Ranking[b]
Sector										
1	3	0.635	8	0.458	8	5	0.573	5	0.549	7
2	1	0.429	3	0.286	1	7	0.368	2	0.257	2
3	2	0.390	1	0.309	4	3	0.429	3	0.315	3
4	5	0.407	2	0.362	2	1	0.328	1	0.251	1
5	6	0.553	5	0.418	5	2	0.435	4	0.337	4
6	4	0.514	4	0.426	6	4	0.741	6	0.495	6
7	7	0.572	6	0.444	7	6	0.781	7	0.465	5
8	8	0.602	7	0.357	3	n.a.	n.a.	n.a.	n.a.	n.a.
City		0.649		0.508			0.632		0.470	
Intergroup contribution to inequality (percent)										
Sectors		21.6		26.9			22.7		22.5	
Rings		—		6.0			—		4.0	
Comunas		32.6		37.8			37.3		40.6	

n.a. Not applicable.
— Not available.
Note: HINCAP = household income per capita.
a. Ranked in ascending order of mean HINCAP.
b. Ranked in ascending order of inequality.
Source: Mohan (1986), tables 4-9, 4-10, and 4-11.

term deleterious effects on the efficient and harmonious working of a city, the trend in Bogotá is a cause for concern. This kind of segregation can lead to increasing distance between the different social groups of a city and impede social mobility.

As an example, the problem of educational segregation has received great attention in the United States. One solution attempted there has been to bus children to school across neighborhoods, particularly to provide better opportunities to children coming from spatially disadvantaged neighborhoods. Busing caused considerable social tension. If significant spatial differences start emerging in cities in developing countries, social problems similar to those experienced in developed countries may well arise. For example, spatial separation, by reducing the personal contacts that are so important in transmitting information about the labor market, could contribute to labor market segmentation.

If similar studies are carried out in many cities, it may also be possible to identify the reasons behind higher and lower levels of spatial differentiation in cities and their effects on labor markets and social welfare as a whole. For example, are such phenomena caused by high rates of growth where similar people congregate near each other to begin with? Over time does further sorting take place and the city become less a collection of differentiated neighborhoods and more like an organic whole? Or are such tendencies exacerbated as the city stabilizes?

Clearly, whatever the answers to these larger questions, the spatial distribution of income in Bogotá and Cali does not conform to expectations from the theory for largely monocentric cities, despite regular and expected patterns of population densities and land values. It is therefore important to study cities in greater spatial detail even if they conform to overall recognizable patterns.

Distribution and Characteristics of the Poor

To identify the correlates and composition of poverty in Bogotá and Cali, we have to address the problem of how to define and measure poverty. Despite the high quality and large quantity of data at hand, it is possible to identify only the people who must, in all probability, be poor. And it is difficult to identify *all* the people who are poor, except within rather large ranges of estimates. It is much easier to identify relative poverty, defined merely as the bottom x percent of the population—say, 30 percent. We adopt a mixture of these approaches. A lower bound is first placed on the proportion of people who must be poor. We can then trace the movement of this proportion over time, compute a range of estimates of others who might be poor, and, finally, collate the characteristics of the bottom 30 percent, who roughly coincide with those who have been identified as poor.

The notion of absolute poverty has been linked with that of malnutrition. Because food is the first necessity of household consumption, if people are malnourished, they can scarcely be consuming other things. Estimates of malnutrition and poverty have therefore been made on this basis for countries (for example, Ohja 1970 and Dandekar and Rath 1971 for India) and for the world as a whole (for example, Reutlinger and Selowsky 1976). In these studies, estimates of minimum expenditures on food required for adequate nutrition were compared with estimates of actual consumption by income or consumption groups. Although nutrition involves the intake of various elements such as calories, vitamins, proteins, and minerals, it is generally agreed that if consumption of calories (that is, energy) is adequate, other elements are also usually adequately consumed (see, for example, Sukhatme 1978). Thus, if we know the caloric content of foods, the usual food basket for different income groups, the prices of foods, the expenditure on food by different types of families, and the share of food in total consumption or total income, we can relate the likely level of nutrition to income levels.

The key problem in using such a procedure is that each individual's norm is different; some individuals, for example, need only 1,800 calories a day, while others need 2,500. The minimum caloric consumption is around the usual requirement levels. A small percentage change in the minimum caloric consumption used as the basis for estimating the number of malnourished people can lead to substantial differences in the estimate of malnourished people. For Colombia, the Instituto Colombiano de Bienestar Familiar (Colombian Institute for Family Welfare) has established 1,970 calories as the average minimum for adequate daily caloric intake, taking into account Colombian conditions and the age and sex distribution of the population.

Using the same data sources as earlier (the 1973 population census and the 1978 World Bank–DANE Household Survey), we attempted to calculate the proportion of people in Bogotá and Cali who can in all probability be classified as malnourished and therefore poor. Because we had only income data from these sources, we used other information to translate the income level of each household into likely calories consumed per person, taking into account the age and sex composition of the household and its likely consumption pattern. Even if it is assumed that anyone consuming less than 80 percent of required mean calories must be malnourished, different methods gave us a likely range of 30 to 50 percent malnutrition in Bogotá and Cali in 1973 and about 15 to 25 percent in 1978. One problematic issue was the undercoverage of incomes in 1973 alluded to in the last section. Another issue is that low-income people typically eat foods that are calorie-rich; that is, the price of each calorie is lower for many cheap food items typically consumed by the poor. Taking that into account, we concluded that our estimate of the share of the population that must be malnourished could be narrowed down to about 25 to 30 percent in 1973 and 12 to 15 percent in 1978. These are the people whose incomes do not allow for adequate nutrition. There may well be additional numbers of people who have adequate incomes but suffer from malnutrition for other reasons.

Clearly, identifying poverty is not a simple task even with detailed data. Table 4-4 provides a quantitative idea of the kind of misclassification that can result if we take, say, the bottom 30 percent of the income distribution as poor. The first row gives the breakdown, by decile, of people who consume less than 80 percent of required calories ($0.8R$). Virtually all the malnourished, so defined, fall within the bottom 30 percent. The next three rows give the percentage in each decile that falls into each nutritional range—less than $0.8R$, between $0.8R$ and $1.0R$, and more than $1.0R$. If we defined all the bottom 30 percent as poor, we would misclassify as poor as many as 32 percent in the second decile and 58 percent in the third decile who are not necessarily malnourished (with 80 percent of requirements as the norm). Conversely, it is only in the top five deciles that we can be sure there are no malnourished or poor. As the table shows, household size declines monotonically with income, suggesting that the malnourished are predominantly in large families with high dependency ratios.[8]

It is useful to compare the minimum wage (1,738 pesos in 1978) with the average incomes presented in the last two rows of the table. Because the majority of the second decile and part of the third decile are malnourished, an intermediate household income level in the range of 4,000 to 5,000 pesos (1978) can be utilized as necessary to attain minimum adequate nutrition. It is clear, then, that for adequate nutrition those households need roughly 2.5 workers per household at minimum wages. In fact, they characteristically have higher dependency ratios; that is, they have fewer than 2.5 workers per household. It would seem that the minimum wage does not provide even a small family with enough income for the barest minimum of nutrition. The monthly wages of fully employed people in typical low-income occupations—construction workers, cooks, waiters, and so on—were between 2.0 and 2.5 times the minimum wage in 1973 and 1978. Moreover, monthly wages had grown at an average of 8 to 9 percent a year between these years. It would be difficult, therefore, to argue that minimum wages were too high during that period or that they contributed to protecting the formal sector.

In conclusion, our results are mixed. First, we must be wary of malnutrition or poverty estimates reached with the use of simple income cut-

Table 4-4. Mapping Malnutrition into Income Deciles in Bogotá, 1978

Item	Decile[a]										Total
	1	2	3	4	5	6	7	8	9	10	
Percentage of 0.8R in decile	46	32	20	1	1	0	0	0	0	0	100
Percentage of decile in nutritional category											
0.8R	100	68	42	1.7	2.5	0	0	0	0	0	21
0.8R to 1.0R	0	28	35	40	16	3	0	0	0	0	12
1.0R+	0	4	23	58	82	97	100	100	100	100	67
Total	100	100	100	100	100	100	100	100	100	100	100
Percentage of population in decile	9.8	10.0	9.8	9.7	10.0	10.4	9.8	10.1	10.3	10.3	100
Average household size (persons)	6.1	5.5	5.4	5.3	5.2	4.8	4.6	4.3	4.1	3.5	4.8
Average monthly household income per capita[b] (1978 pesos)	440	720	925	1,200	1,470	1,818	2,300	3,110	4,780	12,640	2,980
Average monthly household income (1978 pesos)	2,580	3,980	5,050	6,340	7,680	8,710	10,675	13,400	19,670	51,790	18,140

Note: 0.8R refers to people who consume less than 80 percent of the minimum nutrition requirements. 1.0R refers to people who consume less than the minimum requirements. 1.0R+ refers to those who meet or exceed the minimum requirements.
a. The population (3.5 million) is ranked from poorest decile (1) to richest (10) according to household income per capita.
b. The minimum monthly wage in 1978 was 1,738 pesos.
Source: Mohan (1986), table 5-7.

off levels. Second, one can get a sense of the likely ranges of malnutrition and poverty through rather detailed work. For 1978, for example, there is almost zero probability that any malnourished people are in the top five deciles, a small probability that they are in the fourth and fifth deciles, and a high probability that they are in the bottom 30 percent. Taking the bottom 30 percent in this case leaves out the few who are in higher deciles but does include some who are not necessarily malnourished in the bottom three. Third, there is a high likelihood that the definitely malnourished and poor decreased from about 25 to 30 percent in 1973 to 12 to 15 percent of the population in Bogotá and Cali in 1978.

Having found reasonable estimates of people who must be poor, we now need to identify their demographic, spatial, and economic characteristics. The concentration of the poor in particular identifiable groups according to each of these dimensions is notable. The incidence of malnutrition is strikingly high among children between the ages of 5 and 14 in large households of more than six members, a high proportion of which are located on the periphery of the two cities and in the particularly poor sectors (in the south in Bogotá and the east in Cali). (For Bogotá, see table 4-5; the situation in Cali is similar.) An index of between 140 and 150 for children ages 5 to 14 in sector 2 means that the children are 1.4 to 1.5 times more likely to be malnourished than the mean of about 28 to 35 percent of this group. Note that this mean is itself much higher than the overall mean of 21.1 percent.

A few other features stand out from this table. Although, on average, the old are less likely to be malnourished and poor, those on the periphery (ring 5) and in the southern part of Bogotá (sector 2) are exceptions and disproportionately so. The children in these areas are not particularly hard hit, but the adults are worse off compared with the city average. Since malnutrition is accentuated by bad sanitation, poor hygiene, disease, and crowding, the purely income-based estimates of malnutrition are more likely to be understated for the poor neighborhoods. There, even people with somewhat higher incomes who can afford more food could suffer from malnutrition because of chronic stomach disorders and other neighborhood effects.[9]

We can now bring together a number of results that are important for understanding the structure of Bogotá. We have pointed out in chapter 3 that densities in the poorer parts of Bogotá and Cali are relatively uniform and do not decline with distance, even though land values do. We now find that many of the households on the distant periphery are large, poor households with high dependency ratios; that is, households have responded to lower land prices and located at the periphery, but because of higher household size, population density continues to be high in these areas. It would seem that poor households with more older people incapable of working tend to descend further into poverty.

Table 4-5. Spatial Distribution of Malnutrition by Age Group in Bogotá, 1978

Age group	Index of malnutrition[a]						Percentage malnourished in age group
	Ring						
	1	2	3	4	5	6	
0–4	160	92	54	77	117	101	19.7
5–9	28	76	77	81	120	112	28.4
10–14	126	82	76	86	112	98	34.1
15–54	77	65	45	84	133	92	17.7
55+	131	97	51	68	140	88	15.4
Total	101	73	55	82	127	98	21.1

Age group	Sector								Percentage malnourished in age group
	1	2	3	4	5	6	7	8	
0–4	160	147	94	54	81	103	75	40	19.7
5–9	28	144	98	73	55	96	70	77	28.4
10–14	126	147	95	88	67	94	70	58	34.1
15–54	77	156	97	85	71	120	57	29	17.7
55+	131	188	108	83	141	84	51	23	15.4
Total	101	155	98	80	72	14	61	38	21.1

a. The index of malnutrition is calculated as:

$$A_{ij} = \frac{\text{Percentage } 0.8R \text{ in age group } i \text{ in sector } j}{\text{Percentage } 0.8R \text{ in age group } i}$$

where $0.8R$ refers to people who consume less than 80 percent of the minimum nutritional requirements set by the Instituto Colombiano de Bienestar Familiar.

Source: Mohan (1986), table 5-12.

This tendency is exacerbated for income earners with relatively flat age-earnings profiles. As is well known (and documented for Bogotá in chapter 5), people who are poorly educated and unskilled do not earn more with experience. As these workers get older and enter the stage of household formation, they have to support more people on the same income. Children of the unskilled are therefore disproportionately poor on the whole. The situation is exacerbated when old people are present in the household. It is interesting to observe how this process works itself out and how spatial effects can be identified in terms of residence patterns. Although economic growth in the mid- to late 1970s was quite effective in reducing the number of people who have no potential of achieving minimally adequate nutrition, the concentration of the poor in particular areas remains striking. The concentration does, however, allow easier targeting of antipoverty, nutrition, and education programs.

Having established the demographic and spatial dimensions of poverty, we now need to look in a little more detail at who the workers are who happen to be poor. For this purpose, poor workers are identified as being in the bottom 30 percent of households ranked by HINCAP.

The very fact of working does much to alleviate poverty. Only about 20 percent of male workers and 15 percent of female workers fall into the bottom 30 percent. Most women are secondary workers (that is, not household heads). A household is better off if there is more than one income earner. As might be expected, almost half of all male workers with no education and about one-third with a primary education are classified as poor. An analysis of poverty by age and education groups confirms that children suffer disproportionately from poverty. Among both males and females, workers in the 35–44 age group are more likely to be poor. Thus, whereas about 20 percent of all male workers are classified as poor, more than one-third of the 35–44 age group is so classified. Most of these are workers with little or no education, but about 15 percent have a secondary-level education. Workers with little education have relatively flat age-income profiles (see chapter 5), and it is these workers who appear to fall into poverty during the period in their lives when their households are expanding and their children are going to school. This highlights the real economic hardship undergone by the poor in educating their children into their teens rather than sending them out to work. Of those in the 12–14 age group who work (and the sample of this group is not large), very few are found in poverty. Those who work clearly contribute to household income and help lift the household out of poverty.

Poor workers are concentrated among a few occupations and corresponding industries. Blue-collar occupations account for about 70 to 75 percent of poor workers but only 55 to 57 percent of all workers. Produc-

tion, construction, and transport workers are particularly likely to
be poor; along with service workers, these groups make up about 70 percent of all poor male workers. Among women, it is notable that maids
(domestics), who account for about 20 percent of the female labor force,
are not particularly poor. Almost one-third of poor female workers are
service workers (excluding maids). Among the production workers, the
traditional industries of textiles and footwear, lumber and wood products, and printing and publishing account for the majority of the poor
workers. Female participation in production activities is mainly in the
textile and footwear industries, which do not seem to pay women well.

Do poor workers work long hours or are they short of work? Poor
men are strikingly overrepresented among workers who work long
hours; about 20 percent of poor, male workers are in this category. Only
about 8 percent of the poor work fewer than forty hours a week, and
about 55 to 60 percent work the "normal" forty- to forty-eight-hour
week. Sales, construction, and transport workers work the longest
hours; among the poor, only professional and technical workers work
relatively short hours. The story is different for female workers; they
appear to be overrepresented among those working shorter hours. (It is
mainly sales workers and maids who work very long hours.) It seems that
many poor, female, part-time workers would like more work but find it
difficult to get or else cannot work longer hours because of responsibilities at home.

Overall, it appears that poor male workers are not lacking for work.
There is little overt underemployment; indeed, if anything, the poor are
overworked but are locked into low-productivity occupations, implying
a need for training programs to improve people's skills. The sales workers may actually be underemployed—that is, idle for a substantial part of
their working hours—but they comprise only about 25 percent of all
poor workers. Almost half of the poor, overworked men are transport or
construction workers. It is unlikely that they are idle during much of
their working day. On the other hand, a substantial portion of the
women are either genuinely underemployed (willing and able to work
more hours) or unable to work longer hours. Poverty will therefore not
be alleviated by mere expansion of employment opportunities. Poor
women need greater employment opportunities, but they could also
benefit from day-care programs—which themselves generate employment for the providers.

It is often said that recent migrants earn less than others and have to
take very low-paying jobs while waiting for better-paid opportunities.
The evidence is mixed. In Bogotá in 1975, 22 percent of the most recent
arrivals earned less than the minimum wage, compared with about 38
percent of all workers. Among those who had been in Bogotá eleven
and twenty years, however, as many as 20 percent earned less than mini-

mum wage. It appears that low wages are spread fairly evenly among workers of all vintages and that experience in the city does not guarantee a higher wage. On the whole, it is clear that recent migrants have no monopoly on poverty; indeed, 60 to 70 percent of all workers earning below minimum wages have been in Bogotá for more than ten years.

We also examined in detail who the unemployed are. Because we have information about current income only, it is difficult to distinguish between people who are poor because they are unemployed and those who are unemployed because they are poor. This problem is partially addressed by looking at primary and secondary workers separately and examining in detail the incidence of unemployment in each decile. Even if we regard all unemployed primary workers as temporarily out of work, the unemployment rate in the bottom 30 percent would still be disproportionately high. We therefore conclude that the probability of unemployment is higher among the chronically poor (see table 4-6). Our conjectures are further supported by the particularly low participation rates in the bottom deciles, which contain a substantial proportion of people who are not working. Male participation rates rise and then flatten out.

We emerge with a distinctive profile of the unemployed. In the bottom decile—that is, among the very poorest—only about 40 to 50 percent of males and 15 percent of females over 12 years of age participate in the labor force compared with the overall participation rate of about 70 percent for men and about 30 percent for women. Among males (over age 12) in the bottom decile who do participate in the labor force, almost 30 percent were out of work. Consequently, only about 35 percent of all males and about 8 to 10 percent of all females over age 12 in the bottom decile have jobs. Of the remainder, some are discouraged workers and others are incapacitated by sickness or injury. Generating employment and upgrading skills are therefore only partial solutions for poverty removal. Many of the poor are probably unemployable, and their poverty must be dealt with directly through welfare measures.

Summary

The 1970s marked a turning point in Colombia's economic history. Prudent macroeconomic and trade policies, along with the successful support of agricultural growth during the late 1960s and the early to mid-1970s, had helped create a growth-oriented, labor-using environment. Colombia's unprecedented expansion of employment during the 1970s brought about a palpable tightening of the labor market. This process was aided by the boom in international coffee prices during the late 1970s. In addition, this was a period of demographic transition and the

Table 4-6. Unemployment in Bogotá by Income Decile and Sex

Sex and year	Income decile[a]										All	Total Number in the labor force (thousands)
	1	2	3	4	5	6	7	8	9	10		
	Unemployment rate (percent)											
Male												
1975	30.8	11.4	7.3	8.7	8.0	5.2	3.8	2.5	2.6	0.4	6.9	624
1977	30.2	12.2	6.2	6.5	6.6	5.5	3.9	4.4	2.7	0.5	6.2	782
1978	19.8	10.2	6.1	5.6	4.2	2.7	2.0	2.9	0.7	0.6	4.7	753[b]
Female												
1975	29.2	12.1	12.7	9.6	7.9	7.8	6.1	3.7	1.9	1.1	6.4	337
1977	16.3	11.1	9.4	9.5	7.7	6.4	5.8	4.2	1.7	2.1	5.8	469
1978	6.2	7.3	5.1	8.9	7.3	4.3	2.5	1.9	1.7	0.4	4.3	463[b]
	Distribution of the unemployed (percent)											Number unemployed
Male												
1975	23.8	15.5	11.2	14.2	12.4	8.1	6.6	3.7	4.0	0.6	100.0	43
1977	23.2	15.0	9.0	10.7	10.3	10.2	7.1	8.1	5.0	1.5	100.0	49
1978	30.9	16.2	10.3	11.2	9.4	6.0	4.7	7.9	1.8	1.6	100.0	35
Female												
1975	13.0	11.8	13.0	12.4	11.2	12.4	10.6	8.1	4.3	3.1	100.0	21
1977	15.1	10.0	11.0	10.7	11.1	10.5	11.0	9.7	5.1	6.0	100.0	28
1978	21.9	16.7	9.5	13.6	13.8	7.9	5.5	5.0	5.2	1.0	100.0	20

Note: Percentages may not add to 100 because of rounding.

a. Ranked from poorest (1) to richest (10), based on monthly household income per capita.

b. The estimated population of Bogotá was lower than expected in 1978. The estimated labor force in 1978 is also low because the estimates for 1975 and 1977 use the original DANE expansion factors.

Source: 1975 DANE Special Bogotá Household Survey; 1977 DANE Household Survey; 1978 World Bank–DANE Household Survey.

achievement of an urbanization level of more than 60 percent. The result was a slowing of urbanization that was somewhat unexpected after almost fifty years of rapid urban growth.

The tightening of the labor market led to measurable growth in household income, and poverty decreased in Bogotá and Cali during the 1970s. According to the data at hand, the distribution of income in the two cities seems to have improved somewhat between 1973 and 1978. The quality of the data is not robust enough for this to be stated conclusively, but such a tendency would be consistent with the other changes in the national economy. Despite this improvement, inequality in the two cities remained very high: the Gini coefficient remained between 0.50 and 0.55.

The spatial separation of rich and poor appears to have increased during the period under study, despite the overall improvement in income distribution. The spatial separation is more pronounced by radial sectors than by distance from the city center, the norm in cities in developed countries.

In this study, we have placed great emphasis on understanding the spatial distribution of households according to their income levels and other characteristics. This is important as a prelude to comprehending the changes that take place in patterns of housing demand, transportation, and demand for infrastructure as a city grows. Whereas some of the specific patterns found, particularly the high degree of spatial segregation of the rich and poor, may be peculiar to Bogotá and Cali, our findings illustrate the importance of understanding these patterns in order to make policy regarding infrastructure and other urban services.

Spatial disparities in an urban area can increase segmentation in the labor market by exacerbating differences in educational background, family background, and other determinants of earnings. The deficiencies in household environment and school quality that a poor child is subject to can be worsened by such segregation. If there is a large concentration of poorly educated or illiterate people in specific areas of the city, it becomes much more difficult to operate good schools in those areas. It is difficult to find good teachers, the student peer group consists of equally disadvantaged children, and the quality of education suffers. Similarly, the peer group of poor workers or of the chronically unemployed usually comprises other poor workers and those who are chronically unemployed. The diminution of aspirations and contacts decreases the worker's chances of moving out of the low-income or unemployment trap.

The richer areas of a city are typically better served by public utilities than poorer areas. Richer residents are simply more effective in voicing their demand for urban public services. If an area has a mix of both rich and poor residents, the poor benefit from the better sanitation, water supply, roads, schools, medical services, and the like that may exist because of the influence of the rich. If, however, the poor live in large, separate tracts, as in the southern part of Bogotá and the eastern part of Cali, it becomes easier for hard-pressed authorities to neglect them. In Bogotá and Cali the severity of the potential spatial disadvantage has been mitigated by the operation of decentralized housing markets and private land development. The decentralized nature of the urban public service agencies has also helped make these agencies more responsive to demands, including the demands of the poor, and the service deficits in the poor areas have not been as large as they might have been.

There is some indication that the land-use zoning policies have contributed to the prevailing spatial development pattern. Residential-density zoning often consciously separates lower-density areas from high-density areas. Although there are market forces that tend to separate the rich and the poor through the operation of the land and housing markets, care must be taken in land-use zoning not to exacerbate such natural tendencies, but instead to promote more mixed land use.

Although we have indicated in this chapter the difficulties of measuring the extent of poverty in a city, we have also demonstrated the possibility of arriving at some robust estimates. The areas of Bogotá and Cali that have high malnutrition and poverty levels are characterized by large, low-income families with high dependency ratios because of the presence of many children. Workers who have low lifetime earnings sink into greater poverty as their households expand. In cities in developing countries large numbers of workers with low education levels have flat age-earnings profiles. The expansion of their families during their middle age pushes them into poverty, and hence an atypically large proportion of children are found in the malnourished or poverty group. This finding provides powerful support for the idea that child-directed nutrition and health programs are effective weapons against poverty. If poverty is concentrated spatially, it becomes easier to target such programs, but knowledge of city structure is then essential.

Another important finding has been that many people who are fully employed are poor: their low productivity, not unemployment, is the cause of poverty. We also found that unemployment is more likely to occur among poor households. The removal of core poverty therefore involves basic welfare measures: mere increases in employment, although essential, will not be sufficient. Investments in human capital—both of adults and of those who are potential workers—would enhance productivity and therefore earnings (see chapter 5).

Notes

1. See, for example, Urrutia (1985) and Anand (1983) for excellent studies of Colombia and Malaysia, respectively.

2. Estimates for 1964 are available in Selowsky (1979) and Berry and Urrutia (1976); see Berry and Soligo (1980) for 1974 estimates.

3. Morrison (1984) claimed that this share is similar for capitalist and socialist countries.

4. See Anand (1983) and Mohan (1986), chapter 4, for an exposition on the derivation of the two measures. Both indexes vary between 0 and 1, with 0 being equivalent to complete equality. The Theil index may be interpreted as measuring the departure of an income distribution from an even distribution.

5. A word about these different measures is in order here. The most common distribution used has been that of households ranked by household income. It has been argued by Datta and Meerman (1980) and Anand (1983) that this distribution does not provide a good indication of differences in the level of living in the population. Our general concern is with the welfare of individuals rather than of households. Moreover, households vary by size as well as by age and sex composition. Hence, for true comparisons, adjustments should be made to account for these variations. The best solution would be to make adjustments by deriving "adult equivalent" measures of consumption. Practically speaking, this is difficult; the next-best strategy is to use HINCAP to rank individuals (or households) for welfare comparisons. As Datta and Meerman also found, although the rankings of particular individuals change substantially when ranked by HINCAP as opposed to household income, the overall result does not. The particular rankings are clearly important when the aim is to find out the characteristics of the poor or the rich, but the distribution is not too different.

6. Reported in detail in Mohan (1984), which also reports estimates of other inequality measures.

7. See Anand (1983) and Mohan (1984, 1986) for a derivation of the decomposition of the Theil index. The within-group contribution is essentially a weighted average of the indexes of inequality within each group, and the between-group contribution is a measure of the differences in the means, appropriately weighted. In the Theil index the weight used is the group share in income. It can be shown that this decomposition is additive.

8. The dependency ratio is the ratio of the dependent population (defined as under 15 or over 64 years old) to the working-age population (ages 15–64).

9. This has been confirmed to be the case from detailed clinical nutrition studies in Cali associated with those reported in McKay and others (1978).

Chapter 5

Workers and Their Earnings

In this chapter we describe the structure of employment and the associated pattern of labor earnings. We also report on the determinants of these earnings in order to understand the changes in income that have already been documented. And we briefly discuss segmentation in the labor market in terms of the identification of an informal sector. One very interesting feature of the labor market in the late 1970s was the increasing participation of women in the labor force; this is also analyzed. Although estimations were conducted for both Bogotá and Cali, for ease of presentation we provide the results for Bogotá only. The findings for Cali were generally consistent with those for Bogotá. Only the main results are presented here, because details of model structure and estimation procedures are available in Mohan (1986, chaps. 6, 7, 8, and 9).

The overwhelming message that emerges is that high urban unemployment, long-term employment problems, high poverty levels, and segmented labor markets are not inherent in a situation of rapid urban growth. An appropriate economic environment bolstered with a judicious mix of policies can lead to positive results, as occurred in Bogotá and in Cali in the late 1970s.

For background it is important to be aware of the overall changes in the employment structure that have taken place in Colombia over the past fifty years. We documented earlier that Colombia went through an intensive phase of urbanization over this period, going from a level of about 30 percent to 65 percent. As happens in many countries, the change in employment structure followed that in sectoral output, with some lag. Hence, as is evident from the data below showing each sector's percentage share in total employment, a dramatic change in the structure of employment occurred in the relatively short period after the mid-1960s.

Sector	1925	1938	1951	1964	1973	1978
Primary	67.1	67.1	57.3	50.6	41.9	35.2
Secondary	15.7	17.8	16.3	17.7	20.6	22.4
Tertiary	17.2	15.1	20.4	31.7	37.5	42.4

The increase in the share of the secondary and tertiary sectors, which are primarily urban, is remarkable over the 1973–78 period. The expansion of education (see table 5-1) that occurred during the 1950s and 1960s increased the quality of the labor force very rapidly. Employment change, however, was more marked in the late 1970s (see table 5-2). In absolute terms it is clear that the tertiary sector was the most important component of this growth in employment, but the rates of growth were also high for manufacturing and construction—between 7 and 9 percent a year, higher than output growth in all these sectors. The output growth in agriculture was higher than employment growth over the same period, thereby implying significant improvements in agricultural labor productivity. Hence the predominantly urban sectors have grown in a labor-using manner. This is contrary to the usual scenario in developing countries, where the urban sectors are regarded as capital-using and agriculture as labor-using. Structural change in production usually takes place faster than the change in employment structure: output growth in manufacturing usually occurs much faster than employment growth, and it is the agricultural sector that tends to absorb the expanding labor force in the absence of employment opportunities in the manufacturing and tertiary sectors. This is the distinctive phenomenon that occurred in Colombia in the late 1970s, which makes this study of the Bogotá labor market and earnings determination particularly interesting as an example of rapid population growth in a city accompanied by employment and income growth.

There was a remarkable downturn in unemployment rates in Colombia in the late 1970s, implying a considerable tightening in the labor market: participation rates rose until the mid-1970s because of the massive expansion in education but then began to stabilize. The last column of table 5-1, labeled "Other," includes mainly housewives: their increased participation in market work between 1973 and 1978 is clear. The expansion of education has applied equally to women, and this has begun to manifest itself in their greater inclination to participate in market work.

Given its large share of the total urban population and its role as capital city, the course of Bogotá in the 1970s was generally that of urban Colombia. It had more than its share of the employment boom: its unemployment rates were consistently below those of other cities. The constellation of economic policies after 1966 tended to promote exports, which are usually more labor-using. The government was also

Table 5-1. Changes in Labor Use in Colombia, 1951–78

Year	Total population age 15 and over (thousands)	Percentage of total			
		In school	Employed	Unemployed	Other[a]
1951	6,910	2.4	54.1	1.7	41.8
1964	9,528	5.3	50.2	3.4	41.1
1973	12,449	9.4	45.5	5.4	39.7
1978	14,698	10.3	52.1	3.1	34.5
		Average annual rate of change (percent)			
1951–64	2.4	8.5	1.9	8.1	2.4
1964–73	3.0	7.8	1.9	8.4	2.6
1973–78	3.4	5.4	6.2	-7.7	0.5

a. Mainly housewives.
Source: 1951, 1964, 1973 population censuses; 1978 DANE National Household Survey (June); Sokol and others (1984).

more oriented toward a pattern of public expenditures that helped the poor: for example, expenditures in public health and education were emphasized. The improvement in the availability of public services is also quite evident in Bogotá during the 1960s and 1970s (see chapter 9). All this combined to produce increased demand for labor in urban Colombia and, specifically, in Bogotá.

We observed a marked increase in the participation of working-age women in the tightened labor market of Bogotá in the late 1970s. Because the participation rate of prime-age men (ages 25–55) in the labor market is usually close to 100 percent in any case, the increase in the labor force has to come from people not traditionally in the labor force—prime-age women, young men, and young women. Because of the expansion of educational opportunities, however, young men and young women defer their entry into the labor force and opt to stay in

Table 5-2. Employment Change in Colombia, 1973–78

Sector	Thousands of workers, 1973	Thousands of workers, 1978	Net change, 1973–78 (thousands)	Percentage of total change	Annual rate of change (percent)
Agriculture	2,305	2,629	324	16	2.7
Mining	68	69	1	0	0.0
Manufacturing	912	1,357	445	22	8.3
Construction	255	360	105	6	7.1
Tertiary	2,124	3,249	1,125	56	8.9
Total	5,664	7,664	2,000	100	6.2

Source: Sokol and others (1984).

school longer. This tends to have a lagged effect in that people with higher education are more likely to participate in the labor force. The participation rates of women with higher education increased from about 43 to 53 percent between 1973 and 1978, compared with participation rates of about 36 percent and 28 percent of women with primary and secondary education, respectively, in 1978 (having changed from 30 percent and 31 percent, respectively, in 1973). The increasing trend in participation was at the low and high ends of the education spectrum during this time of labor market tightening.

Some of the improvement in poverty and income distribution indexes is attributable to the increased utilization of female unskilled labor during the boom years of the late 1970s in Bogotá. The participation rate of females in the bottom 30 percent as classified by household income per capita (HINCAP) increased from about 17 to 34 percent in the short time between 1975 and 1978. A detailed analysis of the participation behavior of women showed that the own-wage elasticity of all married women was between 0.6 and 0.8, whereas that of prime-age nonmarried women was much lower—about 0.15 (see Mohan 1986, chap. 7). The latter group included widows and never-married women. The analysis indicates that women in cities in developing countries can be expected to participate in market work in much greater numbers in the future. Both a secular increase in education levels, which raises the opportunity cost of not working, and the pure wage response under conditions of a tightening labor market will motivate the rise.

The education level of the work force changed along with its makeup (see table 5-3). By the late 1970s the Bogotá work force was almost fully literate. Education was more advanced as well as more widespread. In 1973 about 40 percent of the labor force was educated up to at least the secondary level in Bogotá; just five years later this proportion had increased to about 55 percent. The expansion of higher education was quite dramatic, especially for the women. With this vastly increased supply of workers with higher education, the earnings differentials between higher and primary education have declined—which is another explanation of the overall improvement in income distribution (see table 5-4).

Education expanded at very high rates in Colombia right through the 1960s and 1970s. In 1960 primary school enrollment was about 75 percent; by the mid-1970s it was 100 percent. Enrollment in secondary schools increased even more dramatically, from about 12 percent of the relevant age cohort in 1960 to about 40 percent by 1975 and just under 50 percent by 1980. Enrollment in higher education increased from 2 percent in 1960 to 9 percent in 1975 and 12 percent by 1980. The speed of expansion was particularly marked between about 1965 and 1975. The private sector has played a substantial role in the expansion of education in Colombia. At the primary level, almost 20 percent of enroll-

Table 5-3. Distribution of Workers by Sex and Education Level
(percent)

Education level	1973			1978		
	Males	Females	All	Males	Females	All
None	5.1	9.2	6.5	2.3	5.7	3.6
Primary	55.0	53.9	54.7	42.0	42.3	42.1
Secondary	31.1	32.5	31.6	38.8	37.6	38.4
Higher	8.8	4.3	7.3	16.8	14.4	15.9
Total	100.0	100.0	100.0	100.0	100.0	100.0
Total number of workers	488,000	249,000	738,000	732,000	454,000	1,186,000
Total number in sample	45,080	23,041	68,121	3,078	1,914	4,992

Note: Percentages in 1973 do not total 100 because of some omitted categories.
Source: 1973 population census sample; 1978 World Bank–DANE Household Survey.

ments were in private schools; this rose to about 54 percent at the secondary level and remained fairly steady at 47 percent at the higher-education level in the late 1960s (see Jallade 1974). During the 1960s the private sector increased its share at the primary and higher levels, whereas the public sector expanded much faster at the secondary level. Hence, the expansion of the Colombian education system was due as much to private initiative as to specific governmental initiatives.

Total government expenditures on education increased from less than 2 percent of GDP in 1960 to about 3 percent by 1970. As might be

Table 5-4. Mean Income Ratios for Workers by Sex and Education Level

Education level	1973			1978		
	Males[a]	Females[a]	Female/male	Males[a]	Females[a]	Female/male
None	0.66	0.66	0.51	0.69	0.80	0.75
Primary	1.00	1.00	0.51	1.00	1.00	0.65
	(1,175)	(595)	n.a.	(4,903)	(3,176)	n.a.
Secondary	2.11	2.62	0.63	0.159	1.81	0.74
Higher	6.75	6.22	0.47	4.82	3.10	0.42
Total	1.83	1.72	0.48	1.87	1.59	0.55
Total number of workers	488,000	249,000	n.a.	732,000	454,000	n.a.

n.a. Not applicable.
a. Ratio of mean earnings, with those of workers with primary education used as a base.
Note: Numbers in parentheses are actual earnings (in 1973 or 1978 pesos) of workers with primary education.
Source: 1973 population census sample; 1978 World Bank–DANE Household Survey.

expected, private-sector schools were more prominent in the larger cities: government expenditures on primary and secondary education were more directed to smaller towns and the rural areas. Education financing was quite complex; it included substantial subvention from the federal government to state (departmental) and local governments and to other decentralized agencies. As will be seen in chapter 9, much of Colombia's developmental public expenditure is routed through decentralized, relatively autonomous agencies, and this was true in education as in other areas.

The period under study immediately followed this very substantial educational expansion. The participation of the private sector indicates that the public perceived high returns to education. Moreover, employment expansion in the 1970s was such that there was adequate demand for this educated labor.

The proportion of professional and technical workers increased considerably between 1973 and 1978 among both men and women. In other respects, the distribution of workers among occupations was quite similar from one year to the other. Among males, production workers accounted for about one-third of the labor force, construction and transport workers for about 16 percent, professional administrative and technical for another 15 percent, and other service for the remaining third. Among females, domestic servants constituted the largest group, accounting for one-fifth of all women workers; professional administrative and technical workers were about 11 percent, office workers 19 percent, and production workers about 15 percent, with other services making up the remaining third. The increase in the professional and technical workers was for both men and women. We found that overall mean nominal earnings increased by more than 400 percent between 1973 and 1978, exceeding the inflation rate of 250 to 300 percent over that period. It is quite striking that, consistent with earlier observations of the decline in earnings differentials between higher and less-educated workers, the rate of increase in the less-skilled occupations was higher than that for the professionals, who on average barely kept pace with inflation. The larger increases occurred in lower-paid fields like production, construction, and transport. Production workers were among the lowest paid. Among women, even domestic servants were better remunerated than the production workers, if the servants' income in kind is also accounted for. Domestic servants typically live in with their employers and get free food and some clothes in addition to their monetary wages.

As might be expected from the spatial distribution of income described in the chapter 4, the lower-paid, less-skilled workers live predominantly in the southern part of Bogotá, and the professionals and administrators live in the north (see map 5-1). Sectors 2 in the south

Map 5-1. Bogotá: Distribution of Occupations by Sector

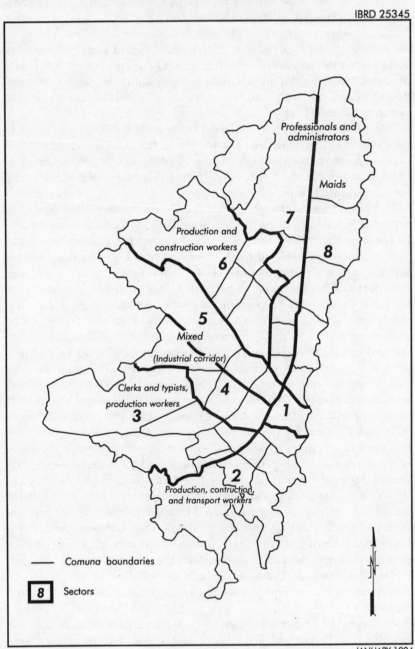

IBRD 25345

Professionals and administrators

Maids

7

Production and construction workers

6

8

5

Mixed

(Industrial corridor)

Clerks and typists, production workers

3

4

1

2

Production, contruction, and transport workers

—— Comuna boundaries

8   Sectors

JANUARY 1994

Source: Mohan 1986, map 5-1.

and 6 in the west are quite similar in their worker composition, although workers in sector 2 are poorer on average. The starkest contrast is between sectors 2 and 8, the poorest and richest sectors. Sixty percent of the workers who live in sector 2 have only primary education or less; in contrast, more than 45 percent of the workers in sector 8 have higher education. This picture has not changed over the years except for a slightly increased tendency for workers with similar occupations to cluster together—a pattern consistent with the increasing spatial inequality based on incomes. Despite these spatial differences in terms of income and occupation we find no evidence of similar differences in participation rates. People in the poorer areas are not less likely to work.

In summary, we observe that the recorded increases in income in Bogotá have resulted from changes in both the demand and the supply sides of the labor market. On the demand side, the continuing overall changes in the structure from a predominantly agricultural economy to an industry- and service-oriented one has resulted in continuing expansion of employment in these sectors. These sectors' expansion was labor-using in the late 1970s, with employment expansion being greater than output expansion. On the supply side, these changes have been matched by continuing migration from rural areas, increased participation of women in the labor force, and the improvement in educational quality of the labor force. We therefore observed overall increases in labor earnings. There was little perceptible change in the structure of employment within Bogotá, with industry- or production-related employment accounting for just under one-third of total employment through the 1970s, although there was a clear shift toward more highly skilled occupations. Workers lived where they might be expected to, given spatial income distribution, with less-skilled workers concentrating in the south and west of Bogotá and the professional and administrative workers in the north.

Because the earnings distribution in urban areas is often said to result from the segmentation of labor markets into the formal and informal sectors, this issue is emphasized in the rest of this chapter. We estimate earnings functions to be the predominant analytical tool used to distinguish the determinants of earnings and to test whether similar people earn different incomes in different sectors, however defined. Overall, we find little evidence of segmentation in the tight labor market conditions of Bogotá in the late 1970s. We also explore the earnings differences that persist across space in Bogotá.

The Benefits of Education and Experience

There has been considerable controversy over the interpretation of returns to education as measured by differences in earnings, and much effort has gone into estimating these returns. Psacharapoulos (1980) summarized the results for different countries. Among the more accessible works on the economic benefits of education for urban workers are Anand (1983) and Mazumdar (1981) on Malaysia and Bourguignon (1983) and Fields and Schultz (1980) on Colombia. Most estimates are lower for developed countries than for developing countries. This is partly a measurement issue, because the variance in education levels is typically lower in developed countries and it becomes more important to measure the quality of schooling. The private returns to schooling range between 12 and 18 percent for developing countries and between 7 and 10 percent for middle- and high-income countries. The highest rates of return seem to be found in Latin America. The typical pattern in other regions is for primary education to bring the highest marginal returns and secondary education the lowest. Colombia conforms to the broad Latin American pattern, but the returns for higher education exceed those for primary and secondary education. Most of these returns are calculated with the assumption of no tuition costs during the time of schooling and are therefore somewhat overestimated. We estimate the returns to schooling in Bogotá in some detail in order to understand the measured pattern of income distribution and to follow the changes that have been observed.

We build on the human-capital model of labor earnings as developed by Schultz (1961), Becker (1964), and Mincer (1974).[1] One of the key criticisms of the traditional human capital earnings function (equation 5-3 in note 1) attempting to estimate the returns to education has been the omission of a measure of "ability"—that is, a measure of v. It is argued that the productivity of schooling depends on the level of initial ability, and ability itself is affected by family and other background. The earnings function should therefore, at a minimum, contain measures of ability as well as background variables.

The data sets we used for Bogotá were rich but did not have any direct measures of ability, family background, or schooling quality. We did, however, have somewhat comparable data sets for four different years between 1973 and 1978, so some time trends could be observed. The only background variables that were available, however, were the location of current residence, location of previous residence, and place of birth. In view of the distinct characteristics observed for different parts of the city, we regard the location of residence as a good background proxy. We also use place of birth, categorized by size of town or rural community, as another proxy. These variables may be argued to be good proxies for family background and schooling quality because children typically go to neighborhood schools. The hypothesis is that quality and intensity of schooling might vary positively with city size and the overall quality of neighborhood. If these are good proxies, we correct at least partially for the omitted variables bias, and the resulting estimated rates of return to schooling may be relied on.

So far, we have neglected on-the-job training as a component of human capital. This is a straightforward extension, and we add the years of experience as another explanatory variable. To test for segmentation we can also add different variables measuring characteristics of employment. The final equations that we estimate are then of the form:[2]

$$y = f \quad \text{(schooling, experience, region of origin, current location of residence, characteristics of employment).}$$

The overwhelming result of our estimations is that the simple human capital model, using merely schooling and on-the-job-training as explanations of earnings, works well in Bogotá and explains as much as 50 percent of the variance in earnings.

We paid particular attention to a couple of issues. The major expansion in education has been documented and commented on. It has been suggested that this may have led to a decrease in the returns to education. The availability of data sets for four different years enabled us to test for this hypothesis between 1973 and 1978. We have also commented on the particular expansion of higher education. It was therefore of interest to measure the rates of return to education distinguished by different levels: primary, secondary, and higher. Another important issue was screening. It is alleged that part of the returns to education are actually returns to certification, rather than to the knowledge gained from an additional year of schooling: employers are willing to pay a premium to someone with a high school diploma or a completed college degree but not to others with similar years of schooling who lack the certification.

The schooling variable was introduced into the regressions in two ways. First was the conventional schooling variable—the years of schooling completed by the worker. The second was a "splined" variable.[3] The years of schooling were broken down into different chunks for primary, higher, and postgraduate education. In addition, separate dummy variables were used for those completing primary, secondary, or higher education in order to test for the certification premium. Both specifications were used for all the years in order to trace changes.

The overall rate of return estimated for the marginal year of education was between 12 and 14 percent for 1978. It had declined from between 17 and 18 percent in 1973. This decline occurred across different specifications and can therefore be stated confidently. Moreover, Bourguignon (1983) has collected results from various studies and added his own estimates to obtain a profile of the returns to education in Bogotá from the mid-1960s to mid-1970s and also showed a consistent decline.

The return to higher education was found to be much greater than that to secondary education, which in itself was greater than that of primary education; and the estimated returns to each level of schooling declined over time. Because about half of total secondary and college enrollment was in private schools with significant tuition costs, however, the estimated rates of return to higher and secondary schooling as calculated from earnings functions are then overstated, given the assumption of low tuition costs. Nonetheless, the magnitudes of these returns are probably higher than those of other investments, and continue to be so despite the declines documented.

The splined specification mentioned earlier permits us to measure the certification bonus. The additional bonus for high school graduation was about 20 percent and for college graduation about 25 percent. That is, people who graduate can be expected to earn 20–25 percent more than their counterparts who attended as many years of school but did not graduate. There was no measurable bonus for completing primary education. These estimates imply that the economic benefits of completing education can be quite high, and people have high incentives to receive certification. The low bonus for primary school completion suggests that the Bogotá labor market has become quite sophisticated, with a greater demand for more highly skilled, better-educated labor. It is also possible that completing and receiving certification for a specific education level provides more information on ability and should not be interpreted merely as certification. Certification in itself implies the ability to carry out a task to completion: a trait that is valuable in most employment situations.

We also tested the declining returns for education by making separate estimates for different age cohorts: 15–24, 25–34, 35–44, 45–54, and 55–64. As might be expected, the mean years of schooling increase with each younger cohort—except for the youngest, many of whom are still in school. The returns to education were the highest for the 35–44 age group. This is consistent with our other results on high mean returns to education earlier in the 1970s. There are two processes at work. Initially, as the proportion of people with higher and secondary education increases, the variance in skill levels also increases, and those with higher education are rewarded for their scarce skills. The average return to education rises as a result of "educational deepening." As this deepening continues, the relative shares change, the return to higher education starts declining, and the composition effect becomes predominant. The age cohort results suggest that the 25–34 age group is not getting as high returns to education as the preceding cohort (see Mohan and Sabot 1988).

We now have a much better understanding of the income distribution in Bogotá and Cali. A portion of the high inequality observed can be explained by the larger returns to higher education and certification, which had a greater scarcity value in previous years. Given these high returns, public policy and private initiative have responded by expanding the supply of education. It is also clear that people have opted to attend school longer and enter the labor force increasing ages later. We can expect these trends to continue until the returns to education decline further and become comparable to returns to other investments.

How does experience affect earnings? It is argued in the literature that as people work they add to their human capital as they do with schooling but at a lower rate, because schooling is usually full time and on-the-job training (OJT) is only part time. While working, a person partly consumes, or gets returns from, his previous schooling and partially invests in learning by doing. Some of the segmentation literature suggests the existence of an internal labor market for firms. It is argued that only firm-specific experience leads to improvements in a worker's performance. There is also an information asymmetry: firms may not be able to evaluate a person's previous experience as well as they can evaluate time spent with the firm. If this were true, labor mobility would decrease. It would also be the case that workers who join better firms to begin with would be expected to earn more than people of otherwise equivalent training and ability. We would then expect higher returns to firm-specific experience, measured as time elapsed since leaving school. Another specific measure of experience is the number of years spent in the same occupation. It may be expected that the returns to occupation-specific experience would be higher than those to generalized work experience.

The data enabled us to test for these hypotheses because the 1978 World Bank–DANE survey asked respondents how long they had worked for their current firm and how long they had worked in their current occupation. It was surprising to find that job mobility has been quite high in Bogotá. Although the mean value of the generalized experience variable (EXPER)[4] was about 20, the mean value of years spent with the current firm (YRSFIRM) was 5.6, and in the current occupation (YRSOC-CUP), 8.5. Workers thus appear to be quite mobile between jobs as well as occupations—a finding contrary to the general impression that urban labor markets in developing countries are rigid.

The standard specification of the experience variable is to enter it as a quadratic in the earnings function along with education.[5] The quadratic term was expected to have a negative coefficient reflecting the decline in the returns to each marginal year of experience after some point. The marginal returns to an additional year of experience, on average, were 4.6, 2.8, and 1.0 percent after ten, twenty, and thirty years of work experience. The earnings for those with primary education peak early, at the age of about forty-five, for those with secondary education at about fifty-two, and for those with higher education at about fifty-seven.

Each of the three different specifications of the experience variable was entered in a similar way. The results were:

	EXPER	YRSOCCUP	YRSFIRM
β_{21}	0.063	0.040	0.044
β_{22}	−0.0009	−0.0006	−0.0008

where YRSOCCUP is the number of years spent in the same occupation and YRSFIRM is the number of years spent with the same firm. These coefficients indicate that, contrary to expectations, firm-specific experience and occupation-specific experience are not valued more highly than generalized work experience. The marginal contribution of an additional year of YRSOCCUP and YRSFIRM was in each case only about 2.8 percent after ten years, which is much less than the 4.6 percent estimated for EXPER. There is little evidence of strong firm-specific internal labor markets. In developing countries this is said to exist particularly in large firms in the formal or protected sector, which reportedly pay much higher wages than other firms. This hypothesis is not borne out for the labor market in Bogotá or for our estimation for Cali.

Having established the relatively regular nature of the determination of earnings in Bogotá in relation to the usual human capital variables of education and length of work experience, we now investigate further some of the other influences on earnings: worker backgrounds on the supply side and firms' characteristics on the demand side.

How Segmented is the Bogotá Labor Market?

Much analysis of labor markets is motivated by a desire to understand what the determinants of existing inequalities are. In the preceding section we found that differences in education and work experience alone explain about half the variation in labor earnings. We now investigate different kinds of labor market imperfections that could result in different levels of earnings for otherwise similar people.[6] The task for analysis then becomes measurement of "similarity" and of differences in earnings after this similarity has been accounted for. Some of the confusion in the discussion of labor market segmentation arises from the possible relationship between what might be termed the human capital market and the physical capital market. Given an unequal physical capital distribution, to the extent that acquisition of human capital is related to the initial income and wealth distribution, the resulting human capital distribution would be correlated with the initial asset and income distribution. Without deliberate policy intervention this situation could perpetuate itself indefinitely. The main traditional intervention to break the link between the asset and human capital distributions has been the provision of free education to all or the provision of tuition fee concessions linked to means tests. We have already found that the massive expansion of education in Colombia has been the result of both private initiative and explicit government policy and that there is at least some evidence that this expansion might have served to reduce the scarcity returns to higher education and thereby to reduce the inequality in earnings. This massive expansion also means that a larger proportion of people now have easier access to higher levels of education.

The Measurement of Labor Market Segmentation

Considerable methodological progress has taken place in the discussion of segmentation in recent years. Early arguments were based merely on the observation of heterogeneity in the labor market. Differences in means in earnings between different groups were seen as evidence of segmentation. Now much of the work is devoted to identifying differences after accounting for similarities between human capital variables. Thus it is argued that differences arising from differences in human capital endowments are in some sense justified, or at least to be expected. Other differences are generally attributed to market imperfections, and their removal would be argued to lead to greater efficiency. An econometric identification problem remains even in this approach, which is followed here. If there is a protected sector that, for whatever reasons, pays higher wages, it could make its selection criteria such that the more highly educated people would be found in these higher-paying jobs, even if the jobs do not actually require skills resulting from higher education. An earnings function would then attribute these higher earnings to human capital variables rather than to segmentation resulting from protection. However, the existence of such a situation is a little difficult to argue persuasively for private profit-seeking firms. It may be a little more defensible for public sector jobs, which often use educational achievements as screening criteria. Because the marginal contribution of public sector jobs is more difficult to measure, it is possible that the official requirements could be higher than necessary. Using similar arguments it is also possible to adduce such a situation for larger firms, which also have much greater indirect office activity in support of their production activities.

In this section we investigate the issue of market imperfections from both the supply and the demand sides. The main issue from the supply side is that the measurement of years of schooling masks differences in ability, in family background, and in schooling quality. The other key supply-side influence in earnings is hypothesized to be the existence of unions. From the demand side, the issue is usually posed as the existence of a formal or protected sector in urban labor markets, where some workers earn more than other workers because of various kinds of restrictive practices. Such practices can result from the government setting a minimum wage, which has the effect of limiting employment and keeping wages in the "legal" or "formal" sector higher than the rest. Similar effects can be caused by government-legislated social security payments, which employers may be required to make. It is common to suggest that these characteristics are highly correlated and exist mostly in larger firms, which are often owned by foreign enterprises. The size of a firm is then used as the indicator variable separating the formal and informal sector. All of government is usually assigned to the formal sector. The basic idea is to identify intervening or segmenting variables that serve to restrict mobility within the labor market and can then help to explain unequal earnings between people who would otherwise be regarded as equivalent. In this study we attempt to identify the formal sector by variables such as firm size, the existence of formal social security systems and contracts in firms, and the type of industry or activity a firm is engaged in.

The overall finding is that the supply-side variables have a slightly greater influence on earnings than do the demand-side effects. The protected sector is simply difficult to find in Bogotá. It is possible, however, that these results are partly due to the boom conditions that prevailed in Colombia during the period of this study.

The Influence of Workers' Backgrounds on Earnings

There are two ways to measure the effects of background. We can either hypothesize that people from more advantaged backgrounds have a higher return to schooling, or that the effect of their background is manifested as a premium on earnings. In the first case the sample would need to be stratified by the background variable, and we would test for differences in the returns to schooling—that is, differences in the education coefficient. In the second case a dummy variable for background would be used in the estimation test for the existence of a premium. We have utilized both methods, even though the first method causes some econometric problems. If the dependent variable—that is, earnings—is highly correlated with the stratifying variable, the resulting coefficients would be highly biased. In this case, if people of a specific background are particularly poor, the estimated returns to their education would be biased and on the low side. This procedure must be used judiciously, and conclusions drawn carefully.

The region-of-origin variable used was the place of birth, distinguished by size of settlement: rural, small town (less than 100,000 population), large town (between 100,000 and 1 million population), city (more than 1 million population but excluding Bogotá), and Bogotá. Because our interest is in environmental effects on quality of schooling, Bogotá is also regarded as the place of origin for people who migrated to Bogotá before the age of ten and presumably received the bulk of their schooling there. In addition to the possible difference in quality of education, it is reasonable to hypothesize that people who grow up in metropolitan areas are exposed to more varied influences and a wider variety of information, with the result that their schooling may be formed into human capital stock more efficiently. The schools in larger cities are also likely to have better teachers. It is also often suggested that migrants are at a disadvantage in competing with natives in the urban labor market.

These background variables did not affect the education coefficients, however. There seems to be little correlation between place of origin and returns to schooling. The dummy variables for region of origin, on the other hand, were all substantially significant, the base comparison being with workers from rural backgrounds:

Place of origin	Percentage in Bogotá	Coefficient
Bogotá	46	0.10 to 0.11
Large city	3	0.15 to 0.18
Large town	6	0.19 to 0.23
Small town	26	0.08 to 0.10
Rural (base)	19	0

Both the Bogotá natives and migrants from other urban areas appear to be 10 to 20 percent better off than rural migrants, but there is little to differentiate Bogotá natives from migrants from other urban areas. If anything, migrants from other large towns are better off than native-born Bogotános—and this may be a result of self-selection. The estimate of returns to education from the stratified samples of workers produced similar results. There was little difference in the returns to education for Bogotá natives, workers in big cities, and other urban migrants, but the rural migrants did get significantly lower returns. Given the consistency between the two methods, it is reasonable to conclude that, on average, there is no evidence of differences in the quality of education between small and large towns and Bogotá, but the rural folk probably do suffer from poor schooling and other negative environmental influences.

Using the location of residence within Bogotá as a variable in earnings functions estimations is one of the more controversial aspects of this study. Is it reasonable to hypothesize that within a city the location of residence "causes" a different rate of return to education, or that it influences earnings in other ways? Is the labor market in fact segmented in this manner? The argument is that current location is acting as a proxy for unmeasured variables. One can expect the quality of schooling to differ by location within the city. To measure only the years of schooling is to ignore differences in quality; however, the location of residence could be a proxy for schooling quality. Parents' education and income, which largely determine where the family lives, then affect the children's schooling by virtue of location. Residence in a low-income neighborhood can also affect a person's network of contacts for obtaining a high-income job. Because the lower-income neighborhoods show rather flat age-earnings profiles, one can also expect that the demonstration effect dampens residents' expectations and aspirations.[7] This can have a cumulative effect on earnings, similar to the discouraged-worker hypothesis for nonparticipators. Finally, location of residence is also a proxy for social class, which probably has significant effects on earnings. The larger question is whether this pattern is peculiar to Bogotá or whether it exists in other cities as well. Clearly, all cities have their poor and rich neighborhoods; the question is whether they are clustered in the same way as they are in Bogotá. We also need to ask how much spatial mobility there is across different parts of the cities. To what extent does current location affect the current earnings and streams of future earnings?

All large cities in the world have rich and poor neighborhoods. People choose their place of residence according to their income, the location of their work, and their preferences regarding the amenities and other characteristics of the neighborhood. Normally, income is the main factor in the choice of residential location. People also sort themselves out by ethnic origin and, to some extent, by occupation and class. The issue here is a feedback mechanism that reverses the causation somewhat so that a person's location affects his or her earning potential.

We have documented that both Bogotá and Cali are characterized by a high degree of spatial inequality in incomes. Recalling the pattern in Bogotá, the north (sector 8) is particularly rich, and the south (sector 2) is particularly poor. The other sectors are more heterogeneous, but the ranking of the radial sectors in ascending order of household income per capita is 2, 3, 6, 4, 5, 7, and 8. Although there are virtually no rich people in the south, there are poor people in almost every part of the city. Historically, it seems that the rich have continuously moved north while the poor have located in the south and later in the west. This makes it even more likely that the better schools would largely be in the north. When large areas of a city are known as rich and poor, as in Bogotá, people's addresses can become screening devices. Employers, for example, may use an applicant's address to gauge his or her likely characteristics—reliability, home background, and so forth—in much the same way that names of schools are used as screening devices.

In summary, if the residential location variables are found to have a significant effect on earnings, there are at least three explanations. First, in the human capital tradition, it may be argued that these location variables act as proxies for ability, schooling quality, and the like, which are unmeasured otherwise. Second, also in the human capital tradition, it may be argued that they act as proxies for other productivity characteristics of workers (class, status, aspiration, attitudes, and contacts) that are correlated with their residence location. The third possibility is that location is being used as a partial screening device in a city characterized by notable spatial differences in income.

There are essentially two location variables that have been used. First are the dummies for each residential sector, using sector 2, the poorest, as the comparator base. Second is the distance of residence from the center of the city. Dummy coefficients for sectors 3 through 7 are all between about 0.15 to 0.25 and are not significantly different from 0.2. Sector 8 is obviously different, with coefficients of about 0.6. These coefficients measure the systematic deviation in log income from sector 2 means, keeping everything else constant, including distance from the city center. Thus, workers in sectors 3 through 7 receive about 20 percent more in earnings than otherwise equivalent workers in sector 2, whereas workers in sector 8 receive about 60 percent more. The addition of these variables does not appreciably increase the level of explanation (R^2) that is the proportion of log variance of earnings that is accounted for. But all these coefficients are highly significant. We have also discussed at some length the location of many of the poor at the periphery. The estimated coefficient of the distance variable implies that workers' earnings decline by about 2.5 percent per kilometer from the city center, on average. Furthermore, the addition of the distance variable makes the differences in earnings between radial sectors more pronounced.

As before, we also estimated the returns to education by stratifying the sample by residential sector. Although this procedure suffers from truncation bias, particularly for the largely poor sector 2, the estimated returns are found to vary systematically by sector; the coefficients for schooling are 0.08, 0.09, 0.10, 0.11, 0.11, 0.14, and 0.16 for sectors 2, 3, 4, 5, 6, 7, and 8, respectively. These differences are not statistically significant between sectors 2 and 3 and between sectors 4, 5, and 6, but the overall pattern is consistent with dummy variable coefficients.

These results were further investigated in different ways. First, do the low-income workers who live in richer areas earn more than similar workers in the poorer areas? The indication is that they do not. It seems that the differences are mainly among the better-educated workers. A worker from the poorer areas who manages to get secondary and higher education does earn less than someone from the richer areas with an equivalent education. Schooling quality differences presumably explain this finding. For the relatively unskilled, less-educated workers, schooling quality makes little differences. Second, how mobile are people? Do people who move "down" from richer to poorer locations carry their work characteristics with them, and vice versa? The data contained information about the last move of the household. We classified as upwardly mobile movers those who had moved from a poorer sector to a richer sector in the last ten years; those who had moved from a richer to a poorer sector were classified as downwardly mobile. For the 1978 data, the former comprised 40 percent of the workers and the latter about 15 percent. Most of the moves were between adjacent sectors.[8] Bogotá households were therefore quite mobile, but the intersectoral mobility is between relatively similar sectors. The addition of these dummies did not alter other results but did increase the level of explanation of earnings slightly. The downwardly mobile movers appear to earn about 10 percent more than similar people elsewhere. This suggests that schooling quality does matter and that people from higher-income locations who move to lower-income ones retain some of the higher-income characteristics. The upwardly mobile people seem to be no different than other similar workers. These results argue against the labeling or screening hypothesis and support the hypothesis that location acts as a proxy for schooling and other aspects of background.

The last supply-side segmenting variable is that of union membership. Only about one-quarter of the male workers in both Bogotá and Cali belonged to unions. When union membership was introduced as another dummy variable in the earnings functions, the average earnings premium for union members was about 6 percent in Bogotá and 12 percent in Cali. It is striking that this appears to be more important for migrants from rural areas and small towns than for others. Given the earlier finding that it was only these migrants who were disadvantaged, and not other migrants or natives, this finding suggests that union membership is more important and serves as a screening device when there are few other distinctions of labor skill or quality.

Results from both the place-of-origin variable and the location-of-residence investigations support the idea that these variables are essentially proxies for background, particularly schooling quality and ability as influenced by background. Although migrants are no worse off than natives in general, rural migrants do appear to be somewhat worse off.

The results imply that there might be income feedback effects from prolonged residence in disadvantaged neighborhoods. One way of compensating for some of these effects is to belong to a union. The importance of the background effects should not, however, be exaggerated; they add only about 3 to 6 percent to the level of explanation in the log variance of earnings, even though each of the coefficients estimated is highly significant statistically.

There seems to be little evidence of the spatial disadvantage hypothesis usually expounded for cities in the United States. High inner-city unemployment rates are often explained by the flight of jobs to the suburbs and the resulting deterioration in the access of poor workers, usually blacks, to these jobs. In Bogotá, even though the poorer parts of the city have far fewer jobs than richer areas do in relation to their population, there is no measurable difference between participation rates and unemployment rates. The differences are essentially those in earnings. Access to jobs does not seem to be a problem for the urban poor in Colombia. This may be partly because of Bogotá's relatively cheap public transportation system and flat bus fares (see chapter 8).

The Protected Sector

On the demand side, we have attempted to identify the protected sector by a number of different variables. First, it was hypothesized that firms with formal social security schemes and/or formal employment contracts must belong to the formal sector. Second, consistent with much other work on the subject, it is expected that large firms pay their workers more than other smaller firms do. Third, different types of work status (for example, employees versus self-employed workers) may give different returns. Fourth, we test to determine if different kinds of industry give varying returns. Last, we see if there is any measurable distinction between the government and the private sector, government being an easily identifiable protected sector and often alleged to pay much more for comparable jobs than the private sector. It is difficult to find labor market segmentation in Bogotá according to any of these criteria. There are some measurable differences, but protected-sector premiums or returns to education, measured as earnings received, are seldom higher than 10 to 15 percent.

We first introduce dummy variables for the existence of social security schemes or employment contracts in the workers' place of work. About half the workers, both male and female, work for employers who have these benefits. The male workers who have contracts earn about 5 percent more than other equivalent workers. Similarly, workers in firms with social security schemes earn about 7 to 9 percent more than other equivalent workers. The correlation coefficient between these two variables is 0.5. Next, a variable measuring the logarithm of firm size is introduced.[9] Its coefficient implies that a doubling of firm size increases earnings by about 2.5 percent. This means that an employee of a firm with 100 employees would earn about 10 percent more than a similar employee of a firm with fewer than 5 employees. These results mean that workers in large firms (with, say, more than 100 employees) that also have other formal sector characteristics would earn about 10 to 20 percent more than similar employees in very small firms (with 1 to 5 employees). Although these differences are significant, they are not large and can scarcely be said to imply the existence of a strong protected sector in Bogotá. The existence of relatively high labor mobility is consistent with this finding, as are the relatively low returns to firm specific experience. Similar workers in different kinds of firms, formal and informal, receive roughly similar earnings.

We next examine other characteristics of work that could possibly segment the labor market in an identifiable manner. First, earnings functions were estimated for different types of workers: blue-collar and white-collar employees, and employers and the self-employed. Because the earnings and education of blue-collar workers are uniformly low, the estimation for these workers suffers from truncation bias, and returns to education for them are found to be low. But there is no statistically significant difference between the returns to education for white-collar employees and those for employers and the self-employed. Second, earning functions were again estimated, stratified by industry of activity classified by the standard industrial classification at the one-digit level. Again, no statistically significant differences were found in the returns to education between manufacturing, construction, trade and commerce, public administration and other services, and financial establishments. Workers in the transportation and communication sectors, however, seem to get somewhat lower returns; in this case it does not appear to be a truncation problem. Finally, different estimates were also made for the government and private sectors.

The mean earnings for workers in government were significantly higher than for workers in the private sector. The rate of return to education, however, was not significantly different. The main difference is that union members in government get about 20 percent higher earnings (compared to about 6 percent higher in the private sector). A notable feature of the earnings function estimation for government workers was that R^2, at 0.68, was the highest earnings function estimated in this study. The human capital variables—in particular, years of education—explained more than two-thirds of the variance in earnings in government jobs. This reflects the higher degree of codification in earnings structure in the government: earning levels are more clearly related to formal qualifications. The returns to work experience were lower in the government than in the private sector. This probably reflects a tendency in the government to do more formal screening at the time of entry and then to provide slow growth in earnings with experience. Government employees accounted for about 15 percent of the total in Bogotá.

Given these results, it is difficult to argue that the Bogotá labor market is highly segmented. Most of the variation in labor earnings is explained by the traditional human capital variables. Although differences in background add little to the overall level of explanation, they make a substantial difference in the prediction of earnings for workers with specific backgrounds. Although these differences have been measured as the place of origin or current residence location, they are attributed to schooling quality and other background influences. On the demand side, a strong protected sector is simply difficult to identify, although workers in formal sector firms do earn about 10 to 20 percent more than other equivalent workers. The only sector that seems to be particularly protected is the government sector, with premiums of about 15 to 20 percent being paid to workers thanks to the efforts of strong government unions. Outside the government, union membership makes little difference except among relatively unskilled rural migrants.

Operation of the Urban Labor Market: What Have We Learned?

The results reported in this chapter are in marked contrast to most other studies of urban labor markets and to popular impressions of the employment situation in cities in developing countries. The improvement in the urban employment situation in Colombia in the 1970s was partly related to the existence of boom conditions there in the latter part of the decade. The rapid growth in GDP during this period resulted from policies that favored agricultural growth and expansion of export-related manufacturing activities. Governmental programs for infrastructure investment also helped provide high growth in tertiary-sector employment in urban areas. The boom in coffee prices during the late 1970s contributed to prosperity in the agricultural sector and to unprecedented tightening of the labor market in rural areas, which was reflected in higher wages for unskilled workers in urban areas.

The late 1960s and the 1970s were also periods of significant demographic changes: fertility declined remarkably, resulting in slowdowns in urban population growth, overall population growth, and rural-urban migration. In Colombia this also coincided with the turning point in the pattern of urbanization; the effervescent urbanization between 1940 and 1980, when the urban population rose from 30 to 65 percent of the total population, gave way to a rather slower rural-urban transformation. This is a familiar S-shaped urbanization pattern.

The other reason our findings in this chapter differ from those in other studies is that most other studies, particularly those of the informal sector, suffer from the use of biased samples. The informal sector is often identified by analyzing the characteristics of workers from slums, from specific occupations or types of firms, and so on. Appropriate comparisons are seldom made. Doing so means keeping other things constant, and this is difficult without using a carefully drawn, citywide or all-urban sample.

The labor market was found to operate quite efficiently. There is scant evidence of segmentation; similarly qualified people earn similar incomes in different activities; there is high labor mobility; and returns to human capital are similar to those in other countries. Part of the tendency toward better income distribution is attributed to the "deepening" of education, with consistent and rapid improvements in average education attainment (see Mohan and Sabot 1988). There is evidence of declines in the returns to secondary and higher education as the stock of people in these categories has increased. Concurrently, the real wages of the unskilled have improved—a consequence of tightening labor market conditions in both rural and urban areas and improved overall labor quality with the universalization of primary education. These forces have resulted in a decline in the ratio of earnings between the more-educated and the less-educated. These results suggest very strongly that the continued expansion of education, along with a reduction in the dispersion of completed education, will be quite effective in reducing the levels of inequality, at least in personal labor earnings over the long run.

The evidence from Bogotá and Cali indicates that the labor market is not characterized by a strong protected sector. Individuals working in establishments with formalized employment arrangements (with unions, social security schemes, and written contracts) and those in large enterprises earn only slightly more than others. Moreover, the stability of the estimated rates of return to schooling and experience across the different occupational and industrial categories argue against the existence of a highly segmented labor market in Bogotá and Cali. Much of the writing on the existence of informal and protected sectors in cities in developing countries is connected with high rural–urban migration. Contrary to popular misconceptions, migrants are not especially poor; they do not concentrate in specific areas of the city—the center or the periphery; they are not concentrated in particular occupations or activities; and they are not less educated or less skilled than natives, on average. In short, they are not found to be disadvantaged in any respect.

Women earn less than men in every occupation and industry. The ratio of average female earnings to male earnings is between one-half and two-thirds in most developing countries. In Bogotá and Cali it is nearer one-half. What evidence there is suggests that women get rates of return for education similar to those of men but do not get comparable returns for experience. Thus, women's earnings differentials increase with age. Women with higher education are far more likely to work than others. The fact that women's access to education is now similar to that of men suggests that women in developing countries are likely to enter the labor force in unprecedented numbers, much as they did in developed countries but perhaps even faster.

Notes

1. We can express the basic human capital model as follows:

(5-1) $Y = P_h \cdot H \cdot e^u$
(5-2) $H = e^s \cdot e^v$
(5-3) $y = \ln y = \ln P_h + S + u + v$

where Y is labor earnings, H is the unobserved quantity of human capital, P_h is the market rental price of a unit of human capital (which may vary over time and space), and u represents other influences on wages. Equation 5.2 may be interpreted as a production function for human capital, using schooling (S) as one input and using ability, efficiency, and so forth (denoted by v) as other inputs. $P_h H$ then gives the flow of returns from the stock of human capital H, with u subsuming other influences on earnings.

2. The equation estimated was $\ln(Y) = \beta_0 + X_1\beta_1 + X_2\beta_2 + X_3\beta_3 + X_4\beta_4 + X_5\beta_5 + \varepsilon$, where X_1 = education variables, X_2 = experience variables, X_3 = place-of-origin shift variables, X_4 = location-of-residence shift variables, and X_5 = characteristics of employment. See Mohan (1986, chap. 8) for a more detailed specification, the actual variables used, and other details.

3. Smith and Welch (1977) also used a splined education variable to obtain estimates of the differential returns to different levels of education. In our specification, the splined variable essentially decomposes the education variable into stepwise dummy (the certification premium) and slope variables (years of education at each level).

4. EXPER = (age – years of education – 6) years.

5. That is,

$\ln Y = \beta_0 + \beta_1$ YRSEDU $+ \beta_{21}$ EXPER $+ \beta_{22}$ (EXPER)$^2 + X_3\beta_3 + X_4\beta_4 + X_5\beta_5 + \varepsilon$
(earnings)   (schooling)

where X_3 = place-of-origin variables; X_4 = location-of-residence variables, X_5 = employment characteristic variables, and ε is the error term.

6. This section summarizes work found in Fields (1980) and in Mohan (1980, 1981, 1984, and 1986, chap. 9).

7. See McGregor (1977) for similar arguments in relation to Glasgow.

8. See Hamer (1981) for more details on residential mobility.

9. The firm size itself was also tried, but the coefficient was negligible and insignificant.

Chapter 6

Firms and Their Location Behavior

The preceding chapter examined the supply side of the labor market. This chapter looks at the demand side of urban employment—more specifically, at the location patterns of firms and the behavior underlying these patterns.[1] Household behavior is, in general, better understood than the behavior of firms. This is partly because the characteristics of households are more homogenous than the characteristics of firms. Firms in retail or wholesale trade are quite different, for example, from manufacturing firms, which themselves can be different in each industry. The location imperatives for banks are quite distinct from those of government departments. Moreover, bank branches are quite different in behavior from their head offices. The study of employment location therefore has to account for a number of differences between firms and in different dimensions—in terms of their function, size, age, and so forth. Understanding workplace location is crucial to understanding residence location and emerging urban travel patterns.

Although we established the general location patterns of the different economic activities that existed in Bogotá and Cali, we paid special attention to manufacturing activities because they are usually regarded as leading other activities in a city. Their extensive backward and forward linkages often determine the location of other activities. In order to focus on behavior, we intensively studied firms in a couple of selected industries. Before we discuss our findings, however, let us consider the composition of employment as a whole, the spatial distribution of different types of employment, and the changes that have recently taken place in Bogotá and Cali.

Decentralization in the two cities has been so thorough that in the late 1970s, the central business districts of Bogotá and Cali provided only about 15 percent and 18 percent of employment, respectively, with net new employment almost entirely outside the center. Employment location trends are vital components of the urban dynamic. For one thing, place of residence is closely related to place of work: families look for housing in areas not too far from their jobs. For another, the different economic activities linked in a production process often need to be located near one another to reduce costs and facilitate tasks to be performed. If one of the segments (that is, firms) forming part of such a technological chain moves to another location, the other segments are likely to move to the same area, thus instituting a substantial change in the spatial distribution of employment and probably also in the population, housing, physical infrastructure, trip patterns, and demand for transportation—in other words, altering the spatial structure of the city.

In charting the changes that have taken place in Bogotá and Cali in employment location, we resorted to a large array of data sets (see the appendix). The broad patterns of employment location were established from the World Bank–DANE Household Survey of 1978 in which each worker was asked to provide the characteristics of the firm where he or she worked, including its location within the city. Trend changes were established by comparing the 1978 pattern with that in 1972, when another household survey—the Phase II Survey—was conducted in Bogotá. We also had access to the 1976 Social Security establishment files for Bogotá and the 1978 files for Cali. This source naturally provides poor coverage of small firms but is useful for checking the quality of information in the 1978 Household Survey. For a detailed analysis of the manufacturing sector we resorted to two additional sets of data. DANE publishes an annual directory of industrial firms that employ ten or more employees. The directory includes information about individual establishments, including location, production, sales, and inputs used in manufacturing. Based on these files for each year from 1970 to 1975, we were able to trace the movement of each firm over this period. A special survey of a sample of manufacturing firms was conducted for the City Study in 1978 to obtain further detail. It is unusual to have such rich data in any city in developed or developing countries. We hope, therefore, that this analysis of employment location behavior has applicability beyond Bogotá and Cali.

Among the questions this chapter raises and attempts to answer are these: What kinds of firms move? Which remain stationary? Where do new firms locate? Why do the firms that move do so? How do new firms decide where to locate? Are there differences in the behavior of small and large firms? What can we expect in the future? What is the magnitude of capital land substitution? How does this affect location in the presence of land price gradients?

Trends in the Location of Employment

In both Bogotá and Cali, employment in all sectors (manufacturing, commerce, and services) has historically been concentrated in and around the CBD, but this situation has been changing rapidly since the 1960s as the two cities grew. The most significant and best-documented locational shift may be seen in the case of manufacturing firms that have been moving out of the CBD to peripheral locations, thus reducing the absolute number of manufacturing jobs in the CBD. This is consistent with the worldwide trend observed in all large cities in both developed and developing countries for which data about employment location are available. In Bogotá and Cali this decentralization has been occurring in conjunction with rapid growth in manufacturing employment: annual average growth rates were almost 8 percent between 1973 and 1978. Employment in the commerce and service sectors also decentralized but more slowly. The larger retail and wholesale trade firms continued to locate in or near the CBD while there was some decentralization of the smaller firms. This was also true of the service sector, although the pattern was not as clear as for trade and commercial firms. Consequently, the CBD became more specialized in its commerce and service functions, while the periphery is specializing in manufacturing. Overall CBD employment has remained constant in absolute terms, but because of total employment growth, its share has been falling.

The employment structure of Bogotá and Cali is not very different from that of other large cities in the world (see Mohan 1986, chapter 3). The share of manufacturing employment in Bogotá is 24 percent, that of commerce 20 percent, and that of services (including finance) 41 percent. The last is a little higher than in many cities because of the presence of the national government in Bogotá, but it is similar to the share in other large capital cities in the world. Cali is a little different in that the share of manufacturing is about 30 percent and that of services about 33 percent. Almost all large cities in the developing world have more than 20 percent employment in manufacturing. Noncapital cities such as Calcutta, Bombay, and São Paulo have a higher share of manufacturing employment, as might be expected. Similarly, in a typical large North American city the structure is about 30 percent manufacturing, 30 percent commerce, and 25 percent services; utilities, construction, transport, and communication account for the rest. The structure of employment in Bogotá has remained relatively stable since at least 1950, and it may be regarded as a well-balanced metropolitan city. No particular sector is overrepresented in Cali either. About half of all employment in both the cities was in small firms, that is, firms employing fewer than ten employees (see table 6-1). The commerce and service sectors

Table 6-1. Employment by Firm Size and Major Industry Group, 1978
(percent)

	All industries[a]	Manufac- turing	Commerce	Finance	Services
Bogotá					
Small[b]	52.0	42.0	71.6	43.2	59.8
Large[c]	48.0	58.0	28.4	56.8	40.2
Total	100.0	100.0	100.0	100.0	100.0
Thousands of people employed	1,212	286	246	98	394
Percentage share of total employment	100.0	23.6	20.3	8.1	35.0
Cali					
Small[b]	55.2	36.3	77.0	55.6	72.9
Large[c]	44.8	63.7	23.0	44.4	27.1
Total	100.0	100.0	100.0	100.0	100.0
Thousands of people employed	368	115	80	13	107
Percentage share of total employment	100.0	31.2	21.5	3.7	29.0

a. Includes other sectors in addition to manufacturing, commerce, finance, and services.
b. Firms with fewer than ten employees.
c. Firms with ten or more employees.
Source: K. S. Lee (1989, table 2-3), based on World Bank–DANE Household Survey 1978.

were characterized by the presence of many small firms, whereas 60 to 65 percent of total manufacturing employment was in large firms.

How was this employment distributed across the two cities? We employ the same spatial scheme used earlier—that is, rings and sectors (see table 6-2). As might be expected, Cali, the smaller city, is more centralized overall than Bogotá. The large firms in the commerce and finance sectors locate in the center, with rings 1 and 2 accounting for half or more of total employment in these groups. Manufacturing is the most decentralized, and the small and large firms seem similar in their location behavior. Small retail (commerce) firms are almost as decentralized as firms in the manufacturing sector.

The distribution of employment by radial sectors (see table 6-3) reflects the pattern of land use specialization referred to earlier. In Bogotá, manufacturing employment is concentrated in the "industrial corridor"—sectors 4 and 5. Sectors 3 (the Bosa area in the southwest) and 6 (near the airport) have recently begun to attract manufacturing activities at their peripheries. Jobs in the commerce, finance, and service sectors are located primarily in the rich sectors 7 and 8 in the north, as well as in the CBD.[2] This reflects the northward movement of high-

Table 6-2. Employment Distribution by Ring, Firm Size, and Major Industry Group, 1978
(percent)

	Manufacturing		Commerce		Finance		Services	
Ring	Small firms	Large firms	Small firms	Large firms	Small firms	Large firms	Small firms	Large firms
Bogotá								
1	4.66	7.00	13.13	22.57	52.14	33.99	8.77	18.60
2	13.42	13.17	17.69	24.84	14.52	39.77	16.02	22.52
3	16.16	24.60	13.18	17.99	11.23	11.29	16.00	18.19
4	26.70	23.58	19.50	18.68	11.58	11.03	24.75	20.11
5	34.37	24.88	33.74	14.00	8.52	3.17	27.93	13.71
6	4.21	1.09	1.95	0.21	1.51	0.00	5.50	3.18
N.i.e.	0.49	5.68	0.82	1.70	0.49	0.76	1.02	3.69
Total	100.00	100.00	100.00	100.00	100.00	100.00	100.00	100.00
Cali								
1	7.02	12.61	17.02	52.76	57.20	76.04	9.53	23.51
2	28.74	22.81	23.29	23.42	28.51	13.51	35.38	29.87
3	41.14	39.06	36.64	15.03	6.25	0.00	·37.76	15.26
4	18.24	9.31	14.42	4.77	3.12	0.00	12.89	22.61
5	2.58	0.63	6.06	0.00	4.91	10.45	2.59	1.53
N.i.e.	2.27	15.57	2.57	4.03	0.00	0.00	1.85	7.22
Total	100.00	100.00	100.00	100.00	100.00	100.00	100.00	100.00

N.i.e. Not included elsewhere.
Note: Small firms are those with fewer than ten employees; large firms, those with ten or more employees.
Source: K. S. Lee (1989, tables 2-5 and 2-6), based on World Bank–DANE Household Survey 1978.

income residents over the past several decades and the subsequent growth of financial and services activities in that area. This pattern of employment location corresponds remarkably closely to the residence patterns of workers shown in the last chapter. Production workers were found to be concentrated in sectors 2 and 6, and professionals were found in sectors 7 and 8. Firms have followed the rich to some extent, and the poor have adjusted their residence locations to the resulting pattern of employment location. An examination of Cali shows the existence of an "industrial corridor" in sector 3 and the tendency of service employment to follow the rich households south. In both Bogotá and Cali there was little manufacturing employment in the rich residential sectors. The rich succeeded in keeping their environment relatively pollution-free.

Again, it has been useful to study the spatial distribution of employment by both concentric rings and radial sectors. An examination by rings reveals the decentralized nature of employment and the concentration of certain activities in the CBD. An examination of radial sectors

Table 6-3. Employment Distribution in Bogotá by Radial Sector, Firm Size, and Major Industry Group, 1978
(percent)

Radial sector	Manufacturing		Commerce		Finance		Services	
	Small firms	Large firms	Small firms	Large firms	Small firms	Large firms	Small firms	Large firms
1	4.66	7.00	13.13	22.57	52.14	33.99	8.77	18.60
2	14.36	4.65	14.91	1.16	2.10	1.57	10.85	4.84
3	24.97	14.89	18.16	8.26	6.52	0.82	12.90	7.98
4	8.75	20.33	12.54	7.46	2.81	2.98	7.60	4.21
5	8.10	27.28	7.36	17.09	4.45	13.59	7.52	12.12
6	18.75	7.77	11.74	4.75	5.07	2.27	11.77	16.87
7	11.50	5.81	8.09	13.53	8.44	11.73	13.92	9.23
8	8.43	6.60	13.26	23.48	17.98	32.29	25.65	22.44
N.i.e.	0.49	5.68	0.82	1.70	0.49	0.76	1.02	3.69
Total	100.00	100.00	100.00	100.00	100.00	100.00	100.00	100.00

N.i.e. Not included elsewhere.
Note: Small firms are those with fewer than ten employees; large firms, those with ten or more employees.
Source: K. S. Lee (1989, table 2-8), based on World Bank–DANE Household Survey 1978.

shows the previously noted pattern of land use specialization and the relationship of employment and residential location a little more clearly.

We now use the 1972 Phase II Survey and the 1978 World Bank–DANE Household Survey to observe Bogotá's changing structure of employment location (see table 6-4). The two surveys were not exactly comparable, but they give an idea of the broad decentralization trend in employment. Specifically, because of the nature of the question asked in that survey, employment in the CBD is exaggerated for 1972. The main difference from 1972 to 1978 is the increased importance of ring 5 in its share of employment. Although definitional patterns alluded to previously do not allow strict comparisons, it is likely that ring 2 also increased its share in employment over this period. We might say that, in effect, the CBD has expanded into ring 2 and that we should really think of both rings 1 and 2 as the CBD now. The construction of the new city center, the Centro Internacional in the northern part of ring 2 has contributed to this expansion. In fact, a detailed analysis of the CBD and the Centro Internacional reveals that the sum of employment in the two locations remained roughly constant over the period. We conclude that overall the center of Bogotá can be regarded as stable in absolute magnitude of employment but that its share in the total has decreased. It is clear, however, that manufacturing employment has decreased in absolute terms as well. The CBD is now more and more a specialized trade and financial center. It is difficult to track trends in Cali because earlier

Table 6-4. Employment Location in Bogotá, 1972 and 1978
(percent)

Ring	All industries[a]		Manufacturing		Commerce		Finance		Services	
	1972	1978	1972	1978	1972	1978	1972	1978	1972	1978
1	23.03	13.95	18.20	6.01	19.43	15.75	42.11	41.43	22.62	12.91
2	13.61	17.74	16.07	13.47	12.18	19.77	13.69	29.38	12.74	18.68
3	14.62	16.40	18.94	21.54	13.35	14.83	6.89	11.43	15.88	16.87
4	18.80	20.60	20.27	24.89	21.83	19.37	10.00	10.88	20.74	23.18
5	18.61	24.94	21.76	28.25	21.52	27.72	14.64	5.65	17.89	21.79
6	1.67	3.43	1.04	2.19	3.42	1.51	0.55	0.60	1.88	4.41
N.i.e.	9.67	2.96	3.72	3.66	8.27	1.05	12.12	0.63	8.25	2.15
Total	100.00	100.00	100.00	100.00	100.00	100.00	100.00	100.00	100.00	100.00

N.i.e. Not included elsewhere.

a. Includes other sectors in addition to manufacturing, commerce, finance, and services.

Source: K. S. Lee (1989, table 2-10), based on World Bank–DANE Household Survey 1978 and Phase II Survey 1972.

data are simply not available. A comparison of social security files between 1976 and 1978 suggests that the CBD there has also lost manufacturing jobs but has attracted more trade and finance jobs.

The 1978 survey allowed a rough tracking of firms in both Bogotá and Cali over the preceding five years. This was very useful, because information on movement was otherwise available only for manufacturing firms. The information is, however, inexact because it was derived from the workers' own knowledge about the current and previous location of their employers. The decentralization pattern was clear in both cities. Existing firms were found generally to move outward, whereas new firms also generally located in outer rings. In Bogotá there was a net movement of firms out of the CBD. Net losses also occurred in ring 3. The outer rings 4 and 5 clearly gained in all activities. It was interesting to note that ring 2 gained in commerce, finance, and service jobs because of the expansion of the Centro Internacional adjacent to the old CBD. The city center had effectively expanded and moved slightly northward. Outer ring 5 received about one-third of all new jobs. In Cali, too, there was a net loss of jobs from the city center, but all the other rings experienced net increases in employment. Because it is a smaller city, each ring outside the CBD was experiencing net employment growth. The decentralization trend was strongest in manufacturing jobs in both cities. It should be noted that the decentralization trend is composed of both existing firms moving out toward the periphery and new firms locating toward the periphery. Nonmanufacturing firms replaced some of the manufacturing employment that moved out.

Patterns of Employment Location in Manufacturing

Given the availability of the time series data in the DANE industrial directory files from 1970 to 1975, the changing location of manufacturing jobs could be charted over this period in detail. The methods employed were similar to the empirical studies of employment location in the United Kingdom and the United States, where a typical approach was both to investigate not only the growth and decline of stationary firms but also the location choices of newly established firms and relocating firms and to analyze location patterns.[3]

It is perhaps useful to compare the manufacturing firms in Bogotá and Cali with those in large U.S. cities. The employment dynamics in the Colombian cities are quite different. Reflecting the vibrant growth of manufacturing employment documented earlier, the birth rate of firms in Bogotá and Cali was between 7 and 9 percent annually from 1970 to 1975. The rate for typical American cities was more like 3 to 4 percent. The death rates of firms, however, were similar: between 3 and

5 percent. Thus, both Bogotá and Cali have been going through a phase of continual increase in manufacturing establishments, whereas the number of establishments in American cities is now essentially stable. It is also notable that the majority of firms that die and the ones that are born are small. In the mid-1970s the average firm size in Bogotá was about forty, approximately half the average for U.S. cities. The average firm size in Cali was a little higher, about fifty, reflecting the presence of a few very large firms employing more than 500 people. Such firms (with at least 500 employees) typically account for 35 to 50 percent of all manufacturing employment in U.S. cities, while in Bogotá they account for only about 15 percent, and in Cali 25 percent. These figures ignore the employment in the smallest firms, those employing fewer than ten people.

In order to trace the spatial changes in manufacturing employment, the industrial directory data were again classified by location according to the ring and sector framework in both Bogotá and Cali. As might be expected, the decentralization trend is confirmed (see table 6-5). Moving outward, the rate of growth increases with each ring (except for a slight decline in growth rate from ring 5 to ring 6 in Bogotá). Note that in Bogotá the absolute increases in manufacturing employment were similar in rings 3 and 5. It would seem that the center of the city, rings 1 and 2, had become saturated, and firms were moving out to get larger space. Many moved small distances to ring 3, and others moved still farther out. Cali was more centralized, with the bulk of manufacturing employment still concentrated in rings 1, 2, and 3.

Similar tabulation of sectors confirmed earlier findings. The industrial corridor (in sectors 4 and 5) continued to provide about three-quarters of all manufacturing employment in Bogotá; in Cali the industrial corridor (located in sector 3) provided about 60 percent. There was clear evidence of the increasing importance of sector 3 in southwestern Bogotá, the Bosa area, where manufacturing employment expanded from about 8 percent in 1970 to 11 percent in 1975. Most of this increase is in the periphery of the sector.

Both Bogotá and Cali reveal clear land use specialization, with little mixing of residential areas with manufacturing employment. In Bogotá the residential areas are predominantly in the north (rich) and in the south and southwest (poor), and these areas are separated by the industrial corridor in the west. Much of this pattern originally resulted from land-use zoning but has been emphasized by people's residential choices in recent years.

We now analyze changes by the underlying components: changes in employment in stationary firms; birth of new firms; disappearance from the directory and presumed death of firms; and relocation of firms within the city between 1970 and 1975 (see table 6-6). About 25,000 jobs

Table 6-5. Distribution of Manufacturing Employment by Ring: Bogotá and Cali, 1970–75

Ring	1970		1975		Annual average growth rate (percent)
	Persons	Percentage	Persons	Percentage	
Bogotá					
1	4,538	5.60	4,102	3.47	−2.00
2	11,767	14.53	14,898	12.59	4.83
3	34,351	42.42	47,858	40.44	6.86
4	18,112	22.37	25,958	21.94	7.46
5	11,548	14.26	24,047	20.32	15.80
6	391	0.48	729	0.62	13.27
N.i.e.	266	0.33	741	0.63	—
Total	80,973	100.00	118,333	100.00	7.88
Cali					
1	2,600	7.65	3,064	6.95	3.34
2	13,836	40.74	14,381	32.60	0.78
3	15,192	44.73	21,704	49.21	7.40
4	1,761	5.18	3,361	7.62	13.80
5	367	1.05	100	0.23	−22.90
N.i.e.	219	0.64	1,499	3.40	—
Total	33,965	100.00	44,109	100.00	5.37

— Not available.
N.i.e. Not included elsewhere.
Note: Data are from establishments with ten or more employees.
Source: K. S. Lee (1989, table 3-3), based on DANE industrial directory file.

were added by the birth of new firms and about 15,000 new jobs resulted from the growth of stationary firms during the period. The rate of growth in jobs in each ring is similar for stationary and new firms except in ring 2, where there is high growth in new firms and low growth in stationary firms. The total employment of firms that moved was higher in their new locations than in their old ones.

This pattern supports the incubator hypothesis, which suggests that small new firms locate in centralized areas where there are already many similar firms and where it is easy to obtain specialized essential services such as ready production spaces and financial services (see Hoover and Vernon 1959; Struyk and James 1975). New firms need the benefit of agglomeration economies to start. A more disaggregated spatial analysis showed that the incubation area was concentrated in the inner area of the industrial corridor, that is, the part of the corridor that fell in ring 2. This area was characterized by a high concentration of firm births, by a higher increase in employment due to births rather than to the expansion of existing firms, and by the small average size of new firms. An area with similar characteristics was also found in the Chapinero district in northwest Bogotá, in ring 2, sector 7. Cali had a similar area just south of the CBD. In both cities the average size of new firms in the outer areas was large—about 100 employees.

An examination of the firms that relocated strengthened the incubator hypothesis. A large number of small firms moved out of the incubator areas, but most moved short distances—40 percent stayed within the ring, and most of the others moved from one ring to the next ring out. Most of the firms that moved greater distances, to rings 4 and 5, were large.

To understand the location patterns better, we further disaggregated the data by industries. Decentralization occurred in most industries, except plastics, which was already predominantly found in ring 5. As in other cities, only the printing and apparel industries were concentrated in the center, with more than 30 percent of employment in rings 1 and 2.[4] These industries did decentralize between 1970 and 1975 but to a lesser extent than other industries. An attempt was also made to measure the clustering of industries: how close to each other do firms in the same industry locate? It was surprising to find no particular pattern among industries. Firms do not seem to gain by locating near similar firms in any industry.[5] The evidence of agglomeration economies is then only present in the incubator area, where small new firms gain by locating where there are all necessary facilities.

In summary, then, we found overwhelming evidence of decentralization in manufacturing employment in Bogotá and Cali in even the short period of 1970–75. Firms that relocate generally move outward and expand their size, but they usually move only short distances. New, small

Table 6-6. Changes in Manufacturing Employment by Ring: Bogotá, 1970–75

Ring	Annual growth rate of stationary firms (percent)	Annual birth rate (percentage of new firms)[a]	Annual death rate (percentage of firms going out of business)[a]	Origin/destination ratio of relocating firms[b]
1	3.6	4.1	2.4	3.8
2	2.9	6.4	2.7	1.5
3	4.5	4.5	2.1	1.0
4	3.9	4.6	1.7	0.5
5	7.3	7.9	2.8	0.1
6	n.a.	17.6	2.2	1.2
Total	4.7	5.4	2.2	0.8

n.a. Not applicable.

Note: Data are for firms with more than ten employees.

a. Based on total 1970 manufacturing employment.

b. Calculated as the ratio of the number of people employed in firms that moved out of the ring to the number of people employed in firms that moved into the ring.

Source: K. S. Lee (1989, table 3-6), based on DANE industrial directory file.

firms locate in the incubator area—in the industrial corridor but near the CBD. They replace other new firms that either succeed and move out or fail and die. Firms locating at the far periphery are usually large enough (with an average of 100 employees) not to need the agglomeration economies of the city center. The decentralization trend is common to all industries.

Factors Influencing the Location of Manufacturing Firms

To explain these changing location patterns, a special sample survey of Bogotá's manufacturing establishments was conducted in 1978, using the industrial directory as the sample base. Data from this survey were used to model the location behavior of manufacturing firms. The underlying theoretical framework is that a particular type of firm will choose a site with particular attributes that are optimal to the firm in terms of such criteria as profits and costs. The determining characteristics of the firms include type of product, production process, building characteristics, lot size, floor space, and level of skill in the work force. Important site attributes include proximity to product markets and suppliers, commuting distance for employees, transportation modes, and the quality and availability of public utilities and municipal services.

A sample of 126 firms was chosen from the roughly 2,600 firm records in the directory. The sample was stratified by location history (new firms, movers, stationary firms), current zone of location, type of industry, and establishment size as defined by the number of employees. To obtain reasonable homogeneity among firms, the sample was focused on textile- and metal-fabricating firms, which covered about 50 percent of total manufacturing employment in Bogotá. Both industries can be regarded as relatively footloose in that they require no special site characteristics for their location. Being footloose, they are also presumably more susceptible to government policy regarding location. A third group, "other industries," was added for descriptive variety. In order to maximize coverage of employees in this limited sample, larger firms were oversampled in the survey. The geographical coverage was good in that twenty-seven of the thirty-eight *comunas*, located mostly in rings 3, 4, and 5 but with some in ring 2, were covered in the survey. Of the 126 firms, 50 were movers (that is, firms that were relocating), 18 were new, and 58 were stationary. The homogeneity of firms from similar industries allowed the testing of behavioral hypotheses with reasonable degrees of freedom.

The incubator hypothesis is supported by firms in this sample. The new firms were smaller than others; they worked in single-shift batch processes; they were housed in relatively older buildings, often with more than one floor; and they had little land for expansion. Thus small, new firms begin operations in the more centralized locations and move to the periphery into larger sites only after they have achieved some success.

The use of trucks has been well documented as a major explanatory factor in the decentralization of employment in the United States (Hoover and Vernon 1959; Moses and Williamson 1967). The same phenomenon was of great importance in Bogotá: 95 percent of all goods going to and from firms were carried in trucks in Bogotá at the time of this survey. This is remarkable considering that the train station in the center of the city was an important reason for the central location of firms until just two decades ago. The change is all the more important given that 40 to 50 percent of the manufacturing output of these firms is exported outside Bogotá.

To gain insight into why firms located where they did, managers were asked to evaluate their firms' locations. On the whole, the respondents were very satisfied with road access, proximity to clients and suppliers, and the availability of unskilled workers, but they were dissatisfied with the quality of municipal services, zonal amenities, the availability of skilled workers, and the cost of land for expansion. Managers of firms that had moved were usually satisfied with their current plant capacity, in contrast to managers of many of the stationary firms. Reflecting their more centralized locations, managers of the new firms were largely happy with the quality of municipal services. Indeed, that quality is yet another reason for the centralized location of new firms. Dissatisfaction with municipal and public services increased with distance from the center. This suggests that when firms move to the periphery they lead infrastructure investments, which follow them with some lag. This negative aspect of the new locations is traded off against advantages associated with greater space.

Moves are usually associated with changes in technology and expansion of production; the new technology often requires more space to spread out. Thus the larger firms move longer distances to the periphery, whereas smaller firms move just one or two kilometers. This is presumably important in order to keep the same labor force: about 80 percent of employees remain with the same firm even after the move. The average commuting distance does not change after the move, which suggests either that firms move short distances or that employees change their places of residence to suit their new job location.

In the firms' own evaluation of factors affecting their move, the expansion of plant capacity was the most significant. Rent payments, proximity to suppliers, and zone amenities were also important. The proximity of clients, quality of public services, and cost of land carried less weight but did enter into their decisionmaking. The firms' responses suggest that they pay little attention to public sector decisions concerning infrastructure availability; they assume that infrastructure will follow with a lag.

Modeling the Intra-Urban Location Behavior of Manufacturing Firms

How can these firms' location decisions be modeled and estimated econometrically? Unfortunately, theoretical and empirical literature on firm location behavior is quite rare, which makes it difficult to draw generalizations from our work.[6] The general idea, however, is that because firms can be assumed to be profit-maximizing, they would be expected to respond to the existing land price gradients and any other input price gradients in deciding their location. The results obtained were certainly consistent with such a hypothesis. Although firms did not explicitly give much importance to land prices, the desire for plant expansion was often given as the main reason for relocation. Lower land prices at the periphery attract such relocating firms: hence land prices are indirectly seen as an important variable affecting location.

Careful consideration was given in the City Study to developing a systematic modeling framework in order to further the understanding of manufacturing firms' location behavior. Because the full derivation of the model and its detailed estimates are available elsewhere,[7] here we merely sketch the principles behind the modeling effort and provide its main results.

A firm's production function may be written as $0 = f(L,\mathbf{X};\mathbf{Z})$, where 0 = output, L = lot size, $\mathbf{X}$ = vector of variable inputs such as labor and capital, and $\mathbf{Z}$ = vector of site characteristics. These site characteristics are independent of lot size and represent local public goods at a particular location.

The relevant cost components are wages, capital costs, input materials' costs, delivery costs of inputs and outputs, and land rent. These would be the main variables of interest for calculating the optimum combination of inputs and for optimum site selection. Following standard urban economic theory based on bid rents, a particular plant site can be seen as being occupied by the firm willing to pay the highest price. The bid price will depend on the attractiveness of the site to a particular firm.

In a locational equilibrium, all firms of a particular type in an urban area would make the same rate of profit, and no firm would have an incentive to relocate. In this case the cost tradeoff calculations by individual businesses determine the spatial distribution of firms. For example, a large manufacturing plant may choose a site in a low-rent area near the urban periphery to meet its need for more space, in spite of a greater delivery distance. Small firms, in contrast, may prefer a central location where the availability of various externalities more than compensates for high rents.

The preceding theoretical framework leads to an empirical framework for predicting the probability that a firm of a particular type will occupy a site with particular attributes ($\mathbf{Z}$). Because the firm with the highest bid will occupy a given site, the relevant random variable for determining this probability is the maximum amount a group of firms with similar attributes would pay (that is, the maximum bid). The probability distribution of the random variable associated with the maximum bid leads to a multinomial logit specification for the firm location model.[8] Such specifications are useful in modeling any behavior dealing with choice.

As chapter 8 discusses, the issue in travel demand modeling is how to model an individual's choice between different modes. Similarly, the issue in residential location is how to model a consumer's choice of particular types of houses and locations. Here we have the employment location problem of firms having to choose among locations. An application of such models to residential location choice by Ellickson (1977, 1981) has suggested the approach adopted in this study. He formulated his problem: given a site of certain characteristics, what is the probability that a household of a certain type will occupy it? Our problem here is similar: given sites of certain characteristics ($\mathbf{Z}$), what is the probability that certain kinds of firms will occupy it? Another approach would be to define certain zones in the city and to find the probability associated with each type of firm locating in each zone. This would necessitate dividing the city into arbitrary zones such as rings and sectors and finding the type of firm most likely to locate in each zone. The approach that has been adopted here is more general; sites are specified by more general characteristics. The most important advantage of this approach is that the model allows the observation of a wide range of spatial variation in site characteristics and the sample does not have to be broken up by zones. This type of specification also allows policy analysis. It predicts the probability that a particular type of firm will occupy a site with particular attributes. The marginal effect of changes in these attributes on the probability of these firms' location can also then be estimated and analyzed. Hence, conclusions can be drawn on the efficacy of different kinds of policy instruments that affect these attributes.

In this study, the data collected in the survey of 126 manufacturing firms were utilized for estimating the model. The firms were grouped into four types: small and large; textile-manufacturing and metal-fabricating. Of the 126 firms surveyed, 87 fell into these categories. Large metal-fabricating firms were used as the reference group. The effect of different location attributes on the probability of location of the remaining three types of firms was seen in relation to the location attributes' effect on the reference group.

The independent variables included:

- Access to local markets for output (PRODSOLD) = percentage of product sold in Bogotá
- Access to local markets for inputs (INPUTBT) = percentage of input bought in Bogotá
- Proximity to residential location of production workers (WKSOUTH) = percentage of workers living in southern part of Bogotá
- Proximity to residential location of administrative workers (ADM-NORTH) = percentage of workers living in northern part of Bogotá
- Index of quality of local public services (ELECINT) = frequency of electricity interruption
- Presence of agglomeration economics (LOCQT) = location quotient defined as *comuna's* (*j*) share of industry (*i*) in relation to its share in total manufacturing employment
- Intensity of economic activity (POPDENS) = population density of the *comuna* in which the firm was located
- Measure of accessibility to the city center (DISTCBD) = airline distance from the CBD of the center of the *comuna* in which the firm was located

The estimation procedure provides measures of the influence of each independent variable on the probability of a firm being in the group specified in the dependent variable. For example, the coefficient of the proximity of firms to residential areas provides a measure of the importance of this variable to small textile firms as compared to the base. The estimated coefficients are translated into elasticities such that policy conclusions can then be drawn. The overall goodness of fit was found to be high, providing some confidence in the results.

The multinomial logit estimation method was used to perform these investigations. It became clear that small firms are quite distinct from large firms in their location behavior and that textile firms display behavior different from that of metal-fabricating firms. These results indicate the interaction between generic differences found in different industries according to their size, the nature of their relationship with their suppliers, types of product markets, and their location.

Small textile firms were the most likely to locate near the city center and in close proximity to their input suppliers and the homes of their production workers. In Bogotá this meant locations in rings 2 and 3 and nearer the southern and southwestern parts of the city. Large textile firms, in contrast, choose sites farther from the city center—about three times farther away, in fact—and proximity to the homes of their professional and administrative workers seems to be more important. They are also more sensitive to locating in areas with better public services (for example, a more reliable electricity supply). They are not sensitive to proximity to local markets and are farther away from dense residential areas. Small metal-fabricating firms are similar, in many ways, to small textile firms: they like to be near their inputs and product markets but are not likely to be near the city center. All these findings are consistent with the idea that smaller firms need to take advantage of agglomeration economies that are realized by locating in areas where both input and produce markets are close by and where production workers are easily available. Large firms, on the other hand, are oriented more toward markets outside the city and are less dependent on the city in which they are located. They tend to internalize many of the agglomeration economies that smaller firms take advantage of by being near other firms.

To strengthen confidence in these findings, the dependent variable could be specified in different ways (that is, firms could be grouped in different ways). Location choice could be modeled more directly by grouping the firms by ring location. In this case, firms were divided into four groups: rings 1 and 2 combined; ring 3; ring 4; and rings 5 and 6 combined. As noted earlier, this was an arbitrary grouping procedure, but it was used here to bolster the results found earlier. The estimations were found to be very robust. Firms that sold a large proportion of their output within Bogotá tend to choose sites near the center, and export-oriented firms locate nearer the periphery. Similarly, firms that rely on local suppliers tend to be near the center. Moreover, locally oriented firms tend to be small. Firms that recently moved are extremely unlikely to be in or near the CBD: they almost always move to outer areas where more space is available, thus contributing to the decentralization of manufacturing employment.

All of these results imply that manufacturing firms in Bogotá behave in an optimizing fashion in choosing their location to minimize overall costs. But we still have little sense of how responsive they are to changes in factor prices. When firms move to more peripheral locations in order to expand, how responsive are they to the land price gradient that exists in the city (see chapter 3)? Is there also a wage gradient? Additional estimations were made to address these questions.

It is clear that a land price gradient exists. The 1976–78 land price gradient was about 0.10 to 0.12; that is, land price can be expected to decline by about 10 to 12 percent with each kilometer from the city center. The sample of 126 manufacturing firms also had direct information about the value of the land where these firms were located. Remarkably, the gradient calculated from these observations—about 0.11—was exactly consistent with the other independent data. The other major factor of production is labor. There are few good reasons to expect the existence of a wage gradient in a city. Firms located in the center of a city need to pay slightly higher wages to attract workers who might have a longer commute from outer areas. But the same justification could be found for higher wages in outlying areas. Hence there are few estimates that suggest the existence of clear wage gradients in cities. Nevertheless, in Bogotá, even after adjusting for the usual human capital variables, wages are found to have a gradient of about 0.05 as one goes out from the center of the city.

How do firms respond to these locational changes in factor prices? The elasticities of substitution between capital and land and between land and labor are good measures for this response. A low elasticity of capital/land substitution would suggest a greater degree of decentralization in the presence of a land price gradient. The elasticity of substitution measures the percentage of change in capital/land ratio in response to a change in factor prices—that is, the ratio of land price to capital price. As land prices vary, then, how does the capital/land ratio vary?

Again, there were few estimates of these elasticities for manufacturing firms in other cities. The capital/land elasticities that have been estimated are mostly for urban housing. They range between about 0.4 and 0.8 in most cases (see McDonald 1981 for a review). In this study we utilized the 84 firms (out of the 126) who were owner-occupiers, and we used the market value of plant and equipment as the capital value. The resulting elasticity of substitution was about 0.31—much less than estimates made for urban housing in the United States. This result supports the a priori assumption that the elasticity of capital land substitution for manufacturing is likely to be smaller than for housing because the possibilities of locating manufacturing activity in multistoried structures are limited. Similarly, the land/labor elasticity was calculated by using the wage bill for each firm. The value of this elasticity was also about 0.30; that is, as land price increases, firms increase the intensity of labor used per unit of land. As expected, we see greater crowding in factories in central areas of the city.

In summary, the results from all these econometric investigations suggest that firm location behavior is by no means random. The estimated model was derived for profit-maximizing firms, which were found to behave much as would be predicted. The goodness of fit was satisfactory, and the estimated model was capable of predicting, in probability terms, which types of firms are likely to occupy a site with particular characteristics. The location patterns that the model predicted were consistent with those expected. Among small firms, accessibility to local input and output markets was the most important factor in the location decision; the benefits of accessibility to the central area compensated for the high rents and congestion. Large establishments, which were more export oriented and required more plant space with modern production technology, located in outer areas, where more space was available at lower cost. The estimation results also indicated that the quality of public utility services is very important for large firms and that proximity to the residences of administrative workers is more important to such firms than is proximity to the homes of production workers.

The precise modeling framework used here was specific to Bogotá. The independent variables chosen were those available from the survey and considered important in Bogotá. Similar investigations in other cities could involve different specifications and different variables suitable for those cities. Our study has, however, indicated a modeling framework that is systematically derived from urban economic theory and contributes to an understanding of the behavior of manufacturing firms.

Trade and Service Employment Patterns

It is much easier to model the location of establishments that are in some sense people-serving—for example, schools, local government agencies, retail trade establishments, and banks—than it is to model the location of manufacturing companies. Access to local markets is the main determinant of the location of employment in people-serving activities. Considerable work has been done in this area,[9] and the model used is a simple analog of Newton's Law of Gravity: the level of interaction is directly proportional to the mass of interacting bodies (size of the groups of sectors) and inversely proportional to the distance between them. This approach is therefore referred to as the social physics approach. Although the model is then not couched in terms of economic behavior, it may be interpreted as reflecting firm-optimizing behavior. A firm chooses its location in order to optimize its access to the customers who are likely to demand its services. Implicit in this formulation is that proximity to inputs is less important to such firms than proximity to customers or that prices of inputs are invariant with respect to location. The model framework assumes that each subarea in the metropolis attracts the various activities in relation to its relevant location attributes. These attributes will vary with the activity group considered but will include both "policy" attributes such as available land for the activity and "given" attributes such as current population or employment levels and land value (Lakshmanan 1964). Only the broad outline of the model and the main results are provided here; details are available in K. S. Lee (1989).

Because we did not conduct a special firm survey of firms in these activities at the establishment level, information was not available for this exercise. Instead, the activity location information in the 1978 Household Survey had to be used. From this survey we knew the location of employment of all the workers in the sample. The behavior of firms was therefore deduced from the location of workers in those trade and service sector activities. The specific activities considered in these exercises were wholesale trades; retail trades; restaurants and hotels; financial establishments; real estate and business services; government services; sanitary services; social and community services; recreation and entertainment; and personal and household services.

The standard model represents the hypothesis that the trade and service firms in the ith zone serve people in all zones in the city but the likelihood of service declines with distance.[10] This implies that a firm of a particular type will locate in a zone with particular attributes.

Three measures of market potential were used in the estimates. The first two were the number of households and population in each zone. As might be expected, they gave similar results. The third was purchasing power of a zone. The dependent variable used was employment density of each different activity in each of the thirty-eight *comunas* in Bogotá. The model was quite successful in explaining the location of these trade and service activities. The more directly people-serving an activity was, the better the model performed. Thus, the best fits were obtained for retail trade, social and community services (which included education), and personal and household services (which included domestic workers). The least satisfactory explanation was found for the location of government workers and sanitary service workers. This is as expected, since these latter groups serve the public less directly.

The purchasing-power model performed better than the population and household measures of market potential for all activities except retail trade, where it was about the same. This is consistent with the overall employment location pattern mentioned earlier—that is, the location of many more employment activities in the richer parts of the city. Specifically, the purchasing-power measure improves the degree of explanation significantly for the location of employment in restaurants and hotels, finance, recreation and entertainment, and personal and household service. Clearly, all of these activities are highly dependent on customers with high incomes. Banks, restaurants, and domestic servants are all more likely to be found in the richer areas of the city.

One other experiment was performed to test the degree of association between the market potential proxy and employment density of each zone. Sensitivity tests were performed by varying the value of g— that is, changing the decay factor of market potential by distance. If a higher g results in better goodness of fit, the more localized the activity is. Recreation and entertainment, social and community services, personal and household services, and restaurants and hotels turn out to have significantly improved goodness of fit with an increase in g: these activities are more dependent on local clientele.

In summary, it was again found that the location of employment in different activities was as would be expected from rational profit-maximizing kinds of behavior. Employment in retail trades, social and community services, and personal and household services follow the patterns of residential location. Other activities, such as recreation and entertainment, restaurants, hotels, and financial services, need to be near high-income districts of the city. Government services and wholesalers are relatively independent of the residential location of households. These investigations illuminate the interaction between residential and employment location and highlight the importance of high-income residential locations.

Implications for Location Policy

This chapter emphasizes the phenomenon of decentralization that accompanies the growth of cities. It focuses on the role of the manufacturing sector as the leading factor in the decentralization of growing cities. In trying to understand the economic forces at work in this process, we have also begun to better understand that certain activities are likely to continue to locate near the center of the city as it grows and that therefore the CBD is likely to remain an important concentration of employment in large cities. What do we learn from all these findings that could help shape policy in regard to the structure of cities?

The growth and diversification of industry in a large city would almost inevitably lead to decentralization of the more successful segments of industry. The most important reason for firms to relocate toward the periphery of Bogotá was their desire for expansion, usually accompanied by technological change in the production process. Mass production requires assembly lines or continuous flow process technology, which implies the need for single-floor plants and therefore more space. This is another way of saying that for such processes the elasticity of capital/land substitution is low, and firms move down the rent gradient to the periphery to acquire the larger plots they need for production, gaining space for future expansion in the bargain. Moreover, large plots of land that are not built up are usually available only at the periphery.

In contrast to larger firms, smaller manufacturing firms, especially newer ones, still prefer locations close to the city center. They locate in premises vacated by other firms and near to the many input services—financial institutions, raw materials suppliers, equipment repair shops, and residences of prospective workers—that they typically require for their day-to-day functioning. A clue to this behavior is found in the high birth and death rates of firms in Bogotá during the period under study. New, small entrants into the manufacturing business are inherently unstable and therefore naturally likely to economize on overhead and fixed costs of all kinds. Many services that a larger firm would internalize are rented temporarily by such a firm until it reaches greater stability. Many new entrepreneurs, for example, are technicians with little capital, starting out on their own after breaking away from their original employers (see Cortes, Berry, and Ishaq 1987). They can afford to take few risks. A thriving, concentrated area of manufacturing firms that gives agglomeration economies to budding entrants is therefore likely to impart health to a city seeking industrial expansion.

Many urban policies are designed to thwart the location of new manufacturing firms in large cities. In countries as different from one another as India, the Republic of Korea, and Venezuela, similar policies prohibiting manufacturing firms from locating in the large metropolitan cities have been followed. These policies have ignored the important role of large cities as incubators of entrepreneurship. They have resulted from a lack of understanding of the locational dynamics of industrial growth. Prohibiting new manufacturing activity in large cities also has the effect of reducing effective death of sick firms. The death of firms is easier for a city's economy to sustain if the displaced labor has a good opportunity to find work in new firms. If births are prohibited, resistance to death increases and the city acquires an environment of stagnation. Apart from enforcing pollution regulations and preventing hazardous industries from locating in densely populated areas, it should be understood that the locational dynamics of manufacturing firms are such that large firms or expanding and successful small firms will themselves decentralize away from central cities.

It is also commonplace to find industrial estates located on the periphery of cities; these are often designed to attract small firms. They have seldom been successful. Our results provide persuasive explanations for such failure. Industrial estates are unlikely to become incubators of entrepreneurship until a large number of successful firms are located there already. Moreover, new firms cannot tolerate interruptions in basic services like electricity, water, and transportation. New developments in cities typically suffer from teething troubles in early stages; if they do not, it is at very high investment costs. Enlightened industrial location policy in cities would therefore not aim for premature decentralization of industrial activities; it would occur anyway with successful growth. The role of policy is to facilitate such growth and plan for the provision of public services in response to such growth. It is the larger firms that are more likely to move to peripheral locations and they are also more likely to be able to pay for the various necessary public services.

Attempts are also often made, at very high initial infrastructure costs, to persuade small and medium-size manufacturing firms to locate in new "satellite" cities, which are typically 30 kilometers to 100 kilometers from the large city. Examples of such attempts include Banweol, near Seoul in Korea, and Kalyan, near Calcutta in India. Attempts at such development are usually miserable failures. The actual cost of locating in such places usually far exceeds the benefits from any tax or other incentives offered by the government.

The pressures for decentralization are relentless with growth, however, so public policy must also be careful not to thwart it. Public transportation routes, for example, are typically radially oriented toward the center of the city, in response to the traditional location of jobs. An expanding city with a growing and decentralizing manufacturing sector also suggests the need to institute circumferential routes so that poor workers can reach their destination without wasteful trips through the center (see chapter 8).

Many of the relocating large firms in Bogotá planned their moves well before the availability of public services in the new location. There seemed to be a general belief that once they moved, public services like roads, water supply, and power would follow. This may have been peculiar to Bogotá, where the decentralized agencies (see chapter 9) are particularly responsive to demand and have the autonomy to act. It was also the case that much industrial location in and around Bogotá conformed to the industrial zones provided according to land use regulations. This points to the value of realistic land use zoning that is itself responsive to firms' preference and able to give public authorities the flexibility to provide services in response to demand.

What about other activities? Manufacturing, after all, seldom employs more than one-third of the workers in a city. For most commerce and service employment, we have found a pattern opposite to that of manufacturing. Larger firms locate much more in the center, whereas smaller firms are more decentralized. Overall, as we also saw in chapter 3, employment in manufacturing is more decentralized than in services and commerce. Indeed, it can be said that the CBD is specializing more and more in nonmanufacturing employment, and the periphery, in manufacturing. The reason, although this has not been determined empirically, seems to be that office activities, trade activities, and other similar activities are likely to have a higher capital/land substitution elasticity. It is easy to pile up such activities in multistory buildings. At the same time, many activities that are directly people-serving, such as small retail stores, other personal services, local government services, and schools, have to be near their customers and therefore decentralize as their customers do. Residential location and manufacturing location therefore lead these other activities in their decentralization pattern as a city grows. But most of these activities are sensitive more to purchasing power rather than to mere mass of people, so they are much more likely to be found in the richer areas than in the poorer ones. In fact, the many retail activities found in the CBD are located there because of the lack of effective demand in the many poor areas of cities in developing countries. A poor neighborhood cannot support many activities. This explains why some activities are likely to continue to be more centralized in cities in developing countries until incomes increase in those countries and cities.

It has also been observed that competing peripheral "city centers" emerge as a city expands. The indication is that the relative poverty of cities in developing countries makes this process slow, however. City planners often prematurely plan competing centers for retail, wholesale, office, and other activities, whereas they attempt to restrict the accretion of new activity in the traditional city center. Our study suggests that this should be done only after careful consideration of the population's demand for such activities. Otherwise, much inefficiency can result from the loss of agglomeration economies inherent in the city center.

These observations illustrate the strong linkage between the pattern of residence location, the spatial distribution of income, and the location of employment, and show how their mutual interaction produces the city structure. The spatial inequality of incomes influences the distribution of employment location and explains the lack of employment in the poor areas of Bogotá. Once again, the effect on the design of public transportation is clear. We can better predict the course of a city's growth once we understand these linkages.

Notes

1. This chapter summarizes the work reported in K. S. Lee (1989).

2. The traditional commercial district (Chapinero area) in sector 7 used to be the "Fifth Avenue" of Bogotá; in recent years, however, retail stores and restaurants have sprung up along 15th Avenue northward, and a large shopping center (called Unicentro) was developed in the northern part of sector 8. The determinants of commercial and service employment location were also tested using a gravity model. For details, see K. S. Lee (1989, chapter 6).

3. As reviewed in Kemper (1973). See also Struyk and James (1975), Hanushek and Quigley (1978), Leone (1971), Schmenner (1973, 1982), and Cameron (1973).

4. See Henderson (1988) for a broader discussion of the kinds of firms that are found to continue in large cities.

5. Henderson (1988) reached a similar conclusion.

6. Works on this subject as it applies in the United States include Hanushek and Song (1978), Erikson and Wayslenko (1980), Schmenner (1973, 1982), and Carlton (1979, 1983).

7. The derivation was first provided in K. S. Lee (1982) and is also available in K. S. Lee (1989, chapter 5).

8. The application of the multinomial logit method to urban economic research became popular with McFadden's work on travel demand studies (1973, 1974, 1976) and with work by Friedman (1975), Lerman (1977), and Quigley (1976) on residential location studies.

9. There was much interest in the location of service-oriented establishments in the United States in the early 1960s (for example, Lowry 1964; Lakshmanan 1965; W. G. Hansen 1959; W. B. Hansen 1961; Pendleton 1963; Huff 1961).

10. Details of the model may be found in K. S. Lee (1989, chapter 6). Briefly, the model framework is as follows:

$$E_i^k = f(G_i, E_i^T)$$

where E_i^k = number of jobs in activity k in zone i; G_i = a gravity measure of the market potential of zone i; and E_i^T = the total number of jobs in zone i.

The measure of market potential can be expressed as

$$G_i = \sum_j \frac{Z_{ij}}{d_{ij}^g} \qquad i, j = 1, \dots, n$$

where Z_{ij} = proxy for market potential of zone i with respect to zone j; d_{ij}^g = distance between zone i and zone j; and g = distance decay weight.

If, for example, we measure market proxy by the population in each zone, and if there are, say, three zones in the city and $g = 2$, then:

$$G_1 = \frac{P_1}{d_{11}^2} + \frac{P_1 P_2}{d_{12}^2} + \frac{P_1 P_2}{d_{13}^2}$$

where d_{11} is a measure of the size of zone 1—for example, the radius of zone 1. G_1 is then a measure of interaction between zone 1 and all other zones in the city: the influence of each zone on zone 1 decreases by the square of the distance between the two zones. A retail store, for example, is likely to consider the people in nearby neighborhoods much more important than those in far-off neighborhoods.

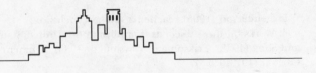

Chapter 7

Shelter in a Growing City

Colombia has been exceptional in the level of importance it has assigned to housing throughout the past several decades. Although the lack of adequate shelter is seen as a serious social problem in most developing countries, higher priority has generally been given to other pressing economic issues, such as agricultural development, poverty alleviation, nutrition, and industrial development. In Colombia the government consciously attempted to use housing as a leading sector to promote economic development in the late 1960s and early 1970s. Moreover, it is probable that Colombia was one of the first developing countries to create an organized system of housing finance. It is therefore of great interest to assess the housing situation in Bogotá and to examine the efficacy of different housing policies.

A country undergoing rapid urbanization faces special difficulties in expanding housing supply quickly enough to keep pace with the burgeoning demand. In countries that are already highly urbanized, the annual increase in housing demand is essentially a combination of growth in the number of households and the need to replace depreciated housing. In countries with extremely low levels and growth rates of urbanization, similarly low growth rates of housing demand are encountered. It is in the large group of middle-income and rapidly urbanizing countries that the problem of adequate supply of urban housing is most serious. Because of the movement of households from rural habitats to urban areas, and the unusually high rates of growth in income during such periods, the increase in demand for urban housing far exceeds the rate of growth in the total number of households in the country. Not only do materials have to be provided in adequate quantity, but land has to be developed and infrastructure services provided at an accelerated pace. At the same time, there is a natural tendency for the price of each of these commodities and services to rise; failing this, the public sector tends to ration these services. The expansion of infrastructure and public services is typically a responsibility of the government or public utilities, and they are often hampered by a lack of adequate resources. Even if the pricing of public resources is appropriate, such activities still need external resources for investment purposes. Hence, there is typically a lag between the expression of housing demand and the supply of the full range of housing and infrastructure services needed to satisfy such demand. The result is pressure on prices and/or rationing.

Colombia experienced this type of expansion from the early 1940s to the late 1970s. Overall, Bogotá may have been exceptional in coping with the problems usually associated with this phase of development. This has happened somewhat fortuitously as private households, private developers, public utilities, local governments, and the national government have separately responded with relatively innovative and flexible solutions in the face of adversity. Between 1964 and 1978, for example, the supply of housing in Bogotá grew faster than the population did, leading to improved dwelling conditions. The housing stock in Bogotá remained crowded, however: the average number of households per dwelling unit was 1.4 in 1978, a small increase from 1.3 in 1964. Despite this increase, there were actually fewer persons per dwelling unit (a decline from about 8 to 7) because of a precipitous drop in average household size. This fell from 6.2 members in 1964 to 5.2 in 1973 and 4.9 in 1978.

The traditional approach to housing has been to estimate a housing deficit or shortage. "Quantitative deficit refers to the material lack of housing, the result of subtracting the existing 'adequate' houses from the total number of families in the city. Qualitative deficit refers to those houses which fail to meet habitability requirements and are then classified as subnormal (dirt floor, lack of water supply, lack of sewerage system and the like)" (Stevenson 1984, p. 2). This kind of approach typically results in a massive estimate of a housing shortage that has little hope of being met in the immediate or foreseeable future. Such an estimate paralyzes policymakers into complete inaction.

Housing in Bogotá: The Institutional Setting

The main public institution responsible for housing in Colombia has been the Land Credit Institute (Instituto de Credito Territorial, or ICT). Originally founded in 1939 to help finance sanitary housing for fieldworkers in rural areas, it became a primarily urban housing institution in 1956 when the rural housing functions were transferred to the Agrarian Credit Bank. Its approach has been essentially a physical, construction-oriented one, initiating major projects in the larger and medium-size cities. It has always attempted to promote organized physical urban development planning, but it has met with only limited success. Although its professed aim has been to provide mainly low-income housing, its own periodic assessments indicated that it felt unable to do so. For example, in a document issued by the ICT in 1955, it was estimated that 83 percent of all Colombian families could not pay for adequate housing (ICT 1955). Furthermore, the "housing deficit" was projected to increase continuously as the city grew. Although in its report the ICT recognized the problems of delivering fully finished units to low-income households, its actual approach remained one of building units for sale or rental.

The ICT achieved a degree of success during the early 1960s, when low-cost funds were readily available from the United States through the Alliance for Progress started by the Kennedy administration. Large housing programs such as Ciudad Kennedy, Timiza, La Esmeralda, and Garcés Navas were implemented in Bogotá at that time, but the programs were halted when the funds dried up. These programs only served the elite among low- and lower-middle-income groups, and even then the ICT suffered from low collection rates and erosion in its resource base because of inflation and large increases in building costs. As a result, the ICT suffered from constant problems of decapitalization.

Throughout most of its operations, until the mid-1970s, the ICT built about 25 to 35 percent of all its units in Bogotá, accounting for 25 to 50 percent of its investments. The greatest number of units built in Bogotá was about 10,000 in 1962; it varied between 3,000 and 5,000 throughout the late 1960s up to the mid-1970s, a period when the number of households was increasing by about 40,000 to 50,000 annually in Bogotá. It was calculated in 1971 that, according to the ICT's repayment requirements, about 60 percent of families in Bogotá simply would not qualify for loans from the ICT (Stevenson 1984). Other studies reached similar conclusions during the 1970s: more than half of Bogotá's households were ineligible for the cheapest public housing (Valenzuela 1970; Vernez 1976; Arias 1977).

All accounts suggest that the ICT's public housing programs are likely to have reached groups in the sixtieth to ninetieth percentiles of income distribution. Thus, despite its explicit mandate to serve the housing needs of low-income, urban residents, the ICT was not able to reach the poor. Its financial base was never well structured; forced channeling of funds at low cost formed the main portion of its financial resources, and this was never a secure and self-sustaining base. One observer concluded that, in an attempt to reach the elusive low-income market, the ICT had adopted a strategy of building very small shoddily constructed units on land far from the center (Laun 1977).

The other main housing finance institution that has existed for a long time is the Banco Central Hipotecario (BCH), which was founded in 1932, replacing an earlier entity, the Central Mortgage Bank of Bogotá, founded in 1905. The BCH has administered the mortgage bond market and raised funds from other instruments such as social security bonds and indexed bonds. It was the main financial institution operating as a savings and loan institution for housing loans to builders as well as consumers. Until 1972, when the indexation savings and loan system for housing came into being, the BCH essentially catered to the top 10 to 15 percent of the income distribution, accounting for about 4,000 to 9,000 housing loans annually in Bogotá in the late 1960s and early 1970s. This constituted about 35 percent of its loans nationwide and 40 to 50 percent of the total amount loaned. Through the 1960s and early 1970s its average loan amounted to between Col$250,000 and Col$300,000 (1975 pesos). Until 1972 the BCH typically accounted for 70 to 80 percent of all formal housing credit in Colombia, with the ICT accounting for most of the rest. Since the institution of indexed mortgages in 1972, the BCH has shifted its lending to low- and middle-income households.

The big change in housing policies came in 1972 with the announcement of the Cuatro Estrategias, or the "Four Strategies" (DNP 1972). Urban construction was to be given the highest priority, and housing would be treated as a leading agent or promoter of development. The government believed that housing construction would not be import-intensive and that its expansion would help promote demand for domestic industrial and agricultural products as well as for transportation and services. The main innovation was the introduction of the Unidad de Poder Adquisitivo Constante (UPAC) system of indexed deposits and mortgages. It financed mortgages at positive ex ante real interest rates and paid depositors a similarly indexed return. These financial flows were to be routed through new Caja de Ahorro y Vivienda (Savings and Loan Associations) regulated by the Fondo de Ahorro y Vivienda created by the Banco de la Republica, the central bank.

This was a major policy initiative and had wider ramifications for the financial sector in Colombia. Because Colombia has typically had regularly high rates of inflation (20 to 30 percent per year), the availability of an indexed financial instrument also provided an avenue of safe investment for funds that would otherwise have gone into other inflation-proof investments, such as land. Although investments in housing through formal channels did increase substantially as a result of this reform, it is not clear how much difference it made in overall housing investment. Some of the shift may have been from the informal housing markets to the formal markets. As will be seen, the poor are not generally able to avail themselves of these formal channels. This policy initiative did serve to indicate forcefully that the government was concerned about raising housing investment in the country. One result of this policy initiative was that the funds controlled by the BCH fell dramatically, and most of the formal housing credit (70 to 80 percent) began to be channeled through these savings and loan associations. Total investment in housing through formal channels increased from about Col\$3.2 billion in 1972 to Col\$10.3 billion in 1976. It has been argued by some that this system was even more effective in denying low-income families access to formal housing credit (see, for example, Stevenson 1984). There was clearly a construction boom in Bogotá between 1973 and 1975, but there is little evidence of any longer-lasting effect on increased housing investment rates.

The new development plan for 1975–78, Para Cerrar la Brecha, did not mount any new specific initiatives on housing, but it shifted the emphasis toward providing public services and encouraging community participation. On the private supply side, there appeared to be a competitive, legal, housing construction business supplying housing to middle- and higher-income groups. The ten largest firms supplied less than one-quarter of the units offered for sale on the legal market. In 1969 the construction sector in Bogotá included 741 companies, of which 40 percent were individually owned, 41 percent were limited liability companies, and 3 percent were corporations. Of these companies, 35 percent were very small, employing fewer than 10 workers, while the top 5 percent had more than 200 workers each. About fifty firms accounted for 20 percent of the total construction market in Bogotá. Of the total construction, about 80 percent was for housing. Thus, there was a relatively vibrant housing construction business sector that did not seem to be concentrated and hence could be expected to operate relatively competitively.

Formal institutional initiatives had very little impact on the housing of low-income families in Bogotá. The vast majority of households in the bottom 60 percent of income distribution had little or no access to the formal housing market, which is characterized by formal tenure, formal credit systems, and the concept of a house as a fully finished, delivered unit. Yet the quality and quantity of housing in Bogotá as it existed by the end of the 1970s was relatively good for the level of per capita income that Colombia had achieved. More interestingly, there was even a high level of public service in most housing settlements. Most infrastructure investments typically followed the formation of settlements, but people seem to have felt reasonably sure that such investments would appear at some point.

How did this happen? Most of the rest of this chapter is devoted to describing and analyzing the housing responses in the unorganized market, which resulted in a relatively high level of housing services in

Bogotá. This has been made possible by unbundling the usual bundle associated with housing. Most households could not qualify for even subsidized low-income housing because the unit price of the complete home was beyond their reach. The cost of a house consists of five main components: the cost of land, the cost of building materials, the cost of the labor that goes into construction, the cost of obtaining access to infrastructure and other public utilities, and the cost of obtaining access to housing financing.

The informal housing market helped households reduce the access price of each of these components. At the time of occupation, land was often only semideveloped and hence much cheaper than a fully developed plot. Furthermore, many families moved into semifinished units at first. At the same time, building materials used (including recycled materials) were also often cheaper. Hence, at the time of entry, the unit cost of the finished unit was also reduced. Expenditure on wages was reduced through full or partial use of unpaid family labor. A plot was usually occupied before public services like paved lanes, water supply, and sanitation services had reached the subdivision (alternatively, utilities were tapped into illegally). Again, the effect was to reduce the price of public service access at the beginning. The developers themselves usually provided credit for land purchase, thereby opening access to financing for low-income households. The process of incremental development then upgraded the dwelling unit, with the household building up equity in the house in the process. The incremental construction was often financed by income gained from the rental of rooms.

The informal nature of the supply side helped in this process. The developers obtained largely undeveloped land at low prices and then passed on semideveloped lots to the consumers while financing a significant portion of the lot price; their intermediation and transaction costs were probably lower than a formal credit institution's would be. They were able to do the financing because they were reaping the unearned gains in land values inherent in any land development business; but they clearly shared a portion of this with the lot buyers. In this process, the effective cost of financing was reduced for the buyers.

The public sector also participated in this process by providing access to public services, albeit with some delay and by tolerating a certain level of illegal activity. The public sector itself unbundled its investment activities in infrastructure through agency decentralization. As will be seen, there was explicit recognition of the need to lower infrastructure standards in order to make housing affordable to the poor: this was demonstrated through the launching of the *Normas Minimas* program (discussed below). Even this proved too expensive for the poor, however. In general, public infrastructure services were extended in response to demand and as the need arose. Demand was often expressed through political means at the time of local elections or through particularly influential or vociferous local representatives. This institutional process of decentralized and relatively unplanned development (see chapter 9) can be seen as having promoted more rapid housing development in Bogotá than in many other cities, where more comprehensive attempts are made to deliver fully completed housing units with a full complement of infrastructure services.

This process effectively enabled people in the low- and lower-middle-income categories (perhaps the thirtieth to seventieth percentiles of income distribution) to enter the housing market. The poorest were still unable to participate as homeowners, but they were able to live as renters in the dwellings of those slightly better off.

Many of the first-time entrants in the housing market among the less well-off consist of *inquilinatos:* usually single people with uncertain employment who live as roomers in other low-income households. As their employment situation improves and as they are able to form families or to bring their families from rural areas or smaller towns, they move to other rental dwellings. Much of the older housing stock in the city center has also been subdivided to provide for such low-income roomers. If their income levels improve substantially, they are then able to become homeowners, typically in an *urbanizacion pirata*, or pirate subdivision.

We examine this process by (a) analyzing in detail the extralegal housing settlements in Bogotá known as *barrios piratas*, (b) looking at the mobility and tenure patterns of households, and (c) modeling housing demand behavior in Bogotá. The 1978 World Bank–DANE Household Survey information was supplemented by information from special data collected from *pirata* developers (*urbanizadores piratas*) themselves, from a sample of low-income households, and from a special mobility survey.

Bogotá's Unregulated Housing Market: The Myths and Realities of Incremental Development

The gap between the conventionally estimated housing supply and demand has been successfully filled in Bogotá through the widespread system of *pirata* subdivisions. This system is different from the widely observed squatter settlements in other Latin American cities and in other developing countries. The difference is that these *pirata* subdivision settlements did not result from land invasions: the land has actually changed hands through legal purchases. It is the subdivision itself that is usually illegal. But these settlements are better described as extralegal rather than illegal. Low-, lower-middle-, and middle-income families, having been shut out of the formal housing market, buy lots from entrepreneurs who acquire tracts of undeveloped land and subdivide them without conforming to zoning laws, subdivision regulations, or service provision standards. The lots sold usually provide only a bare minimum of services, often nothing more than some streets and water standposts. Typically, this rudimentary infrastructure is incrementally upgraded after initial settlement has taken place. It was found that buyers typically made down payments of about one-quarter to one-third of the lot price and then paid off the balance in monthly installments over one to four years. The pirate developer himself usually financed these installments.

There have been no accurate land records in Bogotá to indicate the extent of *pirata*-supplied housing. Most estimates suggest that 30 to 40 percent of the total residential land in Bogotá has been developed in this fashion; this implies that about 50 to 60 percent of the city's dwelling units have been constructed incrementally in these developments—residential density in these areas is higher than in other areas of the city (DAPD 1980; Vernez 1973; Borrero and Sanchez 1973). Our own household survey in 1978 indicated that between 1971 and 1976, about 60 percent of all construction was unlicensed. According to Valenzuela and Vernez (1974), in the early 1970s, 45 percent of households in Bogotá lived in units developed as *pirata* developments, about 43 percent in legal private developments, 11 percent in public developments, and only 1 percent in squatter developments. Various studies corroborate the notion that *pirata* developments cater mainly to low- and lower-middle-income households. For example, Vernez (1973) calculated that these dwellings provided shelter for only 28 percent of the poorest 10 percent of households in Bogotá, about 75 percent of the next quarter of households, about 65 percent for the next quarter, and about 10 percent of the top 40 percent.

Many of the originally illegal *pirata* developments were eventually legalized. By 1980 both the area covered by illegal development and the percentage of the population living in unauthorized settlements had declined substantially. Various estimates, including official estimates made by the District of Bogotá, suggest that only 10 to 15 percent of households lived in *pirata* developments in 1980. There is also evidence that new residential land development in the late 1970s had increasing proportions of legal development. This may have resulted from both a slowed city growth rate and an accelerated process of legalization.

Government Response

The significance of *pirata* development was recognized increasingly by the government starting in the early 1970s. One governmental response was the *Normas Minimas* approach to development (see Consultécnicos 1971). *Normas Minimas* are planned and approved "sites-and-services" projects. The idea behind such projects is to provide a developed site, often with a core sanitary structure, along with full public services, and to let the household do its own unit construction. Regulations were amended in 1972 to lower minimum design standards for residential developments and to allow private sector participation in these developments. The idea was to replicate the incremental development pattern of *pirata* developments in a legal and more organized manner, with a higher level of public services. The implementation of this new concept faced many obstacles. First, the approval process itself was very cumbersome, consisting of two stages of review and approval. Between 1973 and 1977, for example, only 28 *Normas Minimas* subdivisions were given final approval—out of more than 250 applications. Second, there was a lack of land zoned as high-density residential within the urban perimeter, and such land was the only kind eligible for *Normas Minimas* development (Paredes 1984). Third, there was social opposition to the zoning of such land because it was seen as legitimizing slums. Fourth, the approval process took one to two years—long enough to discourage many would-be developers. The simplification of the approval process from two stages to one improved matters somewhat and in 1979 allowed developers to begin selling lots before making infrastructure investments.

Under laws passed in 1963 and 1972, the district government has pursued a policy of systematically legalizing unauthorized subdivisions. The legalization process includes upgrading public services with contributions coming in different proportions from the government, developers, and the community itself. Since 1972 the legalization process has also included the installation of provisional sources of water supply and other public services such as road lighting. That the district government had a relatively positive attitude to the legalization of these developments is signified by the fact that the government was required to pay for these emergency services.

The legalization process involved reaching an agreement between the original developer or the neighborhood association and the district. This agreement specified a subdivision plan and the provision of a number of collective services. Although the developer was legally required to provide some minimum services, in practice there were loopholes that permitted the developer to plead ignorance of these provisions and yet be legalized. For subdivisions created after 1972, there was an effort in the late 1970s to enforce stricter standards and greater financial contributions from developers for the infrastructure provision. In practice, this did not prove too effective. Although legalization was supposed to take place only if certain minimum standards in public services had been met, legalization was actually much more liberal: in effect, a subdivision became legal if the district government simply pronounced it as such.

Once the subdivision was legalized, it became feasible for lot owners to get legal lot titles, but this process was made very difficult by the legal requirements. Once the lot purchaser had paid for the lot in full, he could have the title transferred from the developer. But he was required to have the following documents: a draft contract of sale; evidence of possession of title by the seller; income tax payment certificates of both the buyer and the seller; a property tax payment certificate; a municipal tax payment certificate; citizenship papers; registry of certificates; and, for males over eighteen, a certificate of military service. As might be expected, it was extremely difficult for low-income households to assemble all these documents; moreover, it was expensive. As a result, few people had legal titles to their lots, even if they were entitled to them. The contract documents between the buyer and seller (*promesa de venta, escritura de compraventa*) became recognized as adequate for extralegal lot sales. Despite the legal obstacles, considerable tenure stability was achieved in these informal markets, and lot sales were surprisingly brisk, despite the extralegality of the system. The main disadvantage, of course, was that the lack of legal title still impeded access to the organized housing finance system, which required legal mortgages. Because households usually possess at least one document giving proof of ownership, though with varying degrees of legal recognition, the fully legal title has little effective value, except for those owners who want access to financing from the official sector.

These legal and economic obstacles to authorized development have given rise to widespread *pirata* development in Bogotá. The need for shelter has inspired innovative responses essential to cope with the requirements of a rapidly expanding city. Unlike many other cities, where land invasions are encouraged by extensive government ownership of land, in Bogotá there has been a large supply of privately owned land on the periphery of the city. The original owners of this usually rural/agricultural land were induced to sell to *urbanizadores pirata* for a number of reasons: the developers were often offering the best price; legal transfer procedures took longer than sales to *pirata* developers; or the land might not have been zoned for development. *Piratas* have also been known to coerce landowners with the threat or fact of squatting.

The developer sells the lots on an installment plan. Lot buyers are usually first-time entrants in the housing market, with limited resources; they are often renters who have been in Bogotá for some time. The transfer of the lot typically takes place without an adequate supply of utilities. Most buyers do not have access to the organized credit market and therefore have to resort to financing from the developers themselves. The terms of such financing are rarely explicit, and it was seldom possible to find the cash price and installment price of lots separately, so estimates of the implied rate of interest could only be calculated indirectly. Carroll (1980) estimated these implied rates of interest from hedonic price equations at the aggregate subdivision level and from disaggregated data at the lot level. The aggregate estimate was 46 percent, whereas the estimate derived from lot level data was 13 percent. The lower estimate was considered more reliable. Given average inflation rates of 20 to 25 percent, it seemed that the lot financing was done at relatively low or even negative rates of interest by the developers.

Once the lot is bought, the structure is built incrementally according to available resources and the housing needs of a growing household. The resources are commonly augmented by renting a room or two to renters, and family members and friends provide significant unpaid labor. Some labor, mostly for specialized tasks, is hired; the extent depends on the family's circumstances.

Amparo de Ardila conducted a special survey of 212 representative low-income households for the City Study in 1978 (see the appendix for details of this data set). Of these households, about two-thirds were living in substantial structures of three to six rooms. About 90 percent of these households had been tenants prior to their current residence; and two-thirds had lived in one-room quarters. This clearly indicates the improvements achieved by means of *pirata* development. The economic necessity of entering the housing market by way of *pirata* development can also be illustrated by citing actual costs of acquiring land and building in 1978: a 120-square-meter lot would have cost about Col$60,000; a modest 40-square-meter structure would have cost about Col$80,000; and the cost of full utility services would have added another Col$20,000, for a total of about Col$160,000. The median household monthly income was about Col$8,000 in Bogotá, and the median monthly income among the households in the low-income homeowners survey was Col$5,000. Such a household would have to pay about eight months' salary as a 25 percent down payment and then about two-thirds of total monthly income in installments if these were paid over three years—and without interest. Given that such a household would typically spend almost 60 percent of its income on food alone, this would be clearly impossible. Hence, the only way to enter the market is through incremental development. The household typically buys an unserviced lot and resorts to clandestine utility hookups to save on utility connection as well as running costs. Occupancy of the lot would then typically be delayed to build up resources for building the structure, which would be a modest one initially. It is also common to delay installment payments; the developers, on the other side, have to factor these eventualities into their lot prices.

According to the survey, two-thirds of recent lot occupants reported no official connection to the water network, yet two-thirds of the same group reported access to piped water; similarly, 90 percent had no official power connection, yet 90 percent had actual connections; and 80 percent had no official sewer connections, yet almost half had toilets connected to a septic tank or sewer system. The discrepancies seem to be excessive. Part of this may have been the result of imprecise questioning. For example, those reporting "access" to piped water supply do not necessarily have an individual water connection in their home but could have effective access to public standposts. In any case, these data indicate the ways in which low-income households achieve effective access to public services. Even if many connections are illegal to begin with, they tend to be regularized later with appropriate payments to the utility company. This may have been why the utility companies tolerated illegal connections to begin with; effective policing would, in any case, be too difficult. Overall, it was found that water and electricity were widely available in Bogotá, and some kind of road existed in most areas. Only the sewerage system was slow to catch up.

About one-quarter of households were found to have delayed occupancy of their lot by a year or more. Missed or delayed installment payments were common among one-third to half of all households, as was the practice of building only small core structures initially. Resales of lots were common—between one-third and half of current homeowners had bought their lot from prior lot owners rather than from the developers themselves.

It is interesting that the mean size of vacant lots acquired in these subdivisions was about 160 square meters, quite a substantial lot size for low-income households. The initial structure built was typically about 25 square meters or less, leaving considerable scope for expansion. About two-thirds of the households in the 1978 survey reported some form of incremental construction. Almost half of the reporting households did this incremental construction using only unpaid labor; one-fifth used paid labor only and another fifth used both paid and unpaid labor. As might be expected, the tendency to use paid labor was higher among households that had higher incomes or were headed by older people or females. The major part of financing for construction comes from savings or sale of other assets. But almost half of the households reported reliance on unspecified loans and *cesantias*, as compared with only a third who used these sources to finance their purchase of the vacant lot.[1]

Because *pirata* development has formed such a large part of Bogotá's housing supply, it is important to understand the workings of this market. We were fortunate in gaining access to a special survey conducted by the Superintendencia Bancaria in 1977.[2] About 120 *pirata* developers were questioned about approximately 150 subdivisions (see the appendix and Carroll 1980). Data included acquisition price of the land tract, when the land was bought, the time profile and prices of lot sales, and public services and infrastructure installation. Information was also obtained about the *Normas Minimas* developments. These data were used to asses the rate of return to *pirata* developers, to compare the *pirata* and *Normas Minimas* developments, and to understand the determinants of lot prices.

As noted earlier, the *Normas Minimas* subdivisions were intended to supplement and preferably replace *pirata* developments. That this did not work in practice is illustrated by the comparative data obtained from this survey (see table 7-1). On average, the *Normas Minimas* lot was significantly smaller than the *pirata* lot but substantially more expensive per square meter. Whereas the average down payment (1976 prices) for a *Normas Minimas* lot was Col\$14,700 and the monthly installment was Col\$700, for a *pirata* lot they were Col\$9,500 and Col\$615, respectively. Thus, *Normas Minimas* developments catered to somewhat higher-income groups; for the lower-income households, access to the housing market still had to be through the *pirata* market. Because the *Normas Minimas* developments had to follow formal (although considerably diluted from the normal) planning standards, they typically devoted

Table 7-1. Average Data for *Pirata* and *Normas Minimas* Subdivisions, Mid-1970s

Characteristic (average)	Pirata inside urban perimeter	Normas Minimas[a]	Pirata outside urban perimeter
Tract price per square meter[b] (1976 pesos)	50	64	18
Tract size[b] (square meters)	35,528	98,700	84,758
Number of lots	156	585	150
Lot size (square meters)	125	92	315
Lot price per square meter (1976 pesos)	253	456	109
Total lot price[c] (1976 pesos)	31,625	41,952	23,008
Subdivider expenditure (1976 pesos) on infrastructure per salable square meter (usable area)	22	64	9
Subdivider expenditure on infrastructure per lot (1976 pesos)	3,256	5,955	3,695
Percentage of subdivision in open space	10	22	10
Open space per lot (square meters)	26	39	38
Total number of subdivisions	109	14	24
Total number of lots subdivided	16,994	8,191	3,604
Total number of lots with sale data	11,540	5,916	2,099

a. All *Normas Minimas* subdivisions are inside the urban perimeter.

b. "Tract" refers to the whole parcel of land that is purchased for subdivision.

c. Total lot price is the sum of undiscounted installments plus the down payment, per standard practice in the *pirata* subdivision business.

Source: Carroll (1980).

about 20 percent of their area to communal and green areas—about double the proportion for *pirata* developments. Accounting for another 20 percent devoted to streets, that left about 55 to 60 percent for salable area in the *Normas Minimas* and 70 to 75 percent in *pirata* developments. This also contributed to higher unit land prices in the *Normas Minimas*.

Infrastructure investments usually took place well after initial subdivision: at least a year elapsed between the sale of lots and the installation of infrastructure in three-quarters of the subdivisions studied. Even in some *Normas Minimas* subdivisions, investment did not begin until almost all the lots had been sold. The developers clearly use lot sale proceeds for infrastructure expenditures: they simply do not have resources prior to the sales. The absolutely essential components—streets and water standposts—are the first elements of infrastructure to be installed. The community itself ended up financing infrastructure investment to a considerable extent—more than 30 percent of costs in most cases (see table 7-2). In formal sector land development in most cities, the government usually bears the initial cost of infrastructure investment and then attempts to recover varying degrees of costs through user charges or taxes. A novel feature of the *pirata* development scenario is the ex ante sharing of costs among the developers, households, and the government. This situation has resulted from sheer force of circumstance but has resulted in faster availability of public services in Bogotá than elsewhere.

Lot buyers end up participating in this cost sharing in two ways. First, if the *pirata* developer does not install the infrastructure he is supposed to, and cannot be persuaded, the lot buyers have little choice but to make the investment themselves. This is sometimes done by explicitly

Table 7-2. Financing of Infrastructure in *Pirata* Subdivisions

Item	Percentage of infrastructure costs paid by				Number of subdivisions with service
	Subdivider	Community	Both subdivider and community	Government	
Sewers	43.5	32.2	16.1	8.1	62
Water	62.8	23.2	5.8	8.0	86
Electricity	48.8	31.7	6.1	13.4	82
Telephone hookups	4.8	61.9	4.8	28.6	21
Streets	81.4	12.8	2.3	3.5	86
Sidewalks	21.0	47.4	5.3	26.3	19
Curbs	53.3	30.0	3.3	13.3	30

Note: In all fourteen *Normas Minimas* subdivisions, 100 percent of all services were financed by the subdividers. The *Normas Minimas* subdivisions are excluded from this table.

Source: Carroll (1980).

sharing costs with the developer. Second, the lot buyers often have to pay when obtaining services from the government or the utility companies. In any case, this process was cost-effective: for example, average infrastructure costs per square meter in these developments were only 25 to 33 percent of costs budgeted for similar investments by the World Bank in sites-and-services projects in El Salvador in the mid-1970s.

One of the main reasons for antipathy toward *pirata* land developers in Bogotá was a general perception that they made high unearned profits. It is always difficult to judge what is a "high" undeserved rate of return and what is reasonable. One yardstick is the existing rate of return in alternative investments. In Colombia in 1979 it was easy to obtain relatively safe nominal returns of more than 30 percent from investments in officially available financial instruments. In some instruments, such as the *Títulos de Ahorro Cafetero* (coffee savings bonds), the rate of return was just over 50 percent. Hence, a *pirata* developer would have to get nominal annual returns of substantially more than 30 percent to compensate him for his risk in an economic environment where the average rate of inflation between 1972 and 1977 was about 25 percent.[3] The most realistic estimates are with payment default assumptions, where the median rate of return is only 25 percent for *piratas* within the urban perimeter, 33 percent outside the urban perimeter, and 39 percent for *Normas Minimas* (see table 7-3). These are clearly modest rates of return, given the risk taking and effort involved in *pirata* developments. Of great interest is the wide variation among developers: a minority of developers clearly do make extremely high profits, and popular impressions are obviously keyed to these high flyers.

These results help explain the reluctance of developers to make adequate infrastructure investments: most simply would not have the resources to do so without losing money. This exercise also focuses attention on the much higher returns made by *Normas Minimas* developers: they were clearly making rents from the district's restrictive approval process. The high returns also suggest that people are willing to pay some premium for legality.

An attempt was also made to understand the determinants of lot prices. As might be expected, lot prices were higher nearer the city center and for preferred locations in the north and west of the city (the predominantly poor areas being in the south). Among elements of infrastructure, there seemed to be specific willingness to pay for water and sewerage. This may partly result from an inadequate degree of variation in other infrastructure such as streets, which are available almost universally. Proximity to water sources is clearly valued, as is hygienic waste disposal.

In summary, the *pirata* development process in Bogotá operated relatively well in responding to the heterogeneous needs of a fast-growing

Table 7-3. Alternative Average Nominal Rates of Return to Subdividers
(annual percentages unadjusted for inflation)

Alternatives for rate of return estimates	Pirata subdivisions inside urban perimeter	Normas Minimas	Pirata subdivisions outside urban perimeter
Payment default assumptions[a]			
Median	25	39	33
Mean	38	101	55
Standard deviation	42	94	75
(N)	(101)	(14)	(21)
Medium assumptions[b]			
Median	33	78	41
Mean	53	125	64
Standard deviation	53	92	78
(N)	(102)	(14)	(21)
Favorable assumptions[c]			
Median	46	146	60
Mean	72	246	90
Standard deviation	80	315	106
(N)	(95)	(13)	(20)

Note: Rates of return are internal rates (IRR) averaged for individual subdivisions. Calculations are based on complete revenue and expenditure figures, with dates, for each subdivision. Basic assumptions in all IRR calculations: All lots in the subdivision are sold; if the total number of lots is greater than the number of lots for which sale data are given, the "excess" lots are counted as sold at the average price (in 1977 pesos) and on the last date of sale among the lots.

a. The data assume that a certain proportion of defaulting lot buyers is given per subdivision; this incidence of default is assumed to occur randomly over the period of lot sales; and defaulting lot buyers are assumed to pay only the down payment.

b. Assumptions are that no default occurs; all lots are fully paid for on time.

c. Assumptions are that overhead costs are limited to one standard deviation above the mean of figures for *Normas Minimas* developments.

Source: Carroll (1980).

city. It would have been difficult for the government to improve on this process in terms of response speed and flexibility or cost-effectiveness. It is difficult for the formal sector to do this kind of incremental development of land, infrastructure, and house construction. The unbundling of these components of shelter is essential in order to make affordable shelter accessible to low-income households.

Mobility and Tenure Choice

Household mobility rates are another measure of a city's housing market. The characteristics of households change over time in various ways that alter their requirements for housing. An increase in household

income enables consumption of greater housing space. Expansion of a
household through marriage and child rearing increases the demand
for space. The relocation of workplaces through job change or the workplace itself changes the proximity of a dwelling unit. Changes in city
structure and in availability of transportation services also alter the characteristics of a dwelling unit. We have observed that in Bogotá, particularly among low-income households, much adjustment takes place
through the process of incremental construction. The other means of
adjustment is to move to a new dwelling unit. High rates of mobility may
be regarded as one sign of a housing market that is functioning well.
Mobility, however, involves costs. These costs are expected to be much
less for renters than for owners. Transaction costs in buying and selling
real estate can be quite substantial. Hence, one expects significant differences in the mobility behavior of renters and owners. It may be
expected that a household is far more likely to own a house when it has
reached stability or does not expect to need to move rapidly.

The need for mobility is likely to be greater during a phase of rapid
city growth. In many cities this need may remain unfulfilled because of
rigidities in the housing market. As we saw in the last chapter, employment decentralized fairly rapidly in Bogotá during the 1970s. This was
partly because of the relocation of existing workplaces and partly
because of a changing location pattern of new employment. Both kinds
of change imply continually evolving city structure in terms of proximity
or desirability characteristics of different neighborhoods. Chapter 3 also
discussed the changing nature of the land price profile over time in
Bogotá. Neighborhoods change through densification and sometimes
through physical deterioration. All these factors point to the need for
households to move in response to varying circumstances. Rigidities
related to housing supply conditions, legal provisions concerning rent-
als and tenure, land sales regulation, and other factors can contribute to
reduced mobility and to mismatches between household requirements
and dwelling unit characteristics. A high mobility rate implies the
absence of such rigidities and probably contributes to a higher level of
household welfare. As household characteristics change, people have to
move to find a dwelling to match their new requirements. If they cannot
do so, their quality of life may decline.

One of the more striking features of household behavior emerging
from the World Bank–DANE 1978 Household Survey was the rather high
rate of household mobility. In both Bogotá and Cali, 23 percent of
households had resided in their present dwelling for less than one year.
Just over one-third of households had lived at their current address for
less than two years and just over half for less than four years. These rates
were similar to moving rates observed in the 1972 Phase II Household
Survey. What is most remarkable is that these rates are almost identical

to mobility rates observed in U.S. metropolitan areas. Further corroboration of mobility rates in Bogotá and Cali was obtained from a more detailed, longitudinal record of moves in a special household survey conducted by Roberto Corno in 1975. This survey focused on a sample of 1,730 adults between the ages of twenty and forty-five and recorded all moves throughout their lives. We concluded that the mobility rates observed were quite reliable and stable across time and cities in Colombia. It would be very interesting if similar data were available for cities in other countries to help us determine whether Bogotá is typical or atypical in this respect.

What were the characteristics of the movers? How does household income affect the tendency to move? Higher income implies both a greater ability to move and less need to move. Higher-income households would be more stable and more likely to be owners rather than renters. Accordingly, higher-income households exhibited lower mobility rates than lower-income households did: only 17 to 20 percent of households with incomes over the median level were moved in the previous years, compared with 27 to 30 percent among the lower half. As might be expected, multiple-worker households move less often, but the differences were not large. The age of household head is probably the best predictor of household mobility: the older the household head, the more stable household characteristics would be and the less likely the household to move (see table 7-4). As might be expected, workplace location correlated closely with residence location. Between 40 and 50 percent of households whose head changed jobs within the previous year moved. As discussed, tenure status and mobility are highly correlated. In 1978 about 40 percent of all renters had moved in the previous year, but less than 10 percent of owner-occupiers had done so. It also appears that a large proportion of those who move do so frequently. Furthermore, recent migrants who have been in the city for less than five years are the most frequent movers.

These insights were gained by merely examining the various characteristics of movers. Given the expected correlations between variables such as income, age of household head, and length of time in current job, it was instructive to model the mobility behavior. The basic hypothesis was that the various household characteristics can be used to predict the probability of moving. Estimation was done by using both the OLS and LOGIT techniques, and the results were essentially as expected (see Hamer 1981 for details). When household income is controlled for, the probability of moving declines as household size and length of residence in current location increase. The probability of moving is clearly the highest for the most recent migrants. A couple of other results are worth mentioning. It may be expected that once household income has been controlled for, the location of residence should have no effect on

Table 7-4. Moving Rates by Tenure Choice, Time Spent in Previous Residence, and Age of Household Head
(percent)

			Time in previous residence		Age of household head			
	Tenure choice		Less than one year	More than one year	30 and under	Over 31–40	40	All movers
City/period	Own	Rent						
Bogotá, 1972								
Moved in 1971–72	15	54	—	—	—	37	20	32
Bogotá, 1978								
Moved within past year	8	37	45	20	41	21	14	23
Cali, 1978								
Moved within past year	5	43	49	20	42	25	13	23

— Not available.
Source: Hamer (1981).

mobility. A dummy variable for the poorer sectors was used to test their independent effect and found to be significant. Poorer neighborhoods seem to have a more unstable pattern of residence. Finally, it was found that female-headed households exhibit no significantly different mobility behavior than male-headed households: both were equally likely to move. Overall, a priori conjectures were confirmed by the systematic estimations. Moreover, the LOGIT estimates were quite similar to the OLS procedure (see table 7-5, which gives comparable elasticities). For purposes such as this, where the reason for estimation is essentially to obtain an idea of independent influences on mobility, as distinguished from specific interest in the magnitude of variables, it would probably be adequate to conduct OLS estimations rather than the more complex LOGIT procedure.

What is most remarkable, again, about the results obtained is that very similar patterns are generally observed in the United States (see table 7-6). As in Bogotá, income, age of household head, family size, and tenure status are important determinants of mobility, whereas the sex of household head is not.

What is the pattern of household moves? In 1972 there was clear evidence of decentralizing moves (see table 7-7); that is, movement of households away from the center. This tendency was much more moderated in 1978, possibly because of a slowdown in the growth rate of the city. More interestingly, most moves were within the ring of previous residence. In general, households move to relatively nearby locations. In most sectors a majority of relocating households moved to new locations within their sector of previous residence. This tendency was strongest in

Table 7-5. Probability of Moving: Comparison of OLS and LOGIT Elasticities

Variable	Bogotá, 1978				Cali, 1978			
	OLS	LOGIT model I	LOGIT model II	LOGIT sample mean	OLS	LOGIT model I	LOGIT model II	LOGIT sample mean
Income	-0.0981	-0.0940	-0.2580	12.51	-0.10	-0.04	-0.14	11.58
Age of household head	-0.8694	-1.1677	-1.2603	41.24	-1.11	-1.09	1.11	42.80
Family size	-0.5146	-0.6250	-0.6736	4.95	-0.48	-0.51	-0.59	4.92
Years in current residence	-0.1086	-0.0470	-0.0382	5.08	-0.11	-0.17	-0.17	4.55
Years in current job	-0.0487	-0.1068	-0.0840	6.06	-0.06	-0.09	-0.08	6.16
Number of workers in household	0.1377	0.0468	0.0970	1.74	0.11	0.10	0.13	1.72

Note: The probability of moving was 0.346 in Bogotá and 0.356 in Cali.
Source: Hamer (1981).

165

Table 7-6. Mobility Rates in U.S. Metropolitan Areas by Selected Household Characteristics

Characteristic	Percentage of households moving
Income[a]	
$6,999 or less	25
$7,000–$14,999	25
$15,000 or more	18
Age of household head	
Under 30	46
30–45	20
Over 45	8
Family size	
Under 4	24
4 or more	17
Tenure choice	
Rent	38
Own	11
Sex of household head	
Male	22
Female	22

a. 1977 dollars.
Source: Derived from U.S. Department of Commerce (1977), table A-1 data for households inside metropolitan areas.

the sectors of greatest poverty (2, 3, and 6 in Bogotá; see table 7-8). The Corno survey data, which had much longer histories of mobility, found further evidence of this tendency. As expected, migrants into the city showed much greater mobility than natives. Natives were more likely to be found in their sector of birth than migrants in their first sector of residence in the city. Migrants live wherever they can when they first arrive and then adjust their residence after achieving some stability. The poor sectors (2, 3, and 6) showed higher retention rates than other sectors but much more so for natives than migrants. Once they achieve stability in poverty, it would seem, natives are not able to move out of their poor neighborhoods. Migrants, by contrast, appear to be more mobile, residing in the poorer neighborhood to begin with and then moving up.

Much of the discussion of housing supply earlier in this chapter was related to ownership housing. How important is ownership housing in Bogotá? How easily is it accessible? What are the determinants of tenure choice? We have already seen that renters are likely to be more mobile than owners. Hence, one would expect that all the influences that increase mobility rates would decrease the probability of homeowner-

Table 7-7. Moves of Households from One Ring to Another (Recent Movers)
(percent)

Ring of present residence	Moved within same ring	Moved to ring farther from center	Moved to ring closer to center
Bogotá, 1972			
1	35	65	n.a.
2	36	62	2
3	28	56	16
4	59	29	12
5	73	1	26
6	18	n.a.	82
Total	53	31	16
Bogotá, 1978			
1	17	83	n.a.
2	58	30	12
3	35	43	22
4	55	23	22
5	74	2	24
6	46	n.a.	54
Total	59	18	23
Cali, 1978			
1	41	59	n.a.
2	67	33	5
3	73	14	13
4	61	3	36
5	39	n.a.	61
Total	64	19	17

n.a. Not applicable.
Source: Hamer (1981).

ship: the age of household head, the length of residence in the city, size of the household, and income would all be expected to be positively associated with the probability of owning a house. This leads to the question of whether, all other things being equal, people in better-off areas of the city are more likely to own a house.

In both Bogotá and Cali, almost half of all households own the house they live in (see table 7-9), and higher-income households are more likely to be owners than renters. Even among the poorer households, however, one-third or more of the households are homeowners, testifying to the efficiency of the nonformal modes of housing supply. In the late 1970s the overall level of homeownership matched that attained in the United States as late as the early 1950s. A large proportion of the households own houses despite the lack of access to home financing for anyone but the better-off groups.

As expected, homeownership increases rapidly with the age of the household head. Few household heads under the age of thirty own their

**Table 7-8. Moves of Households from One Sector to Another
(Recent Movers)**
(percent)

Sector of present residence	Moved within sector of origin	Moved to other sector
Bogotá, 1972		
1	35	65
2	57	43
3	64	36
4	46	54
5	45	55
6	68	32
7	45	55
8	46	54
Total	56	44
Bogotá, 1978		
1	17	83
2	58	42
3	69	31
4	55	45
5	46	55
6	78	22
7	34	66
8	51	49
Total	58	42
Cali, 1978		
1	41	59
2	57	43
3	59	41
4	65	35
5	76	24
6	76	31
7	0	100
Total	66	34

Source: Hamer (1981).

own homes; those beyond forty are much more likely to own. Similarly, job stability contributes to homeownership: among household heads with less than one year in the current job, as many as 75 percent were renters. Recent migrants, who are also very mobile, are likely to be renters, and older residents are much more likely to be owners (see table 7-10). Female-headed households in Bogotá exhibit tenure choice characteristics similar to those of male-headed households.

How do these patterns compare with other countries? Information about developing countries is still scanty, but it does seem that homeownership rates vary with income levels of countries as a whole. For example, whereas only 33 percent of households in Bangalore, India, were homeowners in the early to mid-1970s, in Korean cities and in

Table 7-9. Tenure Choice by Household Income
(percent)

| | Household income | | | |
Tenure choice	Up to half of median	Half of median to median	Over median	All households
Bogotá, 1972				
Own	33	39	57	46
Rent	67	61	43	54
Bogotá, 1978				
Own	33	39	57	47
Rent	67	61	43	53
Cali, 1978				
Own	40	43	59	51
Rent	60	57	41	49

Source: Hamer (1981).

Dakar, Senegal, almost half were homeowners, and in the United States the figure was as high as 61 percent. Ownership increases more smoothly with income in the United States, but, as in Bogotá and Cali, the jump in ownership comes just above the median income level. One important difference in the United States is that female heads of households are much less likely to own their own homes. This is probably due to the race-related issues in U.S. cities. Although the trends are, in general, similar between the U.S. and Colombian cities, the differences in ownership levels are much greater than differences in mobility levels. Income levels are clearly much more important for homeownership.

The probability of homeownership was also estimated using data available in the World Bank–DANE 1978 Household Survey, and all variables were found to have the predicted signs.[4] The elasticity of each characteristic is nearly identical in magnitude but opposite in sign to

Table 7-10. Tenure Choice by Recency of Household Head's Migration
(percent)

Tenure choice	Arrived within past five years	Long-term resident
Bogotá, 1972		
Own	26	56
Rent	74	44
Bogotá, 1978		
Own	23	50
Rent	77	50
Cali, 1978		
Own	16	56
Rent	84	44

Source: Hamer (1981).

those estimated for mobility decisions (see table 7-11). Hence, decisions about homeownership are clearly very strongly influenced by the household's need to be mobile. As a household matures and becomes more stable, either because of its members' characteristics or because of increased job stability, the household head decides to own a house and expects not to move too frequently. After becoming a homeowner, he is most likely to continue in that status even if he does move.

International comparisons of such elasticities are difficult to obtain, but some sketchy information is provided in table 7-12. These comparisons need to be interpreted with some care, because homeownership is strongly influenced by institutional structures related to housing finance and legal systems. Nonetheless, it is interesting to observe that income elasticities of ownership are surprisingly uniformly low across the three countries compared. The age of the household head is atypically important in Colombia, presumably because of the lack of access of most households to housing finance: they have to save for some time before gaining access to homeownership.

Household characteristics are the main determinants of household mobility and homeownership. The household life cycle is the most important of these. In a fast-growing city such as Bogotá in the 1960s and 1970s, the progress of a migrant household through these life-cycle stages may lag behind those of natives, but the essential behavior is no different. Bogotá and Cali had relatively high mobility rates—quite similar to those in the United States. However, these rates were relatively low among homeowners in Colombia; the relatively higher proportion of renters had higher mobility rates, bringing up the average. The more widespread availability of housing finance and smoothly functioning systems of property transfer help ease mobility among homeowners in the

Table 7-11. Elasticities for Tenure Choice Model Comparison of OLS and LOGIT Specifications

Independent variable	Bogotá			Cali		
	OLS	LOGIT	LOGIT sample mean	OLS	LOGIT	LOGIT sample mean
Income	0.11	0.24	12.51	0.12	0.16	11.58
Age of household head	0.96	1.39	41.24	0.65	1.10	42.78
Family size	0.38	0.73	4.95	0.46	0.60	4.92
Years in previous dwelling unit	0.11	0.06	5.08	0.09	0.13	4.55
Years in present job	0.05	0.06	6.06	0.03	0.03	6.18
Number of workers in household	-0.12	-0.25	1.74	-0.12	-0.16	1.72

Note: The probability of ownership is 0.49 for Bogotá and 0.54 for Cali.
Source: Hamer (1981).

Table 7-12. International Comparisons of Ownership Status Elasticities

Variable	Colombia		Eleven Korean cities			United States	
	Bogotá	Cali	Low	Mean	High	Phila-delphia[a]	Thirty-nine cities
Income	0.11	0.12	0.03	0.06	0.12	0.30	0.18
Age of household head	0.96	0.65	0.06	0.23	0.50	0.19	—
Family size	0.38	0.46	0.20	0.43	0.54	0.25	—
Length of occupancy	0.11	0.09	0.12	0.15	0.18	—	—
Number of workers in household	−0.12	−0.12	—	−0.08	—	—	—
Female household head (coefficient)	−0.01	0.07	—	0.10	—	—	—

— Not available.

a. Estimates are for married couples.

Source: Bogotá and Cali data from OLS estimates in table 2-29 of Hamer (1981); Korean data from Lim, Follain, and Renaud (1980); Philadelphia data from Fredland (1974); other U.S. city data from Struyk and Marshall (1975).

United States. Expectations about mobility seem to determine whether a household owns or rents, and these are based largely on factors exogenous to the household.

Modeling Housing Demand

So far we have attempted to understand the behavior of the household as a demander of housing and the behavior of both public and private suppliers of housing in the particular institutional setting of Bogotá. In this section we focus on the more traditional dimensions of housing demand: how income-elastic and price-elastic is housing demand, and how can this be measured properly? Although there is considerable literature concerning housing demand in the United States, very few studies exist for developing countries.[5] This situation has improved in the last few years,[6] but information available is still limited to a relatively small group of countries, including Egypt, El Salvador, India, the Philippines, and the Republic of Korea.[7]

Modeling housing demand is intrinsically difficult because it is hard to find "correct" measures of both quantity and price. Moreover, housing markets are very heterogeneous, and housing prices typically vary over space within a city. It is difficult to define a "standard" house such that different quantities consumed can be measured. Similarly, in the absence of a natural unit of quantity measurement there can be no associated unit price. What is more readily observed is expenditure on housing and various attributes such as extent of development in the area, size of the lot, number of rooms, location, neighborhood quality, and level of public service. Typically, a means of simplification is then found in order to make the modeling problem tractable. The easiest solution is to assume away price variation in a housing market and regard expenditures as proxies for quantity (see Muth 1969). Another solution is to segment the housing market in a city into neighborhoods within which homogeneity, and thus price uniformity, can be assumed (see King 1975). In more complex approaches, indirect methods are used to derive price indexes by means of hedonic price-index estimation or the estimation of a housing production function with varying input prices (see Polinsky and Elwood 1979; Witte, Sumka, and Erekson 1979).

Each of these approaches causes specification problems that involve the inappropriate limitation of choice. Households typically search within and across neighborhoods: the price variation encountered is then not just within but across neighborhoods. Similarly, estimating hedonic prices unbundles the dwelling into its constituent parts, whereas the household may really regard the house as a composite good. As has been argued, this is an empirical issue, because low-income households have succeeded in unbundling their shelter into different components that are sought in a house sequentially.

The problem, therefore, is to find a tractable method of defining housing quantity and price that conforms to our theoretical understanding of urban housing markets. It would then be possible to estimate housing demand elasticities with respect to income and price variation. Another issue is to understand the biases that result from incorrect data aggregation. It is not always easy to obtain disaggregated data at the household level. Elasticities are then estimated from different kinds of aggregated data that group households in different ways. Are aggregated results consistent with disaggregate demand estimates?

A relatively simple application of residential location theory suggests an alternative way of incorporating price variation into a demand equation for housing as a composite good. We have observed that residential location is related to the workplace location of the household head. The household head can then be seen as optimizing the location of residence in relation to his workplace: housing prices, R, would typically vary with distance, d, from his workplace, whereas travel costs, t, would increase with distance. For any given amount of desired housing, H, the household's problem is to minimize total expenditure on housing, Z_j, including the implied transport expenditure. Thus:

$$(7\text{-}1) \qquad Z_j = R_j(d) \cdot H + t_j(d)$$

where the subscript j refers to workplace j.

For each quantity of H desired, there would be an optimal distance from the workplace—this is essentially the monocentric city model being generalized to a city that has workplaces in all areas. For each individual household, however, the city looks like a monocentric city with the workplace at the center. A different optimal location profile will be obtained for each workplace, because the price variation and transport costs variation would be different for each workplace. The consumption of the same quantity of housing, H_o, will imply a different total cost for each workplace. Thus, for example, the total housing expense for H_o for a person working in the CBD is likely to be higher than for one working on the periphery; this variation in cost across workplaces for consumption of the same housing quantity may be regarded as constituting the price difference within a housing market. This also implies the existence of a wage gradient: a worker at the periphery can be paid less than one at the center and yet have the same housing consumption and the same utility level. This was empirically found to exist in Bogotá (see K. S. Lee 1989).

The procedure used for estimating housing demand was as follows: the city was divided into j work zones, each with Nj households associated with the workplace. The total number of sample households was M. Each household i at workplace j spends R_{ij} on housing that has a set of k characteristics, ijk. A hedonic equation relating housing expenditure R_{ij} with housing characteristics can then be estimated:

$$(7\text{-}2) \qquad R_{ij} = \sum_{k=1}^{K} \beta_{jk} \cdot X_{ijk}$$

Thus β_{jk} can be estimated and

$$(7\text{-}3) \qquad \bar{R}_j = \sum_{k=1}^{K} \beta_{jk} \cdot \bar{X}_k$$

calculated where $\bar{R}_j$ is the expenditure on housing associated with workplace j on a house with standard characteristics X_k. This set of standard characteristics X_k could be defined as the average across the city. This procedure serves to define the different expenditures on the same standard house as related to different workplaces. The housing price index for workplace j is $\pi_j = \bar{R}_j / \bar{R}_1$, where R_1 can be arbitrarily used as the numeraire.

Each household's housing expenditure, R_{ij}, can then be normalized by π_j. R_{ij}/π_j is then the quantity of standard house consumed by household i associated with workplace j. The demand equation

$$(7\text{-}4) \qquad\qquad Q_i = R_{ij}/\pi_j = f(\pi_j, Y_i, HC_{ijc}, d_{ij})$$

can then be estimated relating quantity of housing (Q_i) with price (π_j), income (Y_i), household characteristics (HC_{ijc}), and distance of residence (d_{ij}) from workplace (j). This equation can be estimated across all M households.

Such an equation was estimated for Bogotá for 1972 and 1978 and for Cali for 1978. Bogotá was divided into thirteen work zones for both years. Separate equations were estimated for owners and renters, using value of house and rent paid, respectively, as the dependent variable. For 1972 only renters' equations were estimated because house value information was not available for owners. It may be seen from table 7-13 that there was considerable variation in average commuting distance. For owners the longest commuting distances were for the central zones, 1, 2, 3, and 4, and for zones 8 and 12, which broadly correspond to our standard sectors 7 and 8 in the north. It had been observed earlier that there was considerable in-commuting into the relatively better-off sectors 7 and 8. The commuting pattern for renters was similar except for work zone 2, which had a very low average commuting distance in both 1972 and 1978. This corresponds to one of the "incubator" areas identified in chapter 6. The central areas of the city had many renters, and they appeared to be working in central zones such as zone 2.

The hedonic equations (7-2) were estimated first using several independent variables: area of dwelling unit; lot area; dummy variables for availability of phone, separate kitchen and bathroom, and municipal garbage collection service. The last variable was seen as a proxy for neighborhood quality or amenities. People working in work zones 9 and 10 in the southwest and the south of Bogotá, who were likely to be low-income blue-collar workers, showed the lowest indexes for these facilities. The most striking difference observed between renters and owners was in the size of the dwelling unit area. The average for owners in Bogotá was about 170 square meters, whereas for renters it was about 70 square meters in 1978. The comparable figures for Cali were 125 square meters and 65 square meters. Interestingly, the differences in lot area were not as large: 150 square meters for owners and 125 square meters for renters in Bogotá (130 square meters and 125 square meters, respectively, in Cali). There was much more variation in the dependent variable (rent and value) across work zones than in the independent variables. The variables used for the 1972 estimation were different because the same information was not available in that data set.

The hedonic price equations were estimated for each work zone and for renters and owners in both Bogotá and Cali, resulting in forty-two equations. The most important variable to emerge was dwelling unit area; lot area did not perform as well. People apparently value dwelling

Table 7-13. Characteristics of Residences by Work Zone, Bogotá

Work zone	Average distance of residence from work zone			Derived price index	
	Renters, 1972	Renters, 1978	Owners, 1978	Renters, 1978	Owners, 1978
1	5.7	6.5	8.0	100	100
2	3.8	3.5	6.2	91	63
3	5.2	6.0	6.9	83	90
4	5.6	6.7	8.1	105	107
5	3.2	2.6	3.2	74	76
6	5.8	5.4	6.8	75	85
7	3.1	4.5	5.4	81	80
8	4.9	5.8	7.3	98	101
9	3.3	2.6	3.3	84	61
10	6.0	5.2	4.2	77	64
11	5.8	4.5	6.0	91	79
12	5.9	7.8	7.3	99	136
13	8.6	5.1	6.1	84	87

Note: Zones 1, 2, 3, and 4 are central city zones; 9, 10, 11, and 13 are outer zones; and 5, 6, 7, 8, and 12 are intermediate zones.

Source: Ingram (1984), exhibits 1, 3, and 4.

unit space more than lot area. The dummy variables for phone access, exclusive bath and kitchen facilities, and garbage collection also performed relatively well. These variables do not perform well for work zones 2, 9, and 10, where many of the less well-off workers work. This correlates with dwelling unit area: the workers in these work zones who do have access to these facilities probably have large dwelling unit areas as well. A measure of the explanatory power of these equations is provided in table 7-14: the equations succeed in explaining about 45 to 70 percent of the variation in housing expenditures. The workplace stratification is more important for owners. This is as expected, because the price gradient of owner-occupied units is usually steeper than that of rented units in most urban areas. Finally, the rents and values for the average "standardized" home were obtained by using the average characteristics of each zone along with the estimated price coefficients. The normalized price index for the work zones is displayed in table 7-13, using zone 1 as the normalizing work zone. There is considerable variation, up to 40 percent for owners and 25 percent for renters. The highest price indexes are found for zones 1, 4, 8, and 12—the corridor that extends from the CBD to the north and where much of employment exists, as well as much in-commuting and the longest commuting distances. The lowest indexes for owners are for zones 2, 9, and 10, which also have shorter commutes on average. The higher price indexes are, in some sense, for the more preferred or competitive workplaces where people are willing to work even if it involves a longer commute in order to live in the same quality of house.

Table 7-14. Analysis of Variance: Hedonic Price Equations
(percent)

| Householder | Variation explained by | | Total variation |
	Work zone stratification	Equations	
1972 Bogotá renters	4.7	49.3	54.0
1978 Bogotá renters	2.5	47.6	50.1
1978 Bogotá owners	8.7	36.4	45.1
1978 Cali renters	1.9	64.3	66.2
1978 Cali owners	8.0	60.9	68.9

Source: Ingram (1984), exhibit 13.

Having obtained the price index, π_j, the demand equation (7-4) could then be estimated using household income, price (π_j), distance from workplace, and other household characteristics as the independent variables.[8] Two functional forms—log and linear specifications—were estimated. Income was clearly the most important explanatory variable. The housing price index was significant only in two of the five samples (Bogotá owner 1978 and Bogotá renter 1972). Distance was also found to be generally significant and negative in sign, as expected. Age of household head and family size were usually significant, whereas sex of household head was not, although it was negative in sign. Although the price coefficients were not in general found to be significant, it was important to conduct the elaborate exercise constructing the price indexes because the unbiased estimation of other variable coefficients requires proper price normalization. In addition, the omission of price variables could have led to biases in other coefficients as a result of the omitted variable problem.

The characteristics are calculated at the mean value of each variable in the linear equations except for income. The estimated linear elasticities for Bogotá are shown for approximately the first, second, and third quartiles of each sample's income distribution (see table 7-15). In each case, the sample mean and seventy-fifth percentile of the income distribution are essentially identical. All income elasticities are clearly positive, significant, and less than one, including those for Cali (not reported here). At the sample mean they lie in a narrow range between 0.6 and 0.8. The elasticities seem to increase with increases in income. At low income levels, income elasticities are relatively inelastic. The price elasticities vary more in magnitude but are always negative and less than 1 in absolute magnitude; they become quite small at high income levels. The distance elasticities are usually small and negative. Family size elasticities (not reported here) showed an interesting pattern, being negative for owners and usually positive for renters. Renters apparently vary their house size according to family size. Owners had

much larger houses on average and do not seem to vary their house size
with increases in family size. As might be expected, the age of household head had a consistently positive demand elasticity. When the term
(age of household head)^2 was used in the linear equations, housing
demand seemed at its peak when the household head was between the
ages of fifty and fifty-seven.

How do these results compare with information from other countries? Most income elasticities are between 0.2 and 0.8, with most clustered between 0.5 and 0.8 and some near unity (see table 7-16).[9] In
general, renter elasticities appear to be lower than those for owners.
The median renter elasticity is about 0.45, whereas for owners it is about
0.65. Price elasticities are generally found to be quite low and negative—usually lower in absolute value than income elasticities. However,
comparisons are difficult to make across studies because of different
specification and estimation methodologies. Malpezzi and Mayo (1987)
attempted to solve this problem by estimating a consistent equation for
a large number of different data sets for sixteen cities in eight countries.
These results confirmed the general findings described here. In addition, Malpezzi and Mayo observed that rent-to-income ratios decline systematically within cities (as would be expected from income elasticities
less than unity) *but increase with average income across cities.* They also con-

**Table 7-15. Housing Demand Equations: Estimated Elasticities
for Bogotá**

Percentiles	Renters, 1972		Renters, 1978		Owners, 1978	
	Linear	Log-log	Linear	Log-log	Linear	Log-log
Income						
All income percentiles		0.77		0.72		0.78
25th percentile	0.32		0.55		0.33	
50th percentile	0.45		0.71		0.47	
75th percentile[a]	0.59		0.80		0.60	
Price						
All income percentiles		−0.70		−0.28		−0.44
25th percentile	−0.91		−0.17		−0.31	
50th percentile	−0.75		−0.11		−0.24	
75th percentile[a]	−0.55		−0.08		−0.19	
Distance						
All income percentiles		−0.06		−0.06		−0.02
25th percentile	−0.05		−0.23		−0.02	
50th percentile	−0.04		−0.15		−0.01	
75th percentile[a]	−0.04		−0.10		0.01	

a. Corresponds to sample mean.
Source: Ingram (1984), exhibits 16 and 17.

Table 7-16. Ranges of Housing Demand Elasticities from Various Countries
(based on observations of households)

	Elasticity with respect to				
Country	Current income	Price	Family size	Age of household head	Sex of household head (1 = Male)
Renters					
Colombia	0.2 to 0.8	−0.1 to −0.7	−0.1 to 0.4	0.1 to 0.6	−0.01 to −0.2
United States	0.1 to 0.4	−0.2 to −0.7	Uncertain	Uncertain	Consistently negative
Republic of Korea	0.12	−0.06 to 0.03	0.15 to 0.25	—	—
Egypt	0.25 to 0.5	—	—	—	—
Ghana	0.33	—	—	—	—
El Salvador	0.25 to 0.45	—	—	—	—
India	0.6	—	—	—	—
Philippines	0.6 to 0.9	—	—	—	—
Owners					
Colombia	0.6 to 0.8	−0.15 to −0.40	−0.2 to −0.35	0.1 to 0.4	−00.2 to −0.1
United States	0.2 to 0.5	−0.5 to −0.6	Uncertain	Uncertain	Negative
Egypt	0.2 to 0.4	—	—	—	—
Republic of Korea	0.21	−0.05 to 0.07	−0.02 to 0.15	—	—
El Salvador	0.45 to 1.0	—	—	—	—
India	0.4	—	—	—	—
Philippines	0.6 to 1.0	—	—	—	—

— Not available.
Source: Colombia from Ingram (1984), exhibit 18; United States from Mayo (1981); Korea from Follain, Lim, and Renaud (1980); all others from Malpezzi and Mayo (1987).

firmed that rent-to-income ratios are consistently higher for owners than for renters.

The curious finding across cities was reflected in another finding: permanent income elasticities of demand for housing are greater than current income elasticities. In the short term, housing consumption does not adjust as fast as increases in income levels, but it catches up in the long term. It is also possible that housing and land prices increase along with economic development, thereby leading to higher housing expenditures as proportions of income. Thus, cross-country data tend to show higher proportions of housing expenditure with increases in per capita income. It is also interesting to note that the U.S. results show relatively inelastic estimates that are generally lower than for developing countries. This suggests that the tendency of housing expenditures to be a greater proportion of income might taper off at the highest income levels and be the highest for the middle-income countries. This would be consistent with the fast-increasing housing and property prices observed at middle-income levels during the period of rapid urbanization.

It is too time-consuming to estimate housing demand parameters from disaggregated data, especially when these estimates are needed for policy purposes. The short-cut is usually to take available information from aggregate statistics based on rent and income data for groups of households. Many such estimations result in income elasticities of housing demand of greater than 1, a finding that is now generally agreed to be incorrect. This result is usually the consequence of incorrect aggregation when the stratification procedure used is based on stratification of the *dependent variable*, that is, on categories of housing expenditures itself. The correct aggregation procedure is to stratify by the independent variable—that is, on income categories (see Ingram 1984 for details and simulations).

In summary, we have found that housing demand estimations have to be made with some care in order to separate price and demand effects. Although housing quantity and prices are intrinsically difficult to measure, a careful theoretical appreciation of the nature of the housing market in its spatial setting suggests a computationally tractable procedure for analyzing housing demand. The key theoretical construct is the theory of residence location based on the relation of residence to location of workplace. Our principal findings have been that income elasticity of demand for housing is typically less than 1; that the elasticity is likely to vary with income level, being lower for low-income household; that there are systematic differences in the behavior of owners and renters, with the requirements and characteristics of renters being different; that owners typically spend more on housing; and that other household demographic characteristics also matter. The important policy conclusion is that the heterogeneity in housing demand requires a heterogeneous response. The affordability that may be expected by observing renter behavior is likely to seriously understate the ability of households to pay for housing. It is also a mistake to assume that all households can devote a similar proportion of their income to housing. Finally, housing policy should also ensure provisions for adequate supply of rental housing: ownership housing is not always a substitute for rental housing. Most housing programs in developing countries are designed to promote ownership housing, thus neglecting the needs of renters.

Pirata Developments and Housing Demand: Some Lessons for Housing Programs and Policies

The most remarkable finding of this study was that the supply of housing in Bogotá and Cali grew faster than the population did during the high growth period of the 1960s and early 1970s. The average number of persons per dwelling unit fell from 8 in 1964 to 7 in 1978. Because of a significant drop in household size from 6.2 members in 1964 to 4.9 in 1978, however, the number of households per dwelling unit remained almost constant at between 1.3 and 1.4. At the same time, the access to basic infrastructure improved during the 1960s and 1970s. The populations of Bogotá and Cali clearly had better shelter in 1978 than in the early 1960s or before.

Although the government in Colombia has exhibited deep concern for housing throughout the period under study, the government had little to do with the successful expansion of housing supply. The formal housing credit and construction agencies encountered great difficulty in effectively channeling their efforts toward the poor. If the poor were relatively well housed in urban Colombia by the beginning of the 1980s, it was mostly due to their own efforts and ingenuity. The evidence, however, is that different government authorities acquiesced in providing incremental infrastructure. In this sense the infrastructure development in Bogotá was clearly demand-determined. Infrastructure generally followed development rather than the other way around. The regularization of *pirata* developments was actively pursued by the authorities, thus also contributing to the development of reasonable housing stock and urban public services.

The estimated income elasticity of housing demand was less than unity, varying largely between 0.6 and 0.8 at the sample mean. In fact, the income elasticity increased with rising income, and low-income households effectively exhibited low-income elasticities. The result is that low-income households have to devote a large proportion of their income to housing; as expected, housing behaved as a basic necessity. The average proportion of income spent on housing was 16 percent in

Cali and 22 percent in Bogotá, with some of the poorer households spending as much as 50 percent of their income on housing. These results are quite consistent with those found in other developing countries. One interesting finding from cross-country information is that permanent income elasticities of housing demand are higher than current income elasticities. Although almost all income elasticities are less than 1, rent-to-income ratios increase with income across cities as average income increases. This is one reason that earlier estimates of housing demand elasticities, which are often based on averaged data across cities or countries, were usually found to be greater than 1.

A number of important policy implications arise from these findings. Housing programs that are based on the ability to pay have to be designed very carefully, given the variation of income elasticity of demand with income within a city or country and the variation of average income across cities. The proportion of income devoted to housing would seem to depend on the place of a household in the prevailing internal income distribution, as well as on the absolute average level of income. The latter may also be a result of prices for housing material and land that increase along with average incomes. It is common practice to make affordability calculations based on a fixed rent-to-income ratio. The result is that housing programs ostensibly targeted at specific low-income groups prove unsuccessful, not because implementation is poor (as is usually supposed) but because of design errors. Heterogeneity in the demand for housing must be respected in designing housing programs.

Most housing programs in developing countries are aimed at ownership housing. One of the important findings of our study is that even in a middle-income country like Colombia, the poorest third of urban households have difficulty in achieving effective access to the ownership market. Indeed, the formal legal organized housing market essentially catered to the top third of households, the extralegal market enabled the middle third to buy homes, and the bottom third were basically in the rental market. Apart from problems caused by the low income level, it was household instability—in terms of income itself, job location, and household formation—that made poorer households find shelter in the rental market. As some of these households graduated up, they entered the ownership market. There, low-income renters generally rented from the middle- or lower-middle-income owner-occupants, thereby also helping them finance their housing investments in an interesting symbiotic relationship. It is important for housing policymakers to recognize the predominant preference of the poor to rent (rather than own), so that this section of the housing market can be developed more effectively.

The chief lesson obtained from the extralegal developments of Bogotá is that unbundling the housing package can substantially expand lower-income groups' access to higher levels of shelter satisfaction. This unbundling is done both by separating different elements of a housing package at a given time and by separating them over a period of time. Unbundling is known more popularly as incremental housing development. Given that shelter is usually seen as a package of infrastructure services, house structure, and land, the entry costs of acquiring this package often become prohibitive, effectively excluding all but the top few income deciles in a developing country. In a situation of rapid urban growth, like that experienced in Bogotá, households found shelter by means of such innovative approaches. They were willing to develop the housing package incrementally: to buy undeveloped land with minimal infrastructure, build a core house to begin with, and then achieve access to improved infrastructure while expanding the house over time. This was made possible from the supply side by the intervention of small, independent developers who rapidly jumped in to fill this large demand niche. The government seemed to recognize the effectiveness of this process and responded by incrementally improving public services and eventually legalizing the developments.

Unfortunately, few governments recognize the real potential of this process. The standard model for delivery of housing to the poor consists of public sector construction of fully finished units, or sites and services, along with a full complement of infrastructure. Households are then assisted by the provision of subsidized loans. The cost of formally built housing units is seldom low enough for most households to afford, with the result that governments invest large resources in directing subsidies to the better-off, while the real target group remains unaffected. Despite the relatively good, although seemingly chaotic, results achieved in Bogotá in the 1960s and 1970s, the government of Colombia has reverted to the previously abandoned ICT-led housing construction model, with apparently predictable results (see World Bank 1990). As this study documents, much better results would be achieved if institutions affecting housing supply remain decentralized and demand-determined.

During rapid urban growth, governments seldom have the resources to lead with timely infrastructure development in urban areas. In any case, housing development patterns must be guided by people's preferences. What may work in Bogotá may not work elsewhere. But we do learn that people's requirements and preferences in seeking shelter are sufficiently heterogeneous so that the government must facilitate a flexible supply response to match their demands. Public policy must be able to harness households' own energy in providing shelter for themselves, yet public services must be provided to the households. The finding that *pirata* developers gained returns that were approximately comparable to those from alternative investments in the economy should promote the idea that land and housing development is like any other economic activity. Hence, like other activities, it should be promoted, particularly because substantial infrastructure investment is then made in a relatively cost-effective way.

Notes

This chapter draws on work reported in Carroll (1980), Hamer (1981, 1985), Ingram (1984), Paredes (1984), Stevenson (1984), Pineda (1981), and Ardila and Hamer (1979). Anna María SantAnna participated in the initial stages of the project. The first section of the chapter, which discusses the institutional setting of housing in Bogotá, incorporates research reported in Stevenson (1984) and Paredes (1984). The second section, on Bogotá's unregulated housing market, is based on Carroll (1980), Paredes (1984), Hamer (1985), and Ardila and Hamer (1979).

1. *Cesantias* are severance pay funds that may be given as advances for house construction purposes. They are not technically allowed to be given for *pirata* developments, but this condition does not seem to have been enforced.

2. The Superintendencia Bancaria, which is otherwise concerned with regulating banking operations, was put in charge of regulating land sales controls in 1968.

3. These returns may be compared with effective annual rates of return available in Colombia toward the end of the 1970s:

Instrument	Percent
UPAC (index savings and loan) ordinary deposits	19.30
UPAC savings accounts	24.95
UPAC savings certificates	
Six months	26.14
One year	27.33
Term deposit certificates	
Three months	26.82
Six months	28.07
Savings accounts	19.00
Agroindustrial *Títulos* (bonds)	
Three months	27.50
Six months	28.00
Bonos Cafeteros (coffee bonds)	22.00
Títulos de Ahorro Cafetero (coffee savings bonds)	
at 65 percent for a two-year term	51.29
Certificates of exchange	35.60

These figures are from the June 1979 issue (no. 23) of *Estrategia Economica y Financiera*, page 10, cited in Carroll (1980).

4. See Hamer (1981) for details of model specifications. Here we report only the elasticities estimated.

5. For summaries of U.S. housing demand literature, see Quigley (1979) and Mayo (1981).

6. See Malpezzi and Mayo (1987) and Malpezzi, Mayo, and Gross (1985) for recent reviews.

7. See, for example, Follain and Jimenez (1985); Follain, Lim, and Renaud (1980); Mayo (1982); Jimenez and Keare (1984).

8. Other household characteristics include sex of household head; family size, (family size)^2, age of household head, and (age of household head)^2.

9. See Malpezzi and Mayo (1987) and Malpezzi, Mayo, and Gross (1985), for example, for reviews of other studies.

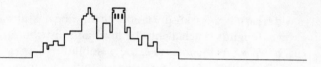

Chapter 8

Autos, Taxis, Buses, and Busetas: The Importance of Choice in Urban Transport

The spatial distribution of population, employment, and income determines transportation patterns in a city. Personal travel almost invariably begins and ends at home. The distribution of employment within a city tells us where people work, shop, and generally transact business. An urban area's growth and the development of its transport network are interdependent. Urban population growth accompanied by spatial growth stretches the transport network required to service the city. At the same time, the availability of an expanding transport network makes city expansion feasible. Thus, the growth of a city is both constrained by the transport network and facilitated by it.

Transportation technology changes over time. Radical changes in transportation technology can also fundamentally change the physical structure of cities. The introduction of streetcars in the latter part of the nineteenth century made it possible for cities to suburbanize. Later, changes in highway construction technology and the availability of trucking made it possible for industrial locations to decentralize. Before the advent of trucking, intracity goods transportation costs were much higher than intercity rail transportation costs. Hence, even heavy industry was typically located adjacent to railheads in large central cities, such as in Sheffield, England.

Technology use changes along with the technology itself. These changes are often linked to income changes. Higher incomes make possible widespread car ownership, for example. This phenomenon leads to the existence of spread-out suburbs; in the United States, for example, the introduction of almost universal automobile ownership is generally held responsible for the proliferation of post–World War II residential suburbs. Cities in developing countries are fortunate in that a wide variety of transportation technology is already available; this choice depends crucially on the level and distribution of income in the city, however. As incomes rise, the possibilities increase, and the introduction of new technologies can have a significant impact on city structure.

Although there are many similarities between the decentralization patterns observed in cities in rich countries and those in developing countries, there are also important differences, and these differences are determinants of people's transportation behavior. In cities in rich countries, generally, the rich live on the periphery and the poor nearer in or within the central city. The resulting transportation pattern includes heavy automobile use. This decentralization also gives rise to vocal demand for rapid modes of public transport such as subways or efficient commuter railways. In developing countries, because of the absence of such rapid transport modes, the lack of highway infrastructure, and the durability of old building structures, the rich continue to live relatively near the central city, and the poor are often found at the periphery. This raises the costs of providing transportation, and the public transport system has to be widespread because the poor do not have access to private transport modes.

Another difference observed in cities in developing countries is that employment is relatively more concentrated in the central city. This makes it feasible to operate high-occupancy vehicles, such as large buses, on radial routes exhibiting high-passenger density. In cities in developed countries, employment often has become so decentralized and auto ownership so high that it is no longer possible to operate high-occupancy transport modes in an economically efficient manner. As a result, public transport systems in developed countries are typically government-owned and run on continual subsidies. Because the structure of cities in developing countries makes it feasible to operate public transport cost-effectively, it is quite common for these cities to have privately run, unsubsidized public transport networks.

It is therefore important to understand the causes, consequences, and patterns of urban decentralization. In general, if residences disperse faster than employment, an increase may be expected in average trip distances and trip times. A continued high concentration of employment encourages a public transport system that is based on high-occupancy public vehicles. An alternative that has emerged in cities in developing countries in the past two to three decades is the use of vans or small buses, known as microbuses or minibuses. Because they are smaller vehicles, they can maintain high occupancy with smaller loads. Because of the low wages paid in developing countries, it is more economical to operate these vehicles there than it is in developed nations. In the United States, for example, the bus drivers' wage costs account for over half the total operating costs whereas, in cities in developing countries, buses are usually operated by two people—the driver and the conductor. On smaller buses, like the *busetas* in Bogotá, the driver can collect the fare. This makes it feasible to run the smaller buses at low fares—not much higher than the fare on a standard full-size bus. These smaller buses bring greater flexibility to the transport system. Indeed, even with the decentralization of employment and residences, mini- and microbuses can be used to run effective public transport systems. This has been the public transport response in Bogotá.

The decentralization of employment in many cities in developed countries has meant the actual loss of jobs from central cities; radial transport networks then become inefficient and the low density of jobs in peripheral areas makes it difficult to operate public transport networks. In cities in developing countries, there are similar declines in the employment density gradients (see chapter 6), but that is because of an increase in jobs in all areas of the city rather than a decline in the central city. Hence, employment density in central Bogotá has remained high, keeping the radial transport system relatively efficient. To the extent that employment remains more densely concentrated in the center than do residences, some of the more distant residence locations can be served efficiently by minibuses.

Much of this chapter focuses on understanding the importance of income in determining transportation patterns and choices. The wealthy have more leisure time and hence indulge in more discretionary travel, a tendency that is reinforced by auto ownership. City structure itself is related to income distribution within the city. As discussed in chapter 6, higher-income residential areas in the city also have more jobs. Higher incomes generate greater demand and hence more jobs. There is then a surplus of jobs in these areas and a large degree of in-commuting. Poor residential areas have significant job deficits. Overall, the poor make long commutes to their jobs. This feature of city structure adds to the disadvantage suffered by poor workers because of adverse residence locations. In Bogotá this is exacerbated by a regular pattern of segregation of residence by income (see chapters 4 and 5). The poor live in the south of the city and the rich predominantly in the north; the poor also tend to live in the outer rings. However, a key finding of this study is that the relatively high service levels provided by Bogotá's public transport network and the prevalence of flat bus fares substantially mitigate the spatial disadvantage suffered by the poor in that city.

Cities in developing countries tend to have larger households than cities in developed countries, and many of these are multiple-worker households. Moreover, as primary and secondary education become universal, the household's decision about where to live becomes more complex. The existence of the informal sector also complicates matters. With many people dependent on irregular employment with a variety of potential job locations, there is a greater tendency to locate in densely populated areas that are likely to have more employment prospects.

The participation of the private sector in the provision of an urban transport system has become quite common in many cities in developing countries. There is often a vacuum in the range of transportation services between the privately owned automobile or two-wheeler (mopeds, scooters, motorcycles) and the publicly provided full-size bus in cities where the minibus has not yet come into widespread use. Cities with a wide range of public transportation services include Istanbul, where the various transportation modes include the *dolmus* (shared taxi), the minibus (8 to 10 seats), the midibus (13 to 15 seats), and the standard large bus; Hong Kong, which has large buses, double-decker buses, minibuses (14 seats), a large taxi fleet, and the metro; Manila, which also has a very large number of "jeepneys" (14 seats) supplementing the full-size buses and a limited light rail system; and Buenos Aires, which, although served by an extensive underground metro system, also has a large fleet of *colectivos* (21-seat minibuses) that are estimated to carry about half the metropolitan-area passengers (Walters 1979; Feibel and Walters 1980).

The introduction of intermediate-size buses makes it possible to serve the varying needs of a large passenger population efficiently. Large-capacity vehicles can operate efficiently only in densely traveled trunk corridors. As cities grow and get more spread out, these vehicles are less able to satisfy the transportation needs of people whose origins and destinations fall between the corridors. Moreover, large-capacity vehicles are better suited to serving radial routes in cities with dominating city centers. As a city expands and both residence and employment locations decentralize, there is an increasing demand for circumferential trips. These routes are unlikely to be densely traveled routes: large-capacity vehicles can then provide only infrequent service. The result is a greater tendency for travelers to opt for private modes in order to avoid the inconvenience and lengthy trip times implied by infrequent services. Although the fares on intermediate-size vehicles are usually higher than those on full-size buses, they are low enough to cater to much of the population. These intermediate-size vehicles provide a low-cost, effective alternative to private modes of transportation: because they are smaller and cheaper, many more people can invest in operating them. A 15-seat minibus can operate three times as often as a 45-seat bus in a corridor of similar transportation density. In Bogotá, for example, the break-even point in terms of load factor was much lower for the *busetas* than for the full-size buses. More frequent service on less dense routes was thus possible, waiting times were reduced, and convenience began to approach that of private vehicles.

All these issues of interdependence between city structure, level and spatial distribution of income, labor market and household characteristics, and transport demand and supply have been found to be important in Bogotá.

The Supply of Transportation Services in Bogotá

The residents of Bogotá and Cali have had a rich supply of transportation services from which to choose. These services include full-size buses (68 passengers), trolley buses (104 passengers), *busetas* (32 passengers), microbuses (15 passengers), and regular and collective taxis (*colectivos*). The full-size buses and *busetas* operate on a flat-fare basis on designated fixed routes but are free to stop to pick up passengers anywhere along the routes: there are no fixed bus stops. The taxis cruise along streets to pick up passengers. The *colectivos* operate on fixed routes, usually during the peak hours, also on a flat-fare basis. Walking and driving privately owned automobiles are two additional options. Motorcycles, scooters, and bicycles are very rarely used in Colombian cities.

Unlike most cities in developed countries, where public transportation is typically government-owned and -subsidized, almost all of the public transportation in Colombian cities is privately owned and provided, although it, too, is subsidized by the government to an extent. Similar systems exist in other Latin American countries, including Argentina, Brazil, and Chile. The District of Bogotá does run a publicly owned bus company (Empresa Distrital de Transporte Urbano [EDTU]), but it accounts for only about 1 percent of the city's transport system. The government provides subsidies for running the full-size buses, which keeps the fares low, but the *busetas* are not subsidized.

Substantial growth took place in Bogotá's transportation services between 1972 and 1978 (see table 8-1). In 1980 the buses and *busetas* were operated by thirty-nine urban transport companies, of which twelve were cooperatives, twenty-five were limited liability companies (affiliated companies), and one was a publicly owned transportation company. Rights to route operation are awarded by the state to the companies, which then lease the rights to affiliated bus owners. Some companies operate their own buses. The managers of these affiliated companies wield considerable power in the transportation sector, but the system of cooperatives and affiliated companies allows the participation of many small owners in the public transport system.

Bogotá has had a high level of public transportation services for some time. In 1980 the buses and *busetas* supplied 123 seats per 1,000 resi-

Table 8-1. Transportation in Bogotá

Type of service	Vehicles	Approximate number of vehicles		Passenger capacity	Fare structure		Ownership
		1972	1978		1978	1980	
Taxi	European and American cars	7,600	13,530	4 and 5 seated		$12 flag $10 per km $25 more from 8 P.M. to 5 A.M. and Sundays	The drivers own approximately 70 percent
Colectivo	European and American cars	370	606	4 and 5 seated		$25 8 A.M. to 5 P.M.	Same as above
Microbus	Small buses w/light truck chassis	996	252	15 seated	$3.00 $3.50	$6 $6.50 nights and Sundays	39 private companies
Buseta	Small buses w/intermediate truck chassis	615	3,289	24 seated 8 standing	$4.00 $4.50	$7.50 $8.00 Sundays	Same as above
Bus	Buses w/school-type body & large truck chassis	2,782	6,289	38 seated 30 standing	$1.50	$3.00 $3.50 nights $4.00 Sundays	Same as above
Bus (diesel)		194	35	38 seated 30 standing	$1.50	$3.00 $3.50 nights $4.00 Sundays	Urban transport district company
Trolley bus	Russian and some American buses	118	37	48 seated 56 standing	$1.50	Same as above	Same as above

Source: Pachon (1981b).

190

dents, and taxis and *colectivos* added another 12 seats per 1,000 residents. This compares very favorably with Hong Kong, a large city generally regarded as being well provided by public transportation services, which had 108 seats per 1,000 supplied by buses and public light buses (minibuses), about 37 by rail services, and an additional 14 by taxis (Hong Kong Government Transport Department 1983). In contrast, the net transportation supply in Lagos was only about 39 per 1,000 residents—15 supplied by buses, 12 by minibuses, 6 by taxis, and another 6 by other informal modes (Transpoconsult 1976; Wilbur Smith and Associates 1979). The supply in Cali was also almost 100 seats per 1,000 residents in 1980.

The level of automobile ownership in Colombia has been relatively low. Automobiles show the highest annual growth rate, at about 8 percent, followed by trucks at 7 percent, and buses at 5.5 percent (see table 8-2). Bogotá accounts for a large proportion of vehicles in the country—about 25 percent (see table 8-3). In 1978, however, there were only about 45 automobiles per 1,000 residents in Bogotá and 32 per 1,000 in Cali—as compared with 78 per 1,000 in Mexico City, 74 per 1,000 in Buenos Aires, and 91 per 1,000 in Caracas (Urrutia 1981).

The Regulation of Supply: Control, Subsidies, and Incentives

This largely private provision of public transportation in Bogotá is governed by a relatively complex system of government regulation and subsidies. Government agencies set routes and fares for buses and *busetas* as well as for taxis and the *colectivos*; subsidies are provided to bus companies for their bus operations; subsidized credit is made available for the purchase of both buses and *busetas*; and the number of licenses granted for bus and *buseta* operation is kept under control. The government

Table 8-2. Vehicle Stock in Colombia, 1970–80

Year	Cars	Buses	Trucks	Total
1970	284,252	28,875	47,318	360,445
1971	303,712	30,065	49,368	382,145
1972	324,712	31,315	51,548	407,575
1973	347,378	32,625	53,843	433,846
1974	374,778	33,782	57,168	465,728
1975	397,641	35,273	60,447	493,361
1976	423,655	37,422	63,894	524,971
1977	463,817	39,810	69,437	573,064
1978	511,822	42,288	79,985	634,095
1979	553,955	46,693	88,316	688,964
1980	601,463	50,167	94,888	746,518

Source: Pachon (1981a).

Table 8-3. Vehicle Stock in Bogotá, Cali, and all of Colombia, December 1977

Vehicle	Bogotá		Cali		Remainder of Colombia		Total	
	Number	Percent	Number	Percent	Number	Percent	Number	Percent
Cars								
Private	95,451	24.69	30,553	7.90	260,543	67.40	386,547	100.00
Public	13,147	15.70	3,580	4.27	67,010	80.02	83,737	100.00
Total[a]	114,057	23.58	35,231	7.28	334,383	69.13	483,671	100.00
Buses								
Private	1,282	22.65	283	5.00	4,094	72.35	5,659	100.00
Public	10,538	25.83	2,800	6.86	27,458	67.30	40,796	100.00
Total[a]	12,402	25.94	3,122	6.53	32,284	67.53	47,808	100.00
Trucks								
Private	15,406	31.43	2,837	5.79	30,770	62.78	49,013	100.00
Public	5,653	10.03	2,310	4.10	48,374	85.87	56,337	100.00
Total[a]	22,297	20.26	5,609	5.10	82,160	74.65	110,066	100.00
Total								
Private	112,139	25.42	33,673	7.63	295,407	66.95	441,219	100.00
Public	29,338	16.22	8,690	4.80	142,842	78.97	180,870	100.00
Total[a]	148,756	23.19	43,962	6.85	448,827	69.96	641,545	100.00

a. Includes vehicles registered for official use as well as publicly and privately owned vehicles.
Source: Pachon (1981a).

maintains a mild policy of restrictive entry—a license known as "nota opción" is needed before a vehicle enters public service. Although the administration of these regulations and subsidies could be made more efficient, the system has provided a high level of transportation services at relatively low social and private cost. Bus subsidies made possible fares that are below the average costs of the suppliers, thus providing the poor with better access to urban transport. Our analysis shows that the whole regulatory and subsidy system performs in favor of the poor.

The responsibility for the overall regulation and policy for an urban transport system rests with the Instituto Nacional de Transporte (INTRA). INTRA typically delegates route setting and enforcement of transportation legislation to the respective mayor's offices. In Bogotá the relevant local authority under the mayor's direction is the Departamento Administrativo de Transporte y Tránsito (DATT). DATT is supposed to review transportation demand constantly and assign new routes or extend existing ones. It does this by inviting tenders for bidding the number of vehicles and frequency of operation. Demand is often identified through pressure from community action boards (Juntas de Acción Comunal). This means that the identification of transportation needs and the subsequent opening of routes are subject to political pressure, and the process is often strongly criticized on this account. Actual route assignment is done on the recommendations of DATT by a committee consisting of the mayor, representatives of INTRA, the Ministry of Public Works and Transportation (Ministerio de Obras Publicas y Transporte), DATT, and the Departamento Administrativo de Planeación Distrital (DAPD) (Cifuentes 1984). The route is generally granted if the bidding company can convince the authorities that there is enough demand and that they would not be crowding out existing operators. Almost all the bus companies are affiliated with one of the two national urban transport organizations—National Corporation of Urban Buses (Corporación Nacional de Buses Urbanos, CORPOBUSES) and the Colombian Federation of Urban Transportation (Federación Colombiano de Transporte Urbano, FECOLTRANS)—which are recognized by the government as representing urban transport interests. Once a company receives the rights to a route, that route is assigned to the individual affiliated operators on a leasing fee basis.

Despite complaints about the politicization of the routing process, the system operates well in matching transportation supply with perceived and expressed demand from consumers. It may be judged superior to most systems, which are centrally run and where routes are assigned in a more technical, information-intensive manner: "It has . . . been established that the existing route assignment system in Colombia produces a network with wide coverage that has adapted to changes in trip demand patterns" (Pachon 1987, p. 146). There are, however, some negative results, such as congestion on some desirable routes, particularly in the center of the city.

Drivers' remuneration is based on the number of passengers transported. This leads to some chaos on the streets as drivers of competing buses rush to get passengers. Drivers get only about 10 to 15 percent of fare box revenues (Avendano and d'Amico 1981)—about 12 percent in 1980—compared with the 83 percent that bus drivers in American cities average (APTA 1980). This emphasizes how different the economics of bus operations are in low-wage countries and why it becomes efficient to operate smaller buses in such cities.

The cost of operating this system is quite low (Urrutia 1981; Interconsulta Ltda 1970). The private operator's cost was about Col$352 per passenger in 1980, and per-kilometer operating cost was about Col$21. The state-owned company, Empresa Distrital de Transporte Urbano (EDTU) had much higher costs, mainly because of higher wage costs per worker as well as the larger number of workers employed per operating bus. Drivers for private companies are relatively poorly paid and work long hours—the average driver worked about twelve hours a day, about half worked seven days a week, and most of the rest worked six days a week. Their wages were just over minimum-wage levels. In 1980 bus drivers earned an average of Col$6,400 per month, whereas *buseta* drivers earned about Col$8,300 per month. They generally have no sick pay, health insurance, or unemployment benefits. Their earnings are roughly what might be expected for their level of education and skills in the Bogotá labor market. When bus services are run directly by government-owned agencies, wages of drivers and other workers generally rise as a result of union and other pressures, leading to higher transportation costs. The relatively low cost of the transport system in Bogotá is in large part a benefit of its privately owned, government-regulated, decentralized status.

The rationale for the urban transport policies maintained by the government is therefore clear. The government has wanted to maintain low public transportation prices so that all city dwellers have reasonable access to employment and education opportunities.

In order to maintain low fare levels, all buses are given flat-rate, per-vehicle monthly subsidies that roughly cover the fixed costs and return to capital. New vehicles receive much larger subsidies than old vehicles in order to encourage companies to purchase newer vehicles with lower operating costs (see table 8-4). The Financial Transportation Corporation (Corporación Financiera de Transporte, CFT) provides subsidized credit for the purchase of new buses; this amounts to nearly one-fifth of the vehicle's value. Overall, the subsidy structure encouraged vehicle replacement and reduced the average age of the fleet. Analysis also showed that it benefited the poor more than others.

Table 8-4. Bus Subsidies in Colombian Cities, 1977 and 1978
(Colombian pesos in current prices)

Year and quarter	1959 and earlier	1960–64	1965–69	1970–73	1974 and later
			Model year of vehicle		
1977					
January–March	9,383	11,133	12,633	13,633	21,133
April–June	9,620	11,370	12,870	13,870	21,370
July–September	10,640	12,390	13,890	14,890	22,390
October–December	10,610	12,360	13,860	14,860	22,360
1978					
January–March	11,630	13,380	14,880	15,880	23,380
April–June	11,600	13,350	14,850	15,850	23,350
July–September	12,630	14,370	15,870	16,870	24,370
October–December	12,590	14,340	15,840	16,840	24,340

Source: Cifuentes (1984).

The fare structure in 1978–80 has already been outlined (see table 8-1). To put the data in perspective, it should be noted that bus travel costs only about 3.8 cents per trip (1978 U.S. dollars), or an average of 0.6 cents per passenger kilometer (average bus trips were 6.5 kilometers per traveler). *Busetas* cost about 10.3 cents per trip. At these rates, even a low-income household in one of the poorer peripheral parts of Bogotá would spend less than 2 or 3 percent of its monthly earnings on work trips. In 1980 revenues from bus fares covered the variable costs of bus operation (about two-thirds of total costs), and subsidies covered the fixed costs and return on capital. Through this system, passengers get the benefit of low transportation costs while bus owners get healthy returns on their capital. In the case of *busetas*, the fare (Col\$7.50 per trip) more than covered total operational costs along with a healthy return on capital, so no subsidies were needed. It is not surprising that the *buseta* fleet grew much faster than the bus fleet in the 1970s. One reason for the existence of these profits is the government's mild policy of restrictive entry.

The subsidy levels are continually varied to account for increasing costs. The authorities maintain an index of input costs to reflect changing transportation costs. The changes in this index help to inform the authorities and bus owners when the fares and subsidies have to be adjusted.

Is there an adequate rationale for giving differential subsidies by age? It is difficult to analyze this issue because many variables enter the actual effective costs of bus operation. Some studies have found no age-related statistical differences in operating costs. These studies did not adjust adequately for the differences in operation between buses of different

Table 8-5. Adjusted Costs, Adjusted Income, and Capital Return for Buses, October 1980
(Colombian pesos per month)

Model	Age (years)	Estimated variable cost[a]	Adjusted fixed cost[b]	Total costs	Estimated income[c]	Subsidies	Capital return
1959	21	55.8	3.7	50.5	47.1	24.9	12.4
1960	20	56.8	3.9	60.7	48.2	25.8	13.3
1961	19	57.9	4.0	61.8	49.2	25.8	13.2
1962	18	58.9	4.1	63.0	50.3	25.8	13.1
1963	17	60.0	4.2	64.2	51.4	25.8	13.0
1964	16	61.1	4.3	65.4	52.5	25.8	13.0
1965	15	62.2	4.4	66.0	53.7	26.7	13.8
1966	14	63.3	4.6	67.9	54.9	26.7	13.7
1967	13	64.5	4.7	69.1	56.0	26.7	13.6
1968	12	65.6	4.8	70.5	57.3	26.7	13.5
1969	11	66.8	4.9	71.8	58.5	26.7	13.4
1970	10	68.1	5.1	73.1	59.8	30.4	17.1
1971	9	69.3	5.2	74.5	61.1	30.4	17.0
1972	8	70.6	5.4	75.9	62.5	30.4	17.0
1973	7	71.9	5.5	77.4	63.8	30.4	16.9
1974	6	73.2	5.7	78.8	65.2	42.8	29.2
1975	5	74.5	5.8	80.3	66.7	42.8	29.1
1976	4	75.9	6.0	81.9	68.1	42.8	29.1
1977	3	77.2	6.2	83.4	69.6	42.8	29.0
1978	2	78.6	6.3	85.0	71.1	42.8	29.0
1979	1	80.1	6.5	86.6	72.7	42.8	28.9
1980	0	81.5	6.7	88.2	74.3	42.8	28.6

Note: In notes a, b, and c above, numbers in parentheses are *t*-statistics.

a. ln (variable costs) = 11.31 − 0.018 (age)b. ln (fixed costs) = 8.81 + 0.028 (age)c. ln (income) = 11.22 − 0.022 (age)

(8.4)   (14.1)   (6.7)

$R^2 = 0.959$ $R^2 = 0.985$ $R^2 = 0.937$

Source: Pachon (1987).

vintages, however. For example, newer buses, being more trouble-free than older buses, are generally used more intensively than older ones. Bus operators may press the older buses into service only in the rush hours, for example. It was estimated that the per-kilometer cost of operation fell by only about 1 percent for every four years of age, but this result itself could be different if all buses were operated for the same distance covered: the operating cost of older buses would be likely to increase with distance traveled.

It may be more useful to examine the effect of age on costs, revenues, and return on capital (including subsidies) on a monthly basis. This would subsume the adjustments in operation made by the bus operators in response to the subsidies offered. Because the subsidy is given monthly, they are free to alter the intensity of bus use in order to maximize income (see table 8-5). Data on bus operating costs and revenues according to model year of buses were obtained from INTRA and FECOL-TRAN, and relationships were found between variable costs, fixed costs, revenues, and age of bus. It may be observed from table 8-5 and from the estimated equations cited that the revenue falls faster with age than do the variable costs. The gap between revenues and costs increased with age. Much of this is clearly related to differences in intensity of use—newer vehicles were used with greater intensity than older vehicles, and higher ratios were obtained with newer vehicles.

Profitability rates must be calibrated with respect to capital prices, however. In order to investigate the comparative profitability of buses and *busetas* in relation to their age, price equations were estimated positing a simple exponential form of depreciation (Pachon 1987).[1] The equation for buses is:

$$\ln P_{1a} = 14.4 - 0.069a \quad R^2 = 0.77$$
$$(141.1) \quad (8.3)$$

and the equation for *busetas* is:

$$\ln P_{2a} = 14.1 - 0.069a \quad R^2 = 0.85$$
$$(141.1) \quad (8.6)$$

where P_{1a} is the price of a bus at age a, and P_{2a} is the price of a *buseta* at age a. (The numbers in parentheses are t-statistics.)

It is remarkable that both equations reveal consistent results of about 7 percent annual depreciation. This is lower than in the cost studies made by the bus companies and used for setting fares and subsidies. The higher depreciation rates actually used help produce higher real profitability rates for older buses.

The results from these equations show that, because of the level of subsidies given, older buses had higher profitability ratios, whereas the profitability profile of *busetas* was constant until the *busetas* were about ten years old, and then it declined somewhat. Because *busetas* did not receive subsidies, their results may be seen as the no-subsidy counterfactual case. Whereas some allowance may be made for errors in price estimation, the result indicates that bus subsidies could be more smoothly and sharply tapered with age. Adopting a more realistic rate of depreciation could help correct the subsidy profile. It is also possible that actual operating costs of older buses may have been underestimated. It is, for example, difficult to account appropriately for the costs arising from the amount of time owners spend on repeated repairs of older buses.

These results suggest ways in which transportation regulations (granting of routes, provision of subsidies) can be analyzed. The system of urban transport that exists in Colombia has been operating remarkably efficiently, benefiting suppliers and demanders alike. There are, however, several areas that could be refined with the help of this type of analysis. Administration of subsidies could be improved. Congestion in some routes could be removed by more careful route assignments or by raising the bid price for routes. Traffic regulation and establishment of bus stops would remove some unnecessary chaos on the streets.

The Impact of Government Regulation, Taxes, and Subsidies

An extensive evaluation of the redistributive impact of government taxes and subsidies in the transportation sector was conducted by Pachon (1981b). In addition to the bus subsidies described earlier, the Colombian government had, for a long time, kept fuel prices low and taxed private automobiles relatively heavily. The task of evaluation is to estimate the net redistributive impact of these subsidies and taxes on different income groups. By convention, a policy can be described as progressive if the fraction of income paid as taxes increases with income level or if the fraction of income received as subsidies decreases with income level. See table 8-6 for a summary of the various tax/subsidy interventions.

Private cars were subject to four taxes in Colombia. In 1980 the customs duty on imported cars was 150 percent, and on components for car assembly it was 10 to 15 percent; sales tax on private cars was 35 percent; a registration fee was collected at both national and state levels, at a rate of about 0.05 percent of capital value; and the value of cars was also assessed as part of the wealth tax. The information about the national registration fee and wealth tax was inadequate to be accounted for in this evaluation.

Table 8-6. Formal and Actual Government Intervention in the Transport Sector, Colombia, 1980

Formal intervention	Actual intervention
Registration fees for vehicles Col$0.40 and $0.50 per each $1,000 of vehicle's value	The same
Sales tax 35% of notionalized value	22% on capital cost
Customs duty 150% CIF value of imported cars; 10–20% CIF value imported components[a]	37% on capital cost; 5.64% on capital cost
Fuel tax 110% on refinery price; 12% sales tax	The same for private vehicles
Bus fares Subsidy for owners according to age of vehicle	Transferred to consumers for public transportation
Fuel subsidy Does not exist	Col$27.00 per gallon

Note: Capital cost is calculated as an annual implicit rental price of capital after accounting for depreciation; return is calculated as an original outlay in real terms.

a. Cost, insurance, and freight.

Source: Pachon (1981b).

A 12 percent sales tax was levied on the wholesale price of fuel, and 110 percent tax for the Highway Trust Fund (HTF), was levied on refinery prices. In 1980 the sales tax amounted to Col$2.48 per gallon and the HTF tax to Col$9.10 per gallon. These taxes were actually based on subsidized fuel prices. The government petroleum agency, ECOPETROL, sold gasoline at a price below opportunity cost: in May 1980 a gallon of fuel was bought at US$1 or Col$47 per gallon but sold by ECOPETROL at Col$20.12, implying a subsidy of about Col$27 per gallon. Taxes reduced this subsidy to Col$15.40 per gallon.

In analyzing the impact of these interventions on income distribution, a number of assumptions had to be made. The travel information gleaned from the 1978 World Bank–DANE Household Survey was used to assign the incidence of taxes and subsidies according to the trip information for each income group. Private cars were assumed to get 40 kilometers per gallon of fuel. Fuel consumption per trip by public transportation was assigned on the basis of average trip distance. Given the information on vehicle makes and age from the survey, it was possible to calculate the average price of cars by make in Bogotá in 1978 and then to find a weighted average for all makes. The incidence of local registration fees could then be assigned. Similarly, the incidence of sales taxes was calculated after accounting for the age distribution of cars and the increase in the vehicle's average price attributable to new vehicle taxes. A sales tax on new vehicles is also passed on to the value of old vehicles: because of high sales taxes, the value of old cars gets inflated and the incidence of sales tax on new vehicles is also passed on to used-car buyers. It was possible to estimate the impact of sales tax on car value by age and then to assign it according to ownership of vehicles by income groups. Differential effects had to be calculated for imported and domestic cars because of the difference in customs duty rates (see tables 8A-1, 8A-2, and 8A-3 in the appendix to this chapter).

The incidence of fuel taxes and subsidies was calculated by assuming an average consumption of fuel at the rate of 1 gallon per 40 kilometers and a distance driven of about 1,250 kilometers per month. The tax/subsidy incidence was estimated according to cars owned and average income by quintile group (see table 8A-4 in the appendix to this chapter). Similarly, the incidence of bus subsidies and of fuel taxes and subsidies on users of public transportation was also assigned by income group according to the pattern of modal choice and trip data collected in the Household Survey.

Vehicle taxes appear to have a V-shaped pattern of incidence, being regressive at low income levels and progressive at high income levels (see table 8-7). It is somewhat puzzling to observe high tax incidence at low-income levels. Two explanations are possible. First, the data used in this exercise were based on current monthly household incomes: the few automobile owners in low-income categories could have been so classified because of transitory low incomes during the period of the survey. As may be seen in tables 8A-1 through 8A-4 in the appendix to this chapter, there were only five to six cars per 100 households in the first two quintiles. With average incomes being very low, the average incidence still comes out high. Second, the calculations have been made

Table 8-7. Vehicle Taxation Incidence in Bogotá, 1978
(estimated tax paid as a percentage of family income)

Income quintiles	Sales tax	Customs duty	Registration fee	Total
1	1.22	1.09	0.14	2.45
2	0.61	0.54	0.07	1.22
3	0.53	0.47	0.06	1.06
4	0.71	0.63	0.08	1.42
5	1.01	0.89	0.12	2.02
City average	0.87	0.77	0.10	1.74

Note: Quintiles are in ascending order of household income.
Source: Tables 8A-1 through 8A-4 in the appendix to this chapter.

Table 8-8. Fuel Policy Incidence in Bogotá, 1980
(net subsidy as a percentage of family income)

Income quintiles	Car	Bus	Buseta	Total
1	0.79	1.17	0.25	2.21
2	0.39	0.87	0.23	1.49
3	0.34	0.65	0.23	1.22
4	0.46	0.35	0.18	0.99
5	0.65	0.06	0.07	0.78
City average	0.57	0.29	0.13	0.99

Note: Quintiles are in ascending order of household income.
Source: Tables 8A-1 through 8A-4 in the appendix to this chapter.

assuming that car ownership and usage are homogeneous over all car-owning households. It is quite likely that low-income car-owning households own, on average, older and cheaper cars and use them less. If this is the case, the methodology used would overstate the incidence of vehicle taxes on low-income groups.

The results from the incidence of net subsidies give an unequivocal progressive incidence (see table 8-8). This is a consequence of the net subsidy (through lower fuel prices) to buses and *busetas*. This somewhat counterintuitive result is a surprise because it has usually been argued that fuel subsidies are essentially regressive in nature. The result is a consequence of the heavy use of public transportation, which overwhelms the effect of fuel subsidies resulting from automobile use. The net result of the subsidies and taxes on Bogotá's transport system is clearly progressive, with the bus transportation subsidy dominating the overall effects of the system (see table 8-9).

These results have been presented in some detail in order to illustrate the possibilities of analyzing quantitatively the effects of government policies. These policies are often made in an ad hoc manner. It is often assumed that it is not possible to conduct such policy analyses. Our task was made feasible by the availability of a rich set of household level data collected especially for this purpose and supplemented by other data on stocks of vehicles available, operational details of public transport, and the like.

Travel Patterns in Bogotá

The design of an urban transport system requires an understanding of travel patterns as they exist in a city. There are various ways to look at travel patterns in a city. One is to look at the outcome of the variegated travel needs of city residents: this may be done by looking at travel flow

Table 8-9. Transport Tax and Subsidy Policy Incidence: Bogotá, 1978–80
(tax or net subsidy as a percentage of family income)

Income quintile	Public				Private			
	Transport subsidy	Bus	Buseta	Total	Vehicle taxation	Fuel	Net tax	Total
1	3.63	1.17	0.25	+5.05	−2.45	+0.79	−1.66	+3.39
2	2.71	0.87	0.28	+3.86	−1.22	+0.39	−0.83	+3.03
3	2.95	0.65	0.23	+3.83	−1.06	+0.34	−0.72	+3.11
4	1.09	0.35	0.18	+1.62	−1.42	+0.46	−0.96	+0.66
5	0.19	0.06	0.07	+0.32	−2.02	+0.65	−1.37	−1.05
City average	0.99	0.29	0.13	+1.41	−1.74	+0.57	−1.17	+0.24

Note: Quintiles are in ascending order of household income. Net subsidies are shown as positive and taxes as negative.
Source: Pachon (1981b).

between various areas, average speeds in different transportation corridors, travel time and distances traversed, and the varied patterns that emerge from travel for different purposes. Another way is to look at the requirements for travel at the household or individual level. Why do people travel within the city? What determines their frequency of travel and the speed and distance traveled? How important are variables like income, age, sex, worker status, and residence and work locations? For some purposes it may be adequate merely to observe the outcomes; for others, particularly long-term planning for urban transport, it is equally important to understand the whys and wherefores.

A standard way of describing travel patterns is to construct origin-destination matrixes based on some spatial disaggregation of the city. In the case of Bogotá, we continue to use our standardized zonal disaggregation by ring and sector. The trips undertaken can also be broken up according to their purpose—commuting between residence and workplace, commuting between residence and school, and trips not related to work or school. Among the latter, if the data are rich enough, it may also be possible to distinguish between necessary trips (such as daily food shopping) and discretionary trips. Once the residential and workplace location pattern is well understood, it is relatively easy to predict the nondiscretionary travel pattern in a city.

It is also necessary to describe the travel pattern according to mode of transportation used. An intensively used public transport system requires less road space than a transport network primarily based on private transportation. Household income levels emerge as prime determinants of transportation mode as well as of travel frequency. A particular concern in evaluating the travel pattern in Bogotá has been the relative accessibility of low-income workers to workplaces and other destinations. The highly income-segregated pattern of residence makes this an especially key issue.

Our main sources of data were the 1972 Phase II Survey and the 1978 World Bank–DANE Household Survey. Whereas the 1972 survey had exhaustive information on all trips, the 1978 survey had information on work trips only.[2] According to the 1972 survey, travel in Bogotá was predominantly nondiscretionary—40 percent of all trips were work trips, 36 percent were school trips, and only 24 percent were other. Of the last category, 18 percent were home-based and 6 percent non-home-based. Hence, nondiscretionary travel probably accounted for more than 80 percent of trips. Information from cities in other developing countries suggests that nondiscretionary travel may be expected to account for 60 to 80 percent of trips in most of these cities. In the United States, by contrast, only about 25 percent of trips in medium-size cities are characterized as work trips, as many as 55 percent may be home-based non-work trips, and almost 20 percent are characterized as non-home-based trips. There is clearly much more discretionary travel in rich countries, because of higher incomes, the flexibility provided by widespread auto ownership, and the spread-out nature of services and employment that makes multiple-destination trips necessary. An interesting finding for Bogotá is that, adjusted for income, automobile-owning households do not make more discretionary trips than similar households without autos.

Distance and Travel Time

The average distance traveled by adult workers was about 8.3 kilometers— 8.5 kilometers for workers without automobiles and 7.6 kilometers for automobile owners. Students' school trips were much shorter—5.3 kilometers on average, 5.1 kilometers for those from households without autos and 5.8 kilometers for those from auto-owning households. For adult nonworkers, the average trip was 7.6 kilometers—8.0 kilometers for those from households without autos and 6.5 kilometers for those from auto-owning households. An interesting fact is that auto-owning workers traveled shorter distances in contrast to patterns found in cities in rich countries. Richer households live closer to the central city and poorer households are disproportionately located at the city periphery. The average time spent in daily travel by workers and students alike was about 110 minutes for non-auto users and 83 minutes for people from auto-owning households. On this basis the speeds work out to 12 kilometers to 15 kilometers an hour. The substantially shorter distances for students are mostly because of the proximity of primary schools to local neighborhoods: many children walk to school, and, although the distance is much less than for workers, the time spent traveling is similar. Automobile travel was about 3 kilometers to 4 kilometers per hour faster than the public transportation.

One issue worth commenting on is Zahavi's theory of travel behavior: he posited that people have relatively fixed "travel-time budgets" independent of income. They choose their residential location partly on the basis of the transportation available (Zahavi 1979). Our data are clearly inconsistent with this conjecture: average time spent traveling per day falls as income rises (see table 8-10). There is much more to a household's behavior regarding its choice of location for residence and its travel pattern than the concept of a fixed "travel-time budget."

Because information was available for work trips made in both 1972 and 1978, a number of useful comparisons can be made. Average travel time increased for all income groups; the larger increases were among middle-income groups (see table 8-10). Travel time increased for both public transportation and automobiles. At the higher income levels, two conflicting trends are at work. Automobile ownership increased sub-

Table 8-10. Work Trip Travel Time by Income Level: Bogotá, 1972 and 1978, and Cali, 1978
(minutes per trip)

Monthly household income (1972 Col$)	Bogotá, 1972[a]	Bogotá, 1978[b]	Cali, 1978[b]
0–500	43.7	41.2	27.3
500–1,000	40.2	43.6	34.1
1,000–1,500	39.3	43.8	30.2
1,500–2,000	40.6	46.6	39.6
2,000–3,000	36.8	48.6	37.4
3,000–5,000	33.3	44.8	36.9
5,000–15,000	28.5	38.4	32.4
15,000–30,000	22.6	30.9	20.9
More than 30,000	24.4	27.6	—
Overall average	35.4	42.3	34.6

— Not available.
a. Calibrated travel times.
b. Reported travel times.
Source: 1972 Phase II Survey; 1978 World Bank–DANE Household Survey.

stantially between 1972 and 1978—this factor would tend to result in reduced travel times. Concurrently, there was an outward shift in residence location patterns. The net result seems to have been an increase in average time traveled, but the increase was much less than the increase in travel time for bus and *buseta* trips (see table 8-11). *Buseta* trips took longer mainly because of the expansion of *buseta* service: in 1972 *buseta* service was rare in peripheral poorer areas. The increased bus trip times are partly the result of increasing congestion in the city center and partly the result of the poor's decentralizing pattern of residence location. The distance data were unfortunately not comparable across the two surveys.

Table 8-11. Work Trip Travel Time by Transportation Mode: Bogotá, 1972 and 1978, and Cali, 1978

	Minutes per trip			Kilometers		
	Car	Bus	Buseta/ microbus	Car	Bus	Buseta/ microbus
Bogotá						
1972	23.5[a]	40.6[a]	33.5[a]	6.7[b]	8.0[b]	6.3[c]
1978	27.6[c]	54.8[c]	47.8[c]	5.0[d]	6.5[d]	6.0[d]
Cali						
1978	24.5[c]	44.7[c]	47.8[c]	3.3[d]	3.3[d]	4.4[d]

a. Calibrated travel time.
b. Reported trip distances, all trip purposes.
c. Reported travel time.
d. Airline distances, centroid to centroid.
Source: 1972 Phase II Survey; 1978 World Bank–DANE Household Survey.

Table 8-12. Ring of Residence and Ring of Employment: Bogotá, 1972 and 1978
(percent)

Residence ring	Employed in ring 1		Employed in ring 2		Employed in ring 3		Employed in ring 4		Employed in ring 5		Employed in ring 6		Total	
	1972	1978	1972	1978	1972	1978	1972	1978	1972	1978	1972	1978	1972	1978
1	66.0	71.9	8.5	16.1	6.6	5.5	10.8	4.6	8.1	1.9	0.0	0.0	100.0	100.0
2	27.1	18.2	50.9	59.6	9.0	8.9	6.7	7.4	5.9	5.2	0.4	0.7	100.0	100.0
3	30.3	12.8	9.5	15.2	43.3	52.1	9.5	10.0	6.1	8.7	1.4	1.2	100.0	100.0
4	25.6	14.7	9.9	15.3	13.6	12.8	39.2	45.1	10.3	11.3	1.3	0.8	100.0	100.0
5	21.1	11.1	11.7	12.4	12.1	11.7	13.0	14.9	40.7	48.1	1.3	1.8	100.0	100.0
6	30.8	10.0	8.8	9.3	9.5	13.2	8.0	16.8	9.4	9.4	33.3	41.3	100.0	100.0
Total	25.5	14.5	15.1	18.7	16.2	15.9	20.8	21.4	20.6	26.1	1.9	3.4	100.0	100.0

Source: 1972 Phase II Survey; 1978 World Bank–DANE Household Survey.

How did the spatial pattern of work travel change between 1972 and 1978? The most striking change was the large decline in the proportion of workers employed in the CBD (ring 1), although the decline was slight in absolute terms. Between 1972 and 1978, employment in the CBD fell from almost 25 percent to about 15 percent of total city employment (see table 8-12). The CBD lost only about 36,000 jobs in this period, but the rest of the city gained almost 350,000 jobs. Another interesting feature of the change was the increase in intra-ring commuting—a sign of employment decentralization that will probably lead to a greater demand for circumferential trips. (A similar table for students' travel patterns in 1972 reveals that the majority of students traveled to school within close proximity of their residences—within the same ring as the location of their residence.) Another way of looking at the pattern of work travel is to observe the "relative employment absorption" by ring of employment (see table 8-12). The index measures the number of jobs in the ring filled by workers who commuted from other rings. The ratio, as might be expected, declines as one moves outward from the CBD. The table clearly points to increasing employment and residential decentralization. The outer rings exhibited a high growth rate in external trips.

This continuing decentralization of employment and residential patterns in Bogotá may have a serious and adverse effect on the quality of Bogotá's public transportation. Mass transit serves radial, concentrated trips more efficiently than it serves less concentrated, circumferential travel. The evident increase in use of intermediate-capacity vehicles may be a direct response to decentralization. As mentioned before, intermediate-capacity vehicles can operate profitably with lower load factors than full-size buses. Break-even load factors for *busetas* were 45 to 50 percent at existing fare levels, compared with 75 to 80 percent for buses. As commuting patterns become less concentrated along specific radial corridors, intermediate-capacity vehicles will begin to supplant larger vehicles.

The Effect of Income and Other Household Characteristics on Travel Time

We found convincing evidence that workers from poor households spent more time traveling and traveled longer distances than workers from better-off households. In both Cali and Bogotá, the richer residential areas have a higher ratio of jobs per resident than do the poorer residential areas. Hence, it seemed that the poor had relatively worse access to work opportunities. In 1978, workers living in the richest sector of Bogotá traveled an average of only 3.7 kilometers per trip—much less than the 6.2 kilometers averaged by the population as a whole. Average speeds of commuters from the poorest sector were more than 25 percent slower than the speeds of commuters from the richest sector.

Table 8-13. Average Commuting Distance by Zone of Work, Type of Worker, and Occupation: Bogotá, 1972 and 1978

(kilometers)

	All zones			Central zones			Other zones		
	1972	1978	Percentage increase	1972	1978	Percentage increase	1972	1978	Percentage increase
Household heads									
Professionals	3.5	4.1	15.7	4.2	4.9	17.6	3.2	3.7	16.8
Employees	4.2	4.4	5.3	4.4	5.1	16.0	4.0	4.1	2.5
Retail employees	2.0	3.4	15.5	4.2	5.1	23.4	2.4	3.1	25.4
Others	3.4	4.0	16.4	4.2	4.6	8.5	3.2	3.9	23.4
Secondary workers									
Professionals	3.5	4.0	12.9	3.9	5.7	47.8	3.3	3.7	12.1
Employees	3.9	4.4	12.9	4.2	4.7	13.9	3.7	4.2	14.0
Retail employees	2.9	3.1	8.4	4.3	4.6	5.5	2.4	2.9	19.0
Others	3.3	4.1	23.6	4.5	4.9	10.7	3.0	4.0	32.5

Source: Pineda (1981).

208

However, if the choice of transportation mode is controlled for, the difference in speeds is small but the distance and time differences remain.

The evidence is that the level of transit service is roughly equal throughout the city. If the poor are transportation-disadvantaged, it is because of the location of activities and not because of the level of transportation services available. Indeed, the relatively high level of service availability throughout the city and the prevalence of the flat-fare system partially mitigate the locational disadvantage of poor workers. Fundamentally, the transport system per se does not contribute to any locational disadvantage suffered by poorer workers in Bogotá and Cali. Instead, locational problems are caused by the imbalance between jobs and workers in rich and poor neighborhoods. However, the longer time that the poor spend traveling does impose higher effective costs on them.

Relocating employment and residence would do a great deal to alleviate the locational disadvantage of poorer workers, but this is typically difficult to accomplish. It has also been found that the net effect of the taxes and subsidies affecting transportation in Bogotá has helped reduce the disadvantage of the poor. More attention could be given to infrastructure investment by further improving the road system in a way that would reduce commuting time for the poor, who reside in disadvantaged locations. Further expansion of public transportation services and some realignment of routes, particularly circumferential routes from the poor southern areas of the city to the wealthy north, would also help.

So far we have focused on one determining characteristic of travel patterns—income. For a richer appreciation of travel patterns, it is necessary to observe the effect of other variables such as household size and composition, occupations of individual workers, employment densities, and housing and ownership status. For example, households with more than one worker have to assess the competing travel needs of different household members in choosing the best residence location. In 1978 as many as half of all households had more than one worker—this had increased from 40 percent in 1972.

This issue was examined in great detail by Pineda (1981) as part of the City Study. His findings suggest that there is a great degree of interdependence in the commuting decisions of multiworker households. Households do tend to optimize the joint satisfaction of different household members' travel needs. Primary workers have longer work journeys than secondary workers. This suggests that residence location is chosen to maximize the secondary workers' access to likely employment prospects; in general, the location of the primary worker's job is likely to be known in advance and would be more fixed. Primary workers were also more likely to be professionals and white-collar employees whose jobs were more likely to be farther away in the central city (see table 8-13). Homeowners travel 1 kilometer more on average than renters; this is consistent with patterns in cities in developed countries. It also conforms to expectations, because renters are likely to be more mobile and therefore to have greater flexibility in their choice of residential location.

In attempting to understand the travel pattern of workers according to type of work done, Pineda found a clear distinction between what he characterized as type I and type II secondary workers. Type I secondary workers had more than a primary education, were neither family workers nor self-employed, and were at least twenty-one years old. Their characteristics resembled those of household heads or primary workers. Type I workers' commutes were longer than those of type II workers and not very different from those of primary workers. Type I workers had increased in proportion from about one-third of all secondary workers in 1972 to about half in 1978. There seems to be a process of "formalization" of the kind of jobs engaged in by secondary workers.

After controlling for other variables such as housing status, mode of travel, and quality of dwelling unit, Pineda also estimated a number of multivariate regressions in order to estimate better the effect of multi-worker households on distance traveled by primary workers. The key result was that the skill mix of workers in a household was important in determining residence location. The more homogeneous the characteristics of different workers in the household, the more likely they were to live close to areas of the city where all could find work. In households with type II secondary workers, the household head commuted farther.

The conclusion of this investigation is that a city with increasing labor force participation has an increasing number of secondary workers whose travel requirements are more variegated than those of primary workers. Hence the city then needs a more flexible transport system.

Travel Schedules

Another useful way to look at urban travel patterns is to observe the frequency of travel and the time profile of travel over the day. Frequency is usually computed on a daily basis, on the basis of trips per person or per household. Analyzing the time profile of travel helps in assessing the adequacy of existing transportation services to meet peak hour demand; travel rates vary widely over the day. Typically, about 75 percent of all trips are made during just 25 to 30 percent of the day. It is also useful to understand why trips take place: household size and composition and individual lifestyle differences all contribute to differences in type of transportation used, as well as time, origin, and destination of trips. Income and access to a private vehicle are other key factors.

Characteristics such as income, household size, and automobile ownership affect trip rates in cities in both developing and developed coun-

Table 8-14. Average Number of Trips per Person and Average Number of Trips per Household: Selected Cities

City	Year	Average household size	Trips per person	Trips per household	Average number of cars per household
Lagos	1975	5.4	0.79	4.3	0.18
Bangkok	1972	6.5	1.11	7.2	0.28
Bogotá	1972	5.7	1.15	6.6	0.17
Hong Kong	1973	4.7	1.27	5.9	0.14
Singapore	1968	5.2	1.40	7.2	0.21
Buenos Aires	1972	3.8	1.42	5.4	0.30
São Paulo	1977	4.8	1.50	7.2	—
Kuala Lumpur	1973	5.8	1.74	10.2	0.42
Mexico City	1972	3.5	1.77	6.4	0.45
Los Angeles	1967	2.9	2.28	6.7	1.28
Chicago	1971	2.9	2.45	7.2	1.04
Denver	1970	3.1	2.83	8.8	1.40

— Not available.

Note: Motorized trips only.

Source: Bogotá—1972 Phase II Survey tabulations; Lagos—TRANSPOCONSULT (1976); Buenos Aires—Ministerio de Obras y Servicios Publicos (1972); São Paulo—EMPLASA (1978); Hong Kong—Wilbur Smith and Associates (1976); Bangkok—cited in Zahavi (1979); Kuala Lumpur—Wilbur Smith and Associates (1974); Singapore—Zahavi (1979); Mexico City—Barton-Aschman Associates (1983); Los Angeles, Denver, and Chicago—Levinson (1978).

tries. (See table 8-14 for a sample of data for motorized trips from the 1970s. Although these data are now somewhat dated, they are still quite instructive. The data exclude walking trips because comparable information for different cities is difficult to obtain.) Trip rates are progressively higher in higher-income countries. There is considerable variation in household size, the average household size being small in richer countries. Automobile ownership seems to lead to higher trip rates.

Trip patterns in Bogotá were examined by level of household income, household size, auto ownership, and individual characteristics—workers, students, nonworkers. Within Bogotá, both trip rates per traveler and number of travelers per household increase as household income rises. A striking fact is that, once household income is controlled for, auto ownership has a minimal impact on trips per traveler but a significant impact on travel participation rates—that is, number of travelers per household. The net effect is that household trip rates are higher for automobile owners than for nonowners at similar income levels. The impact of automobile ownership is greatest on workers: presumably those who travel by private automobile to work are also likely to make many more side trips. Controlling for income, automobile ownership has little impact on travel frequency of other household members such as students and nonworkers. The fact that members of higher-income

Table 8-15. Trip Generation Characteristics of All Travelers: Bogotá, 1972

Monthly household income (Col$)	Average trips per traveler per day			Average travelers per household per day			Average trips per household per day		
	No car	Car	Total	No car	Car	Total	No car	Car	Total
0–500	2.2	—	2.3	1.7	—	1.7	3.9	—	3.9
500–1,000	2.4	—	2.4	2.0	—	2.0	4.8	—	4.9
1,000–1,500	2.4	—	2.4	2.3	—	2.3	5.8	—	5.8
1,500–2,000	2.6	2.7	2.6	2.6	2.6	2.4	6.7	6.4	6.7
2,000–3,000	2.8	2.9	2.8	2.8	3.6	2.9	7.9	10.2	8.2
3,000–5,000	2.8	2.8	2.8	3.0	3.1	3.0	8.1	8.8	8.3
5,000–15,000	2.8	2.8	2.8	3.0	3.4	3.2	8.5	9.7	9.2
More than 15,000	—	2.9	2.9	—	3.5	3.5	—	10.4	10.4
Weighted average	2.6	2.8	2.7	2.5	3.2	2.7	6.7	9.4	7.2

— Not applicable.
Source: Westin (1980); data from 1972 Phase II Survey.

households stay in school longer is brought out very sharply in students' trip rates per household as household income increases.

It is interesting to compare U.S. urban travel characteristics with those in Bogotá (see tables 8-14 and 8-15). At the 1972 exchange rate of Col\$25 to US\$1, a monthly household income of Col\$5,000 in Bogotá was equivalent to annual household income of US\$2,400. This corresponded to the lower end of the income scale in the United States. Automobile ownership in Bogotá was only 0.17 per household, compared with 1.31 in the United States; the average household size was 4.6 in Bogotá, compared with 3.06 for the United States. Travel frequency increased with income in both places; at straight exchange rate equivalents, household trip rates were higher in Bogotá. The data indicate that automobile ownership has a quantitatively larger effect on trip rates in the United States than in Bogotá for a given level of income. This illustrates the benefits gained from the operation of a relatively good and easily accessible transport system such as Bogotá's. In the United States, non-automobile-owning households are put at a disadvantage by the existence of a highly dispersed pattern of residence and employment. Moreover, high levels of automobile ownership put those without cars at a further disadvantage, because it is increasingly difficult to operate a

Table 8-16. Trip Generation Equations: Bogotá, 1972

| Variable | Workers | | Nonworkers |
	Total trips	Work trips	Nonwork trips
Mean trip rate	2.74	2.51	2.54
Sex (female = 1)	-0.12^*	-0.03	-0.11
Age (years)	0.04^{**}	0.04^*	0.08^*
Hours worked	—	0.004^{**}	—
Number of workers in household	—	—	-0.11^*
Transportation accessibility			
Work trips			
Automobile owners	0.57^*	0.19^*	—
Non-owners	-0.29^*	0.28^*	—
Nonwork trips			
Automobile owners	-0.22	—	0.21^{**}
Non-owners	0.07	—	0.40
Intercept	2.83	2.35	2.64
R^2	0.057	0.055	0.051

— Variable not included in the equation.
* Denotes significance at the 99 percent confidence level.
** Denotes significance at the 95 percent confidence level.
Note: Household income not included as a variable.
Source: Kozel (1981).

public transport system economically as fewer people come to depend on it.

Urban transport planners in developing countries must understand this issue well. The continued provision of good public transportation could help slow increases in automobile ownership as incomes rise. The validity of this conclusion was investigated by estimating trip generation models for workers and nonworkers. (See table 8-16. For details, see Kozel 1981.) The most important variable was a measure of transportation accessibility. This index was calculated as a measure of transport system attractiveness as defined by times and costs to desired locations and the availability of transportation modes.[3] The model follows the original specification by Lerman and Ben-Akiva. The estimates shown exclude household income as a determining variable because it was found that income was highly correlated with the index of transportation accessibility.

The equations provide evidence of a strong causal link between frequency of travel and quality of transport system. The measure of access to non-work-related destinations was highly significant for nonworking adults. Households without automobiles were more affected by improvements in the transport system. Although our overall conclusion in this study has been that the transport system serves the poor relatively well, the high correlation between the measure of transportation accessibility and household income suggests that the poorer areas of the city are less well served by the transport system.

In cities in developed countries, peaking takes place during rush hour traffic in the journey from home to work in the morning and the return home in the evening. In many developing countries, particularly in Latin American cities, there is considerable travel from work to home for lunch, creating another peak travel period. The proportion of workers going home for lunch in Bogotá seems to have increased from about 25 percent in 1972 to 31 percent in 1978. In Cali this proportion was about 50 percent. As may be expected, automobile owners are much more likely to lunch at home—about 70 percent of automobile owners do so in Cali and about 40 percent in Bogotá. Among workers without cars, just under 50 percent in Cali and 28 percent in Bogotá lunched at home. This additional trip home contributes to traffic congestion in the middle of the day, hampering the movement of both business-related goods and passengers. An interesting fact is that the number of people lunching at home seems to decline as city size increases—presumably because of longer average commutes. Thus, the increase in lunch travel between 1972 and 1978 in Bogotá is hard to understand.

A close examination of the peaking pattern by transportation mode showed that bus travel peaked earlier in the morning than *buseta* and automobile travel. The morning peak was the highest because trips to school and work coincide. The evening peak was more spread out, because school days end earlier than most jobs. The travel distributions for *busetas* over the course of the day closely resembled automobile travel distributions—again suggesting that *buseta* transportation is a close substitute for private transportation.

Modeling Travel Demand

The design of urban transport systems and infrastructure requires a systematic understanding of how and why people choose among various public and private transportation modes. Understanding their choices and being able to encourage them to use mass transit are particularly important because collective public transportation modes usually make more efficient use of road space and fuel and other resources. It is especially desirable to promote such collective modes in resource-poor developing countries. Private modes, however, provide faster, more comfortable travel, so there is a natural tendency for people to switch to these modes whenever possible. Can behavioral modeling help in understanding the determinants of travel behaviors? What characteristics of urban transport supply do travelers value most? What really irks people in their daily urban travel patterns? What, if anything, can be done to improve urban public transportation services and thus slow the rapid shift to private motorized modes of transportation as incomes increase? The modeling of urban transport demand would be useful if answers to such questions become available.

Every traveler is faced with limited transportation choices, which are, interestingly enough, often greater in cities in developing countries than in developed countries because of the emergence of a number of intermediate modes. Our descriptive work has already shown that model choices are strongly influenced by income. Automobile ownership is particularly influenced by income level and mode choice is then affected by whether or not the household owns an automobile. Trip distance also affects mode choice: very short trip distances, for example, are likely to be traversed by walking. City structure also influences mode choice: if a city has relatively concentrated central city employment, those working in the city center are more likely to use public transportation than those employed in the periphery. Modeling travelers' behavior thus involves the modeling of discrete choice. In chapter 6 we referred to the modeling of location, also a discrete choice problem for the firm. In that formulation, the employer's problem was to choose the location that maximized profit subject to various constraints. This was transformed into an empirical framework for predicting the probability that a firm with certain characteristics would occupy a site with certain attributes. Similarly, in modeling urban transport demand, the individual's problem is to chose the most useful travel mode that maximizes utility subject to various constraints specific to the individual and others specific to the chosen mode. Using this conceptual framework, one can estimate the probability that an individual with certain characteristics will choose a specific travel mode. Among individuals regarded as homogeneous in tastes, except for measured characteristics, the variation in travel choice results from variation in unmeasured characteristics and tastes: the utility function is therefore probabilistic in form. The theoretical derivation and various applications of urban travel demand modeling are found in a number of sources and will therefore not be repeated here.[4] A skeletal introduction to the essential theoretical basis of such modeling is given in the appendix to this chapter, however. The estimation method is the multinomial logit technique that was used for employment location.

This approach, focusing on the behavioral modeling of the individual, may be contrasted with the traditional social physics approach of urban transport modeling. The latter attempts to replicate the observed travel patterns in a statistical fashion by modeling the volumes of traffic flow, for example, based on the available information of residential and workplace densities, the available travel routes, and the like. The goal in such modeling is essentially to observe statistical regularities and to replicate such regularities through modeling. These models do not provide insights into behavior and are very data-intensive. Our approach is more economical in the use of data, although the estimation techniques and modeling theory are quite involved.

In this approach, it is necessary to carefully identify the choices facing each individual. Not all individuals face the same choices. For example, individuals in households without cars do not have the option of traveling by private car.

In Bogotá the available choices were defined as follows (see table 8-17):

Transport mode	Available to:
Private car	All members of automobile-owning households
Taxi and *colectivo*	All persons living on *colectivo* routes and in the inner three rings of Bogotá
Bus	All travelers
Buseta	In 1972, all travelers living within 1 kilometer of a *buseta* route; in 1978, all travelers
Walking	All travelers making a trip of less than 10 kilometers

Table 8-17. Work Trips by Mode of Transportation: Bogotá, 1972 and 1978, and Cali, 1978
(percentage shares)

Mode	Bogotá, 1972	Bogotá, 1978	Cali, 1978
Automobile driver	9.0	9.3	6.2
Automobile passenger	2.9	2.7	2.0
Taxi	1.3	1.2	2.7
Colectivo	0.8	0.3	0.1
Bus	69.0	51.8	62.1
Buseta[a]	8.7	17.7	2.5
Walk	7.3	12.9	16.3
Other[b]	—	4.0	8.1

— Not available.
a. Includes microbuses.
b. Includes bicycle, motorcycle, and vehicle owned by employer.
Source: Kozel (1981); 1972 Bogotá tabulations from Phase II Survey; 1978 Bogotá and Cali figures from 1978 World Bank–DANE Household Survey.

The key determinants of modal choice are household income, comparative costs in terms of both money and time, motorization rates, and urban structure. Other socioeconomic variables such as household size, composition, and the traveler's position in the household (for example, household head) can also affect the mode of travel chosen.

In modeling the mode choice of travelers in such a discrete choice framework, where the probability of choosing a mode is determined by such explanatory variables, a number of useful by-products emerge for policy analysis. The valuation of time by travelers can be estimated. The valuation of time can vary for different modes, and for different levels of income. This is usually done as a proportion of existing wage rates. Is travel time valued by workers at the same rate as wages or at a lower or higher rate? Such travel time valuation is needed for conducting project evaluations of different transportation projects. The estimations also yield direct estimates of elasticities of mode choice (derived in the appendix to this chapter). The evaluation of the elasticities can be used to predict the effect and mode choice resulting from time reductions that may emerge from traffic management improvements or transportation infrastructure investments. Similarly, the effects of increased fares or rising incomes can be evaluated.

In this study, a large number of different specifications were used to model mode choice behavior in both Bogotá and Cali (see Kozel 1981 and 1986 for details). In the case of Bogotá, data were available for both work trips and nonwork trips for 1972. For 1978, data were available for work trips only but on a comparable basis for both Bogotá and Cali. The specifications had to be different in the different years because the 1978 survey had only travel-to-work information and the data available in the two data sets were not on identical variables.

Our interest in modeling is to understand the influence of these variables on the probability of choice. If the model is well specified and the estimation is found to capture the revealed choices well, it can be used to predict future travel demand in response to expected changes. There are several ways to judge the performance of such models. First, as in ordinary least-squares regression, the significance of the coefficient of each variable is an indicator of the importance of each variable in the mode choice decision. Second, statistical measures like log likelihood ratio and likelihood ratio index may be used to measure goodness of fit. Third, the percentage correctly predicted gives a good idea of the model's ability to capture the revealed preferences of the population. Once a model is calibrated on a base year, it can be used to predict the outcomes of projected changes in a future year.

Because of the lack of variation in travel cost caused by the existence of flat bus and *buseta* fares, the cost coefficients were not very robust. Otherwise, the estimated coefficients were significant and of appropriate size and magnitude. The models estimated performed about as well as might be expected from other similar exercises: in general, the models were able to achieve 70 percent predictive capability. Had there been more variation in travel cost, there would have been even better predictive performance. Moreover, when there are more than two choices, as in Bogotá, the modeling problem acquires greater complexity.

It had been hypothesized that time spent in different transportation modes could be valued differently. The time spent in bus travel, for example, would be seen as more undesirable than time spent in a private car. It was found that the generic time coefficient is not significantly different from the alternative specific coefficients, and with the bus being the most dominant mode, the bus-specific time coefficient was the nearest to the generic coefficient. Household characteristics were also found to be important: travelers from better-off households placed a higher value on their travel time; travelers from larger families appeared to be less willing to pay to save time, reflecting lower household income per capita. It was also interesting to note that the time spent walking was found to be the most onerous. It was also found that the travel accessibility variable—distance to the nearest bus or *buseta* route—was significant for automobile owners. Proximity to a public transportation route reduced the probability of automobile use for automobile-owning households. This reduction was particularly pronounced regarding *buseta* accessibility, a fact suggesting that a *buseta* was seen as a possible alternative by automobile-owning households.

Although it is not very useful to provide the detailed estimates of equations here, it is quite instructive to give an indication of the elasticities observed. It is interesting to compute the actual change in modal share resulting from a 1 percent change in the explanatory variable: this is the percentage change in the share (or the elasticity) multiplied by the share itself. Because the elasticity estimates are nonlinear, they have to be evaluated at a given point; in this case the effects are evaluated at the observed modal shares. The results indicate that, whereas automobile use was quite sensitive to cost, walking, bus, and *buseta* use were relatively more sensitive to time variations. In Bogotá, for example, in 1978, a 1 percent increase in time spent walking would have reduced the walking share from 12.9 percent to less than 12.5 percent; and a similar increase in *buseta* time would have reduced its share from 17.7 percent to 17.4 percent. In contrast, a 1 percent increase in automobile time would have had almost no effect on the 9.3 percent share of automobile use (see tables 8-17 and 8-18). Cross-elasticity effects can be calculated in a similar fashion. As may be expected, increases in bus times increase the use of *busetas*, but increases in automobile journeys have negligible effects on other modes.

How do the models perform intertemporally?[5] Because we had data sets for 1972 and 1978, it was possible to test the predictive accuracy of the 1972-based parameters using 1978 data by predicting modal shares in 1978. Parameters were also estimated for 1978 and compared with

Table 8-18. Change in Work Trip Modal Shares—Direct Elasticities: Bogotá, 1972 and 1978 and Cali, 1978

Mode	Time	Cost	Household income
Automobile			
Bogotá, 1972	—	−.0144	—
Bogotá, 1978	−.0026	−.0502	—
Cali, 1978	−.0144	−.0807	.0070
Taxi, Colectivo			
Bogotá, 1972	—	−.0030	—
Bogotá, 1978	—	−.0192	.0176
Cali, 1978	−.1108	−.0775	—
Buseta			
Bogotá, 1972	—	−.0029	—
Bogotá, 1978	−.2936	−.0286	.1704
Cali, 1978	−.0851	−.0175	.0070
Bus			
Bogotá, 1972	—	−.0032	—
Bogotá, 1978	−.3309	−.0211	—
Cali, 1978	−.1440	−.0196	—
Walk			
Bogotá, 1972	—	—	—
Bogotá, 1978	−.4350	—	—
Cali, 1978	−.3194	—	—

— Not available.
Source: Kozel (1982).

the 1972 parameters. It is important to note the main exogenous changes that occurred between 1972 and 1978. Automobile ownership increased from 167 to 217 per 1,000 households; household income increased by about 33 percent in real terms; proportion of total employment in the central city fell from about 40 percent to 33 percent; and all travel times increased with considerable city expansion (particularly bus trips, which increased from 40 minutes to 55 minutes on average, and of *buseta* trips, which increased from 34 minutes to 48 minutes); finally, supply of *busetas* increased tremendously—in 1978 almost all areas were served by both buses and *busetas*.

A number of tests were performed to analyze the transferability of the estimated models. The 1972 Bogotá estimates were simulated to observe how well the 1978 modal split would be predicted. Similarly, the 1978 estimates were used to simulate the 1972 split, and the Bogotá and Cali estimates for 1978 were interchanged. Overall, the model estimation was similar for work trips over the two years (see table 8A-5 in the appendix to this chapter). There were some difficulties, however, in such comparisons. As mentioned earlier, because of differences in data availability, the specifications of models estimated for the two years were different. Hence, the comparison had to be done on the basis of a common set of variables. Another general difficulty encountered was in the cost variable. Because of the prevalence of flat-fare systems in Bogotá, there is no variation in costs between journeys of different distances. Thus, the coefficients of cost variables were generally unsatisfactory, and a significant difference was found between the parameter estimates for the two years. The stability of coefficients across the two models was tested statistically through likelihood ratio tests.

The most interesting test of a model for planning purposes is in its predictive ability. The 1978 predicted modal shares from the 1972 model give good results—the main error being in the share of *buseta* ridership. This is not surprising, because the supply of *busetas* had been limited in 1972. The 1972 coefficients therefore modeled mode choice under such supply constraints. Different simulations were conducted to successively substitute 1978 parameters step-by-step for the 1972 parameters. The predictive success of the model improved with each successive step. In particular, *buseta* ridership is approximated well after these substitutions. Automobile use falls and walking increases, however. Another experiment was done to predict mode choice by income class. The predictions for the lower income groups perform much better than for the higher income groups. Once again, this suggests the greater difficulty in modeling situations where choice is greater than two modes.

One problem found throughout this modeling effort and one that is difficult to explain is that the valuation of time spent in traveling is found to be a multiple (of 3 or 4) of hourly wages. This is quite counterintuitive and very different from modeling efforts in developed countries. Travel time is usually valued at half or three-quarters the rate of hourly wages. There could be two explanations. First is the lack of cost data for bus and *buseta* trips. Second is that the time cost becomes important mainly for the richer, auto-owning travelers. It is possible that the average reduction of time being obtained really reflects the valuation assigned by high-income travelers.

Similar modeling methodology was used to estimate the probability of a household owning an automobile. Overall, the models performed well in predicting automobile ownership levels in 1972 and 1978. As might be expected, income was the key determinant of automobile ownership. Homeownership, used as a proxy for wealth, was also significant. In fact, an alternative specification approximating permanent income was found to be a better explanation. Estimated demand elasticities ranged between 1.0 and 1.3—consistent with cross-section elasticities estimated elsewhere. It was also found that, at similar levels of income, households living farther away from the center were more likely to own an automobile. What was most interesting was that a variable attempting to measure accessibility to transportation performed well: better transportation availability reduced the chances of automobile ownership. This is a most important result: the general inexorable trend toward greater private transportation ownership and use that accompanies increased incomes can at least be slowed with better provision of public transportation. The projection for the year 2000 suggests that automobile ownership levels at that time will be less than one-third of current U.S. levels.

What have we learned from this relatively sophisticated modeling effort? The disaggregated travel demand modeling methodology contrasts with the macro or social physics approach used earlier in modeling urban transportation patterns. This approach is clearly much more economical in data requirements and even estimation; even relatively small data sets can be used. However, it must be admitted that this methodology demands data of high quality, if not heavy volume. Moreover, because it is not easy to gain an intuitive understanding of the theory and estimation technique, it can be difficult to interpret the estimates well. Nonetheless, the models performed quite well and even had reasonably good predictive capability. The estimation of such models also fosters an understanding of the behavioral rationality (or irrationality) of travelers. Overall, the verdict is mixed: better understanding has been achieved, but with considerable effort.

Lessons for a Developing Metropolis

The structure of a city is deeply affected by, and at the same time itself determines, the transport system at any given time. The spatial distribution of activities in a city depends on the quality of the transport system, its spread and coverage, and the costs of transportation. In turn, the pattern of urban transportation is determined by the existing structure of activities in the city: an efficient system responds to effective demands for travel as they become evident. In a city in a developing country, as in Bogotá, income growth causes changes in city structure through changes in housing patterns, residence location, income distribution, and shifts in occupations and activities; these changes then have an impact on travel demand. In addition, income changes affect travel demand more directly through the impact on automobile ownership and the valuation of time.

We found that Bogotá had a rich supply of transport services. People of almost all income levels had easy access to motorized transportation. Bus service was available to most residents within about 500 meters of their home. About 125 seats were available for every 1,000 residents. This compares well with richer cities, such as Hong Kong, which are generally regarded as being well served by public transportation. The cost of travel was low because of the tax and subsidy system adopted by the government.

Unlike most cities in developed countries, and many large cities in developing countries, where the government typically operates public transportation services and usually subsidizes them, in Bogotá the government had a negligible presence in actual supply. Almost all public transportation was privately owned and operated. The government did, however, regulate the system physically through route allocation and control, and regulate the fares through tariff setting and subsidies. Overall, the system succeeded in being progressive: the bottom 40 percent of the population received between 4 and 6 percent of their monthly incomes as transportation subsidies. Although the tax and subsidy system was by no means ideal and could be improved, the combination of fuel subsidy, vehicle taxation, and bus subsidies helped make urban public transportation accessible and affordable to almost all residents of Bogotá. The situation was similar in Cali.

One result of this high level of transportation availability was that Bogotá households exhibit a high level of mobility. The number of trips per household was seven per day, similar to the trip rates recorded for some U.S. cities. The trip rate per person, however—1.4 in Bogotá compared with two in U.S. cities—was much lower because Bogotá households are larger. One interesting feature of trip generation in Bogotá was that automobile ownership was not found to increase the number of journeys per household. This was probably because of the high level of transportation availability: the absence of a private mode did not hamper mobility. This suggests one of the more important findings of this study. In developing countries, it may be possible to slow down the increasing use of private transportation modes, particularly automobiles, if credible alternative modes are provided. In Bogotá, *busetas* appeared to be substitutes for automobiles.

What are the characteristics of private automobile travel? Automobiles provide great convenience: door-to-door service, no waiting time, twenty-four-hour availability, and the possibility of multipurpose trips. The drawback, of course, is the high cost. Automobile use was found to be quite sensitive to costs, so it is clear that automobile travel can be reduced, or at least its growth curbed, if public transport modes can be made sufficiently convenient and economical. The success of the public transport system in Bogotá and in a number of other cities in various middle-income countries has demonstrated that convenience and economy are possible to achieve in developing country systems.

In developed countries, urban public transportation is difficult to run without subsidies. The driver is the most expensive element in the structure of costs of bus operation: typically, more than 80 percent of fare box revenues in U.S. cities go to the bus driver. Economical operation therefore implies large buses serving heavily traveled corridors. Other locations are then difficult to serve economically by means of large vehicles, thus promoting private transportation, which itself reduces public transit ridership.

In developing countries, on the other hand, where wages are low, the driver does not cost much at all: in Bogotá, the typical driver received only 10 to 15 percent of fare box revenues. It is therefore possible to operate smaller buses, with just 10- to 25-passenger capacity. These can approximate the convenience of private transportation. They can serve the less heavily traveled routes at reasonable frequencies and at lower costs than automobiles.

As a city expands and incomes grow, the city decentralizes. In cities in developing countries, although decentralization of jobs commonly occurs, there is seldom a decrease in the absolute number of jobs. Hence the demand for radial travel does not fall in absolute terms. The decentralization of jobs and residence implies a greater demand for circumferential travel and provides new opportunities for distributing loads more evenly in the road system by means of low-capacity vehicles like *busetas* or even smaller vans. A radial and circumferential transit system can coexist: this seemed to be the case in Bogotá as the city expanded in size and the transport system responded to the new demands.

How was the system able to respond so well? The private provision of public transportation through the participation of small bus owners operating as cooperatives lent great flexibility to the system. As the city grew, new neighborhoods sprang up, and employment location patterns changed; it was easy for small independent bus enterprises to respond to new demands. The government authorities, on their part, responded by issuing permits for new route allocations. Such flexible responses in the high-growth situation of Bogotá in the 1950s, 1960s, and 1970s, would probably not have been possible if there had been a monolithic large public transport company.

The government in Bogotá succeeded in inducing private participation by making good use of private initiatives. Overall costs per bus kilometer were low; subsidies amounted to about half of costs; and as a result fares were low, which improved access of the poor to transportation. The presence of many private operators introduced competitive behavior, which helped keep costs low. At the same time, the government was saved from making heavy capital investments in bus purchases. The introduction of *busetas*, which were not subsidized, meant that the bus subsidies helped the poor because the higher-cost, more convenient *busetas* attracted the better-off riders away from the subsidized buses. Lesson: the existence of a full-cost, upmarket service can help concentrate subsidies where they are most needed. Although the results may have been achieved serendipitously, the flexibility inherent in Bogotá's transport system provides good pointers for effective transport policy in cities in developing countries. The introduction of even greater heterogeneity through smaller vans with superior levels of service would have added to this flexibility.

One implication of the patterns observed in Bogotá is that when automobile ownership rates are low, as they were in Bogotá, it is a good time to establish restraints on automobile use. If upmarket residents have a reasonable alternative to driving, controls on automobile use (such as exclusive bus lanes, high fuel prices, parking charges, and restrictions on private cars in congested areas) could do much to slow down the growth of automobile use. None of these measures has been introduced in Bogotá. Such measures are desirable because private transportation uses road space and energy inefficiently, increasing congestion. Reducing automobile ownership would reduce the need for premature heavy investments in road and other infrastructure.

As the city grows and both residences and jobs decentralize, the demand for radial trips decreases while that for circumferential trips increases. In Bogotá, for example, there is a good deal of cross-commuting from poor sector 2 in the south to rich sector 8 in the north. The availability of circumferential routes would reduce both transportation time and central-city congestion. Another lesson from Bogotá was that circumferential roads can eliminate unnecessary radial trips through the center, reducing both congestion on the radial routes and the time required to travel the circumferential routes.

What did we learn from our behavioral modeling efforts? The behavior of Bogotá residents was broadly similar to that observed elsewhere. Choice of transportation modes is more sensitive to income and service levels than it is to relative prices of competing modes. At low income levels, there is effectively no choice: people either walk or use public transit. Between the fiftieth and eightieth percentiles of income distribution, people will switch to better service levels if they are available. At the highest income levels people switch to cars but can be restrained if viable alternatives exist. Whereas automobile ownership rates would continue to increase, it may be possible to restrict automobile use by simultaneously improving public transportation service levels and increasing costs of automobile use.

The main lesson for urban transport provision in developing countries is that, if the system is made flexible enough to respond to changes in demand, it is possible to cope with rapid growth.

Appendix: Theoretical Background for Modeling the Choice of Transport Mode

For an individual, each alternative $j = 1,...,I$ has a vector of observed attributes X^j. Each individual t is also subject to socioeconomic characteristics S, which are invariant with the alternative chosen. The utility function of an individual may then be written as

$$U_t = U_t(X^j, s, \varepsilon)$$

for $j = 1,...,I$, where ε is an unobserved vector containing all the attributes of the alternative and individual characteristics that are not amenable to measurement. Hence the value of U at any X, S, is a random variable depending on the random variable ε.

The individual will choose alternative i if

$$U(X^i, S) > U(X^j, S)$$

for all $j \neq i$ and $j = 1,...,I$. Hence the probability of choice i can be written as

$$P_i = \text{Prob} \left[U(X^i, S) > U(X^j, S) \right]$$

for $j \neq i$, $j = 1,...,I$. The stochastic utility function may be written as

$$U(X, S) = V(X, S) + \eta(X, S)$$

where V is nonstochastic and η is stochastic. The probability of choice i may then be rewritten as

$$P_i = \text{Prob} \left[\eta(X^j, S) - \eta(X^i, S) < V(X^i, S) - V(X^j, S) \right]$$

for $j \neq i,\ j = 1,...,I$. Once the $\eta_j\ (X,\ S)$ are given a functional form Φ, the probability may be written as

$$P_i = \int_{-\infty}^{\infty} \Phi\,(t,\ X,\ S)\ dt$$

where Φ is the cumulative joint distribution function of the random components η_j of the stochastic utility function.

The only computationally tractable distribution function that leads to a plausible stochastic specification is the Weibull distribution, which may be written as

$$\Phi\,(\eta) = e^{-(\eta + \alpha)}\exp\,[-e^{-(\eta - \alpha)}]$$

where α is a parameter.

The Weibull distribution is similar to the normal distribution but is skewed with a thinner left tail and a thicker right tail. Two properties of the Weibull distribution are relevant for the travel choice problem: the maximum of a Weibull distribution is itself a Weibull distribution, and the difference between two Weibull distributions has a binary logistic distribution. Thus,

$$\text{Prob}\,[\,V_i + \eta_i \geq V_j + \eta_j \ \ \text{for}\ j = (1,...,I,\ i \neq j)\,] = \frac{\exp\,(V_i + \alpha_i)}{\displaystyle\sum_{j \in I} \exp\,(V_j - \alpha_j)}$$

which may be rewritten (suppressing α_j) as

$$P_i = \frac{\exp\,[\,V(X_i,\ S)\,]}{\displaystyle\sum_{j \in I} \exp\,[\,V(X_j,\ S)\,]}$$

This provides a formulation for multinomial logit estimation. If V is linear in parameters, V may be written as

$$V(X_j,\ S) = \beta' Z_j$$

and

$$P_i = \frac{\exp{(\beta' Z_j)}}{\displaystyle\sum_{j \in I} \exp{(\beta' Z_j)}}$$

This expression may be transformed to a logit form:

$$\text{logit}\,(P_i) = \ln \frac{P_i}{1 - P_i}$$

where the logit function is estimated by maximum likelihood techniques. It is important to understand that the coefficients β must be estimated to be interpreted correctly. The easiest way to understand them is to derive an expression for the slope of the estimated logit function. It is found that the slope with respect to a specific variable may be written as

$$(\delta P_i) / (\delta Z_{jk}) = \hat{\beta} P_i (1 - P_i)$$

where $\hat{\beta}_k$ is the estimated coefficient. Elasticity of probability P_i with respect to variable Z_{jk} is

$$P_{i_{\eta_{z_{jk}}}} = \hat{\beta}\,(1 - P_i)\, Z_{jk}$$

Here, both the slope and elasticity in such an estimation are nonlinear and need to be evaluated at a specific point.

The Accessibility Index

The accessibility measure used in the trip generation equations was computed from the parameters estimated in the mode choice equations. It was a composite measure of accessibility as perceived by the individual traveler. In principle, this accessibility measure is an index of the maximum utility derived by the traveler by choosing the most appropriate alternative—that is, Max U_{it} for all $i \in I_t$, where I_t is the choice set of traveler t, and U_{it} is the utility of traveler t associated with alternative i. The accessibility measure is the expected value E [Max U_{it}] for all $i \in I_t$ This measure can be computed from the parameter estimates derived in the mode choice equations, using the same stochastic specifications of the utility function as previously derived.

Table 8A-1. Local Registration Tax Incidence: Bogotá, 1980
(1980 Colombian pesos)

Income quintile	Cars per 100 households	Income per month	Local registration fee	Incidence (percentage of monthly income)
1	5.6	3,388	4.9	0.14
2	5.8	7,102	5.1	0.07
3	8.0	11,288	7.0	0.06
4	17.9	18,788	15.7	0.08
5	72.0	53,523	63.0	0.12
Weighted average	21.7	18,659	19.0	0.10

Note: The tax is Col$0.45 per 1,000 pesos of vehicle value; the 1980 vehicle value was estimated from the average value in 1978. Quintiles are by ascending order of household income.

Source: Pachon (1981b); number of cars from 1978 World Bank–DANE Household Survey.

Table 8A-2. Sales Tax Incidence: Bogotá, 1978
(1978 Colombian pesos)

Income quintile	Cars per 100 households	Effect on car price	Effect on income	Monthly income	Incidence (percentage of monthly income)
	(1)	(2)	(3)	(4)	(5)
1	5.6	1,663	29	2,378	1.22
2	5.8	1,712	30	5,019	0.61
3	7.1	2,587	12	7,921	0.53
4	17.9	5,371	94	13,149	0.71
5	72.0	21,602	378	37,569	1.01
Weighted average	21.7	6,518	111	15,094	0.87

Note: Quintiles are by ascending order of household income.
Source: Pachon (1981b).

Table 8A-3. Customs Duty Incidence: Bogotá, 1978
(1978 Colombian pesos)

Income quintile	Effect on car price			Effect on cost of capital			Incidence (percentage of monthly income)
	Imported	Domestic	Weighted average	Imported	Domestic	Weighted average	
1	2,640	443	1,476	46	8	26	1.09
2	2,764	469	1,045	48	8	27	0.54
3	3,789	642	2,118	66	11	37	0.47
4	8,525	1,445	4,765	149	25	83	0.63
5	34,283	5,813	19,164	600	102	335	0.89
Weighted average	10,340[a]	1,753[b]	5,779	181	31	101	0.78

Note: Quintiles are by ascending order of household income.
a. Effect on price for imported cars is 37 percent of the average price of the car.
b. Effect on price for locally assembled cars is 5.64 percent of the average price.
Source: Pachon (1981b).

Table 8A-4. Incidence of Taxes and Subsidies on Fuel Consumption of Private Cars: Bogotá, 1980

Income quintile	Fuel consumption (gallons per month)	Subsidy (pesos per month)	Tax (pesos per month)	Net subsidy (pesos per month)	Subsidy (percentage of income)	Tax (percentage of income)	Net subsidy (percentage of income)
1	1.74	+47	−20	+27	+1.39	−0.60	+0.79
2	1.82	+49	−21	+28	+0.69	−0.30	+0.39
3	2.50	+67	−29	+38	+0.60	−0.26	+0.34
4	5.62	+151	−65	+86	+0.81	−0.35	+0.46
5	22.61	+611	−262	+349	+1.14	−0.49	+0.65
Weighted average	6.82	+184	−79	+105	+0.99	−0.42	+0.57

Note: Quintiles are by ascending order of household income.
Source: Pachon (1981b).

Table 8A-5. Models for Choice of Work Trip Mode: Bogotá, 1972 and 1978

	Estimated coefficient [a]	
Independent variables	Bogotá, 1972	Bogotá, 1978
Travel time (minutes), all motorized modes	−0.0257 (1.3)	−0.0675 (2.5)
Travel time (minutes), walking	−0.0688 (6.0)	−0.1083 (9.4)
Cost of travel (Colombian pesos/ wage rate per minute)[b]	−0.3013 (1.0)	−1.083 (4.0)
Gross family income[c]		
Automobile driver/passenger	0.00013 (3.2)	0.00017 (6.6)
Taxi/colectivo	0.00018 (4.2)	0.00018 (5.8)
Bus	0	0
Buseta/microbus	0.00010 (2.7)	0.00011 (6.1)
Walk (≤30-minute trip)	−0.00003 (0.4)	−0.00002 (0.6)
Head of household (1 = head, 0 otherwise)		
Automobile driver/passenger	1.61 (5.2)	2.192 (7.8)
Taxi/colectivo	0	0
Bus	0	0
Buseta	0	0
Walk	0.263 (0.6)	0.672 (2.5)
Car competition variable (number of vehicles/number of workers)		
Automobile driver/passenger	3.450 (4.0)	1.107 (2.2)
Taxi/colectivo	0	0
Bus	0	0
Buseta	2.333 (3.4)	−0.117 (0.3)
Walk	2.702 (2.4)	−1.707 (2.1)
Buseta/microbus accessibility dummy variables		
Poorly served (1)	−0.465 (1.4)	0
Well served (0)	0	0
Alternative-specific constants		
Automobile driver/passenger	−1.696 (3.0)	−2.410 (4.5)
Taxi/colectivo	−2.167(5.70)	−3.749 (6.9)
Bus	0	0
Buseta	−1.302 (6.2)	−0.761 (6.2)
Walk	0.754 (0.9)	2.287 (4.9)
Model statistics	Bogotá, 1972	Bogotá, 1978
Log likelihood		
At zero	−894	−1,538
At convergence	−524	−1,014
Likelihood ratio index	0.414	0.340
Number of cases	732	1,244

(Table continues on the following page.)

Table 8A-5 (*continued*)

Sample constitution: 1972[d]	Number of travelers in sample who choose
Automobile driver/passenger	223 (305 have alternative in choice set)
Taxi/*colectivo*	38 (338 have alternative in choice set)
Bus	321 (733 have alternative in choice set)
Buseta/microbus	115 (520 have alternative in choice set)
Walk	35 (590 have alternative in choice set)

Sample constitution: 1978	Number of travelers in sample who choose
Automobile driver/passenger	323 (417 have alternative in choice set)
Taxi/*colectivo*	21 (614 have alternative in choice set)
Bus	467 (1,239 have alternative in choice set)
Buseta/microbus	378 (1,239 have alternative in choice set)
Walk	146 (909 have alternative in choice set)

Note. Available alternatives include drive/shared ride, taxi/*colectivo*, bus, *buseta*, and walk.

a. Asymptotic *t*-statistics are in parentheses.

b. Cost of travel measured in Colombian pesos. Wage rate measured in Colombian pesos per minute.

c. Measured in 1972 Colombian pesos per month.

d. All individuals in households owning automobiles have driver/passenger in their choice set. Households living in inner areas of the city (rings 1–3) have taxi/*colectivo*. All travelers are assumed to have access to standard buses. Households living in regions served by *busetas* (according to route maps) have the *buseta*/microbus alternative—all households in 1978. Travelers living within 12 kilometers of their work location are assumed to be able to travel there on foot.

Source: Kozel (1986).

Notes

This chapter is based on work originally reported in Cifuentes (1984), Kozel (1981, 1982, 1986), Pachon (1979, 1981a, 1981b, 1981c), and Westin (1980). Alberto Hernandez and Emilio Latorre also contributed to the research, and Gregory Ingram directed the research design. The section on "Modeling Travel Demand" reports the work in Kozel (1981, 1982, 1986).

1. Data about the value of vehicles by age were available from information assembled by the Centro de Estudios para Desarrollo Economico of the Universidad de Los Andes, Bogotá.

2. A trip, incidentally, is taken as a one-way trip: travel from home to work and return is counted as two trips.

3. See the appendix to this chapter for the derivation of the accessibility index.

4. See Domencich and McFadden (1975), Maddala (1983), Hensher and Johnson (1981), Charles River Associates (1976), Ben-Akiva (1973), Lerman (1975), Manski and Lerman (1977), Hensher and Stopher (1979).

5. See Kozel (1986) for a detailed evaluation of transferability of such models.

Chapter 9

Urban Government and Finances

There is a wide variation in the range of administrative, service, and financial responsibilities borne by local governments. Most cities exhibit a complex web of relationships, usually historically determined, between the local municipal government and state and national governments. These relationships become more complicated in capital cities because the national governments often display greater interest in the running of these cities. Municipal bodies in most cities are responsible for providing local public services, such as water supply, sanitation and sewerage, solid waste disposal, roads, and street lighting. They also regulate such activities as land use, land development, and construction, and they provide public safety services in the form of a police force. In addition, in many cities, local governments are responsible for providing public transportation, power, telephones, public housing, education, and health care. In some cases there is a distinction between investment and maintenance responsibilities, because urban infrastructure investment is characteristically expensive and local bodies seldom have adequate resources for making such investments.

In order to provide services, municipal governments have certain tax-raising powers, most commonly related to taxing real property but also in many cases related to taxing industrial and commercial activities. Because municipal governments are typically responsible for control and regulation of land use, zoning, building by-laws, and development controls, it is also common for them to have overall responsibilities for medium-term investment and physical plans. As may be expected, all these functions have to be performed by some entity: what varies between cities and countries is the degree of private involvement and how responsibilities and powers are shared between the different levels of government, as well as between government and empowered parastatal public agencies.

Urban Government in Bogotá

In the case of Bogotá, the district government is responsible for a larger number of functions than usual for local government in developing countries. The city is an autonomous administrative entity, the Distrito Especial (Special District), and does not form a part of any state. This is a common pattern for many capital cities, including New Delhi, Mexico City, and Washington, D.C. The Distrito Especial was carved out of the state of Cundinamarca in 1954 by consolidating the Municipality of Bogotá with a number of adjacent municipalities. The mayor of Bogotá (the *alcalde*) is directly nominated (and removed) by the president of Colombia. He has no fixed term and is not elected. Over the last seventy years, the average tenure of the mayor has been just over one year!

The district government of Bogotá is responsible for providing almost all public services: health, education, roads, water and sewerage, power, telephones, and waste disposal. It has minimal presence in the supply of public transport and public housing, however. The administrative structure of Bogotá that delivers all these services is highly decentralized but essentially organized along functional lines. The mayor is assisted by a cabinet of five secretaries: Interior (Gobierno), Finance (Hacienda), Education (Educación), Health (Salud), and Public Works (Obras Públicas). In addition, there are four administrative departments (Departamentos Administrativos): the planning department (Departamento Administrativo de Planeación Distrital, DAPD), the transport department (Departamento Administrativo de Transporte y Tránsito, DATT), social welfare (Departamento Administrativo de Bienestar Social), and community development (Departamento Administrativo de Acción Communal). Each department is headed by a director who reports directly to the mayor. There are three other officers: the legal representative (*personero*), the treasurer (*tesorero*), and the controller (*contralor*). Each of these is appointed by the city council, an elected body of twenty members and twenty alternates.

Services are delivered primarily by several decentralized agencies. The main agencies were the power company (Empresa de Energía Eléctrica de Bogotá, EEEB), the water and sewerage company (Empresa de Alcantarillado y Acueducto de Bogotá, EAAB), the telephone company (Empresa de Teléfonos de Bogotá, ETB), and the general public service company (Empresa Distrital de Servicios Públicos, EDIS). The decentralized agencies account for a major portion of the district budget, in particular the capital budget, and are largely self-financing. Another implementing agency, mainly concerned with capital infrastructure works, is the Institute of Urban Development (Instituto de Desarrollo Urbano, IDU). It was funded mainly from valorization charges and was very active in the early 1970s but has declined in importance since. The district also has its own social security agency, the Caja de Previsión Social; a small public housing agency, the Caja de Vivienda Popular; and a small public transport company, Empresa Distrital de Transporte Urbano (EDTU). As this list suggests, most of the local government functions are carried out through relatively autonomous decentralized agencies.

The management of many large cities in the world suffers from excessive geographical fragmentation. It is not unusual for a large metropolitan area to fall into the jurisdictions of a number of local governments, as do the Washington, D.C., Calcutta, and Mexico City metropolitan areas. Such fragmentation creates a number of problems, including uneven tax rates, management of services across boundaries, and varying building and zoning regulations. The problem of fragmentation does not exist in Bogotá because the district covers almost the entire metropolitan area, thanks to annexation of selected adjacent municipalities. After official extension of the urban perimeter, the major public utilities had even begun to service some areas outside the district to which development had spread. As the city expands, it may become more difficult to continue annexing municipalities, however, and fragmentation of jurisdiction may become more of a problem in Bogotá.

An interesting feature of the extensive functional decentralization in Bogotá is that some agencies have to conform to national policies and control despite being essentially autonomous. Service charges for water, electricity, and telephones must conform to national tariff policies. Education and health services are regulated by national tax subventions and controls. The borrowing ability of the agencies is limited by the need for permission and oversight by the national government. However, there is little interference by the national government in the day-to-day administrative activities of the district government and its decentralized agencies. The district government is also quite independent in its authority over urban planning functions and the preparation and implementation of its annual budgets.

There is no centralized consolidated district budget in Bogotá. Indeed, in conducting this study it was not easy to obtain the full picture of district finances over a reasonable historical period.[1] We launched a special effort to compile these data for 1961–79 in order to gain an appreciation of the trends in the district's revenues and expenditures. There was a rapid 23 percent annual growth in total district government expenditure in nominal terms. Between 1961 and 1979 consolidated district expenditure grew by a factor of 37 in current prices. In constant prices there was little growth in per capita expenditures—about 1 percent per year. This trend is not easy to discern, however, because growth in constant prices fluctuates widely along with inflation rates (see figure 9-1). It is obviously difficult to calibrate taxes and user charges so that they keep up with inflation in a regular smooth fashion and so that expenditures can be kept up in real terms. It is interesting to note that expenditures in Cali were at a similar absolute level and exhibited a similar trend over the same period. Although it is creditable for a local government to be able to keep up real per capita revenues and expenditures over a long period of extremely rapid population growth along with inflation, the growth of per capita real income in Bogotá was still higher, at about 1.7 percent per year from 1960 to 1975 (see chapter 3, table 3-2). Local government's share of total city income therefore declined over this period. The revenue yields closely followed expenditures. The district government itself accounted for only about 20 percent of expenditures over the whole period. The various decentralized agencies accounted for the rest: the three big utility companies—EEEB, EAAB, and ETB—had a combined share of more than 60 percent, increasing to almost 75 percent in the late 1970s.

An Overview of Financial Structure

In Bogotá during the period studied, user charges financed more than 50 percent of all expenditures, particularly for the utilities. This might have been expected from the decentralized nature of the city's utility

Figure 9-1. Total Consolidated Expenditure Per Capita of the Bogotá District, 1961–79

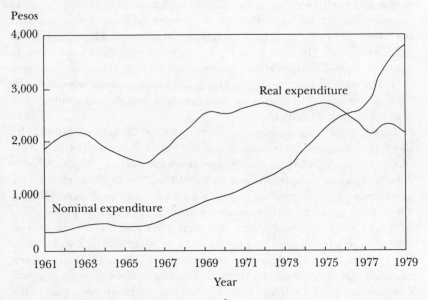

Pesos

Source: Linn (1984).

companies. Similarly, borrowing, at 20 to 30 percent of total revenues, financed much of the capital expenditure. Per capita revenues from taxes fell in real terms over the period, implying a failure of the tax system to fully compensate for inflation. Transfers and revenue sharing showed a slight increase in real per capita terms and went up to about 15 percent of all revenues in 1976. By the late 1970s, the revenue structure was quite changed from that in the early 1960s. The reduction in reliance on tax revenues and transfers was matched by an increasing share of user charges.

As might be expected from the highly decentralized nature of public service agencies in Bogotá, district budgeting and investment planning are highly decentralized. Although there is an elaborate coordination system designed to link the activities of various agencies with those of the district government, there is very little effective coordination. This is partly because of a lack of genuine medium-term urban planning and systematic evaluation of urban investments. It is also a result of the self-financing nature of the main decentralized agencies. Their budgets are considerably larger than that of the city government per se, and they neither receive nor pay any funds to the district budget. Moreover, their staffs have greater continuity than the leaders of the district government. In reality, then, the decentralized agencies are left pretty much alone to plan and implement their projects and programs.

Within the district government, the budget for current expenditures is prepared in the Finance Secretariat (Hacienda) and the investment budget is prepared by the District Planning Department (DAPD). Formally, the budgets have to be approved by the District Council. Additions and amendments to the budget are frequent over the spending year. Similarly, the budgets of the decentralized agencies, after approval by their respective boards of directors, are presented by the secretary of finance to the District Council for approval. When changes in the budgets are approved, implementation can take place, but the payment systems and auditing system are quite bureaucratic. The control experienced is essentially "numerical-legal" rather than administrative (Wolff 1984). The agencies supposed to supervise the execution of the budget, the Finance Secretariat and the DAPD, are too weak professionally to exercise effective control. However, the auditing procedures are quite strict and cumbersome: there is 100 percent auditing rather than random sampling. The controller's office has to verify all expenditures twice—once before and once after the expenditure. For the main decentralized agencies, the auditing agents are *revisores fiscales* who are nominated by the mayor and the District Council.

Credits have historically financed the major part of investment financing. Between 1971 and 1976, credits financed about 60 to 90 percent of investments in different years. To raise any credit over Col$1 million (about US$22,000 in 1980) required formal approval by the national government. This approval consists, at different stages, of the concurrence of the National Planning Department, the Ministry of Finance, and in the case of foreign credits, the Central Bank (Banco de la República). The Monetary Council (Junta Monetaria), attached to the Finance Ministry, also has a say in the approval of credits. The National Planning Department evaluates the economic viability of projects before granting approval. For the decentralized agencies, foreign credits have been the most important source of funding. The existence of these various controls, in addition to the technical supervision of the international lending agencies, has contributed to upgrading the quality of professionalism in the decentralized agencies. In the absence of a coordinated overall investment plan, however, each agency essentially makes investments in response to its own perception of increasing demands and proceeds incrementally. This has often resulted in poor timing or sequencing of investments by the different service agencies.

Overall, the administrative fragmentation of Bogotá is reflected in fragmentation in the budgetary process. Although much attention has been paid to organizing formal mechanisms of control and coordination among the different agencies, in practice there was little effective control. The main decentralized public service agencies are more powerful than the district government and hence operate quite autonomously. The lack of continuity in the district government is another factor in this relationship. As already mentioned, the mayor seldom holds office for much longer than a year. The city council is elected every two years and meets four times a year for a month each time. There is little continuity among council members, unlike the U.S. Congress, for example, where many members are reelected many times. Representatives of the council who serve on agency boards exercise some influence but not a significant amount. The general conclusion is that "the executive units exercise more political power than the legislative District Council" (Wolff 1984). The continual changes in officials, council members, and mayors contribute to the difficulty of making coherent long-term strategies and approaches.

The paradox is that, in spite of all the problems, public service delivery has been relatively efficient in Bogotá in terms of people's access to essential services such as water supply, urban transport, sanitation and sewerage, roads, power, and even telephones. A fragmented structure made up of powerful public service agencies is probably well suited to the needs of a rapidly expanding city. The agencies' relative autonomy contributes to their ability to be more aware of changing needs and then responding to them incrementally. Their fiscal autonomy has also helped make them more reliant on user charges, which in turn probably makes consumers more demanding. This itself contributes to the agencies' sensitivity to consumer demand for their services. It is quite possible that a tight, more centralized governmental system might have performed less well in the context of a rapidly growing city.

The Structure of Revenue

The compilation of the district government's total consolidated revenues, including those of the decentralized agencies, revealed that tax revenues have become less important. In 1961, taxes contributed about 27 percent of total revenues; they had declined to about 16 percent in 1979, an improvement from just 12 percent in 1974. In constant 1976 prices, per capita tax revenue fell from Col$482 in 1961 to Col$381 in 1979. More noteworthy is the significant increase in the contribution of "self-financed" revenues. These included service charges and development contributions. In relative terms these contributions grew from 45 percent of total revenues in 1961 to about 60 percent in 1979. Revenues from borrowing fluctuated significantly over the years, depending essentially on the investment program requirements of the main decentralized agencies. The revenues from national grants and shared taxes varied between 8 and 15 percent over the whole period. Grants had mainly been for education services. Education was "nationalized" in 1976 and these funds transferred to a special education fund. Hence, grants fell to zero by 1979 (see tables 9-1 and 9-2, and figure 9-2).

It is interesting to compare the revenue structure of Bogotá with other cities in developing countries. Comparable data on local finances are not easy to come by, however, and coverage of services by local governments is different in different cities. Broadly comparable data pertaining to the early to mid-1970s were compiled by Linn (1980) and are in table 9-3. Bogotá and Cali are unusual in their degree of self-financing charges as sources of revenue. This pattern is a common one for the Colombian cities listed in the table—Bogotá, Cali, and Cartagena. The other cities exhibiting a similar pattern are Ahmedabad and Bombay in India and Lusaka in Zambia. The only other city with a high degree of borrowing was Karachi, but it had a very low degree of self-financing. It appears that borrowing costs were being financed through high mobilization of local taxes. Bogotá, Cali, and Cartagena are outliers in their low reliance on local taxes as revenue sources. The Colombian cities also have little dependence on grants and other devolution from higher levels of governments. This would be even more pronounced if the education grants were taken out of these data. Overall, Colombian cities

Table 9-1. Consolidated Per Capita Revenues: Bogotá, 1961–79
(1976 Colombian pesos)

Revenue	1961	1962	1963	1964	1965	1966	1967	1968	1969	1970	1971	1972	1973	1974	1975	1976	1977	1978	1979
Tax revenue	482	460	373	338	354	288	325	324	358	248	364	357	383	325	357	350	326	345	380
General non-tax revenue	25	26	21	21	25	8	10	12	9	8	12	8	5	10	8	6	7	10	21
Self-financed revenue	792	847	803	740	815	778	895	1,061	1,285	1,348	1,474	1,373	1,317	1,300	1,241	1,395	1,451	1,560	1,432
Shared taxes	142	131	185	201	179	150	159	141	171	235	284	255	224	233	259	205	191	199	210
Grants	16	48	73	61	50	57	46	79	43	102	107	86	113	108	133	115	22	31	0
Borrowing	327	530	575	440	352	289	572	665	509	488	562	575	557	658	787	516	419	413	322
Total revenue	1,784	2,042	2,030	1,801	1,775	1,570	2,007	2,282	2,375	2,429	2,803	2,654	2,599	2,634	2,785	2,587	2,416	2,558	2,365

Source: Linn (1984b).

Table 9-2. Structure of Consolidated Revenues: Bogotá, 1961–79
(percentage distribution)

Revenue	1961	1962	1963	1964	1965	1966	1967	1968	1969	1970	1971	1972	1973	1974	1975	1976	1977	1978	1979
Tax revenue	27.0	22.5	18.4	18.8	19.9	18.3	16.2	14.2	15.1	13.8	13.0	14.5	14.7	12.4	12.8	13.5	13.5	13.5	16.0
General non-tax revenue	1.4	1.3	1.0	1.2	1.4	0.5	0.5	0.5	0.4	0.3	0.4	0.3	0.2	0.4	0.3	0.3	0.3	0.4	0.9
Self-financed revenue	44.4	41.4	39.5	41.0	45.9	49.3	44.3	46.5	54.1	53.3	52.6	51.7	50.7	49.3	44.5	53.9	60.0	60.9	60.3
Shared taxes	8.0	6.4	9.1	11.2	10.1	9.6	7.9	6.2	7.2	9.3	10.1	9.6	8.6	8.8	9.3	7.9	7.9	7.8	8.8
Grants	0.9	2.4	3.6	3.4	2.8	3.6	2.3	3.5	1.8	4.0	3.8	3.3	4.4	4.1	4.8	4.5	0.9	1.2	0.0
Borrowing	18.3	26.0	28.3	24.4	19.8	18.4	28.5	29.1	21.4	19.3	20.0	21.7	21.4	25.0	28.2	19.9	17.3	16.1	14.0
Total revenue	100.0	100.0	100.0	100.0	100.0	100.0	100.0	100.0	100.0	100.0	100.0	100.0	100.0	100.0	100.0	100.0	100.0	100.0	100.0

Source: Table 9-1.

241

Table 9-3. Financing of Local Public Expenditure in Selected Cities by Type of Revenue
(percent)

City	Year	A Local taxes	B Self-financing services	C Other local revenue	D Total local revenue	X Grants and taxes	Y Net borrowing[a]	Z Total external revenue	T Total
Francistown, Botswana	1972	46.8	56.1	n.a.	102.9	1.9	-4.8	-2.9	100.0
Mexico City, Mexico	1968	70.9	5.2	25.8	101.9	8.9	-10.8	-1.9	100.0
La Paz, Bolivia	1975	61.9	3.6	31.5	97.0	9.0	-6.0	3.0	100.0
Tunis, Tunisia	1972	36.8	7.1	50.0	93.9	0.7	5.4	6.1	100.0
Kitwe, Zambia	1975	35.0	53.1	4.6	92.7	2.2	5.1	7.3	100.0
Valencia, Venezuela	1968	44.8	13.4	32.6	90.8	9.2	n.a.	9.2	100.0
Lubumbashi, Zaire	1972	72.8	n.a.	17.7	90.5	9.5	n.a.	9.5	100.0
Rio de Janeiro, Brazil[b]	1967	74.5	7.2	6.7	88.4	1.7	9.9	11.6	100.0
Ahmedabad, India	1970–71	38.6	41.8	5.9	86.3	4.2	9.5	13.7	100.0
Bombay, India	1970–71	37.9	38.7	8.0	84.6	1.0	14.4	15.4	100.0
Karachi, Pakistan	1974–75	67.6	2.2	14.3	84.1	2.8	13.1	15.9	100.0
Seoul, Korea	1971	30.3	36.3	13.4	80.0	15.8	4.1	19.9	100.0
Jakarta, Indonesia[c]	1972–73	40.6	15.2	23.0	78.8	21.1	n.a.	21.1	100.0
		(43.7)	(15.2)	(23.0)	(81.9)	(18.1)	(n.a.)	(18.1)	

242

		A	B	C	D	X	Y	Z	T
Lusaka, Zambia	1972	39.3	36.9	2.0	78.2	6.0	15.8	21.8	100.0
Cali, Colombia	1972	15.6	57.5	1.3	74.4	2.8	22.9	25.7	100.0
Calcutta Corp., India	1974	64.4	n.a.	9.4	73.8	19.4	6.8	26.2	100.0
Cartagena, Colombia	1972	23.3	43.3	3.8	70.4	12.8	16.8	29.6	100.0
Mbuji-Mayi, Zaire	1971	66.5	n.a.	2.7	70.2	29.8	n.a.	29.8	100.0
Manila, Philippines[d]	1970	10.0	5.0	30.0	55.0	n.a.	n.a.	30.0	100.0
Bukavu, Zaire	1971	67.4	n.a.	2.5	69.9	30.1	n.a.	30.1	100.0
Madras, India	1975	54.5	3.7	11.0	69.2	25.1	5.7	30.8	100.0
Bogotá, Colombia	1972	13.7	48.5	0.3	62.5	14.0	23.5	37.5	100.0
Tehran, Iran	1974	42.8	n.a.	4.1	46.9	45.2	7.9	53.1	100.0
Kingston, Jamaica	1971–72	23.9	2.7	3.4	30.1	67.2	2.7	69.9	100.0
Kinshasa, Zaire	1971	25.4	n.a.	1.5	26.9	73.1	n.a.	73.1	100.0
Median (average)[c]		42.8	7.2	6.7	78.8	9.5	5.1	21.1	100.0
		(46.0)	(19.3)	(11.2)	(76.6)	(17.7)	(5.7)	(23.4)	

n.a. Not applicable.

Note: $D = A + B + C$; $Z = X + Y$; $T = D + Z$.

a. Net borrowing consists of loan financing minus net changes in financial assets or reserves.

b. As a result of the exclusion of autonomous agencies, the contributions of self-financing service revenue and of all locally raised revenue are probably understated, and the remaining entries overstated.

c. Figures not in parentheses include shared taxes under grants; figures in parentheses include shared taxes under local taxes.

d. Total revenues are used instead of total expenditures.

Source: Linn (1980).

243

Figure 9-2. Composition of the Bogotá District's Real Per Capita Total Revenues, 1961–79

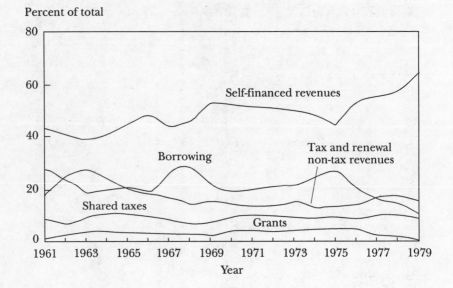

Source: Fawcett (1984).

have a different financing pattern from most other cities in the developing world: they exhibit much greater reliance on user charges as a means of financing urban services.

The property tax is the most commonly levied local tax in almost all countries in the world (see table 9-4). On average about half of all taxes come from the property tax. Another 25 to 40 percent of tax revenue typically comes from some tax related to economic activity. Among most Hispanic countries, this is a tax levied on industry and commerce; in India the corresponding tax is *octroi* (although it is generally agreed that *octroi* should be replaced by a more general tax related to economic activity); in other countries some kind of income tax is levied. In the Colombian cities, the property tax fetches almost 60 percent of tax revenue; the industry and commerce tax are the other major taxes.

Between 1960 and 1979, receipts from the property tax fell in constant per capita terms. (See table 9A-1 for revenues of the Bogotá District Administration from 1960 to 1980). The fall in relative importance of tax revenues via-à-vis the total district revenues is largely the result of the declining performance of the property tax. Why did this happen? The basis for property taxation in Bogotá is capital value of property, as distinguished from the "annual value" taxation found in most former British colonies. Whereas it is difficult to prescribe a normative level of property tax, the rate of property taxation seemed low in the late 1970s. The effective taxation rate—the ratio of property tax collection to estimated market value of properties—was less than 0.5 percent. In the United States it is generally greater than 1 percent. One caveat needs to be expressed here, however: a number of the service user charges in Bogotá are based on property values, so at least a portion of the user charge collection is related to property values, thus raising the effective property tax rate in Bogotá.

The data system related to property taxation is relatively well systematized in Bogotá and has been computerized for some time. The city has also been quite efficient in adding new properties to the system: for example, the number of properties in its files doubled between 1975 and 1979. The District Cadastral Office also maintains a land value map, which is continually updated. It was interesting to find that the assessed values in this data set kept up well with market values: they were even overestimated in many cases. Yet assessment ratios for property tax purposes had declined during the late 1970s. The statutory tax ratio was 0.84, but it was estimated that the effective assessment ratio had probably declined to below 0.4 in the late 1970s. It seemed that values in the land value map were seldom used for revaluing properties for tax purposes. There was also a lag in following up changes in land uses—for example, from residential to commercial uses.

As a result of concern over the performance of the property tax and the overall fiscal system, particularly the sharing of funds and responsibilities among national, departmental (state), and municipal governments, the government appointed a Commission on Intergovernmental Finance in 1980. With changing circumstances at both the local and national levels, it is useful to appoint such special commissions at regular intervals—say, every five or ten years. The actual arrangements made depend on the particular circumstances of the country and its tax system, but the principles should be to make revenue sources commensurate with the responsibilities of providing services and to encourage decentralization of service provision as well as revenue raising.

In this case the commission's basic conclusion was that local government functions should rely on local resources for funding. This resulted in new legislation aimed at strengthening local government institutions and tax sources. Specific attention was given to the administration of the property tax. All cadastral values were updated to a base of 1983 values by inflating all values by an annual increase of 10 percent from the year of their last valuation. Subsequently, there was to be an annual increase by a price index. This adjustment has not kept up with full inflation, but it is, nonetheless, a step in the right direction in injecting greater tax

Table 9-4. **Distribution of Local Tax Revenue in Selected Cities by Source**
(percent)

City	Year	Local taxes as percent of local expenditure	A Property tax	B Property transfer tax	C Income tax	D General sales tax	E Octroi	F Beer tax	G Gasoline tax	H Entertainment tax	I Industry and commerce tax	J Motor vehicle tax	K Gambling tax	L All other taxes	T Total
Managua, Nicaragua	1974	84.3	—	—	—	69.4	—	—	—	2.3	21.1	3.2	—	4.1	100.0
Mexico City, Mexico	1968	70.9	33.5	2.8	—	—	—	—	1.1	2.6	44.2	—	—	15.8	100.0
Valencia, Venezuela	1968	44.8	21.4	—	—	—	—	—	—	—	66.7	11.8	—	—	100.0
Bogotá, Colombia	1972	13.7	58.4	—	—	—	—	—	1.8	7.0	18.2	5.1	—	9.5	100.0
Cali, Colombia	1974	23.2	54.0	—a	—	—	—	—a	—	6.1	27.8	4.3	—	7.8	100.0
Cartagena, Colombia	1972	23.3	61.2	—	—	—	—	—	—	4.4	12.2	2.1	5.8	14.2	100.0
La Paz, Bolivia	1975	61.9	5.2	—	—	—	—	7.1	—	1.5	73.8	—	—	12.4	100.0
Manila, Philippines	1970	55.0	61.9	—	—	—	—	—	2.2	—	32.1	—	—	3.8	100.0
Group average												37.0			
Karachi, Pakistan	1974–75	67.6	46.0	—	—	—	49.9	—	—	—	—	3.0	—	1.0	100.0
Ahmedabad, India	1971–72	38.6	43.0	—	—	—	52.0	—	—	—	—	2.0	—	3.0	100.0
Bombay, India	1971–72	37.9	55.6	—	—	—	37.7	—	—	0.3	—	3.7	—	2.7	100.0
Calcutta Corp. India	1974–75	64.4	64.8	—	—	—	27.1b	—	—	—	—	—	—	8.2	100.0
Group average								41.7							
Francistown, Botswana	1972	48.8	12.9	—	61.1	—	—	—	—	—	—	—	—	26.0	100.0
Lusaka, Zambia	1972	39.3	74.6	—	25.4	—	—	—	—	—	—	—	—	—	100.0
Ndola, Zambia	1972	n.a.	75.6	—	24.4	—	—	—	—	—	—	—	—	—	100.0
Kitwe, Zambia	1972	n.a.	80.0	—	20.0	—	—	—	—	—	—	—	—	—	100.0

246

City	Year	A	B	C	D	E	F	G	H	I	J	K	L	T
Kinshasa, Zaire	1971	25.4	—	—	14.4	—	62.5	—	—	—	—	—	23.1	100.0
Bukavu, Zaire	1971	67.4	—	—	3.7	—	87.0	—	—	—	—	—	9.3	100.0
Mbuji-Mayi, Zaire	1971	66.5	—	—	62.7	—	—	—	—	—	—	—	37.3	100.0
Daegu, Korea	1976	n.a.	49.5	21.2	9.1	—	—	—	10.4	—	5.4	—	3.5	100.0
Gwangju, Korea	1976	n.a.	50.3	23.1	13.2	—	—	—	6.6	—	4.1	—	2.9	100.0
Daejeon, Korea	1976	n.a.	51.0	20.1	9.7	—	—	—	10.7	—	5.5	—	3.0	100.0
Jeonju, Korea	1976	n.a.	52.0	24.4	8.9	—	—	—	7.5	—	4.9	—	2.1	100.0
Group average					23.0									
Seoul, Korea	1971	30.3	20.6	34.8	—	—	—	—	16.4	—	22.2	—	6.0	100.0
Madras, India	1975–76	54.5	68.9	5.1	—	—	—	—	16.0	—	—	—	10.0	100.0
Tehran, Iran	1974	42.8	55.3	—	—	—	—	—	9.1	—	10.1	—	25.6	100.0
Tunis, Tunisia	1973	36.8	82.6	12.8	—	—	—	—	4.6	—	—	—	—	100.0
Jakarta, Indonesia	1972–73	43.7	—	—	—	—	—	—	16.9	—	50.2	26.9	6.0	100.0
Lagos, Nigeria	1962–63	50.9	100.0[a]	—	—	—	—	—	—	—	—	—	—	100.0
Kingston, Jamaica	1972	23.9	100.0	—	—	—	—	—	—	—	—	—	—	100.0
Rio de Janeiro, Brazil	1967	84.4	3.9	1.0	89.2	—	—	—	—	—	—	—	5.9	100.0
Overall median			51.0											
Overall average			44.6											

n.a. Not available.

— Negligible.

Note: Cities grouped roughly according to similarity of financial structure. T = the sum of columns A–L.

a. Share tax receipts not shown under local tax revenue.

b. Share of octroi receipts collected by the Calcutta Metropolitan Development Authority.

Source: Linn (1984b).

buoyancy into the system. Further flexibility has been given to municipal governments to fix the tax ratio at any point between 0.4 and 1.2 percent, compared with a fixed rate earlier. These changes are quite realistic and pragmatic. Most cities in developing countries suffer from the problem of inefficiently updating property tax valuations. Some are constricted by rent control legislation, which naturally provides a cap on possible property valuations. Now that property records can easily be computerized, it is much easier to keep property records up to date. The application of gradual annual increases along with inflation also provides a convenient method of updating values: this is also unlikely to be resisted strenuously by taxpayers, because it is easier to sustain small, regular changes than any large change.

An interesting feature of property tax administration in Bogotá is the apparent progressiveness in the incidence of the property tax. It is often assumed that the property tax has regressive incidence, but in Bogotá and Cali it was found that the exemption of properties of low value does much to promote progressiveness while not losing any significant revenue. There was also a tendency to underassess land values in the poorer areas of the city and to overassess those in the better-off areas, which helped lend a degree of progressiveness to tax incidence.

The other main tax in Bogotá and Cali is the industry and commerce tax. Earlier, the tax was levied on different activities at different rates—mostly specific rates. As a result it had a declining trend until 1974, when it was transformed into a uniform ad valorem rate based on gross sales. This made it into the most buoyant tax in the district. This reform was extended to other Colombian cities by the Commission on Intergovernmental Finance in 1983.

Other taxes include the motor vehicle tax and the urban construction tax. The former is another commonly levied tax in most cities and one that can be a very buoyant source of revenue. Automobiles are major users of infrastructure that is not easily amenable to incremental user charges. Compared with public transport, they are also inefficient users of road space. Ownership, naturally, is also with a small (although increasing) affluent minority in developing countries. Typically, however, taxation of motor vehicles is inadequate because of the natural political and bureaucratic influence of car owners. In Bogotá revenues from automobiles declined in real per capita terms until 1976, but posted a very substantial increase between 1976 and 1980. As with property, it is essential to continually update the tax rate with inflation. Given the indefinitely rising trends in automobile ownership in cities in developing countries, serious thought must be given to making this tax a significant source of revenue for the funds required for urban infrastructure maintenance and investment. It would be rational to link the level of the motor vehicle tax to an index of road maintenance and investment costs.

The Commission on Intergovernmental Finance also recommended increasing the devolution of national tax collections from the sales tax to municipal governments. The sharing was to be increased from 30 percent in 1986 to about 50 percent by 1992, and the sharing formula has been skewed toward smaller municipalities and those who succeed in raising their own resources.

Valorization

The other source of revenue in Bogotá that has been an important means of financing infrastructure investment has been the system of valorization charges, which has frequently been used to finance infrastructure improvements in built-up areas. The idea is to recover the cost of infrastructure investments from properties that are in the vicinity of the improvements and/or likely to benefit from capitalization resulting from these improvements. This method was used extensively in Bogotá during the late 1960s and early 1970s. The implementing agency was the IDU. At the peak of its operations, valorization revenues amounted to almost two-thirds of the property tax revenues in 1969 and financed 16 percent of all consolidated expenditures. This was the phase of heightened urban construction activity, which was then regarded as the lead activity promoting economic development and employment. Valorization-financed expenditures fell to 8.6 percent of the total in 1976 and 3 percent in 1979. The procedure of levying valorization tax has been quite complex: properties are levied a differing rate of tax depending on their proximity to the improvement financed. In the case of road improvement, for example, the rate of valorization varies with distance from the road.

One reason that the importance of valorization-related activities has declined has been that the system has encountered problems in fully recovering its investments. This has been caused both by arrears in collection—particularly from public agencies—and by a feeling that people in low-income neighborhoods could not be expected to pay full valorization charges. The resulting shortfalls have necessitated transfers from the district government, leading to a reduced enthusiasm for valorization projects. Another problem that has cropped up is that legal norms restricted the concurrent coverage of one property by more than one valorization charge. Hence, new projects are difficult to carry out in previously covered areas. Moreover, cost overruns are difficult to pass on through valorization charges: if they result from inefficiency there is no reason the beneficiaries should suffer. Finally, the lack of adequate infrastructure investment planning is also responsible for a slowdown in valorization-financed investments. It should be noted that one element of good planning is the involvement of beneficiaries: when beneficiaries have been involved in planning projects, it has been easier to collect the charges.

Despite the problems encountered, Colombian cities have effectively used the valorization process to raise revenues for financing urban infrastructure investments. The method is well suited for financing investments in built-up areas and can be used to great benefit in other growing cities, although its potential as a method of financing urban infrastructure is limited in cities where government agencies own a large proportion of land and property. Some of the problems encountered in Bogotá also suggest that it may not be feasible to finance improvements in infrastructure from this source repeatedly. Taxpayer resistance is likely to develop if the same properties face valorization charges a second or third time. Some resistance could be avoided by better participation of affected communities. Even if valorization charges cannot be levied to cover the full costs of construction, they could be used to recover a significant portion of the costs.

Revenue Sharing

Shared taxes from the national government have generally ranged from 7 to 10 percent of total consolidated per capita revenues for the Bogotá District. Between 1961 and 1978, real per capita shared taxes grew by a little more than 2 percent a year, a performance that was much better than the growth of local taxes. The shared taxes consisted of the beer consumption tax, the shared sales tax, the gasoline tax, and the tobacco tax. The most important of these for Bogotá has been the beer tax, whose revenues often exceeded those from the property tax. The sales tax revenues were primarily earmarked for education, specifically teachers' salaries. Since 1976 these funds have been directed to the Regional Education Fund (Fondo Educativa Regional, FER) and no longer enter the district's budget. The FER also receives direct grants from the national government under a revenue-sharing program called the Situado Fiscal, which has been in operation since 1969 and formalized since 1971. Fifteen percent of total national revenues, excluding taxes already shared with subnational governments, was assigned for revenue sharing under this program. Funds received by the district government under this program were earmarked solely for education and health: 74 percent for primary education and 26 percent for local health care (see figure 9-3).

The Situado Fiscal was introduced to help reduce disparities, particularly in health and education services, between regions in Colombia. The formula for distribution favored the most rural regions: 30 percent of the fund was distributed equally to all departments (states) and the other 70 percent was based on 1964 census population shares. This obvi-

Figure 9-3. Distribution of Situado Fiscal to the Bogotá District

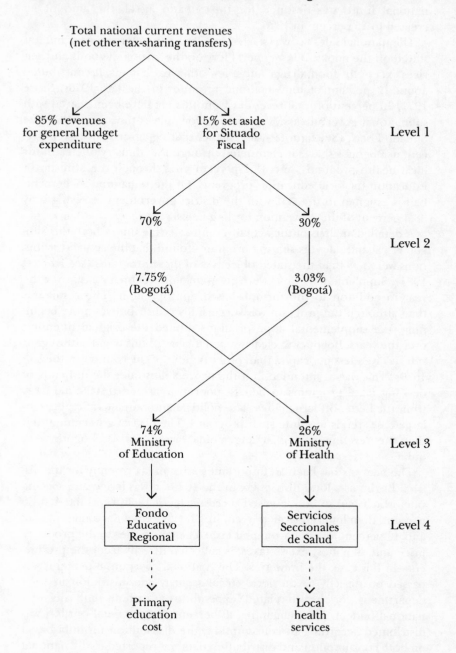

Source: Ruiz Betancourt (1978).

ously acted against the interests of Bogotá. Originally 6.5 percent of national funds was destined for the Situado Fiscal; the amount increased to 15 percent in 1975.

The national sales tax was started in 1965 as an emergency tax but has stayed on the books. It is a general levy on the sale of all goods and services except for food, drugs, and a few other basic items. It contributed about 15 percent of total national revenues in the late 1970s. Since 1971, 30 percent of total revenues from this tax have been shared with subnational governments. The sharing formula is the same as for the Situado Fiscal. (See figure 9-4 for further sharing agreements.) Ten percent of Bogotá's shares is channeled through the Ministry of Health for local health programs, and 13.1 percent goes through the Ministry of Education for local education programs. Of the remaining 77 percent, half is assigned to the FER, with the district government receiving only 38.5 percent of the subvention for its general revenues.

A detailed analysis of the actual revenue sharing under both the Situado Fiscal and sales-tax-sharing programs found that the actual distributions were less than the stated objectives of these programs (see Fawcett 1984). Supplemental grants were given on a discretionary basis over the year in addition to the formula-based appropriation. The result was that, although the program was successfully redistributive in the beginning, the supplemental appropriations diluted the original intention over the years. Bogotá was clearly a beneficiary of this trend, although it still received less per capita than other regions of the country in the late 1970s. This was as intended, but the process illustrates the difficulty of devising fiscal programs to benefit poorer areas and to take aid away from the better-off large cities. The political and bureaucratic power of large cities tends to dilute such programs. The district government felt that the revenue-sharing arrangements biased against Bogotá were unfair.

The beer tax has been an important source of tax revenue for the district. Begun as a local district tax in the 1920s, it was levied at a specific rate, which had to be increased successively. In 1966 it was fixed at 60 percent, then lowered to 48 percent in 1971 (8 percent as a national tax and 40 percent as a departmental tax). The tax applies to the producer price and, like most excise taxes, is collected directly from the producers—in this case, the breweries. The "national" portion, 8 percent, was passed on directly to the local social security administration in each department for health-related expenditures, without entering the national budget. The remaining 40 percent departmental portion was distributed according to consumption; the distribution formula based on both consumption and distribution data was reported to the national tax administration by the department governments (see figure 9-5). Bogotá had the highest per capita beer consumption in the country,

Figure 9-4. Distribution of Sales Tax Revenue to the Bogotá District, 1975–80

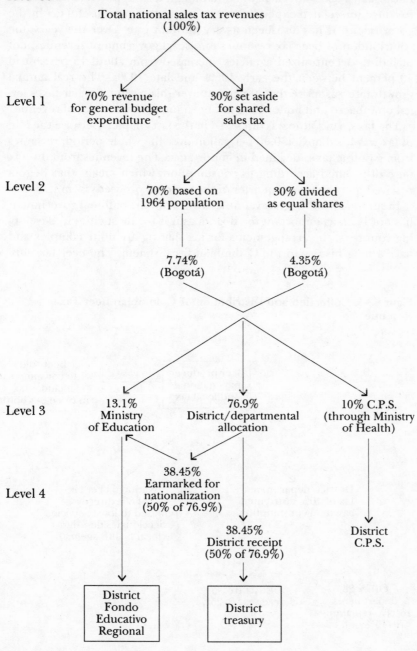

Source: Caceres Bolanos (1978).

and so it received almost one-quarter of the proceeds from the beer tax. Because this tax is not earmarked (although it is supposed to be devoted to education-related expenditures), it is seen as a most useful tax by the government. It has also been a very buoyant one. Over the years, the contribution of beer tax revenues to district government revenues, not including decentralized agencies, increased from about 15 percent to 40 percent between the early 1960s and late 1970s. The real annual growth rate was more than 9 percent over this period. Similar taxes levied on tobacco and liquor have not been important sources of revenue.

The tax on gasoline was discussed in the last chapter. Because the rate of tax was fixed at Col$0.06 per gallon over the whole period, revenues from gasoline taxes declined in importance. The revenues from this tax were distributed according to consumption, which meant that Bogotá received more than one-quarter of the national proceeds from it.

In summary, although revenue sharing from the national government has not been as important for Bogotá as it is for most cities in developing countries, the arrangements for tax sharing are quite complex and have a long history in the Colombian fiscal system. The beer tax illus-

Figure 9-5. Collection and Distribution of Colombian Beer Tax Revenue

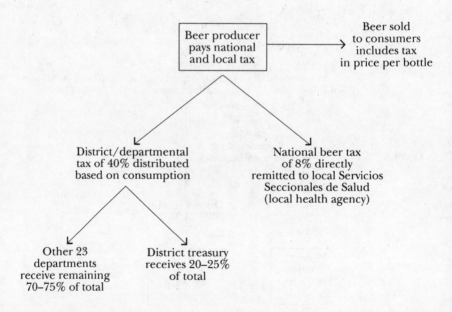

Source: Based on interviews with district administration officials.

trates how important even a single-source tax can be: in this context it was clear that much more could be collected from motor-vehicle-related taxes than has been the case in Bogotá. Not only are both beer and vehicle-related taxes easy to collect, but the tax base is highly income- and population-elastic. These taxes are therefore very useful sources of revenue for fast-expanding cities in developing countries.

The Structure of Expenditures

Expenditures on general administration have generally varied between 6 and 10 percent of total consolidated expenditure in the district: there seems to have been a slight increasing tendency. The average share of general administration expenditure increased from 6.35 percent in the 1960s to about 6.95 percent in the 1970s. There was, however, large variation between different years, largely related to differing inflation and reflecting lags in wage adjustments. The share of the main decentralized agencies on expenditures related to water and sanitation, electricity, and telephones varied between 50 and 60 percent of total consolidated district expenditures throughout the 1960s and 1970s (see figure 9-6), with considerable variation between the agencies.

Until the mid-1960s, expenditures on power predominated, amounting to about one-third of district expenditures. The share of power had fallen to 10 to 15 percent in the early 1970s but rose to about 25 percent in 1979. Obviously, these movements are related to the investment cycles of specific projects, which are typically bunched with construction of large power projects. Water and sewerage expenditures were around 10 percent in the early 1960s; they increased to about 15 to 18 percent in the late 1970s (see table 9-5). These increases in the share of water and sewerage systems and telephones have clearly been reflected in the relatively good availability of these services in Bogotá.

Debt service fluctuated between 14 and 20 percent over the two decades, exhibiting no trend. Each individual agency is prohibited by statute from exceeding a debt service ratio of 20 percent. Some of the agencies have reached this limit from time to time, but the district administration has always been substantially below it.

The expenditures on education show a clear increase in the 1970s compared with the previous decade.[2] (The higher education levels discussed in chapter 5 reflect these expenditures. The increase in schooling in Bogotá was palpable in the 1970s and was clearly a considerable achievement for the district.) Although the financing of these expenditures is now directly controlled by the central government, the district retained important responsibilities in the running of schools and has therefore continued to take considerable interest in the devolution of

Figure 9-6. Composition of the Bogotá District's Total Expenditures Per Capita

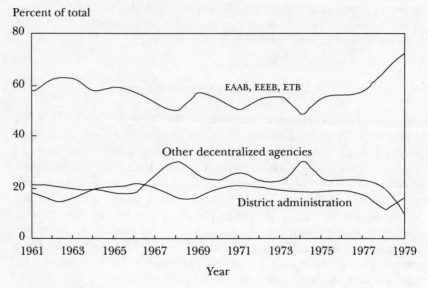

Percent of total

Source: Linn (1984a).

education funds. One issue of interest in this context is that the subventions to the FER can, by law, be applied only to teachers' salaries. The financing of school equipment, teaching materials, textbooks, and so on relies on extremely limited resources, and provision of these items suffered.

Another noteworthy feature in the structure of expenditures in Bogotá was the wide fluctuation in spending on roads and bridges. As already discussed, a significant portion of infrastructure expenditures on roads and bridges came from valorization, and this is reflected in atypically high expenditure between 1966 and 1970 (see table 9-5 and figure 9-7). This was also the period when a conscious effort was made to further the development process of the country through urban housing and infrastructure construction programs. The city's road system was significantly upgraded in both quality and coverage. Major new traffic management schemes, including the building of overpasses and underpasses in the central areas, were undertaken. Apart from the particular circumstances related to the history of valorization in Bogotá, expenditures on roads and bridges are generally related to the rate of expansion of a city. The effervescent growth of Bogotá took place in the 1960s into the early 1970s. One may therefore expect a rising pattern of

Table 9-5. **Structure of Consolidated Total Expenditures: Bogotá, 1961–79**
(percent)

Category	1961	1962	1963	1964	1965	1966	1967	1968	1969	1970	1971	1972	1973	1974	1975	1976	1977	1978	1979
General administration	6.4	5.1	6.0	5.5	5.8	5.8	4.7	6.3	9.4	8.5	7.3	8.6	6.5	10.9	6.0	6.7	9.2	7.9	6.4
Police and prisons	0.9	0.8	0.9	0.9	1.0	1.0	0.8	0.7	0.6	0.5	0.5	0.5	0.5	0.5	0.5	0.4	0.5	0.4	0.5
Fire protection	0.3	0.2	0.2	0.2	0.2	0.2	0.2	0.1	0.2	0.2	0.2	0.2	0.2	0.1	0.2	0.3	0.2	0.2	0.2
Roads and bridges	4.4	3.4	2.7	4.7	4.9	6.4	14.6	17.0	9.9	7.1	6.1	4.5	5.2	8.1	5.1	7.0	6.7	4.5	4.9
Parks and recreation	0.2	0.2	0.2	0.2	0.3	0.3	1.0	1.3	0.9	0.5	0.3	0.5	0.8	0.7	0.8	0.8	0.5	0.6	0.4
Education	6.4	5.9	6.0	6.5	7.6	8.8	7.5	5.7	6.3	10.6	11.2	11.5	10.7	9.8	10.7	10.5	5.1	1.8	1.2
Health	2.1	1.7	1.5	1.8	1.9	2.1	1.5	1.4	1.3	1.4	1.6	1.5	1.5	1.4	1.2	1.2	1.3	1.1	1.3
Transportation	4.3	3.2	3.0	3.0	3.1	2.8	2.2	5.2	2.0	3.7	3.4	2.0	1.7	2.2	5.0	1.9	1.6	1.8	0.6
Welfare	1.6	1.8	2.1	1.3	0.8	0.9	0.7	0.7	1.0	1.3	2.6	2.7	2.6	2.4	1.4	1.8	2.0	1.7	1.7
Water and sewerage	9.1	9.1	9.7	10.7	11.1	13.2	13.9	16.8	23.6	22.5	16.0	19.7	16.6	13.9	19.0	18.0	17.5	15.7	17.0
Other sanitation	2.4	2.2	4.1	6.2	3.2	3.1	2.6	2.7	2.5	3.3	3.8	3.6	3.4	3.9	2.8	3.0	3.4	2.9	3.3
Electricity	34.8	34.2	37.5	32.9	27.7	18.3	13.2	15.1	15.8	12.4	14.1	12.7	16.2	10.7	15.7	15.3	16.4	23.6	24.3
Telephones	5.9	8.2	6.4	5.3	6.9	10.8	15.9	7.4	8.7	10.0	10.4	12.2	9.9	14.1	11.5	12.4	12.4	15.6	19.3
Housing	2.0	1.5	0.9	2.4	2.1	2.6	0.8	1.4	1.0	0.9	1.0	0.6	0.5	1.2	1.6	2.1	2.1	2.1	0.0
District social security	3.8	4.9	4.1	4.4	5.0	4.0	4.6	3.1	2.9	3.2	3.7	3.6	3.9	3.8	3.8	3.7	3.9	4.3	1.6
Debt service	15.5	17.4	14.8	13.9	18.6	19.7	15.7	15.2	14.0	13.9	17.7	15.8	19.8	16.4	14.8	14.8	17.0	16.0	17.3
Transfer to outside district	0.0	0.0	0.0	0.0	0.0	0.0	0.0	0.0	0.0	0.0	0.0	0.0	0.0	0.0	0.0	0.0	0.0	0.0	0.0
Total	100.0	100.0	100.0	100.0	100.0	100.0	100.0	100.0	100.0	100.0	100.0	100.0	100.0	100.0	100.0	100.0	100.0	100.0	100.0

Note: Categories arranged as shown in Bogotá budget.
Source: Linn (1984b).

Figure 9-7. Composition of the Bogotá District's Capital Expenditures

Percent of total

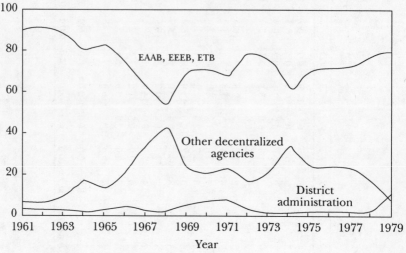

Source: Linn (1984a).

expenditures on such infrastructure to be related to city expansion. Valorization-related expenditures have provided Bogotá with a good road system that provides relatively good access to almost all parts of the city. Unlike many other cities in developing countries, even poor neighborhoods are generally well served by roads. This was also reflected in the almost universal accessibility of bus transport.

One interesting feature of the infrastructure system in Bogotá, although small in terms of expenditure, is the system of community action (*acción communal*) grants. Funds for this program come partly from the national Ministry of the Interior. The district's Community Action Administration (Departamento Administrativo de Acción Communal) channels these funds to six hundred community action groups. The district government is required by law to carry out small public works projects if the community collects a certain percentage of the costs in advance. A number of small projects specifically demanded by the community get implemented under this program. Another provision through which such projects can be executed is that of *auxilios parlamentarios* (parliamentary grants), which are made on the initiative of individual councillors who determine their use. These *auxilios* can be used, for example, to fund minor public works, the neighborhood committees, and scholarships. Typically the District Council adds these funds to the district budget: in 1980 they amounted to about 1.5 percent of the budget (excluding decentralized agencies). This system of direct response to the demands of the community does much to help forge a link between the people and the district government. The principle of matching grants in response to the community's own raising of funds is in itself a good mechanism for inducing community action.

The structure of capital expenditures illustrated in figure 9-7 shows the importance of the main decentralized agencies in infrastructure investment in Bogotá. The dip in the late 1960s and in 1974 is almost fully accounted for by the valorization-related expenditures made by IDU (induced in other decentralized agencies in figure 9-7). Overall, Bogotá has been served relatively well by its local governments through the decentralized agencies, which are discussed in the following section.

The Public Service Enterprises of Bogotá

The three main public utilities of Bogotá—the water and sewerage, electricity, and telephone companies—were all originally founded as private entities in the latter part of the nineteenth century. Each has a history of gradual takeover by the government. The water company was founded in 1888, acquired by the city in 1914, and given its current status as a decentralized autonomous agency, the EAAB, by the city council in 1954. The power company began operating in 1892; it later merged with the Compañía Nacional de Electricidad, founded in 1923, and the city acquired a 51 percent interest. The merged company was fully taken over by the city in 1951, when it became known as the EEEB. The telephone company, founded in 1884, was taken over in 1940 and has operated as the ETB ever since. By contrast, Bogotá's public service company, the EDIS, was government-run from the start. Founded by the district in 1958 as a refuse-collection and street-cleaning company, it expanded in 1960 to cover functions like administering the municipal slaughterhouse, running markets, and maintaining cemeteries.

Each of these decentralized agencies has a similar governing board consisting of six or seven members and presided over by the mayor. Two members of the board of each agency are nominated by the District Council. The other four members of the EAAB board are nominated by the main bond holders of the company—the Banco Central Hipotecario and the Colombian central bank, the Banco de la República. The EEEB has one member nominated by the president of the republic and one each nominated by different associations—the manufacturers, the merchants, and the bankers. The ETB has the *personero* (district legal counsel) on its board, along with two additional members nominated by the mayor and approved by the District Council. The EDIS also has the *personero* on its board, along with two ex-councillors chosen by the Banco de la República and two members recommended by the city banking associations. In each case the board appoints the general manager, who is in charge of all the company's operations. The board, however, has to approve all major decisions involving, for example, the budget, investment plans, changes in tariffs, and changes in administrative structure.

Each of these public utility agencies is a relatively large entity and saw major expansions during the 1960s and 1970s. By 1972 the EAAB had about 2,300 employees, the EEEB about 1,600, the ETB over 2,000, and the EDIS over 3,000. Each had more than doubled its staff size during the 1960s, but the output per employee generally increased at the same time.

The service levels achieved were generally satisfactory by the late 1970s. Over 90 percent of the population received water, supplied by the EAAB. Per capita consumption of electricity grew by about 6 percent annually between the early 1960s and late 1970s; almost all households had a power connection by 1978. Similarly, the EDIS provided more than 95 percent of the city with street cleaning and refuse collection, a level achieved through continual expansion and upgrading of equipment. As many as 60 percent of households reported access to a telephone in 1978.

The autonomy of these public utilities has been useful in insulating them from day-to-day political pressures on their operations. Given the presence of the mayor and District Council members on each board, the agencies are obviously not immune to political pressures. However, the administration of these enterprises is left largely to professional managers and technical personnel more removed from political interference than are the staff of the district administration itself. The enterprises have succeeded in maintaining a high degree of professional competence and technical expertise and in keeping a stable and experienced staff. They have had broad financial autonomy and remained solvent through most of the period under study. They have essentially been self-financing, borrowing for capital expenditures and financing the borrowing by levying overcharges.

The System of User Charges

The tariff rates of all public services in Colombia are regulated by the National Tariff Board. Each enterprise has to follow the guidelines set by that board, which must approve tariff changes. In principle, all agencies apply a long-run average-cost pricing criterion: operating costs and debt charges that finance past borrowing for capital expenditures are supposed to be covered from operating revenues. Capital expenditures should be covered by new borrowing and by connection charges. In addition, equity considerations have been seen as very important in tariff setting in Colombia. Most public service tariffs in Colombia have an equity element built into them: tariff charges paid by more affluent customers are higher, being related to either property values or volume of consumption. Changes in the tariff pattern, guided by these broad principles, were frequent during the 1960s and 1970s.

Most user charges are divided into two segments: monthly charges for services consumed and connection charges payable on initial connection of the service. The monthly charges go into the current revenues of the enterprise, whereas the connection charges are capital contributions financing capital expenditures. Monthly charges for water supply were themselves divided into two parts. One was a lump-sum charge related to a minimum allowance of water supply per connection and the other was a unit charge for consumption beyond the minimum allowance. This lump-sum charge was graduated according to seven classes of property values. The minimum allowance was 15 cubic meters per month and uniform across all property classes. Prior to 1970, the charge was graduated according to twenty-six property classes and the minimum allowance itself ranged from 20 to 60 cubic meters per month. Consumption beyond the minimum allowance was levied a unit charge, which itself increased according to property value as well as progressively with higher consumption. Residential rates at the lower ends were lower than the charges for commercial and industrial use. For higher consumption levels at high property values, however, residential charges were higher than charges for commercial and industrial use. For industrial consumers, the minimum allowance was abolished in 1970. All tariff rates increased in step jumps in 1961, 1965, 1968, 1970, 1973, and 1974. The result was that the average tariff rate (total revenue divided by total sales) in real terms looked like a ratchet pattern, with step increases at the time of tariff revision followed by a decline until the next revision. In the late 1970s small monthly marginal adjustments replaced this pattern. The progressiveness of rates increased over time. The ratio between the highest and lowest increased from just about 6 in the 1961–65 period to over 40 in the late 1970s, if the rates for the minimum allowance are accounted for. For total water consumed, this ratio in the late 1970s was about 10. Almost all connections consumed more than 15 cubic meters per month, or the minimum allowance; this fact suggests the minimum allowance was less than actual minimal household requirements. In other Colombian cities, the minimum allowance was 25 cubic meters per month.

In addition to the monthly charges, the EAAB levied rather stiff connection charges. The connection charge itself had four elements: a connection fee set at 3 percent of the property's assessed cadastral value; a "supply fee" set at a flat rate per square meter of developed land on the property (with a lower rate for certain specified low-income areas); a network fee levied as a capital contribution for the construction of the secondary distribution network designed to connect a new development; and a fee to cover actual installation charges (this also varied according to property value).

Sewerage charges were essentially linked to the water charges because it is difficult to charge according to use. The monthly charge varied from 5 to 20 percent of the water charge depending on property value. The capital charges for sewerage had two components: the network charge analogous to the water network charge, and valorization charges levied by the IDU to finance large-scale sewerage projects.

The EAAB made a great effort to collect user charges. Given the different objectives of levying user charges—the financing of both operating and capital costs on the one hand and promoting equity in order to improve access to basic public services on the other—the resulting tariff structure was quite complex. The tariff structure looked like a large matrix rather than a rate. It turned out that the capital contributions were higher than most poor families could afford, despite the progressive structure. Even if they paid in installments spread out over three or four years, a low-income family would have had to pay 9 to 10 percent of its income for the water supply connection alone. This led to many illegal connections. Over the years the share of capital revenues increased, whereas the share of capital expenditures fell. As a result, during the mid- to late 1970s the capital revenues were helping to fund operational expenditures.

The structure of electricity pricing was guided by similar principles. The aim was to cover the long-run average cost of producing energy while incorporating redistributive criteria in the tariff structure. Residential areas were charged a unit rate in two slabs; the rate increased when users went beyond a certain level of monthly consumption. In earlier years there were a larger number of such slabs and a monthly meter charge. Industrial and commercial users were levied higher rates, with smaller firms receiving preferential rates. Some elements of efficiency pricing were introduced through time-of-day variations with higher peak-period charges. Installation fees were charged according to capacity installed and varied between residential, commercial, and industrial uses.

Electricity connection charges were nowhere near as onerous as those for water supply. An analysis of actual collections showed that commercial consumers paid the highest charges, followed by industrial consumers, and then residential consumers. Residential consumers paid just about the same rates as those paid for public lighting. An element of cross-subsidy was therefore built in on the principle of apparent ability to pay. The actual incidence was difficult to calculate because the industrial and commercial consumers would presumably pass on their higher charges. Clearly, the rate differences were not based on the relative costs of supply to different users.

Unlike the EAAB, the EEEB's revenue structure moved from larger capital revenues in the early 1960s to greater current revenues in the 1970s. The structure of expenditures moved in a broadly consistent direction, and the surplus from current revenues helped finance capital expenditures throughout the whole period.

The tariff structure for the telephone company, the ETB, was also supposed to cover long-run average costs while providing for internal cross- subsidies for different income groups. It is probably unusual for telephone tariff rates to vary according to property values. The main component of the tariff structure was the basic monthly rate, which was levied according to six residential property value categories for residential areas and four registered asset value categories for industrial and commercial users. The difference between the lowest and highest rates widened during the 1960s and 1970s, but all had fallen behind the rate of inflation. The capital contribution was collected in four segments: a lump sum, a returnable security deposit, and an installation charge, all of which were equal for all users, and a connection fee that rose steeply with property value. These rates were revised frequently to keep up with inflation. The ETB's financial position was generally healthy, with current surpluses contributing to capital expenditures throughout the 1960s and 1970s.

Service charges for garbage collection by the EDIS were also levied according to property value assessed at a constant ad valorem rate based on the capital value of properties. Low-value properties were exempted from any charge. The EDIS also charged for its other operations.

This summary of user charges shows the importance attached to cross-subsidization in providing urban services in Colombia—a political system not otherwise known for its concern for the poor. The government's considerable effort to make basic urban services accessible to the poor was partly the result of the self-financing and fragmented nature of urban service enterprises in Bogotá. Because the enterprises had to rely on their own finances and there was no possibility of cross-subsidization between utilities, there had to be stronger cross-subsidization across income groups. In Cali, where all public services are unified in one public utility, Empresas Municipales de Cali (EMCALI), there was significant cross-subsidization between the different services.

For almost all the utilities, average unit costs increased in real terms over time. This implied that unit user charges should have been adjusted more than inflation throughout the period and that marginal cost exceeded average cost: utility pricing based on marginal costs would have more than financed the expanding network of services.

Table 9-6. Subsidies from Public Utility Pricing: Bogotá, 1974

Population decile	Water and sewerage		Electricity		Telephones		Garbage collection		Total	
	Subsidy (Col$ per month)	Subsidy (percent of income)	Subsidy (Col$ per month)	Subsidy (percent of income)	Subsidy (Col$ per month)	Subsidy (percent of income)	Subsidy (Col$ per month)	Subsidy (percent of income)	Subsidy (Col$ per month)	Subsidy (percent of income)
0–10	—	—	1.13	0.18	—	—	—	—	1.13	0.18
10–20	—	—	4.66	0.40	—	—	—	—	4.66	0.40
20–30	—	—	5.07	0.34	—	—	—	—	5.07	0.34
30–40	16.72	0.91	5.37	0.29	—	—	13.75	0.75	25.84	1.95
40–50	16.48	0.72	6.72	0.29	—	—	11.12	0.49	34.22	1.47
50–60	14.10	0.49	6.63	0.23	2.48	0.09	10.72	0.38	33.93	1.18
60–70	14.10	0.38	5.78	0.15	2.96	0.08	3.21	0.09	26.06	0.70
70–80	9.02	0.16	4.28	0.07	2.14	0.04	(1.74)	(0.03)	13.70	0.24
80–90	(15.23)	(0.18)	(8.92)	(0.10)	(2.05)	(0.02)	(9.86)	(0.12)	(36.07)	(0.42)
90–100	(147.65)	(0.82)	(20.33)	(0.11)	(9.57)	(0.05)	(44.94)	(0.25)	(222.50)	(1.24)
Gini coefficients (without charges, 0.5103)	0.5098		0.5074		0.5102		0.5097		0.5070	

— Not applicable.
Note: Figures in parentheses are negative subsidies.
Source: Linn (1976).

How far did the attempts at cross-subsidization succeed? Linn (1976) reported a 1974 study conducted for the National Tariff Board that showed that the top two income deciles of the population essentially subsidized the rest of the population. The main beneficiaries were the third to sixth deciles, who were estimated to gain 1 to 2 percent of their monthly income through these cross-subsidies. The lowest income groups also gained, but not as significantly (see table 9-6). This may be expected; it was observed in chapter 6 that the lowest three deciles also did not benefit as much from *pirata* housing development. It is simply too difficult to pass on public subsidies to the bottom three deciles. Where a significant proportion of households in the bottom three deciles are not homeowners and are not connected to the public service system, a graduated tariff structure cannot hope to succeed in redistributing effective income.

Overall, the existing system of user charges enabled the three main public service enterprises in Bogotá to operate throughout the 1960s and 1970s on a financially self-sufficient basis without receiving or contributing funds to the district government. There was a mild trend of increasing real unit costs for each of the agencies, and hence they ran into difficulties whenever inflation ran ahead of their tariff adjustments. The EAAB was most affected and had to resort to occasional borrowing in order to finance operating deficits as they evolved. In the late 1970s small monthly charges in tariff rates began to be made for water and sewerage as well as electricity in order to alleviate the problem caused by inflation.

How efficient was this system of user charges? It was clearly not based on marginal cost considerations. Hence, for different services, the unit rates differed quite markedly from marginal costs. For electricity, the marginal cost was higher than the average tariff, whereas for water it was lower. There were other inefficiencies, too. Electricity charges for industrial and commercial users were higher than for residential consumers, when the relative marginal costs of supply would be in the opposite direction. It is difficult to evaluate, however, how important these inefficiencies were in comparison with the perceived gains from redistributive tariffs in as unequal a society as Colombia. The driving force behind the tariff structure in Bogotá was the need for financial self-sufficiency. However, the same aim could have been achieved with greater consideration to marginal cost pricing and a different division between marginal unit consumption charges and fixed monthly charges on the one hand and connection charges on the other. Progressive connection charges can be supported strongly: low-income households should not be discouraged from gaining access to these basic public services.

Lessons for a Developing Metropolis: An Evaluative Summary

Bogotá has long had a rather elaborate system of urban government, one that has been supported by public service institutions that also have a relatively long history. Yet Bogotá's government has been more of a follower than a leader in guiding the growth of the city. This was at least partly because of the effervescent growth that the city experienced from the early 1950s to the early 1970s. Few governments in the world could have led such growth. The spatial development of the city has been dominated more by the rapid development of pirate settlements than by legally zoned formal housing developments. It is creditable, however, that public infrastructure was largely able to keep up with this growth and even marginally improve on per capita service levels while certainly improving the coverage of the expanding urban population.

This was accomplished with negligible infusions of funds from outside sources—except for international borrowing that was sustained by manageable and prudent levels of debt servicing. Bogotá and other cities in Colombia have been unusual in the extent to which urban public services have been financed by user charges. Some degree of cross-subsidy between income groups reduced the burden on the poor, but they still had to pay substantial charges for the installation and use of public services, often forcing the poorest among them to resort to illegal tapping of these services. To the extent that each agency was financially solvent, this illegal tapping effectively amounted to a large subsidy from the better-off users to the poor. In many other cities in developing countries, urban public services are designed to subsidize the poor, but the main beneficiaries are the better off. In these cases powerful vested interests then succeed in preventing future increases in user charges. The result is that the expansion of public services is limited by paucity of resources, and the most severely affected are the poor. It is therefore very important to develop sound user-charge-based systems of financing urban public services in order to fund the ever increasing needs of growing cities.

It has been observed that there is no systematic attempt at urban investment planning in the medium term. Zoning and building regulations exist but are frequently breached without fear of effective sanctions. We have also found that accessibility and variety of urban transport provision improved over the period studied. How did all this occur? Paradoxically, the very decentralized nature of urban public service provision in Bogotá made it possible for the government to cope with very rapid city growth. By design or accident, Bogotá's government and public service agencies, as well as the private sector providers of service, have all responded well to expressed demands. This has enabled the unbundling of services that are often a prohibitively expensive package in other cities in developing countries. The key to successful unbundling has been a very effective sharing of costs among all concerned. The urban government system was able to adopt the incremental construction paradigm of informal housing because of the autonomy of the public service enterprises, which in turn enabled greater flexibility in service provision than is generally possible. The valorization and user charge systems institutionalized the idea of cost sharing between public service agencies and the beneficiary public. The private sector contributed by taking part in supplying transportation. The government further contributed through regulation and tariff-setting policies that made the unit costs of services progressive, making it easier for the poor to obtain access to basic services.

It is argued that, paradoxically, the fragmented nature of decision making in Bogotá and its lack of centralized and effective urban investment planning have contributed to the development of a relatively efficient public service delivery system. It is probably the case that the needs of a rapidly growing large city are intrinsically difficult to serve if an attempt is made to meet these needs in a planned and coordinated fashion. It is probably easier for autonomous agencies, which are forced to be financially independent, to perceive the growing demand for services and to respond incrementally. Such a decentralized system lends itself to financial self-sufficiency, achieved through the levy and collection of user charges. Excessive reliance on usually scarce budgetary resources only leads to inadequate growth in the supply of urban public services.

The key lesson to be learned here is that much can be gained by observing people's preferences and devising systems of government that are able to respond to expressed demands. In Bogotá this was done by instituting a fragmented system of city government. In other cities there could be a stronger system of community development, which would also be effective in making perceived demands felt but perhaps in a more organized manner than in Bogotá. There is, however, considerable room for improvement in Bogotá. Although the pricing system performed well in financing the public service enterprises, it could be improved in structure to better reflect efficiency considerations without losing its effectiveness as an adequate resource-raising mechanism. The enterprises could improve their performance further by a little more forward investment budgeting and planning—but not in such a way that would reduce flexibility and become dysfunctional. The valorization system had fallen on hard times: it could be revived to finance further improvement of the infrastructure. Much more needs to be done as well to improve the quality of education and health service in the poorer neighborhoods. Because Bogotá is one of the more spatially differentiated cities by income group, a more directed effort will have to be made to provide services and upgrade neighborhoods in order to integrate the city into an organic whole.

Table 9A-1. Per Capita Revenues of District Administration: Bogotá, 1960–80
(1976 Colombian pesos)

Revenue	1960	1961	1962	1963	1964	1965	1966	1967	1968	1969	1970	1971	1972	1973	1974	1975	1976	1977	1978	1979	1980
Local tax revenue	347.9	456.2	434.1	349.8	315.3	328.4	257.5	290.3	280.2	303.1	314.6	298.3	276.4	276.7	240.0	281.1	269.7	260.7	279.6	317.7	362.6
Property & complement	192.7	258.0	259.7	209.5	192.7	198.9	163.8	189.4	172.0	187.1	188.8	169.4	166.8	172.6	144.0	158.5	141.5	108.7	122.5	121.6	146.0
Industry & commerce	41.6	111.0	94.0	79.4	65.2	70.1	44.6	50.7	48.6	51.9	59.3	56.4	51.9	58.3	51.9	83.7	88.2	95.9	101.2	130.4	130.3
Public entertainment	0.0	1.8	0.4	0.5	0.4	0.0	0.1	1.5	0.0	10.9	10.6	11.1	8.4	6.9	5.9	6.2	5.7	6.2	6.1	6.3	5.5
Advertisement	0.0	0.0	0.5	0.5	0.4	0.04	0.5	1.5	4.0	4.4	4.7	2.3	0.8	0.9	0.9	0.9	0.5	0.6	0.4	0.4	0.3
Vehicles	37.3	44.7	38.9	25.9	21.2	25.4	20.1	18.7	21.3	16.5	18.8	20.0	14.7	10.1	11.7	9.0	8.8	16.3	19.8	29.3	25.0
Urban construction	11.6	10.0	11.9	10.7	14.2	12.3	9.7	9.9	15.1	14.2	15.2	12.5	10.3	10.6	9.9	8.6	9.2	13.8	12.4	13.3	31.2
Public road use	0.6	0.9	0.8	0.8	0.7	0.6	0.5	2.3	1.9	1.4	1.5	1.0	1.1	0.8	1.1	0.7	0.7	3.4	3.9	4.0	9.3
Raffles	0.8	0.8	0.9	0.7	0.9	0.9	0.9	0.9	0.4	1.6	1.1	1.0	1.1	0.5	0.6	1.5	1.1	2.1	2.0	1.5	1.3
Betting	48.5	11.1	10.0	9.2	8.6	9.5	8.4	8.6	8.9	7.5	7.6	9.0	10.7	9.1	10.2	8.5	10.5	8.1	6.4	4.3	3.1
Gasoline ($0.04/gal.)	14.8	17.9	17.0	13.1	11.4	10.7	8.9	8.3	8.0	7.6	7.0	7.1	5.8	5.3	4.2	3.5	3.0	2.5	2.1	1.6	1.3
Foreign cigarettes	0.0	0.0	0.0	0.0	0.0	0.0	0.0	0.0	0.0	0.0	0.0	8.5	4.8	1.5	0.1	0.0	0.5	3.1	2.8	5.0	9.3
Others	0.0	0.0	0.0	0.0	0.0	0.0	0.0	0.0	0.0	0.0	0.0	0.0	0.0	0.0	0.0	0.0	0.0	0.0	0.0	0.0	0.0
Local non-tax revenue	22.4	25.3	26.4	21.0	21.5	25.5	8.6	10.3	12.2	9.8	8.0	12.7	8.3	5.7	10.8	8.8	6.9	7.4	10.4	21.3	43.9
Sanitation licenses	1.7	1.6	1.1	0.8	0.8	0.8	0.7	0.6	0.5	0.4	0.5	0.6	0.1	0.0	0.0	0.0	0.0	0.0	0.0	0.0	0.0
Nomenclatura urbana	0.1	0.1	0.0	0.0	0.0	0.0	0.0	0.0	0.1	0.1	0.0	0.0	0.0	0.0	0.0	0.0	0.0	0.0	0.0	0.0	0.0
Laboratory services	0.9	0.7	0.5	0.4	0.3	0.3	0.2	0.2	0.3	0.2	0.1	0.1	0.0	0.0	0.1	0.1	0.0	0.0	0.0	0.0	0.0
Interest receipts	3.1	10.0	13.6	11.1	12.5	11.7	0.0	0.0	0.0	0.0	0.0	0.2	0.0	0.0	0.1	1.8	1.3	6.2	4.3	10.8	39.8
Fines	7.9	6.4	6.1	6.1	5.9	5.9	5.9	7.2	9.3	7.2	1.6	1.7	4.2	3.9	5.2	5.4	3.4	0.0	4.5	9.4	0.0
Confiscated land sales	0.1	0.1	0.1	0.1	0.1	0.0	0.0	0.0	0.2	0.1	0.1	0.2	0.1	0.1	0.1	0.0	0.0	0.1	0.0	0.0	0.0
Rental receipts	2.6	1.9	1.1	0.5	0.3	0.4	0.1	0.1	0.1	0.0	0.0	0.1	0.1	0.1	0.1	0.1	0.1	0.0	0.0	0.0	0.0
Real estate sales	0.0	0.0	0.1	0.2	0.2	5.1	0.6	0.4	0.0	0.0	0.0	0.2	0.0	0.0	0.0	0.0	0.1	0.1	0.1	0.0	2.4
Others	6.0	4.5	3.8	1.8	1.5	1.3	1.1	1.8	1.7	1.8	5.7	9.6	3.8	1.6	5.4	1.5	2.0	1.0	1.5	1.1	1.7

Shared taxes	105.6	142.4	131.4	185.7	202.0	179.3	150.6	159.6	141.4	171.1	235.2	284.8	255.5	224.1	233.1	259.7	205.5	191.7	199.1	210.1	243.1
Sales tax	0.0	0.0	0.0	0.0	0.0	0.0	11.1	0.7	0.0	6.6	13.9	31.1	36.4	21.5	37.7	62.6	31.0	17.6	28.8	16.1	23.3
Beer tax	84.7	94.1	82.2	145.4	139.6	123.5	116.1	122.8	113.2	133.3	186.0	204.6	177.2	150.2	148.8	157.9	138.1	138.6	138.1	161.0	185.7
Gasoline ($0.06/gal.)	19.3	26.9	25.4	19.6	17.1	16.1	12.6	12.4	11.9	11.2	10.0	10.1	7.9	6.4	6.1	5.7	4.5	3.6	3.1	2.1	2.1
Other	1.6	21.4	23.8	20.7	45.3	39.7	10.8	14.1	13.4	20.0	22.3	22.1	19.1	20.7	23.7	16.1	17.0	16.6	18.1	19.6	21.0
Tobacco tax	0.0	0.0	0.0	0.0	0.0	0.0	0.0	9.6	2.9	0.0	3.0	16.9	14.9	25.3	16.8	17.4	14.9	15.3	11.0	11.3	11.0
Grants	25.1	10.9	31.9	45.7	42.8	38.1	43.0	31.8	40.7	34.5	73.3	80.0	69.1	86.1	82.0	117.8	97.4	0.0	0.0	0.0	1.8
For teachers' salaries	4.6	5.9	29.8	38.2	42.0	37.2	42.3	31.6	26.5	28.5	0.0	0.0	0.0	0.0	0.0	0.0	0.0	0.0	0.0	0.0	0.0
For regional education fund	0.0	0.0	0.0	0.0	0.0	0.0	0.0	0.0	0.0	0.0	71.9	78.5	69.0	86.1	81.5	113.8	97.4	0.0	0.0	0.0	0.0
For school cafeterias	0.0	0.4	0.3	0.2	0.3	0.3	0.2	0.2	0.2	0.0	0.0	0.0	0.0	0.0	0.0	0.0	0.0	0.0	0.0	0.0	0.0
For health services	18.9	3.4	0.8	6.5	0.0	0.0	0.0	0.0	0.0	0.9	1.0	1.5	0.1	0.0	0.0	1.0	0.0	0.0	0.0	0.0	0.0
For social welfare	0.0	0.0	0.0	0.0	0.0	0.0	0.0	0.0	0.0	0.1	0.1	0.0	0.0	0.0	0.0	0.0	0.0	0.0	0.0	0.0	0.0
For economic development works	0.0	0.0	0.0	0.0	0.0	0.0	0.0	0.0	14.0	4.9	0.3	0.0	0.0	0.0	0.0	0.0	0.0	0.0	0.0	0.0	0.0
From decentralized agencies	1.3	1.2	1.0	0.8	0.6	0.6	0.4	0.0	0.0	0.0	0.0	0.0	0.0	0.0	0.5	3.0	0.0	0.0	0.0	0.0	0.0
Capital resources (debt)	75.0	5.1	4.5	0.0	0.0	0.0	0.0	168.9	186.5	4.2	15.9	22.4	3.1	13.4	39.1	91.0	39.0	7.6	7.6	8.8	286.0
Loans	75.0	5.1	4.5	0.0	0.0	0.0	0.0	58.0	11.3	4.2	15.9	17.7	3.1	13.4	39.1	91.0	39.0	7.6	7.6	8.7	216.7
Bond issues	0.0	0.0	0.0	0.0	0.0	0.0	0.0	110.9	175.2	0.0	0.0	4.7	0.0	0.0	0.0	0.0	0.0	0.0	0.0	0.1	69.4
Total revenues	576.0	639.9	628.3	602.2	581.6	571.3	459.7	660.9	661.0	522.7	647.0	698.2	612.4	606.0	605.0	758.4	618.5	467.4	496.7	557.9	937.5

Source: Linn (1984b).

Table 9A-2. Consolidated Capital Expenditures: Bogotá, 1961–79
(percentage distribution)

Revenue	1961	1962	1963	1964	1965	1966	1967	1968	1969	1970	1971	1972	1973	1974	1975	1976	1977	1978	1979
General administration	0.0	0.0	3.0	1.6	1.4	0.0	1.4	5.3	40.2	24.1	12.3	9.9	12.2	20.7	10.8	12.4	2.1	3.3	9.0
Police and prisons	0.0	0.0	1.2	0.0	0.0	0.0	0.0	0.0	0.0	0.0	0.0	0.0	0.0	1.5	0.0	0.0	0.0	0.0	1.8
Fire protection	0.0	0.0	0.0	0.0	0.0	0.0	0.0	0.0	0.0	0.0	0.0	0.0	0.0	0.2	2.5	2.4	0.0	0.1	0.2
Roads and bridges	48.6	38.5	24.2	56.6	50.1	73.3	235.3	323.6	201.4	117.0	110.1	76.0	92.6	173.2	98.8	132.1	97.7	69.7	60.1
Parks and recreation	0.0	0.6	0.1	0.3	0.3	0.4	17.9	27.2	21.3	11.0	6.5	4.5	4.1	4.0	6.9	8.8	3.3	2.3	4.3
Education	4.1	1.1	16.2	3.0	7.1	11.3	21.3	4.2	35.2	37.0	37.6	11.6	4.2	9.8	4.5	5.0	0.5	1.9	6.4
Health	0.0	0.1	0.2	1.2	1.5	4.5	1.9	0.9	1.8	0.8	1.2	0.0	0.0	0.0	0.0	0.0	0.0	0.0	0.0
Transportation	0.0	2.1	0.5	0.0	0.0	0.0	0.0	68.9	0.0	32.3	33.1	0.5	0.0	19.3	99.0	6.2	0.0	0.1	1.5
Welfare	0.0	0.6	6.3	0.9	1.7	0.0	0.0	0.9	6.2	15.9	48.3	51.2	40.6	40.0	8.7	18.6	16.1	10.8	7.4
Water and sewerage	96.4	109.1	126.4	110.6	93.6	110.4	153.6	240.9	463.8	402.7	277.3	370.4	225.2	180.9	335.1	293.5	223.3	222.1	151.7
Other sanitation	0.0	0.0	42.8	71.0	8.6	3.3	1.2	6.1	4.9	12.3	27.2	7.5	4.2	21.2	2.0	0.1	0.0	0.0	1.5
Electricity	572.3	693.1	725.9	518.9	354.5	166.9	105.4	202.7	261.4	157.6	201.9	136.4	236.1	99.9	196.6	131.7	88.1	120.7	57.5
Telephones	53.5	111.3	75.7	46.0	57.2	109.3	228.8	89.5	126.2	141.2	171.6	217.9	135.5	258.4	199.1	191.5	136.2	182.7	191.6
Housing	15.1	13.1	3.2	23.0	17.8	20.6	4.0	18.2	16.2	12.9	15.1	6.5	4.2	27.7	39.1	45.9	36.1	41.8	0.0
District social security	1.4	14.0	5.7	4.3	4.9	12.8	6.4	4.6	11.5	14.2	6.7	1.2	20.1	10.0	0.8	0.2	0.4	0.3	0.2
Debt service	0.0	0.0	0.0	0.0	0.0	0.0	0.0	0.0	0.0	0.0	0.0	0.0	0.0	0.0	0.0	0.0	0.0	0.0	0.0
Transfer to outside district	0.0	0.8	0.0	0.0	0.0	0.0	0.0	0.0	0.0	0.0	0.0	0.0	0.0	0.0	0.0	0.0	0.0	0.0	0.0
Total expenditures	791.4	984.4	1,031.4	837.4	598.7	512.8	777.2	993.0	1,190.1	979.0	948.9	893.6	779.0	866.8	1,003.9	848.4	603.8	655.8	493.0

Source: Linn (1984b)

Notes

This chapter is drawn from works by Linn (see bibliography) and from Contraloría de Bogotá D.E. (1982), Fawcett (1984), Greytak (1984), and Wolff (1984). The section on "The Structure of Revenue" summarizes research reported in Linn (1984a) and Fawcett (1984). The detailed work on consolidating the finances of the district was conducted over a period of three years by Alberto Hernandez, Marco Tulio Ruíz, Jeffrey Lewis, and José Fernando Pineda, directed by Johannes Linn, and published in Contraloría de Bogotá, D.E. (1982). The section on "The Public Service Enterprises of Bogotá" is drawn from research reported in Linn (1976b) and Greytak (1984).

1. One by-product of the City Study was the compilation of the full series of district and agency revenues and expenditures for 1961–81. This information was subsequently published in the statistical bulletin of the controller of Bogotá (Contraloría de Bogotá, *Boletín Estadístico*, vol. 1, no. 5, December 1982).

2. The fall in education expenditures after 1975, shown in table 9-5, reflects the channeling of all education expenditures through the FER.

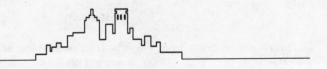

Chapter 10

Coping with City Growth

The aim of this study has been to improve our understanding of the way cities in developing countries work. What have we learned from the various detailed investigations that have been reported in earlier chapters? What are the messages that can be flashed to policymakers in developing countries as they confront the daunting problems posed by the rapid urbanization that most developing countries are experiencing?

One of the broad themes of this book has been that an understanding of cities requires an appreciation of the behavior of economic agents who respond to economic signals in a relatively rational and predictable way. There are no easy or straightforward "policy recommendations" that can be generically prescribed for managing growth in the cities of the developing world. Different cities and countries exist in specific settings that need to be understood and analyzed case by case. Different countries also have quite different administrative systems. Policymakers need to observe and understand the rationale behind the various phenomena observed in cities and to react accordingly. The integrating theme of our study is that the various patterns observed in cities are a result of relatively rational behavior on the part of their various economic constituents—workers and their families, employers, government, housing suppliers, and so on. The problems arising from rapid city growth are best dealt with by observing and understanding these patterns and designing flexible and self-correcting institutional frameworks that are capable of responding to the variegated needs of the city's components.

Bogotá and Cali emerge from this study in an optimistic light. We have depicted them as having had fair success in withstanding the challenges of sustained and extremely rapid growth over the past fifty or so years. Much of this growth was concentrated in the 1940s, 1950s, and 1960s. We also found evidence during the 1970s of a significant increase in household incomes and some decline in the high inequality that had characterized Colombia for a long time. We have documented that the two cities are relatively well served with the essential elements of infrastructure, such as water supply, roads, transport, and electricity.

Consequently, we have an optimistic view of the prospects of managing city growth in developing countries. This is in marked contrast to much writing concerned with urbanization in developing countries. We do not believe that cities in general are growing out of control in developing countries. We do not believe that the vastly expanding urban population in these countries is necessarily condemned to a shelterless existence. We do not believe that it is impossible to provide a modicum of necessary urban services that are affordable and manageable. We do not believe that cities are being swamped by a flood of destitute migrants who have no productive employment prospects. We do believe, however, that some changes in attitude are necessary if this optimistic vision of cities in developing countries is to become a generalizable reality. The study of Bogotá and Cali suggests that many solutions are best found by the urban constituents themselves and that the job of the public authorities is to develop institutions and systems that are sensitive to the emerging needs and preferences of households and firms and are capable of reacting accordingly.

Our observations of Bogotá and Cali are colored by the relatively happy state of the Colombian economy in the 1970s. This was fortuitous in many ways but was also the result of the prudent national economic policies followed during the late 1960s and through the 1970s. The state of the urban labor market and urban income generation is much more conditioned by national economic conditions and policymaking than by any specific local policies.

In retrospect, it turns out that the period during which this research was conducted (1977–81) and the period under study (1972–80) were remarkable in recent Colombian economic history. The average growth rate of real gross national product was 6 percent from 1960 right up to 1980, although it showed signs of slowing toward the end of this period. During the 1973–78 period an unprecedented 6 percent annual expansion in employment took place. It was in this overall national economic climate that we observed the tightening of the urban labor market in Bogotá and Cali that was accompanied by a rise in real wages. The early 1970s witnessed a major turning point for Colombia: real wages in agriculture began to rise after stagnating for at least forty years, and the agricultural labor force began to stabilize or contract in absolute terms. In addition, this was also a period of high world coffee prices, which made possible a more rapid rise in real agricultural wages in Colombia in the 1970s. By the end of the 1970s urbanization had reached a level of about 70 percent. This is beyond the point at which the rate of urban growth typically slows. The process of urbanization in general and the growth of particular cities follow a sigmoid path, with an acceleration in growth followed by deceleration. Colombia had reached the turning point of the curve by the late 1970s. The effervescent growth of the previous fifty years was therefore drawing to a close during our period of observation. This is an important factor since the period encouraged a more optimistic view than that held by earlier observers, whose expectations of unending rapid and bewildering change had been conditioned by the experiences of those fifty years.

One lesson of our study is that understanding city growth requires a knowledge of the overall process of urbanization. The transition from a rural to an urban economy is very rapid in historical terms for most countries. The trajectory for a country moving from a level of about 30 percent urban to about 70 percent urban is steep, and it has usually been traversed over a period of fifty to seventy years. During this period most cities in an urbanizing economy grow at unprecedented rates. It is understandable if observers and administrators are driven to despair during this period of seemingly unending rapid change. The task of meeting all the demands for jobs, shelter, water, roads, transport, and other urban infrastructure is daunting.

It is therefore all the more important to understand that rapid change during such a period is a norm of urban development, not an aberration. Once this is accepted, it follows that policies for urbanization and provision of urban infrastructure and employment must be positive, not negative. Urban growth must be accommodated and institutional mechanisms derived to cope with such growth. Most cities and countries are faced with acute fiscal pressure during such a period. This in itself points to the need for fiscal conservatism in the provision of urban services and for innovative financing mechanisms, like those found in Bogotá and Cali, to provide for the necessary urban infrastructure.

This study differs from others in a number of ways. First, it is probably the most comprehensive study of any city to be undertaken since Hoover and Vernon's (1959) study of New York in the 1950s. Second, whereas some other studies have attempted to understand city structure by developing comprehensive models of cities, we eschewed a large-model approach, preferring to conduct detailed studies of behavior. Partial modeling was done to test hypotheses regarding labor markets, employment location, residence location, housing choice, transport choice and trip patterns, and the effects of some government policies. Third, we have attempted to link the changes in city structure with underlying behavioral patterns, a step seldom taken in other studies. Fourth, and as a direct consequence of the overall approach adopted, this study may be regarded as being an exercise in positive (as distinguished from normative) analysis.

Understanding Behavior

How do households in cities in developing countries behave? Can we understand the workings of labor markets in these cities? Is the labor market highly segmented, thereby constraining household choices? What determines decisions about housing regarding ownership status, location, quantity, and so on? What determines the movement of firms as they grow? Where does a firm locate to begin with and why? How are travel patterns determined? What is the range of effective choice in transport modes for different kinds of households? These are the kinds of questions we addressed in attempting to model behavior.

The broad result is that many of the behavioral relations documented in this study are similar to those obtained from studies in other cities—mainly in developed countries. We may infer that the transfer of behavioral findings is high and that the workings of cities in developing countries are therefore quite comprehensible.

Income level is a key determinant of household behavior. In understanding the determination of income itself, we have found that the human capital model of earnings works well and explains a substantial portion of the variation in earnings. The explanatory power of such a model was higher in Bogotá and Cali than is usually the case in developed countries. Much of the dispersion in earnings is explained by the dispersion in educational achievement. There was little evidence of significant segmentation in the labor markets of Bogotá and Cali; workers with similar backgrounds were found to have similar earnings in different activities. Hence the informal sector was hard to identify. If there was segmentation in the labor market in these cities, it was probably in the government sector, which paid workers with similar backgrounds slightly higher wages than private-sector employers did. There was also evidence of segmentation by sex: by and large, other things being equal, women earned substantially less than their male counterparts.

The other major explanation of household behavior is its stage in the demographic cycle. Participation of household members in the labor force, their demand for housing, and their travel patterns are all conditioned by characteristics that are related to the household's size and the age composition of its members. For a large proportion of workers, who have relatively flat age-earnings profiles, the advance into the middle stages of their life cycle of household formation and expansion also means a descent into relative poverty as family size increases but earnings remain flat. This phenomenon is more noticeable in cities or countries in which average education levels are relatively low, as was still the case in Bogotá and Cali. As may be expected, women's participation in the labor force depends greatly on whether there are small children in the household. Because the value of women's time in child care and other household activities is traded off against the expected benefits of earnings, women with higher education are more likely to work outside the home. The expansion of higher education in the 1970s provided a supply-side reason for increased participation of women in the labor force. Overall, women were found to respond well to earnings opportunities in the labor market: as real wages rose in the late 1970s the labor force participation of women increased measurably. This has been a familiar phenomenon in developed countries in the post–World War II period, which has seen a secular increase in the participation of women in the labor force.

The techniques of analysis and the basic principles of behavior used in investigating labor market behavior and labor force participation were the conventional ones used in developed countries. The results obtained are quite robust and conform to expectations. The understanding of income determination, labor market dynamics, and income growth helped significantly in tracing the changes in city structure brought about by income growth and changes in demographic and household characteristics.

Transport choice is also determined largely by income levels; more journeys are made as income rises. As may be expected, income level also largely determines what mode of transport is chosen. In Bogotá and Cali the level of service provided by *busetas* makes them a credible alternative to private automobiles and provides an important clue to devising strategies aimed at containing the growth of private automobile use. Choice is an essential feature of such a strategy. Transport choice and travel patterns are more dependent on available service levels and indices of accessibility than on price levels. The availability of adequate choice also mitigates the tendency of households to use private transport as their income increases. Understanding the heterogeneity of household characteristics and demands leads to the conclusion that transport supply must also be heterogeneous to reflect such demands.

Similarly, income levels and household characteristics are the main influences on housing demand. As has been documented in developed countries, the income elasticity of housing demand is less than unity, implying that households with low incomes spend a substantial proportion of their income on housing, leaving little discretionary income for other expenditures. The nature of the demand for housing changes with shifts in income levels and movement along the life cycle. People with low and uncertain incomes find it difficult to enter the owner-occupied housing market and prefer to rent, which offers greater choice and mobility. Indeed, the mobility rates for households in Bogotá were found to be similar to those in American cities. The inference is that, as needs change, households change their housing consumption bundle accordingly. The flexibility of supply in the housing markets in Bogotá and Cali has permitted households to exercise a wider degree of choice. Choice is, however, clearly limited for the poor, who—particularly if they have large families—tend to live on the periphery of the city, where they can get more housing for less money because land is cheaper. Average family size was found to increase with distance from the city center in both Bogotá and Cali.

The behavior of the land market also broadly conforms to expectation. The trade-off between land price and transport costs, particularly time costs of travel, are evident in Bogotá and Cali, and regular land value gradients are observed, as in most other cities. Densities are also quite high, however, in the periphery, where the poor live. Whereas the rich tend to substitute capital for land when land prices increase, the poor substitute "crowding" for land. For those with larger families, a slide down the land value gradient is essential to preserve a modicum of housing consumption, but density remains high as more people crowd onto somewhat larger plots. In this case, predictable and understandable behavior leads to a different result: in developing countries the poor live in crowded conditions on the periphery of cities, whereas in developed countries the rich live in large-lot suburban developments.

Central cities have often been observed to be "incubators" for entrepreneurship. The employment location of firms is well explained by location models based on standard profit-maximization or cost-minimization principles. Firms minimize localization costs by locating near their suppliers and their markets. Locations nearer the center of the city are also usually better served with essential infrastructure. New firms respond to the same conditions and tend to prefer these locations. As firms grow and their technology changes, requiring greater space, they move out to areas where more space is available. Failures are intrinsic to new firm development. Firm death rates in Bogotá and Cali were found to be similar to those in North American cities, but firm birth rates in the two Colombian cities were vastly higher, indicating the conditions characteristic of a developing country.

The adaptability of firms and households to rapid change is an all-pervasive characteristic. A city's structure changes in response to demands made by those who live or work there. These constituents in turn adapt to the changing city structure. As land prices rise in the city center, firms and households decentralize. This act itself moderates the rate of increase of land values. New centers of activity develop elsewhere in the city, and households and firms again respond by clustering around these newer centers.

Understanding behavior also means understanding the heterogeneity inherent in the characteristics and consequent demands of both households and firms. This is particularly important in a growing city, where there is much more ferment than in a city that has reached a position of stability. A key lesson from our studies of behavior is the resilience of households and firms in the face of rapid change and their willingness to adapt to changing conditions. City structures and urban policies must take these characteristics into account in order to provide for the variegated demands of a heterogeneous set of city constituents.

Understanding City Structure

A pervasive phenomenon characterizing a growing city is the decentralization of residential and economic activity. Changes in city structure also result from changes in prevailing technologies. Because we have found the transfer of behavioral findings to be high, we also find many broad similarities in urban structure in developed and developing countries.

A conventional method of observing the structure of a city has been to look at the prevailing patterns of population density and land prices, which reflect much of the change that takes place. Both land prices and residential and employment densities are usually highest at the city center and decline exponentially toward the periphery. As a city grows, the gradient of these exponential curves declines and becomes flatter. Within this broad generalization, many subpatterns exist in different cities according to their peculiar circumstances and topographical characteristics.

Bogotá and Cali conform to the generalized pattern. Land value and population density configurations are consistent with expectations, as are the changes in these patterns over time. Land values declined exponentially in all directions from the city center. This suggests that the land market works as might be expected and does not suffer from much distortion. Land values are relatively similar at equivalent distances from the city center, a fact indicating the absence of significant segmentation in the land market. Density gradients, however, differ substantially between the different segments of the city. The density gradient is steep in the rich northern sector, but it is quite flat toward the poor southern part of the city.

How is the density gradient consistent with the regularly declining pattern of land values? The rich sectors have higher land values because of better employment opportunities as well as better neighborhood quality and infrastructure. Because land values are relatively regular, the poor have no choice but to substitute land by crowding. But it is the larger households that locate there. Poor, large households settle at the periphery to take advantage of the lower land prices—although these prices are in fact similar to land prices in the rich areas at equivalent distances. Taking advantage of lower land prices, they (the poor) buy or rent somewhat larger lots. Because the poor are unable to substitute capital for land (that is, to build more floors), their only choice is crowding. The rich can build more floors on the same lot size and reduce the number of persons per room. Hence, even the periphery exhibits high population densities in the poor areas. A flat density gradient is thus consistent with the existence of a relatively strong land value gradient. This example shows how overall regularities of structure can mask significant variations at a more disaggregated level, variations that clearly relate to underlying behavioral patterns.

A significant difference between the decentralization observed in cities in developed countries and the cases of Bogotá and Cali is the persistence of high employment densities at the city center. Whereas in developed countries the decentralization of employment has usually meant an absolute decline in the level of economic activity in central cities, in Bogotá and Cali it did not. This phenomenon is related to the low incomes that continue to prevail for a large proportion of the people. An important aspect of city structure emphasized in this study is the separation of rich and poor in different parts of the city. In addition, the rich parts of the city had more jobs than they had workers. The demand for goods and services being higher in the richer parts of the city, the demand for labor is also higher in these parts. Poor parts of the city, conversely, have a deficit of jobs. Poor households have meager demands because poor sectors can support only a limited number of activities, mainly small retail businesses that satisfy daily subsistence needs. Thus, much of the retail (and wholesale) activity continues to be concentrated in the center in Bogotá and Cali, and there is an excess of workers residing in the southern part of Bogotá. The relatively low income levels in the city therefore explain to a considerable extent the continuation of high levels of economic activity at the center. In richer cities, retail and other service activities decentralize much more in response to demand.

Another consequence of this pattern of residence and employment location is the increasing incidence of cross-commuting as a city grows and employment decentralizes. Much commuting is radially directed toward the central city. As long as employment density gradients are steeper than residential density gradients, the predominant pattern of commuting is inward, toward the city center. With the decentralization of employment, particularly toward the richer section of the city, the poor need to cross-commute across the center to the richer parts. This need leads to a demand for circumferential trips, the availability of which would eliminate the inconvenience of traversing the congested city center. It would be beneficial if road patterns and public transport routes were designed in response to this changed commuting pattern. The example above illustrates the manner in which household behavior (with regard to housing consumption and residence location) and firm behavior (with regard to location) interact with the operation of the land market to produce a predictable and comprehensible city structure. Knowledge of this interaction could lead to the provision of appropriate transport services.

Changes in technology also influence city structure greatly. The movement in manufacturing technology from batch processing to continuous processes that require much greater space has contributed to the decentralization of manufacturing employment. Conceptually, such a technological change reduces the elasticity of substitution between capital and land: it is difficult to stack a continuous manufacturing process on different floors. Hence, there is greater demand for land, and a firm is better off locating at the periphery of a city, where land values are lower.

Older cities—for example, those in Europe—were heavily dependent on the railways for intercity transport of goods. Transport costs therefore induced many manufacturing enterprises to locate close to the railhead, usually in the city center. The advent of trucking and new highway technology has made it profitable for firms to locate at the periphery and so take advantage of the flexibility and convenience of trucking. The decentralization of manufacturing activity in Bogotá and Cali has clearly been related to the convenience of trucking and the increasing availability of roads. There is a natural tendency for manufacturing firms to relocate toward the periphery of a city as they expand. Premature forced location at the periphery, however, would be harmful to the healthy generation of economic activity in the city.

We have documented the importance of income as a determinant of household behavior with regard to demand for housing and transport. How does this affect city structure? Rising incomes lead to a demand for larger houses. A general increase in incomes in a city can be expected to lead to decentralization of residence, with each household demanding more and better housing as incomes rise. Thus, each household would move out to where land values are lower, and the city would decentralize. In fact, in developing countries, income growth is accompanied by a continual increase in population. What is observed therefore is a general increase in densities in most areas of the city and an expansion of the city itself. As each area becomes denser, land values increase and new accretions take place at the edge.

The spatial expansion of cities into the surrounding agricultural areas is sometimes viewed with alarm, yet the densification of cities is also seen as leading to excessive congestion. Our study of behavior and its interrelation with city structure suggests that both patterns are inherent in the dynamics of city growth. The real issues relate to the sequencing of such city growth and the provision of matching urban services.

Encouraging Endogenous Institutional Responses to Rapid Growth

The theme of this study has been the extent to which behavioral adaptation to change is facilitated in the context of the rapid city growth characteristic of developing countries. Observation of the processes of change in Bogotá and Cali has led us to believe that rapid city growth can be managed in such a way that most residents of cities experiencing such growth can be provided with urban services that are commensurate both with their needs and with the delivery capabilities of the government and other public and private agencies. The key lesson from this study is that city growth is easier to manage successfully if the tasks of management are decentralized in such a way as to encourage endogenous responses to the changing situation.

The rate and nature of city growth are seldom precisely predictable, but the broad contours of the process are well known, and even the general patterns of structural change that will be experienced by a growing city can be anticipated. Within these patterns, however, there are considerable uncertainty and unpredictability, requiring the establishment of institutional mechanisms that can respond actively and innovatively to rapidly unfolding, new situations. We have emphasized that this response is more likely to be possible if we understand better the behavior of the various constituents of the city—households, firms, and government agencies—and the impact of their behavior patterns on the evolving city structure.

A standard governmental response to rapid city growth is to prepare comprehensive metropolitan plans. Such plans attempt to shape the growth of a city for perhaps five to twenty years, delineating land use in a detailed manner and freezing city structure for the planned period. It is also typical to do physical planning for all the anticipated infrastructure needs. Often, however, the costs of such infrastructure are not calculated realistically, and, when these costs turn out to be excessive, the plan becomes nonoperational or implementation falls far short of what was intended. Large portions of the growing city are then deprived of essential needs. Success in drawing up physical plans depends heavily on effective forecasting of population growth: as we have seen in Bogotá and Cali, such forecasting is fraught with difficulty and is seldom successful.

The preparation of detailed plans is necessarily time-consuming. Moreover, in most countries the adoption of an urban plan also involves different levels of political consultation—another time-consuming process. By the time a plan becomes operational, it may already have become obsolete.

Largely as a result of these difficulties, the experience with urban planning has been less than happy. But the desire to undertake similar exercises remains widespread. One lesson of our study is that cities would be better advised to decentralize the instruments of infrastructure provision that are able to finance themselves and to respond flexibly to the changing demands of a growing city. The mechanism of self-financing is important because it serves as a self-correcting procedure whereby higher-priority projects are implemented first and realistic planning becomes a necessity. Self-financing by an agency does not necessarily imply commercial financing. It can include government subventions, commercial loans, government loans, and soft loans, as well as public contributions from users. It does, however, mean greater agency autonomy than in a system in which infrastructure programs are fully funded and handed down from above. What is important is that the decentralized autonomous agencies develop the ability to respond to the emerging demands of the growing city.

Given the limited ability of government agencies to deliver the full infrastructure and other requirements of a rapidly growing city, it is also prudent to allow private initiative to flourish whenever possible. This is not so much a matter of ideology as of necessity. The relatively happy experience of Bogotá and Cali with housing provision is a case in point. Public agencies were clearly not in a position to meet the full requirements of land development or housing during the 1950s, 1960s, and 1970s; it was the relatively unhindered operations of the *urbanizadores piratas* that helped house the burgeoning population of these cities during that period. Similarly, the transport system has expanded adequately to cope with the cities' needs, through extensive use of private incentives, although this time within a public regulatory framework. The scarcity of public resources that usually constricts the expansion of public transport was not an issue. Private investment in public transport was allowed to flourish in such a way that high service levels were achieved at low cost. The system was also allowed to respond to the heterogeneous demands arising from increases in household incomes, and an increasing variety of transport modes was encouraged.

It is difficult to assess how much conscious policy-level thinking went into devising the kind of institutional arrangements that were in place in Bogotá and Cali in the 1960s and 1970s. It is likely that institutions and policy responses emerged somewhat endogenously in response to rapid urbanization. It is true, however, that the highest policymaking authorities had a positive attitude toward urban development, investment in urban infrastructure, and housing during that period. Innovative schemes such as the indexed UPAC housing finance instruments were the result of such high-level policy concern. Some of the innovative and flexible policy responses that we observed in Colombia may therefore have emerged as a result of a generally positive attitude, rather than simply fortuitously. It is useful to delineate some of the main institutional developments that were found to assist the rapid growth in these cities.

One problem that a rapidly growing city typically faces is how to manage a fast-expanding supply of developed land for housing and other purposes. Rapid in-migration makes the demand for housing grow much faster than normal population growth, and entirely new areas have to be developed. Land development includes investment in infrastructure such as water supply, sewerage, roads, and power supply. All this requires substantial front-end investment, which public authorities can usually ill afford. On the demand side, households face similar problems: most households do not possess the wherewithal to enter the owner housing market by purchasing a fully finished housing bundle. There is usually a time lag between the expression of housing demand and supply by housing services.

Different cities have attempted to respond to this situation in different ways. In Delhi, for example, the government effectively nationalized all land that could possibly be urbanized with the idea that the public authorities would develop it and make sites-and-services projects available to the poor at affordable prices. In addition, the public authorities would build houses. Thus, undesirable speculation would be avoided and the poor would have better access to shelter.

In fact, the public authorities have not been able to keep pace with the burgeoning demand, and the legal housing they provide is only a small proportion of the total. Because of this supply-demand imbalance, land prices have risen tremendously, limiting access to housing and defeating the original purpose of public land acquisition. In Colombia, too, the national housing agency, the ICT, initially attempted to supply finished houses for the poor. As many as 60 percent of all urban households could not afford the lowest-cost ICT houses, however. This is not atypical—in fact, it is a common situation: houses fully constructed by public agencies are seldom accessible to the poor. Specific housing projects can rarely address the problem of providing shelter for the poor. More general approaches devoted to improving access and reducing effective prices are more likely to be successful.

What, then, is the solution? The conceptual breakthrough is to realize and accept that under almost no circumstances can the poor in developing countries afford a complete housing bundle. In principle, a well-functioning housing finance market should solve this problem. In practice, the earning pattern of the poor is such that financial institutions find it difficult to finance them; moreover, low-income households are loath to get into long-term debt relationships in the face of other pressing consumption demands and uncertainties about their earnings. The predominant solution in Bogotá and Cali, and in many other cities, is to "unbundle" the housing and infrastructure package and to invest in cash and kind in an incremental fashion. The public agencies also solved their problem by supplying infrastructure services piecemeal, unbundling the infrastructure package (a solution not permitted in holistic planning frameworks).

The housing bundle consists of developed land, the actual house structure, and a package of infrastructural services. Households solve their problem by buying relatively undeveloped land to begin with, building a core house, and then obtaining access to improved infrastructure over time, while augmenting the house for household expansion as needed and as increases in income permit. From the supply side this was made possible by the intervention of small, independent developers who jumped in to fill this large demand niche. Although government regulations and other rigidities often do not sanction this kind of incremental solution, it is a rational response to household needs in a rapidly growing city. Buying a semideveloped site reduces the effective land price for the household, which then benefits from the large increases in land values that occur after full development. By reducing this price, the household can afford better and larger housing over time than if it attempted to start with a fully finished unit. The cost of the structure is also reduced, to much less than the cost of an equivalent house built in the conventional way, by the use of recycled materials and family labor. Similarly, at the beginning, the household makes do with a lower quality of urban services. In such an incremental development, various agencies bring in different services at different times. In a fully built-up development all services have to be provided simultaneously, which can be so costly as to be prohibitive; hence the development often does not take place.

The poorest 30 percent were not even able to enter the incremental ownership housing market. They were mostly renters, partly because their incomes were so low they could not afford even core housing sites, but also because of uncertain employment, which necessitated frequent residential moves. The poor therefore rent rooms from people who are slightly better off, thereby becoming housing finance agents for their landlords in the bargain. The slightly better off entering the housing market often rent rooms to the less well off as a source of funds with which to finance their next stage of development. Governments have typically done little to encourage a rental market that facilitates shelter for the urban poor. Most government shelter programs, even sites-and-services projects and other programs targeted at the poor, are aimed at increasing home ownership. The behavior and preferences of poor households, however, clearly indicate that it is not generally feasible to push them into the ownership housing market, nor is it usually in their interest. Closer observation of the operation of housing markets in cities in developing countries and of household behavior would have made this apparent earlier. Yet most government programs continue to focus on ownership housing. The reality that the poor are seldom candidates for homeownership should be reflected in the policies of housing finance agencies that serve this group. Rental of rooms to the poorest by the slightly better off should be made easier; the poorest will then be housed and a general expansion of the housing stock achieved.

The overall lesson of these observations is that government should recognize the effectiveness of this process and facilitate institutional arrangements that enable people to express their preferences and invest their own ingenuity and resources in providing for their own shelter. On the supply side, governments should be more realistic in assessing their own capabilities for supplying the requisite urban services and developed land. It should be possible for small, independent developers to supply the needs that governments are characteristically incapable of supplying. This broad approach may be characterized as promoting the public use of private incentives.

Transport

The management of transport in Bogotá and Cali provides a similar illustration of a public service system's responding well to household needs and with built-in flexibility and adaptability. A rapidly expanding city requires a rapidly expanding transport system. One approach to providing this kind of service is to operate a publicly owned transport company and to develop a metropolitan plan for expansion of services. This requires heavy capital investments in equipment, heavy expenditures on operating costs, and, in a large city, the ability to cope with the management problems inherent in the operation of a large system. It is difficult for such a system to respond to rapidly changing consumer demands and to provide for different levels of service quality demanded by households of different characteristics. It is also difficult to make such systems pay for themselves because of consumer resistance to realistic fare setting in a government-owned public service. Regulatory systems should allow for the entry of different types of transport suppliers who provide a variety of transport services in response to the typically variegated demand found in a growing city in a developing country.

The institutional framework in Bogotá and Cali has allowed for a decentralized system that can respond quickly to changing situations. The route allocation system allows for new routes to be opened in response to consumer demand. The introduction of *busetas* introduced both greater flexibility and a higher level of service. Other cities have allowed even greater heterogeneity in service levels. At the same time, government regulation of fares and routes prevents a free-for-all and injects some order into what might otherwise be too chaotic a system. The system of fare subsidies performs relatively well as a subsidy to the less well off because only the lowest level of transport service—full-size buses—receives such subsidies. Our evaluation of the whole transport subsidy and regulatory system suggests that the system, in general, works well. This underlines the fact that a government subsidy system to private, decentralized operations is probably cheaper to operate than a fully owned public transport system. Another significant feature of the transport system in Bogotá and Cali is that flat fares are effective in mitigating the spatial disadvantage suffered by the poor, who are pushed to distant peripheral residential locations.

We have emphasized that the decentralization of employment suggests that circumferential routes also have to be introduced as a city expands, although the continued concentration of employment in city centers in developing countries makes possible the continued use of large high-occupancy buses on trunk radial routes. (In developed countries the loss of employment in the city center, coupled with high incomes, makes it increasingly difficult to run high-occupancy vehicles often, even on trunk routes, without subsidies.) Low wages in developing countries also make it economically feasible to operate smaller buses and vans, whereas, in richer cities, drivers' wages make it uneconomical to run anything but large buses with a minimum number of passengers.

These arrangements illustrate a point: that in cities in developing countries it is feasible to devise public transportation systems that minimize the use of public resources and respond to the needs of the vast majority of city residents. The specific needs of different cities may vary, but the behavioral principles do not. Household and firm behavior have a bearing on city structure, and such knowledge can help in designing appropriate systems for public transport provisions in a responsive manner. The trick is to devise a system that economizes on information collection and processing and responds positively to emerging needs. Major ex ante public decisionmaking is not needed in such a system.

Infrastructure

The governments of Bogotá and Cali have acted as followers rather than leaders in guiding city growth. There were no systematic attempts at overall urban investment planning for the medium term. Yet the achievement of adequate public service levels has been better than in most cities in developing countries. How did this happen? Our view is that, paradoxically, it is the decentralized nature of urban government in these cities that has led to such a creditable performance. As mentioned earlier, decentralization facilitates the effective sharing of the costs of urbanization among all concerned. A more centralized system tends to shift all present costs to the government, which usually finds it difficult to bear the burden. The result is inadequate investment in urban infrastructure and the emergence of significant public service deficits. The autonomy extended to public service agencies has helped foster a culture of user-financed public services. Capital costs have usually been funded by loans, which have then been effectively serviced by user charges. The autonomy of public service entities also helps them concentrate on providing service and responding to demand.

During the period of particularly high growth, the system of valorization helped provide for road infrastructure, which is usually seen as a classic public good, financed solely from the government budget. Although the system fell into disuse later because of practical difficulties, it served its purpose at a crucial time. Again, the principle was that people benefiting from the development of infrastructure should be aware of such development and should share in paying for its costs.

This system stands in sharp contrast to more centralized systems that are based on a priori impressions of requirements and are not geared to meeting the preferences of urban residents. Our observation of urban behavior, of the unfolding city structure, and of the government agencies supplying services in Bogotá and Cali leads us to the conclusion that city growth is manageable only if institutions are designed to be responsive to the behavior and needs of the various constituents that make up a city. The institutional framework must have an endogenous ability to serve greatly heterogeneous demands, and an ability to change as these demands change in a rapidly growing city.

Appendix: The Data

The City Study assembled a data bank of existing sources of information about Bogotá and Cali in the form of copies of the original computer tapes prepared by the respective originators of the data. All have been documented in detail by Valverde (1978) and Y. J. Lee (1979, 1981). A number of primary surveys were also carried out specifically for the project. The main comprehensive primary data collection effort was the 1978 World Bank–DANE Household Survey conducted in Bogotá and Cali, a joint project of the Bank and the Departamento Adminstrativo Nacional de Estadísticas, Colombia's national statistical agency. The main data sources used in the study are briefly described in this appendix.

The 1973 Population Census

Before 1985, the most recent censuses taken in Colombia were in 1964 and 1973. Unfortunately, the 1964 census did not report incomes. There was widespread skepticism about the coverage of the 1973 census,[1] but Potter and Ordonez (1976) concluded, after careful demographic analysis of an advance sample, that the information appeared to be of good quality, at least in relation to previous censuses. They estimated that the overall undercounting for Colombia as a whole was probably 7 percent. The tape provided by DANE for public use was a 4 percent sample of households. For Bogotá, however, the tape covered all households living in the buildings that happened to house the 4 percent sample. We used the entire sample for the tabulations in this book and expanded it to reflect the size of the city's population and estimated undercounting. Because this study was particularly concerned with spatial distributions within the city, the expanded sample was used so that it would be representative of the various subdivisions within the city's boundaries.

The census contains information about dwelling and household characteristics, demographic data for all individuals, labor force information for workers, and fertility information for females. Although we cannot comment on its coverage, we agree with Potter and Ordonez (1976) that the overall quality of the information in the sample appears to be good. Nonresponses seem to be distributed randomly; the only obvious bias is that single-person households predominate in the "no information" categories for income and the labor force. One of the most useful distinguishing features of this data set is that the location of respondents is coded down to the block (*manzana*) of residence. Income data were obtained from only one question: "What was your income from all sources last month?" Only about 12 percent of the sample did not report income information—a proportion that compares well with nonresponses in the U.S. census.

The extent of income coverage of the 1973 census as well as the 1977 Household Survey and the 1978 World Bank–DANE Household Survey was estimated (see Mohan 1986, appendix C, for details). The aggregation of all incomes reported in the census appeared to be no more than 50 percent of the estimated total personal income for Bogotá. Various factors are responsible for this underreporting:

- Twelve percent of the people gave no information.
- When only one question is asked, much of the nonlabor income is probably not reported.
- Income in kind—for example, as received by domestic servants—is probably not reported.
- Many earners receive end-of-the-year bonuses; these are characteristically not covered in one-shot cross-sectional surveys such as the census, unless the question is asked specifically.

In view of these factors, it is not surprising that the income coverage of the census was only 50 percent.[2]

Household Surveys

DANE has conducted a regular program of household surveys since 1970; the main objective has been to collect information about the labor force. Since 1975, these surveys have been conducted quarterly, alternating between Colombia's four largest and seven largest cities,[3] along with an occasional national survey. We obtained the computer tapes for 1972 (Encuesta de Hogares 6, Fuerza de Trabajo: EH 6-FY), 1975 (EH8E), and 1977 (EH15).[4] The 1972 survey was a national one and covered 6,371 households, of which 1,348 were in Bogotá. It contained information about housing as well as demographic and labor force characteristics. The survey did not provide the intracity location of the respondents. The 1975 survey was a special one for the city of Bogotá; it sampled 3,953 households and contained information on labor force and demographic characteristics only. The 1977 survey was conducted in the four largest cities and sampled 6,082 households, 3,161 of which were in Bogotá. Starting with this survey, DANE began to use "rotational sampling": 67 percent of dwelling units sampled remain in the next survey and 33 percent are new. Both the 1975 and 1977 surveys contain the location of respondents' residences. The 1972 and 1975 surveys had information about the number of workers in each respondent's workplace. This question was not included in the 1977 sample.

In these samples, DANE classified neighborhoods into six socioeconomic strata: (1) low-low; (2) low; (3) medium-low; (4) medium; (5) medium-high; and (6) high. At the conclusion of a survey, weights were assigned to each of these strata and applied to the members of the strata for all expansions of the sample. These "expansion factors" are supposed to take into account the over- and undersampling that may occur over the course of the survey. The expanded sample should then be correctly representative of the city as a whole.

The 1977 survey is unusual in that as many as 20 percent of the working respondents did not report their incomes, a proportion that compares unfavorably with the census. Consequently, a method was devised to impute incomes to them. (See Mohan 1986, appendix B, which describes the calculation of incomes for all respondents and the imputation method for nonrespondents.)

The coverage of income in the 1977 survey was only slightly better than that in the 1973 census, despite the more detailed questions asked. Labor and nonlabor income data were taken separately, and income in kind was estimated as well. Even when the imputed incomes were included, the survey covered only about 61 percent of the estimated total of personal incomes in Bogotá. It also appears that the highest incomes were either underreported or undersampled. If the incomes reported in the 1977 sample are converted to 1973 pesos, there is little real income growth on average, and those in the highest categories actually decline.

The 1978 World Bank–DANE Household Survey

In 1978 the World Bank's City Study team and DANE jointly conducted a survey of about 3,000 households in Bogotá and 1,000 households in Cali. This was larger and more carefully conducted than previous surveys. It had five main parts: household and dwelling characteristics; demographic characteristics of all individuals; worker characteristics, including information on workplace; information about the unemployed; and information about the vehicle ownership and journey-to-work characteristics for the employed.

A partial recount of dwelling units was done to take into account the expansion of Bogotá since the 1973 census (earlier surveys were all based on a 1972 sample frame). Information about income was elicited more carefully. In earlier surveys, data on the earnings of all workers in a household were usually obtained from any available adult respondent. In this survey, all worker information was obtained from each worker directly, even if this required more than one visit to the household. Furthermore, income questions were asked of all members of the household even if they did not work. Two questions were asked to obtain labor income: the amount and periodicity of wage payments and total earnings in the previous month. Income in kind was imputed. Various nonlabor sources of income were specifically mentioned to obtain nonlabor income. As a result, the income coverage of this survey was about 90 percent, which was a great improvement over previous surveys.

Only about 3.6 percent of responses gave no information about income, and these responses have been imputed by the same method used in the 1977 Household Survey. All regressions were conducted after weighting each observation with expansion factors, as in the procedure for 1977. These expansion factors take into account over- and undersampling.

Note on Household Survey Samples and the Spatial Disaggregation of Bogotá and Cali

In map 3-1 Bogotá was divided into *comunas,* rings, and sectors, but the basic socioeconomic spatial unit in the city is a barrio, or neighborhood, of which there were about 500 in 1973 and about 700 in 1978. DANE geocoded each of these units with a four-digit number. The first two digits identify a *comuna*—a collection of barrios. The last two digits identify barrios within the *comuna*. The *comunas* were then further aggregated for City Study purposes into rings and sectors. The boundaries of the *comunas* shown in map 3-1 are the principal streets in Bogotá. The city is bounded on the east by mountains and therefore has an approximately semicircular shape, although the north-south axis is longer. Note that the first digit goes from 1 to 9 and roughly rotates (increasing) from south to north by sectors (or pie slices). The second digit ranges from 1 to 6 and corresponds roughly to rings centered in *comunas* 31 and 81, increasing from south to north. Similar principles were followed in geocoding Cali (map 3-2) so that rings and sectors could be identified there.

DANE, along with the Ministry of Health, compiled an inventory of *manzanas* and of dwelling units within the city before the 1973 census, and that inventory has continued to form the sample frame of all subsequent surveys in Bogotá. Thus, none of these surveys had sampled the new neighborhoods that had developed since 1972. The sample frame was therefore updated for the 1978 World Bank–DANE Survey. The sampling was designed to make equiprobable the possibility that any dwelling unit in the city according to the 1972 inventory might be selected. The basic sampling unit (*unidad primaria de muestra*) is a block, within which all households in all dwelling units are interviewed. Provision is made for different sizes of blocks. Since all the sampling was based on the 1972 sample frame, it was difficult to trace time trends for changes within the city. Moreover, caution must be exercised in drawing any conclusions about the changing character of neighborhoods. If different regions of the city differ systematically from one another and if one region changes character over time, the later samples will no longer be representative. Sampling is based on the classification of neighborhoods into the six socioeconomic strata. If neighborhoods change character— that is, filter up or down in the socioeconomic scale—the resulting sample will no longer be representative. Hence, drawing conclusions about fine changes in the income distribution from two household surveys at two points in time is hazardous in the absence of detailed knowledge of the sampling procedures used. If, however, rates of change are not high, such difficulties are minimal—but then one would have less interest in tracing time trends anyway! These remarks can be extended to national surveys, where the heterogeneity of regions is perhaps typically more pronounced than within a city.

These details have been offered here because they are seldom given by users of household survey data. They become particularly important when comparisons are made between surveys undertaken in different years; information about each data source is necessary in order to be aware of biases that may arise from differences in survey design and coverage.

The 1972 Phase II Household Survey

Phase II of the Bogotá Urban Development Study occurred in 1971–72 and was funded by the United Nations Development Programme (UNDP) under the auspices of the World Bank. The project included a survey of 4,675 households in 1972 (for a detailed description of the data set, see Valverde 1978). Although the survey focused on demographic and housing characteristics, it also included questions about the respondent's workplace, including its location and type of industry. Extensive information about work trips was also collected. This data set was used extensively in the City Study to obtain a comparative picture of Bogotá in 1972, particularly in the employment location, housing, and transportation segments of the study.

The Social Security Files on Establishments

These data (see K. S. Lee 1989) provide a complete listing of all establishments affiliated with the social security system. The Colombian Social Security Agency (Instituto de Seguros Sociales) released to the City Study a copy of the complete files of Bogotá for 1978 and 1979 and of Cali for 1976. For each firm, the tapes contain the address, the number of workers, and the SIC (Standard Industrial Classification) code; each establishment's location was then geocoded at the barrio level at the Corporación Centro Regional de Población in Bogotá.

The main limitation of this data set was its poor coverage of small firms. Even though the law requires that all employees in private and public enterprises and self-employed individuals register with the social security system, those with small family shops and independent and casual workers tend to avoid membership. Government employees and military personnel have separate social security programs.

For the country as a whole, the social security data compare favorably with other information, such as the industrial census and labor force surveys, particularly for the manufacturing and finance sectors (DANE 1975; further descriptions and analyses of the data appear in DANE 1974 and 1976). DANE concluded that the coverage is almost complete for large manufacturing establishments (with ten or more workers) and firms of all sizes in finance but is poor in the commerce and service sectors (which include many small firms).

DANE's Annual Industrial Directory File

DANE compiles an annual directory of all industrial establishments. This data set is very similar to the Dun & Bradstreet Market Identifier (DMI) data in the United States, which have been used in a number of employment location studies. The DANE directory includes information about all establishments with ten or more employees. This covers about 70 percent of total manufacturing employment in Bogotá. The data in this directory include information about location, production, sales, and input uses of individual establishments. The annual directories for the years 1970 to 1975 were computerized for Bogotá and Cali in order to study the trends in employment, births and deaths of firms, and location of jobs.

The World Bank City Study Survey of Manufacturing Establishments

In 1978 K. S. Lee organized and conducted a survey of manufacturing establishments in Bogotá to explain the changing location patterns found from analyzing the data from the DANE industrial directories.[5] The establishments in the industrial directory were used as a sample base. The sample of 126 establishments interviewed in the survey was drawn from DANE's records of 2,629 firms in the industrial directory file from 1970 to 1975. The sample of firms was stratified by location history (that is, whether they were new or mature firms or movers); zone of location, defined by thirty-eight *comunas*; type of industry, defined by three-digit SIC codes; and size, defined by the number of employees.

To minimize the cost of sampling while obtaining a sufficient number of observations for econometric estimation, the survey focused on textiles and fabricated metals. These industries have no particular locational requirements, such as proximity to a river or mines, and should be more amenable to spatial policies than others such as cement or steel. Moreover, together these two industries accounted for 50 percent of total manufacturing employment in Bogotá. The homogeneity of firms within each industry also makes it possible to test behavioral hypotheses with sufficient degrees of freedom. A third group of "other industries" was added, however, to allow descriptive studies of other kinds of firms.

The second major consideration in the sampling process was to oversample large firms in order to maximize the number of workers included. Moreover, there was an attempt to cover a wide geographic area that would allow estimation of rent and wage gradients for the entire city. The goal was to obtain a sample of at least 120 firms, with equal representation of the three types of firms. There were 58 mature firms, 50 movers (including 2 firms that moved to Bogotá from outside the city), and 18 new firms. The sample coverage across zones was satisfactory; twenty-seven *comunas* were represented and allowed a fairly even spread over the three rings with high densities of manufacturing employment. Only a small number of establishments, however, were selected from ring 1 (the central business district [CDB]) and ring 6 (three residential *comunas* in the north).

In some cases the four-way stratification severely limited the possibility of drawing sample establishments from a specific population category. For example, not enough textile firms were located in certain *comunas*.

Additional establishments were therefore selected from the apparel industry to supplement the textile industry sample and from the non-electric machinery industry to supplement the fabricated metal industry sample. The final sample had fairly even shares among the three industry groups: about 35 percent each for the two main industry groups and 30 percent for the "other" category.

The average size of mature firms in the sample was about four times larger than that of new firms, and more than twice that of movers. This results from the oversampling of large firms; the average size of firms in the sample (135 employees) is about twice as large as the average among Bogotá's manufacturing establishments.

The World Bank Housing Survey of Low-Income Households

Twenty-six barrios were drawn from two separate universes of low and very low socioeconomic status subdivisions created either between 1963 and 1971 or after 1971 (see Hamer 1985 for details).[6] These lists were further reduced to exclude barrios for which there was no information on legal standing at the District Planning Office. In addition, areas of the city with little new low- or very low status subdivision formation were eliminated from consideration. Given these two universes, one for each time period, a stratified random sample of 10 percent of the barrios was extracted from each, reflecting the geographic location, legal standing, and socioeconomic status inherent in the sample frames. From the set of twenty-six barrios, thirteen were eliminated from the household survey sample frame because they were government-sponsored, had very low lot occupancy (below 50 percent), or were very small (fewer than fifty dwelling units). Another barrio was eliminated because it had been extensively surveyed in a previous study. Other corrections were subsequently made, and the result was the set of twelve barrios listed in table A-1.[7]

The number of structures in the surveyed barrios totaled 2,433; of these, 9 percent were surveyed. Following the recommendations of local consultants, a decision was made not to take a completely random sample. Instead, given the paramount interest in the characteristics of the different prevailing dwelling types and in the way they were modified over time, an effort was made to sample roughly the same number of households in each of several dwelling types in the barrio. In each barrio roughly twenty households were interviewed. The dwelling types surveyed in any given barrio did not necessarily correspond to the distribution in place. In addition, on entering any given barrio, the surveyors carried instructions about which types of units to sample randomly on that particular day, in order to maintain the required structural diversity at the aggregate twelve-barrio level. That could result, for example, in

Table A-1. Households Interviewed, by Barrio

Barrio name	DANE code number	Number of households
Quindio Viejo	1318	13
Quindio Nuevo	1399	8
Managua	1406	14
Molinos del Sur	2506	20
Pachon de la Torre	2528	21
Pastranita	4525	21
De Gaulle	4527	21
San Ignacio	5607	21
Prado Pinzon	9105	12
Los Naranjos	9204	20
Rincon	9205	21
Tibabuyes	9209	20

Source: Hamer (1985).

the inclusion of only one or two dwelling types in a given barrio, simply because earlier survey work had not managed to uncover enough units with those characteristics in other barrios. Thus the survey could be used to characterize the conditions in any one barrio. Finally, and by definition, the survey was not designed to derive means and medians even for the barrios as a whole, except for illustrative and very rough approximations of actual behavior. It is only a felicitous coincidence that the distribution of sampled structure types corresponds in a rough way with the actual distribution of structures in the barrios, as noted in table A-2. Such a coincidence allows the cited means and/or medians to be taken more seriously than would otherwise be possible, because it can be shown that the different structure types are associated with a fairly predictable and distinct set of characteristics.[8] Table A-1 presents a breakdown of actual interviews by neighborhood, and table A-3 provides a review of selected characteristics of the barrios surveyed.

Table A-2. Distribution of Structure Types: Survey and Universe
(percent)

Category	Survey	Universe
Tugurio[a]	14	16
Casalote[b]	26	24
Single-story	32	39
Multistory	29	21

Note: These categories are aggregations of yet more carefully differentiated structure types.
a. A shack, usually of very small dimension and intended as temporary shelter.
b. One or two multiple-use rooms attached to the wall defining the perimeter of the lot.
Source: Hamer (1985).

Table A-3. General Characteristics of Surveyed Subdivisions

Characteristic	Quindio Viejo	Pachon de la Torre	Molinos del Sur	Rincon	Los Naranjos	Prado Pinzon	De Gaulle	Managua	Pastranita	San Ignacio	Tibabuyes	Quindio Nuevo
Age[a]	1	1	1	1	1	1	1	2	2	2	2	2
Stratum[b]	1	1	2	2	2	3[c]	1	2	1	2	1	1
Distance[d]	2	3	2	3	3	3	3	2	3	2	3	2
Legal 78[e]	3	4	2[f]	4	3	3	4	3	3	3	4	5
Legal 72[g]	2	2	1[f]	2	1	1	2	2	2	2	0	3
Water[h]	78	77	62	74	75	64	0	73	75	70	75	0
Sewer[h]	0	0	62	78	0	72	0	0	0	74	0	0
Power[h]	62	73	62	64	65	64	10	73	70	68	75	0
Units 77[i]	370	218	541	195	119	497	88	221	195	209	54	223
Gross area[j]	20	7	13	6	4	24	1	8	5	8	2	3
Net area[k]	7	5	9	5	3	18	1	5	4	6	1	2
Pop DEN-N[l]	430	320	400	308	300	222	508	300	303	300	260	659
Pop DEN-G[m]	300	228	266	243	225	166	430	170	236	225	175	467
One floor[n]	99	99	56	82	87	76	91	90	85	85	96	99
Two floors[n]	1	1	42	17	13	22	9	10	15	15	4	1
Three floors[n]	0	0	2	1	0	2	0	0	0	0	0	0
Casa 77[o]	15	27	10	25	20	20	39	31	25	30	31	1
Tugurios 77[o]	32	19	1	6	2	7	9	11	1	10	15	54

(Table continues on the following page.)

297

Table A-3 (*continued*)

a. Age: 1 = barrio formed between 1963 and 1971; 2 = barrio formed after 1971.

b. Barrios classified in ascending order of socioeconomic rank, "1" being the lowest; the ranking in the whole city runs from 1 to 5.

c. Although the Prado Pinzon barrio as a whole was classified as having a middle-low status, the area interviewed was then a recent nucleus that had an atypical, low status.

d. Distance: 2 = barrios located at intermediate distance from the central business district (CBD), between 1,750 and 8,750 meters; 3 = barrios located farther than 8,750 meters.

e. 1978 status of barrio provided by Bogotá District Planning Department (Departamento Administrativo de Planeación Distrital [DAPD]): 1 = minimum norm development; 2 = legal, standard barrio; 3 = barrio in process of being regularized; 4 = unauthorized barrio; 5 = squatter settlement.

f. Although the Molinos barrio as a whole was classified as legal, the area interviewed was a then-recent nucleus that had been developed illegally.

g. 1972 status of barrio provided by DAPD: 1 = legal; 2 = in process of regularization; 3 = illegal; 0 = not applicable.

h. Year of barrio's connection to service; 0 = no connection.

i. Barrio dwelling units in place in 1977.

j. Total area in hectares.

k. Total area in hectares excluding nonresidential use in 1977.

l. Net residential density in persons per hectare.

m. Gross residential density in persons per hectare.

n. Percentage distribution of dwelling units in barrio according to number of floors.

o. Percentage of dwelling units classified as such in 1977.

Source: Hamer (1985).

298

Survey of *Pirata* Developers Conducted by Superintendencia Bancaria

In 1977 the Superintendencia Bancaria in Bogotá collected data on 135 *pirata* subdivisions as well as 14 *Normas Minimas* developments (Carroll 1980). The Housing Division sent out questionnaires to some 200 subdividers whose names were in its files and in records of the District Planning Department. The respondents were informed that they were legally bound to supply the information and that their subdivisions could be "regularized" if they cooperated. Data requested for each subdivision included the size of the original tract; its price and date of acquisition; the number of lots; the total street and open space areas; the amounts and costs of services installed (sewer, water, telephone, electricity, and paving); and, for each lot sold, its size, price, terms, and date of sale (see table A-4 for a complete list of variables included in the survey). The 149 *pirata* and *Normas Minimas* subdivisions for which completed questionnaires were returned represented the efforts of 121 individual subdividers. No data on dwelling units or on the characteristics of families buying lots were collected.

Table A-4. Variables in Superintendencia Bancaria *Pirata* Subdivision Survey, 1977
(from questionnaires)

Serial number	Variable description
1.	Name of subdivision
2.	Name of DANE (census) barrio of subdivision
3.	ID number of DANE barrio (1973 codes)
4.	Date of initiation of physical works
5.	Number of lots
6.	Date of DAPD approval, if any
7.	Date of Superintendencia Bancaria approval, if any
8.	Size of tract (square meters)
9.	Date of acquisition of tract
10.	Date of tract acquisition document
11.	Price of tract
12.	Value of installments (up to five) for tract
13.	Dates of installments
14.	Interest rate on tract installments
15.	Number of bus routes within ten minutes' walk
16.	Existence of neighboring subdivision with water network
17.	Subdivision inside or outside urban perimeter?
18.	Subdivision above or below water company elevation limit?
19.	If above, source of water supply
20.	For sewer, water pipes, standpipes, electricity, telephones, streets, sidewalks, and curbs: quantity installed, cost of installation, source of financing, date of installation

Notes

1. See, for example, Lubell and McCallum (1978, p. 126), who regard the Bogotá 1973 results as "simply not usable" and therefore do not rely on the census. Their calculations and projections are based on the 1972 Urban Development Study Household Survey, which covered 4,675 households.

2. This may be compared with an estimate of undercoverage in the Brazil 1960 and 1970 censuses by Pfefferman and Webb (1979, p. 16), who find that the censuses cover about 57 to 58 percent of incomes.

3. In descending order by size, these are Bogotá, Cali, Medellín, Barranquilla, Bucamaranga, Manizales, and Pasto.

4. EH = Encuesta de Hogares; E = Especial (special sample of Bogotá).

5. For more details about firms in the sample, see chapter 4 of this book; for a copy of the questionnaire used, see K. S. Lee (1989, appendix B).

6. The classification scheme was developed for the Special District of Bogotá by Jairo Arias and reported in "Estudio de Estratificación de Desarrollo Social," Departamento Administrativo de Planeación Distrital, n.d. The scheme was based on a points index based on type of dwelling, type of structure, type of construction, level of crowding, availability of public services, and family income.

7. One barrio on the original list was replaced by another because of community hostility. Another of the barrios chosen for the survey terminated its involvement in mid-stream, and a substitute barrio was chosen to complete the requisite number of interviews. See table A-1 for the final list of barrios and table A-3 for a listing of general barrio characteristics.

8. This can be demonstrated from the survey data, even though these suffer from a peculiarity, namely that the bulk of the *casalote* dwellers are drawn from barrios with a somewhat higher socioeconomic ranking than those from which single-story occupants were selected. Thus, for example, the mean household income of *tugurio* dwellers is Col$4,400; for *casalote* and single- story occupants it is Col$6,500; for households living in two-story structures it is Col$9,300; and for families found in three-story structures it is Col$13,900. (See table A-2 for definitions of *casalote* and *tugurio*.)

Bibliography

The word "processed" describes informally reproduced works that may not be commonly available through libraries.

Abt Associates; Dames & Moore; General Organization for Housing, Building, and Planning Research; and USAID. 1982. *Informal Housing in Egypt.* Cambridge, Mass.: Abt Associates.

Amato, Peter. 1968. "An Analysis of the Changing Patterns of Elite Residential Locations in Bogotá, Colombia." Latin American Studies Program, Dissertation Series, no. 7. Ithaca, N.Y.: Cornell University.

———. 1970a. "A Comparison of Population Densities, Land Value and Socio-Economic Class in Four Latin American Cities." *Land Economics* 46 (4): 447-55.

———. 1970b. "Elitism and Settlement Patterns in the Latin American City." *Journal of American Institute of Planners* (March).

Anand, Sudhir. 1983. *Inequality and Poverty in Malaysia: Measurement and Decomposition.* New York: Oxford University Press.

Anderson, John E. 1982. "Cubic-Spline Urban Density Functions." *Journal of Urban Economics* 2 (2): 155–67.

APTA (American Public Transport Association). 1980. *Transit Fact Book, 78–79.* Washington, D.C.

Ardila, Amparo de, and Andrew M. Hamer. 1979. "Selected Characteristics of the Barrios of Bogotá." City Study Intermediate Paper, no. 21. World Bank, Development Economics Department, Washington, D.C. Processed.

Arias, Jairo. 1977. "Modelo de Desarrollo Urbano." In Colcultura: *Vida Urbana y Urbanismo.* Bogotá, D.E.: Colcultura.

Asabere, Paul K., and K. Owusu-Banahere. 1983. "Population Density Functions for Ghanaian (African) Cities: An Empirical Note." *Journal of Urban Economics* 14 (3): 370–79.

Avendano, R., and A. d'Amico. 1981. "Bogotá Bus Drivers: Asesinos o Santos." Bogotá. Processed.

Avramovic, Dragoslav, and Associates. 1972. *Economic Growth of Colombia: Problems and Prospects.* Baltimore: Johns Hopkins University Press.

Barton-Aschman Associates. 1983. "Transportation Planning Technical Assistance for Metropolitan Mexico City: Narrative Summary and Technical Summary," technical appendices. Mexico City. June. Processed.

Becker, Gary S. 1964. *Human Capital: A Theoretical and Empirical Analysis*. New York: Columbia University Press.

Ben-Akiva, M. E. 1973. "Structure of Passenger Travel Demand Models." Ph.D. diss., Massachusetts Institute of Technology, Cambridge, Mass.

Ben-Akiva, M. E., and Steven Lerman. 1986. *Travel Behavior: Theory, Models, and Prediction Methods*. Cambridge, Mass.: MIT Press.

Berry, Brian J. L. 1973. *The Human Consequences of Urbanization*. New York: St. Martin's Press.

Berry, R. Albert. 1975a. "Open Unemployment as a Social Problem in Urban Colombia: Myth and Reality." *Economic Development and Cultural Change* 23 (January): 276–91.

———. 1975b. "Wage Employment, Dualism and Labor Utilization in Colombia: Trends over Time." *Journal of Developing Areas* 9 (July): 563–76.

Berry, R. Albert, and Ronald Soligo. 1980. *Economic Policy and Income Distribution in Colombia*. Boulder, Colo.: Westview.

Berry, R. Albert, and Miguel Urrutia. 1976. *Income Distribution in Colombia*. New Haven, Conn.: Yale University Press.

Borrero, Oscar. 1979. "Actividad Edificadora Según Firmas Constructoras." City Study Intermediate Paper, no. 8. World Bank, Development Economics Department, Washington, D.C. Processed.

Borrero, Oscar, and Sonia Sánchez. 1973. "Mercados de Tierras en Barrios Clandestinos de Bogotá." Bogotá, D.E.: Departamento Administrativo de Planeación Distrital.

Bourguignon, François. 1983. "The Role of Education in the Urban Labour Market During the Process of Development: The Case of Colombia." In Victor L. Urquidi and Saul Trejo Reyes, eds., *Human Resources, Employment, and Development*. Vol. 4. London: Macmillan.

Bowden, Martyn J. 1975. "Growth of Central Districts in Large Cities." In Leo F. Schnore, ed., *The New Urban History*. Princeton, N.J.: Princeton University Press.

Caceres Bolanos, Robert. 1978. "La Situación Financiera de Cundinamarca." *Revista Cámara de Comercio de Bogotá* 30–31 (June–September 1978): 123–33.

Cameron, Gordon C. 1973. "Intra-Urban Location and the New Plant." *Papers of the Regional Science Association* 31: 125–44.

Carlton, Dennis W. 1979. "Models of New Business Locations." In William C. Wheaton, ed., *Interregional Movements and Regional Growth*. Washington, D.C.: Urban Institute.

———. 1983. "The Location and Employment Choices of New Firms: An Economic Model with Discrete and Continuous Endogenous Variables." *Review of Economics and Statistics* 65 (3): 440–49.

Carroll, Alan. 1980. *Pirate Subdivisions and the Market for Residential Lots in Bogotá*. Staff Working Paper 435. Washington, D.C.: World Bank. (In Spanish as Alan Carroll, "Las Subdivisiones Piratas y el Mercado para Lotes Residenciales en Bogotá," *Revista Cámara de Comercio de Bogotá* 41–42 [December 1980–March 1981].)

Charles River Associates, Inc. 1976. *Disaggregate Travel Demand Models.* Vols. 1 and 2. Boston: National Cooperative Highway Research Program.

Cifuentes, J. I. 1984. "Urban Transport in Bogotá." In "Housing and Urban Development in Bogotá, D.E.: The Institutional Backdrop." Discussion Paper 51. World Bank, Water Supply and Urban Development Department, Washington, D.C. (First published in Spanish as "El Transporte en Bogotá," *Revista Cámara de Comercio de Bogotá* 43 [June 1981]: 151–84.)

Consultécnicos Ltda. 1971. *Estudios de Normas Mínimas de Urbanización.* Bogotá.

Contraloría de Bogotá, D.E. 1982. "Finanzas Públicas Consolidadas del Distrito Especial de Bogotá 1961–1981." *Boletín Estadístico* 2 (5).

Cortes, Mariluz, R. Albert Berry, and Ashfaq Ishaq. 1987. *Success in Small and Medium-Scale Enterprises: The Evidence from Colombia.* New York: Oxford University Press.

Dandeker, V. M., and Nilakantha Rath. 1971. *Poverty in India.* Bombay: Sameeksha Trust.

DANE (Departamento Administrativo Nacional de Estadísticas). 1974. *Statistical Bulletin* 279 (October).

———. 1975. *Statistical Bulletin* 293 (December).

———. 1976. *Statistical Bulletin* 301 (August).

DAPD (Departamento Administrativo de Planeación Distrital. 1978. *Applicación de las Normas Mínimas de Urbanización y de Servicios.* Bogotá, D.E.: Unidad de Mejoramiento y Coordinación de Barrios.

———. 1980. "Crecimiento de Bogotá, D.E. Colombia. 1890–1980." Bogotá.

Datta, Gautam, and Jacob Meerman. 1980. *Household Income or Household Income per Capita in Welfare Comparison.* Staff Working Paper 378. Washington, D.C.: World Bank.

DNP (Departamento Nacional de Planeación). 1972. *Cuatro Estrategias: Plan Nacional.* Bogotá, D.E.

———. 1977. *Cuentas Regionales de Colombia, 1960–75.* Bogotá, D.E.

Doebele, William. 1975. "The Pirate Subdivision of Bogotá." Discussion Paper D75-11. Harvard University, Department of City and Regional Planning, Cambridge, Mass.

Doebele, William, Orville F. Grimes, and Johannes F. Linn. 1979. "Participation of Beneficiaries in Financing Urban Services: Valorization Charges in Bogotá, Colombia." *Land Economics* 55 (1): 73–92.

Domencich, Thomas A., and Daniel McFadden. 1975. *Urban Travel Demand: A Behavioural Analysis.* Amsterdam: North-Holland.

Ellickson, Bryan. 1977. *Economic Analysis of Urban Housing Markets: A New Approach.* Santa Monica, Calif.: Rand Corporation.

———. 1981. "An Alternative Test of the Hedonic Theory of Housing Markets?" *Journal of Urban Economics* 9 (1): 56–79.

EMPLASA (Empresa Metropolitana de Planejamento de Grande São Paulo). 1978. "Basic Results of the 1977 Origin Destination Survey." São Paulo. Processed.

Erikson, R. A., and M. Wayslenko. 1980. "Firm Relocation and Site Selection in Suburban Municipalities." *Journal of Urban Economics* 8 (1): 69–85.

Fawcett, Caroline S. 1984. "The Revenue Sharing System in Colombia: A Case Study of Bogotá." In Johannes F. Linn, ed., "Urban Finances in Bogotá,

Colombia." Discussion Paper 39. World Bank, Water Supply and Urban Development Department. Washington, D.C. Processed.

Feibel, Charles, and Alan A. Walters. 1980. *Ownership and Efficiency in Urban Buses.* Staff Working Paper 371. Washington, D.C.: World Bank.

Fields, Gary S. 1975. "Rural Urban Migration, Urban Employment and Under-Employment and Job Search Activity in LDCs." *Journal of Development Economics* 2 (2): 165–87.

————. 1980. *How Segmented Is the Bogotá Labor Market?* Staff Working Paper 434. Washington, D.C.: World Bank.(In Spanish as "Qué Tan Segmentado es el Mercado Laboral in Bogotá?" *Revista Cámara de Comercio de Bogotá* 41–42 [December 1980–March 1981]: 293–353.)

Fields, Gary S., and Nohra de Marulanda. 1976. "Intersectoral Wage Structure in Colombia." Economic Growth Center Discussion Paper 251. Yale University, New Haven, Conn.

Fields, Gary S., and T. Paul Schultz. 1980. "Regional Inequality and Other Sources of Income Variation in Colombia." *Economic Development and Cultural Change* 28 (3): 447–67.

Follain, James, and Emmanuel Jimenez. 1985. "The Demand for HousingCharacteristics in Developing Countries." *Urban Studies* 22 (5): 421–32.

Follain, James, Gill-Chin Lim, and Bertrand Renaud. 1980. "The Demand for Housing in Developing Countries: The Case of Korea." *Journal of Urban Economics* 7 (3): 315–36.

Fredland, D. R. 1974. *Residential Mobility and Home Purchase: A Longitudinal Perspective on the Family Life Cycle and the Housing Market.* Lexington, Mass: Lexington Books.

Friedman, Joseph. 1975. *Housing Location and the Supply of Local Public Services.* Santa Monica, Calif.: Rand Corporation.

Fuentes, Alfredo, and Rodrigo Losada. 1978. "Implicaciones Socioeconómicas de la Ilegalidad en la Tenencía de la Tierra Urbana de Colombia." *Coyuntura Económica* 8 (1).

García, Jorge G. 1983. "Aspects of Agricultural Development in Colombia." World Bank. Washington, D.C. Processed.

García, Jorge G., and Sisira Jayasuriya. Forthcoming. *Stability, Adjustment, and Growth: The Colombian Economy since the 1960s.* Washington, D.C.: World Bank.

Gilbert, Alan, and Joseph Gugler. 1982. *Cities, Poverty and Development: Urbanization in the Third World.* Oxford, U.K.: Oxford University Press.

Glickman, Norman J. 1979. *The Growth and Management of the Japanese Urban Management System.* New York: Academic.

Greytak, David. 1984. "Revenue and Expenditure Forecasting in Bogotá." In Johannes F. Linn, ed., "Urban Finances in Bogotá, Colombia." Discussion Paper 39. World Bank, Water Supply and Urban Development Department. Washington, D.C. Processed.

Griffith, Daniel A. 1981. "Modelling Urban Population Density in a Multicentered City." *Journal of Urban Economics* 9 (3): 289–310.

Hamer, Andrew M. 1981. "Households and Housing: Residential Mobility, Tenure Choice, and Space Consumption in the Developing Metropolis." Urban and Regional Report 81-20. World Bank, Development Economics Department, Washington, D.C. Processed.

————. 1985. *Bogotá's Unregulated Subdivisions: The Myths and Realities of Incremental Housing Construction.* Staff Working Paper 734. Washington, D.C.: World Bank. (In Spanish as "Los Mitos y Realidades de la Construcción de Vivienda Suplementaria," *Revista Cámara de Comercio de Bogotá* 45–46 [December 1981].)

Hansen, Walter G. 1959. "How Accessibility Shapes Land Use." *Journal of American Institute of Planners* 25 (1): 73–76.

Hansen, Willard B. 1961. "An Approach to the Analysis of Residential Extension." *Journal of Regional Science* 3 (1): 37–55.

Hanushek, Eric A., and John Quigley. 1978. "An Explicit Model of Intra-Metropolitan Mobility." *Land Economics* 54 (November): 411–29.

————. 1979. "The Dynamics of the Housing Market: A Stock Adjustment Model of Housing Consumption." *Journal of Urban Economics* 6 (1): 90–111.

Hanushek, Eric A., and Byung Nak Song. 1978. "The Dynamics of Postwar Industrial Location." *Review of Economics and Statistics* 60 (4): 515–22.

Harrison, David, Jr., and John F. Kain. 1974. "Cumulative Urban Growth and Urban Density Function." *Journal of Urban Economics* 1 (1): 61–96.

Henderson, J. Vernon. 1988. *Urban Development Theory, Fact, Illusion.* New York: Oxford University Press.

Hensher, D. A., and L. W. Johnson. 1981. *Applied Discrete Choice Modelling.* London: Croom Helm.

Hensher, D. A., and P. R. Stopher. 1979. *Behavioral Travel Modelling.* London: Croom Helm.

Hirschman, Albert. 1958. *The Strategy of Economic Development.* New Haven, Conn.: Yale University Press.

Hong Kong Government Transport Department. 1983. *Traffic and Transport Digest.* Hong Kong.

Hoover, Edgar M., and Raymond Vernon. 1959. *Anatomy of a Metropolis.* Cambridge, Mass.: Harvard University Press.

Hoyt, Homer. 1939. *The Structure and Growth of Residential Neighborhoods in American Cities.* Washington, D.C.: U.S. Government Printing Office.

————. 1966. *Where the Rich and Poor Live: The Location of Residential Areas Occupied by the Highest and Lowest Income Families in American Cities.* Washington, D.C.: Urban Institute.

Huff, P. L. 1961. "Determination of Intra-Urban Retail Trade Areas." Real Estate Research Program, University of California, Los Angeles, 1961.

ICT (Instituto de Crédito Territorial). 1955. *Una Política de Vivienda Para Colombia.* Bogotá.

Ingram, Gregory. 1982. "Land in Perspective: Its Role in the Structure of Cities." In Matthew Cullen and Sharon Woolery, eds., *World Congress on Land Policy, 1980, Proceedings.* Lexington, Mass.: D. C. Heath.

————. 1984. *Housing Demand in the Developing Metropolis.* Staff Working Paper 663. Washington, D.C: World Bank. (In Spanish as "Demanda de Vivienda en las Metrópolis en Vía de Desarrollo," in *Revista Cámara de Comercio de Bogotá* 45–46 [December 1981]: 82–121.)

Ingram, Gregory, and Alan Carroll. 1981. "The Spatial Structure of Latin American Cities." *Journal of Urban Economics* 9 (2): 257–73. (In Spanish as "Estructura Espacial de las Ciudades de América Latina," *Revista Cámara de Comercio de Bogotá* 43 [June]: 9–28.)

Ingram, Gregory K., José Fernando Pineda, and Alvaro Pachon. 1986. "El Estudio Urbano: Resumen de Resultados e Implicaciones de Política." In Alvaro Pachon, ed., *Lecturas Sobre Economía Urbana.* Bogotá, D.E.: Fundación Simón Bolívar, Instituto de Estudios Políticos.

Interconsulta Ltda. 1970. "Estudio de Organización Administrativa del Transporte Colectivo de Bogotá." Bogotá, D.E.: INTRA (Instituto Nacional de Transporte).

International Labour Office. 1970. *Toward Full Employment: A Program for Colombia.* Geneva.

Jacobs, Jane. 1961. *The Death and Life of Great American Cities.* New York: Vintage Books.

Jallade, Jean Piere. 1974. *Public Expenditures on Education and Income Distribution in Colombia.* Baltimore: Johns Hopkins University Press.

Jimenez, Emmanuel, and Douglas H. Keare. 1984. "Housing Consumption and Permanent Income in Developing Countries: Estimates from Panel Data in El Salvador." *Journal of Urban Economics* 15 (March): 172–94.

Kemper, Peter. 1973. "The Location Decisions of Manufacturing Firms within the New York Metropolitan Area." Ph.D. diss., Yale University, New Haven, Conn., Department of Economics.

King, Thomas. 1975. "The Demand for Housing: Integrating the Roles of Journey to Work, Neighbourhood Quality and Prices." In N. Terleckyj, ed., *Household Production and Consumption.* New York: Columbia University Press.

Kozel, Valerie. 1981. "Travel Demand Models for Developing Countries: The Case of Bogotá, Colombia." Urban and Regional Report 81-26. World Bank, Development Economics Department, Washington, D.C. Processed.

———. 1982. "Comparisons of Disaggregate Demand Model Parameter Stability Over Time in a Developing Country: A Colombian Example." Urban and Regional Report 82-2. World Bank, Development Economics Department, Washington, D.C. Processed.

———. 1986. "Temporal Stability of Transport Demand Models in a Colombian City." In *Behavioural Research for Transport Policy.* Proceedings of the 1985 International Conference on Travel Behaviour. Amsterdam: North-Holland.

Kuznets, Simon. 1966. *Modern Economic Growth.* New Haven, Conn.: Yale University Press.

Lakshmanan, T. R. 1964. "A Model for the Distribution of Urban Activities: Formulation, Evaluation, and Reformulation." Paper presented at the seminar on Models of Land Use Development, University of Pennsylvania, Institute of Urban Studies, October 22–26. Alan M. Voorhees and Associates, Washington, D.C.

———. 1965. "A Theoretical and Empirical Analysis of Intra-Urban Retail Location." Ph.D. diss., Ohio State University.

Latorre, Emilio. 1981. *El Modelo de Demanda de Transporte para Cali: Tassim- Cali, Descripción y Utilización.* Working Paper 10. Bogotá, D.E.: Corporación Centro Regional de Población.

Laun, J. 1977. "Analisis de Urbanizaciones del I.C.T." In Colcultura, *Vida Urbana y Urbanismo.* Bogotá, D.E.: Colcultura.

Lee, Kyu Sik. 1978. "Distribution of Manufacturing Establishments and Employment in Bogotá and Cali." City Study Workshop Paper. World Bank, Development Economics Department, Washington, D.C. Processed.

————. 1981. "Intra-Urban Location of Manufacturing Jobs in Colombia." *Journal of Urban Economics* 9 (2): 222–41. (In Spanish as "Localización Intra-urbana del Empleo Manufacturero en Colombia," *Revista Cámara de Comercio de Bogotá* 43 [June]: 49–72.)

————. 1982. "A Model of Intra-Urban Employment Location: An Application to Bogotá, Colombia." *Journal of Urban Economics* 12 (3): 263–79. (In Spanish as "Modelo de Localización del Empleo Manufacturero en Bogotá," *Revista Cámara de Comercio de Bogotá* 43 [June 1981]: 29–48.)

————. 1989. *The Location of Jobs in a Developing Metropolis: Patterns of Growth in Bogotá and Cali, Colombia.* New York: Oxford University Press.

Lee, Yoon Joo. 1979. "The City Study: The Available Data." Vol. 2. Urban and Regional Report 79-13. World Bank, Development Economics Department, Washington, D.C. Processed.

————. 1981. "The City Study: The Available Data." Vol. 3. Urban and Regional Report 81-15. World Bank, Development Economics Department, Washington, D.C. Processed.

————. 1985. *The Spatial Structure of the Metropolitan Regions of Brazil.* Staff Working Paper 722. Washington, D.C.: World Bank.

Leone, Robert. 1971. "Location of Manufacturing Activity in the New York Metropolitan Area." Ph.D. diss. Yale University, New Haven, Conn., Department of Economics.

Lerman, S. R. 1975. "A Disaggregate Behavioral Model of Urban Mobility Decisions." Ph.D. diss., Massachusetts Institute of Technology, Cambridge, Mass.

————. 1977. "Location, Housing, Automobile Ownership and Mode to Work: A Joint Choice Model." *Transportation Research Board Record* (Washington, D.C.) 610: 6–11.

Lerman, S. R., and M. Ben-Akiva. 1975. "A Behavioral Analysis of Automobile Ownership and Modes of Travel." Washington, D.C.: U.S. Department of Transportation, Office of the Secretary and the Federal Highway Administration. Processed.

Levinson, Herbert S. 1978. *Characteristics of Urban Transport Demand: A Handbook for Transportation Planners.* Washington, D.C.: U.S. Department of Transportation.

Lim, Gill-Chin, James Follain, and Bertrand Renaud. 1980. "Determinants of Home-Ownership in a Developing Economy—Case of Korea." *Urban Sudies* 17 (1): 13–23.

Linn, Johannes F. 1976a. *The Distributive Effects of Local Government Finances in Colombia: A Review of Evidence.* Staff Working Paper 235. Washington, D.C.: World Bank.

————. 1976b. "Public Utilities in Metropolitan Bogotá: Organization, Service Levels and Financing." Urban and Regional Report 76-9. World Bank, Development Economics Department, Washington, D.C. Processed.

————. 1979. "The Incidence of Urban Property Taxation in Colombia." In Roy W. Bahl, ed., *The Taxation of Urban Property in Less Developed Countries.* Madison, Wis.: University of Wisconsin Press.

————. 1980a. "Property Taxation in Bogotá, Colombia: An Analysis of Poor Revenue Performance." *Public Finance Quarterly* 8 (October): 457–76.

————. 1980b. "Urban Finances in Developing Countries." In Roy W. Bahl ed., *Urban Government Finance: Emerging Trends.* Beverly Hills, Calif.: Sage Publications.

————. 1981a. "Administración y Financiamiento de Servicios Públicos en el Distrito Especial de Bogotá." Working Paper 11. Bogotá, D.E.: Corporación Centro Regional de Población.

————. 1981b. "Impuesto Predial en Bogotá, Colombia: Un Analisís de Bajo Rendimiento de los Ingresos por este Concepto." *Revista Cámara de Comercio de Bogotá* 43 (June): 73–90.

————. 1984a. "Administration and Financing of Public Services in Bogotá, D.E.: Summary of Findings." In Johannes F. Linn, ed., "Urban Finances in Bogotá, Colombia." Discussion Paper 39. World Bank, Water Supply and Urban Development Department. Washington, D.C. Processed.

———— (ed.). 1984b. "Urban Finances in Bogotá, Colombia." Discussion Paper 39. World Bank, Water Supply and Urban Development Department. Washington, D.C. Processed.

Losada, Rodrigo, and Hernando Gómez. 1976. *La Tierra en el Mercado Pirata de Bogotá*. Bogotá, D.E.: Fedesarrollo.

Losada, Rodrigo, and L. Pinilla. 1980. *Los Barrios Ilegales de Bogotá*. Bogotá, D.E.: Centro de Investigación y Desarrollo de Pedro Gómez y Cía.

Lowry, I. S. 1964. *A Model of Metropolis*. Santa Monica, Calif.: Rand Corporation.

Lubell, Harold, and Douglas McCallum. 1978. *Bogotá: Urban Development and Employment*. Geneva: International Labour Office.

Maddala, G. S. 1983. *Limited Dependent and Qualitative Variables in Econometrics*. Cambridge: Cambridge University Press.

Malpezzi, Stephen, and Stephen K. Mayo. 1987. "The Demand for Housing in Developing Countries: Empirical Estimates from Household Data." *Economic Development and Cultural Change* 34 (4): 687–721.

Malpezzi, Stephen, Stephen K. Mayo, and David J. Gross. 1985. *Housing Demand in Developing Countries*. Staff Working Paper 733. Washington, D.C.: World Bank.

Manski, Charles F., and S. R. Lerman. 1977. "The Estimation of Choice Probabilities from Choice Based Samples." *Econometrica* 45 (80): 1977–88.

Mayo, Stephen K. 1981. "Theory and Estimation in the Economics of Housing Demand." *Journal of Urban Economics* 10 (1): 95–116.

Mazumdar, Dipak. 1976. "The Urban Informal Sector." *World Development* 4 (8): 655–79

————. 1981. *Urban Labor Market and Income Distribution: A Study of Malaysia*. New York: Oxford University Press.

McDonald, John F. 1981. "Capital-Land Substitution in Urban Housing: A Survey of Empirical Estimates." *Journal of Urban Economics* 9 (2): 190–211.

McFadden, Daniel. 1973. "Conditional Logit Analysis of Qualitative Choice Behavior." In Paul Zarembka, ed., *Frontiers in Econometrics*. New York: Academic.

————. 1974. "The Measurement of Urban Travel Demand." *Journal of Public Economics* 3 (4): 303–28.

————. 1976. "The Theory and Practice of Disaggregate Demand Forecasting for Various Modes of Urban Transportation." Urban Travel Demand Forecasting Project, Working Paper 76-23. Berkeley: Institute of Transportation Studies, University of California.

McGregor, Alan. 1977. "Inter-Urban Variations in Unemployment Duration: A Case Study." *Urban Studies* 14: 303–13.

McKay, Harrison, and others. 1978. "Improving Cognitive Ability in Chronically Deprived Children." *Science* 200 (4339): 270–79.

Mills, Edwin S. 1967. "Aggregative Model of Resource Allocation in a Metropolitan Area." *American Economic Review* 57 (2): 197–210.

———. 1972. *Studies in the Structure of the Urban Economy.* Baltimore: Johns Hopkins University Press.

Mills, Edwin S., and Katsutoshi Ohta. 1976. "Urbanization and Urban Problems." In Hugh T. Patrick and Henry Rosovsky, eds., *Asia's New Giant: How the Japanese Economy Works.* Washington, D.C.: Brookings Institution.

Mills, Edwin S., and Byung Nak Song. 1979. *Korea's Urbanization and Urban Problems, 1945–1975.* Cambridge, Mass.: Harvard University Press.

Mills, Edwin S., and Jee-Peng Tan. 1980. "A Comparison of Urban Population Density Function in Developed and Developing Countries." *Urban Studies* 17 (December): 313–21.

Mincer, Jacob. 1974. *Schooling, Experience and Earnings.* New York: Columbia University Press.

Mohan, Rakesh. 1979. *Urban Economic and Planning Models.* Baltimore: Johns Hopkins University Press.

———. 1980. *The People of Bogotá: Who They Are, What They Earn, Where They Live.* Staff Working Paper 390. Washington, D.C.: World Bank. (In Spanish as "Población, Ingresos y Empleo en Una Metrópoli en Desarrollo," *Revista Cámara de Comercio de Bogotá,* 41–42 [December 1980–March 1981]: 9–116.)

———. 1981. *The Determinants of Labor Earnings in Developing Metropolises: Estimates from Bogotá and Cali, Colombia.* Staff Working Paper 498. Washington, D.C.: World Bank. (In Spanish as "Determinantes de los Ingresos Laborales en Una Metrópoli en Desarrollo," in Alvaro Pachon, ed., 1986, *Lecturas Sobre Economía Urbana,* Bogotá, D.E., Fundación Simón Bolívar, Instituto Estudios Políticos.)

———. 1984. *An Anatomy of the Distribution of Urban Income: A Tale of Two Cities in Colombia.* Staff Working Paper 650. Washington, D.C.: World Bank.

———. 1986. *Work, Wages, and Welfare in a Developing Metropolis: Consequences of Growth in Bogotá, Colombia.* New York: Oxford University Press.

Mohan, Rakesh, and Nancy Hartline. 1984. *The Poor of Bogotá: Who They Are, What They Do, and Where They Live.* Staff Working Paper 635. Washington, D.C.: World Bank.

Mohan, Rakesh, and Richard Sabot. 1988. "Educational Expansion and the Inequality of Pay: Colombia 1973–1978." *Oxford Bulletin of Economics and Statistics* 50 (May): 175–82.

Mohan, Rakesh, and Rodrigo Villamizar. 1982. "The Evolution of Land Values in the Context of Rapid Urban Growth." In Matthew Cullen and Sharon Woolery, eds., *World Congress on Land Policy, Proceedings.* Lexington, Mass.: D.C. Heath. (In Spanish as "La Evolución de Los Precios de la Tierra en el Contexto de un Rápido Crecimiento Urbano," in Alvaro Pachon, ed., *Lecturas Sobre Economía Urbana,* Bogotá, D.E.: Fundación Simón Bolívar, Instituto de Estudios Políticos.)

Mohan, Rakesh, M. Wilhelm Wagner, and Jorge García. 1981. *Measuring Urban Malnutrition and Poverty: A Case Study of Bogotá and Cali, Colombia*. Staff Working Paper 447. Washington, D.C.: World Bank.

Morrisson, Christian. 1984. "Income Distribution in East European and Western Countries." *Journal of Comparative Economics* 8 (2): 121–38.

Moses, Leon, and H. F. Williamson, Jr. 1967. "The Location of Economic Activity." *American Economic Review* 57 (2): 211–22.

Muth, Richard F. 1969. *Cities and Housing*. Chicago: University of Chicago Press.

Nelson, Richard R., T. Paul Schultz, and Robert L. Slighton. 1971. *Structural Change in a Developing Economy: Colombia's Problems and Prospects*. Princeton, N.J.: Princeton University Press.

Ojha, P. D. 1970. "Configuration of Indian Poverty: Inequality and Levels of Learning." *Reserve Bank of India Bulletin* 24 (January): 16–27.

Pachon, Alvaro. 1979. "Urban Structure, Modal Choice, and Auto Ownership in Bogotá, 1972." City Study Intermediate Paper no. 31. World Bank, Development Economics Department, Washington, D.C. Processed.

———. 1981a. "El Automóvil en Dos Metrópolis del Tercer Mundo." *Revista Cámara de Comercio de Bogotá* 45–46 (December):188–222.

———. 1981b. "El Impacto Redistributivo de la Intervención del Gobierno en el Transporte Urbano." *Revista Cámara de Comercio de Bogotá* 43 (June): 185–216.

———. 1981c. "Situación del Transporte en Cali y Bogotá Decada de los Setenta." Documento del Trabajo 18, Corporación Centro Regional de Población, Bogotá.

———. 1987. "Urban Transport Policy: Colombia." In George Tolley and Vinod Thomas, eds., *The Economics of Urbanization and Urban Policies in Developing Countries*. Washington, D.C.: World Bank.

Paredes, L. Ricardo. 1984. "Colombia's Urban Legal Framework." In "Housing and Urban Development in Bogotá: The Institutional Backdrop." Discussion Paper 51. World Bank, Water Supply and Urban Development Department, Washington, D.C. Processed.

Pendleton, W. C. 1963. "The Value of Highway Accessibility." Ph.D. diss., University of Chicago.

Pfeffermann, Guy P., and Richard C. Webb. 1979. *The Distribution of Income in Brazil*. Staff Working Paper 356. Washington, D.C.: World Bank.

Pineda, José Fernando. 1981a. "Residential Location Decisions of Multiple Worker Households in Bogotá, Colombia." Ph.D. diss., University of California, Berkeley, Department of City and Regional Planning.

———. 1981b. "Residential Location Decisions of Multiple Worker Households in Bogotá, Colombia." (In Spanish in "Decisiones de Localización Residencial en Hogares con Multiples Trajabadores en Bogotá, Colombia," *Revista Cámara de Comercio de Bogotá* 45–46 [December]:163–87.)

Pineda, José Fernando, and Sonia Rodriguez. 1982. *La Población de Bogotá*. Working Paper 26. Bogotá: Corporación Centro Regional de Población.

Polinsky, A. Mitchell, and David M. Elwood. 1979. "An Empirical Reconciliation of Micro and Grouped Estimates of the Demand for Housing." *Review of Economics and Statistics* 61 (2): 199–205 .

Potter, Joseph, and Myriam Ordonez. 1976. "The Completeness of Enumeration in the 1973 Census of the Population of Colombia." *Population Index* 42 (July): 377–403.

Preston, Samuel H. 1979. "Urban Growth in Developing Countries: A Demographic Reappraisal." *Population and Development Review* 5 (2): 195–215.

Psacharapoulos, George. 1980. "Returns to Education: An Updated International Comparison." In Timothy King, ed., *Education and Income.* Staff Working Paper 402. Washington, D.C.: World Bank.

Quigley, John M. 1976. "Housing Demand in the Short Run: An Analysis of Polytomous Choice." *Explorations in Economic Research* 3 (1): 76–102.

———. 1979. "What Have We Learned About Urban Housing Markets?" In Peter Mieszkowski and Mahlon Straszheim, eds., *Current Issues in Urban Economics.* Baltimore: Johns Hopkins University Press.

Renaud, Bertrand. 1981. *National Urbanization Policy in Developing Countries.* New York: Oxford University Press.

Reutlinger, Shlomo, and Marcelo Selowsky. 1976. *Malnutrition and Poverty: Magnitude and Policy Options.* Baltimore: Johns Hopkins University Press.

Ribe, Helena. 1979. "Income of Migrants Relative to Non-Migrants in Colombia: An Economic Analysis of the 1973 Census Sample." Ph.D. diss., Yale University, New Haven, Conn., Department of Economics.

Ruiz Betancourt, Mario Christina. 1978. "El Situado Discal." Investigación de Grado para optar al Título de Economista. Universidad de Gran Colombia. Processed.

Schmenner, Roger W. 1973. "City Taxes and Industry Location." Ph.D. diss., Yale University, New Haven, Conn., Department of Economics.

———. 1982. *Making Business Location Decisions.* Englewood Cliffs, N.J.: Prentice Hall.

Schultz, T. Paul. 1969. "Population Growth and Internal Migration in Colombia." Rand Corporation Memorandum 5765, Santa Monica, Calif.

Schultz, T. W. 1961. "Investment in Human Capital." *American Economic Review* 51 (1): 1–17.

Selowsky, Marcelo. 1979. *Who Benefits from Government Expenditure? A Case Study of Colombia.* New York: Oxford University Press.

Sethuraman, S. V. 1976. "Towards Definition of the Informal Sector." Research Working Paper. International Labour Office, World Employment Program, Geneva. Processed.

Slighton, Robert. 1987. *Relative Wages, Skill Shortages, and Changes in Income Distribution in Developing Countries.* Washington, D.C.: World Bank.

Smith, James P., and Finis Welch. 1977. "Black-White Male Wage Ratios 1960–1970." *American Economic Review* 67 (3): 323–38.

Stevenson, Rafael. 1984. "Housing Programs and Policies in Bogotá: A Historical and Descriptive Analysis." In "Housing and Urban Development in Bogotá: The Institutional Backdrop." Discussion Paper 51. World Bank, Water Supply and Urban Development Department, Washington, D.C.

Struyk, Raymond J., and Franklin J. James. 1975. *Intrametropolitan Industrial Location.* Lexington, Mass.: Lexington Books.

Struyk, Raymond J., and S. A. Marshall. 1975. "Income and Urban Home Ownership." *Review of Economics and Statistics* 57 (1): 19–25.

Sukhatme, P. V. 1978. "Assessment of Adequacy of Diets at Different Income Levels." *Economic and Political Weekly* 13 (31, 32, 33): 1373–85.

Tabares, Henry. 1979. "Población de Cali: Series Históricas y Características." PIDECA, Document 3, Planeación Municipal, Cali. Processed.

Thomas, Vinod. 1985. *Linking Macroeconomic and Agricultural Policies for Adjustment with Growth: The Colombian Experience.* Baltimore: Johns Hopkins University Press.

Tolley, George S., and Vinod Thomas, eds. 1987. *The Economics of Urbanization and Urban Policies in the Developing Countries.* Washington, D.C.: World Bank.

Transpoconsult. 1976. *Lagos: Metropolitan Area Transport Study.* Lagos, Nigeria.

Urrutia, Miguel. 1969. *The Development of the Colombian Labor Movement.* New Haven, Conn.: Yale University Press.

————. 1981. "Evaluación del Sistema de Transporte Público en Bogotá." In Fedesarrollo, *Evaluación del Transporte Urbano de Bogotá.* Bogotá, D.E.: Fedesarrollo.

————. 1985. *Winners and Losers in Colombia's Recent Growth Experience.* Baltimore: Johns Hopkins University Press.

U.S. Department of Commerce. 1979. *Annual Housing Survey: 1977.* Part O. Housing Characteristics of Recent Movers. Washington, D.C.: Government Printing Office.

Valenzuela, Jaime. 1970. "El Papel de la Vivienda Popular: El Caso de Colombia." Centro de Investigaciónes en Desarrollo (CID). Bogotá, D.E. Processed.

Valenzuela, Jaime, and George Vernez. 1974. "Construcción Popular y Estructura del Mercado de Vivienda: El Caso de Bogotá." *Revista SIP,* no. 31 (September).

Valverde, Nelson. 1978. "The City Study: The Available Data." Vol. 1. Urban and Regional Report, no. 70-6. World Bank, Development Economics Department, Washington, D.C. Processed.

Velasco, Juliana, and Gilberto R. Mier. 1980. "Valores y Características de la Tierra en Cali." Planeación Municipal, Cali. Processed.

Vernez, Georges. 1973a. "Bogotá's Pirate Settlements: An Opportunity for Metropolitan Development." Ph.D. diss., University of California, Berkeley.

————. 1973b. "Pirate Settlements, Housing Development by Incremental Housing Development and Low Income Housing Policies in Bogotá, Colombia." New York: Rand Institute. Processed.

————. 1976. "Traslados Residenciales de Migrantes de Bajos Ingresos." Bogotá, D.E.: Corporación Centro Regionales de Población (CCRP). Processed.

Villamizar, Rodrigo. 1981. "Land Prices in Bogotá between 1955 and 1978." In J. Vernon Henderson, ed., *Research in Urban Economics.* Greenwich, Conn.: JAI Press. (In Spanish as "Los Precios de la Tierra en Bogotá [1955–1978]," *Revista Cámara de Comercio de Bogotá* 41–42 [December 1980–March 1981]: 117–70.

Wagner, M. Wilhelm. 1984. *The Market Prices and Assessed Values in the Urban Land Market in Bogotá, Colombia.* Staff Working Paper 651. Washington, D.C.: World Bank.

Walters, Alan A. 1979. *Cost and Scale of Bus Services.* Staff Working Paper 325. Washington, D.C.: World Bank.

Webb, Richard C. 1977. *Government Policy and the Distribution of Income in Peru 1963–1973.* Cambridge, Mass.: Harvard University Press.

Weber, Adna F. 1963. *The Growth of Cities in the Nineteenth Century.* Ithaca, N.Y.: Cornell University Press.

Westin, Richard. 1980. "Travel Patterns in Bogotá." City Study Intermediate Paper no. 45. World Bank, Development Economics Department, Washington, D.C. Processed.

Wheaton, William. 1982a. "Urban Residential Growth under Perfect Foresight." *Journal of Urban Economics* 12 (1): 1–21.

———. 1982b. "Urban Spatial Development with Durable and Replaceable Capital." *Journal of Urban Economics* 12 (1): 53–67 .

White, Michelle J. 1977. "On Cumulative Urban Growth and Urban Density Functions." *Journal of Urban Economics* 4 (1): 104–12.

Wiesner, Guillermo. 1980. "The History of Land Prices in Bogotá between 1878 and 1978." (In Spanish as "Cien Años de Desarrollo Histórico de los Precios de la Tierra en Bogotá," R*evista Cámara de Comerico de Bogotá* 41–42 [December]: 171–208.)

Wilbur Smith and Associates. 1974. "Urban Transport Policy and Planning Study for Metropolitan Kuala Lumpur." Kuala Lumpur, Malaysia. Processed.

———. 1976. "Hong Kong Comprehensive Transport Study." Hong Kong. Processed.

———. 1979. "Masterplan for Metropolitan Lagos." Lagos, Nigeria. Processed.

Witte, Ann D., Howard Sumka, and Homer Erekson. 1979. "An Estimate of a Structural Hedonic Price Model of the Housing Market: An Application of Rosen's Theory of Implicit Markets." *Econometrica* 47 (5): 1151–73.

Wolff, Juergen H. 1984. "Budgeting and Investment Planning in Bogotá." In Johannes F. Linn, ed., "Urban Finances in Bogotá, Colombia." Discussion Paper 39. World Bank, Water Supply and Urban Development Department. Washington, D.C. Processed.

World Bank. 1977. *World Bank Atlas.* Washington, D.C.

———. 1990. *Colombia: Social Programs for the Alleviation of Poverty.* Washington, D.C.

World Bank and José Sokol. 1984. *Colombia: Economic Development and Policy under Changing Conditions.* World Bank Country Study. Washington, D.C.: World Bank.

Zahavi, Yacor. 1979. "Urban Travel Patterns." Washington, D.C. World Bank, Economic Development Institute. Processed.

Index

African cities, 24–25
Agencies. See Public service agencies
Agglomeration economies: city expansion and, 19, 20; for new firms, 130, 141–42
Agrarian Credit Bank, 147
Agricultural sector: decentralization and, 36; output growth in, 97; primary activities in, 19; prosperity in, 13–14, 117; transition from, 75–76
Ahmedabad (India), 239
Alliance for Progress, 148
Amato, Peter, 6, 79
Anand, Sudhir, 81, 95 n5, 104
Anderson, John E., 37 n5
Ardila, Amparo de, 156
Asabere, Paul K., 24–25
Automobile ownership. See Car ownership
Auxilios parlamentarios (parliamentary grants), 258

Banco Central Hipotecario (BCH), 149, 150, 259
Banco de la República (Central Bank), 149, 238, 259
Bangalore (India), 168
Banking Regulatory Agency. See Superintendencia Bancaria
Banweol (Korea), 143
Barco government (1987–90), 13
Barrios: and density gradients, 56, 72 n2; in survey data, 291, 295–96, 299, 300 n7, 300 n8
Barrios piratas. See Pirata subdivisions
BCH (Banco Central Hipotecario), 149, 150, 259
Becker, Gary S., 104
Belo Horizonte, 30, 56
Ben-Akiva, M. E., 214
Berry, R. Albert, 6, 75
Bogotá: beer consumption in, 252, 254; car ownership in, 191, 214; City Study's selection of, 5–6; employment densities in, 63–64, 279; employment diversification in, 43, 123; employment location in, 121–22, 124–25, 126, 128, 129; firm size in, 129, 131; GDP in, 38; growth characteristics of, 15–16; home-ownership in, 167–68; household mobility in, 114, 162–63, 170; housing patterns in, 67–68; income distribution in, 77–78, 79, 81, 83, 101, 103, 112; infrastructure expenditures in, 256, 258; labor force in, 89–91; labor market segmentation in, 117, 118, 275; land use in, 42–43; land values in, 58, 60, 70–71; malnutrition in, 84–85; manufacturing sector in, 10, 43, 123, 128–29, 130–32, 143; *1970s* employment in, 97–98; occupational distribution in, 101, 103; peripheral development in, 25; physical characteristics of, 40–41, 42; *pirata* subdivisions in, 152–53; population densities in, 39–40, 43, 50–51, 55–56, 63; prior research on, 6–7; public housing programs in, 148–49; public services in, 94, 234–35, 259–60, 266–67; residential lot size in, 70; returns to education in, 106–107, 111–12; revenue sources in, 239, 244–45, 248–50, 254–55; transportation services in, 187, 189, 190, 222, 223–24, 285–86; travel characteristics of, 203, 204, 213, 214; union membership in, 114. *See also* CBD (central business district); Government, district
Bombay, 40, 43, 239
Bourguignon, François, 105
Bowden, Martyn J., 21
Bridges, 256
Brunner, Karl, 42
Budgets, district, 235–36, 237, 258–59
Buenos Aires, 188
Buses: fare structure of, 195, 223; government subsidy of, 189, 191, 193, 194, 195–96, 198; operating costs of, 194; ownership of, 189; profitability of, 196, 198; seats per 1,000 residents on, 189, 191, 222; sizes of, 189; travel peaks on, 214–15; travel times on, 205, 220